The Best and Worst of Everything

Editor-in-Chief: Les Krantz

PRENTICE HALL GENERAL REFERENCE
New York London Toronto Sydney Tokyo Singapore

PRENTICE HALL GENERAL REFERENCE
15 Columbus Circle
New York, New York, 10023

Copyright © 1991 Facts That Matter, Inc.
Correspondence: 2210 N. Burling, Chicago, Illinois 60614

Library of Congress Cataloging-in-Publication Data
Krantz, Les.
    The best and worst of everything / Les Krantz.
        p. cm.
    ISBN 0-13-026337-0 : $25.00. — ISBN 0-13-026345-1 (pbk.) : $15.00
    1. World Records. 2. Success — United States — Evaluation.
I. Title.
AG243.K73 1991
031 – dc 20   91-13965
                                                                          CIP

Designed by Les Krantz.

Manufactured in the United States of America

10 9 8 7 6 5 4 3 2

First Prentice Hall Edition

To Kate Kelly, for luck

Editor : **Les Krantz**

Editorial Director: **Mark Mravic**

Photo Editor: **Sharon Exley**

Contributors: **Michael Weinberg, Jordan Wankoff, Jessica Copen, Leif Madsen, Alan Enzer, Emily Rovnick**

Research: **Maureen Okicki**

CONTENTS

INTRODUCTION

WELCOME TO THE BEST AND WORST

"And never the twain shall meet. . . ." That is what the best and the worst is all about, and it's what makes this volume different from all other references, which usually deal with the stuff that lies in between.

For some two years, our staff surveyed, measured and compiled data on the most relevant aspects of our lives—the people, places and things that we confront on a regular basis. Not so surprisingly, we found that much research on bests and worsts had already been done. Some of the existing measures, though, were more fun than informative—such as "Black's Ten Worst Dressed List" or *People* magazine's "50 Most Beautiful People" issue. We thought someone should take up the task of finding the best and worst in a more serious and more practical vein.

The measurements we used had to meet several criteria before we accepted them. We sought measures from reliable sources, which based their measurements on numerical data and not opinion. We also sought the most current available data compiled by reliable sources. These sources were quite diverse, including agencies of the U.S. government, trade associations, authoritative publications, broad-based opinion polls and hundreds more. We also required that the data be based on a large sampling of the category in question. In most cases we wanted a world-wide or national sample.

Sometimes our lofty criteria could not be met by quantitative measurements. For example, who can reasonably measure the best hamburger? Matters of taste are hard to rate. But even with the absence of hard data, we thought at least some objective evaluation practicable. In such cases, we relied on several methods. Expert opinion was one, but it had to be backed by *some* reasonable data before we accepted it.

In many instances, we devised our own formulas or criteria for measuring the best and worst, which we have dubbed "Best and Worst original." These entries are marked as such under the ratings, where the source is identified. This process involved identifying factors that determine quality and applying scores accordingly. Such scores were derived by an array of data, including measurements such as citation analysis, critical acceptance, numbers of awards or honors, and sometimes even sales, which is often a barometer of public acceptance. This method, we admit, is "pseudo-scientific," but it does have merit where no other quantitative measures are available.

Although we believe our book is entertaining, we endeavored, above all else, to make it informative and useful. For instance, we included "fast food" items, not because we think franchise-land is the idyllic dining spot, but because we know meals on the run are a relevant part of American life for most who will read and use this book. We also examined the seamy side of life. Crime, alcohol consumption, poverty and other aspects of our culture are issues we need to be informed about.

Some of our findings were unpleasant. For example, we learned that Chicago, the city from which we work, was the nation's most segregated. But we also found that it was the most architecturally significant metro in America. Washington, D.C., was among the most blighted city, but it is also contains the most educated and best-paid populace. Enigmas, indeed, but facts we had to relate.

Some things we did not attempt to rate. In the main, these were products. Publications and research institutions such as Consumers Union and Underwriters Laboratories already do a credible job, and we did not think we could outdo them. What you will find on the pages that follow are people, place and things that are seldom ranked, but should be. In many instances, we were the first to rank them in a public forum, aptly named *The Best and Worst of Everything*. We believe the best of our rankings are the ones you, the reader, will act upon. Do so with your eye on the best and your guard on the worst. And remember, nothing's perfect, even our rankings—but we painstakingly tried to portray our world so that you could get the best out of it. You can, and we believe *The Best and Worst of Everything* will help you do it.

GENERAL INDEX

GENERAL INDEX

GENERAL INDEX

GENERAL INDEX

GENERAL INDEX

GENERAL INDEX

PEOPLE

ACTORS AND ACTRESSES
Highest Grossing

Film acting is an art, but also very much of a business. Public tastes are fickle at best, but among the disposable dozens in the Hollywood ranks, there are always a few who stick tenaciously at the top of the financial mountain. The success of these golden few seldom derives from any single factor — talent, determination and old fashioned hype all play major roles in this production. The following are the stars whose films have grossed the most over the past year, along with their astronomical takes.

Star	Gross
1. Eddie Murphy	$86 Million
2. Tom Cruise	$83 Million
3. Michael Douglas	$79 Million
4. Jack Nicholson	$73 Million
5. Kim Basinger	$64 Million
6. Sigourney Weaver	$55 Million
7. Cher	$48 Million
8. Bette Midler	$46 Million
9. Sylvester Stallone	$40 Million
Arnold Schwarzenegger	$40 Million

ACTORS AND ACTRESSES
Highest Paid

The movie industry pretty much reflects society — the Equal Rights Amendment wouldn't succeed there either. According to box office receipts, *Rambo* is more popular than *Sophie's Choice*, and in the mysterious mind of Hollywood, that means Stallone is worth more than Streep. However, even when an actress's movies are more popular than those of her male counterpart, as is the case of Kim Basinger and Sylvester Stallone, she'll still make less than him. The following are estimates of what the top ten stars command for a picture. Note that some stars, in addition to the base pay shown here, also have deals that give them a percentage of the movie profits; how much a dud like Stallone's *Over the Top* yielded the Italian Stallion is hard to determine.

Actors	Pay Per Film (Millions)
1. Sylvester Stallone	$20
2. Jack Nicholson	$11
3. Eddie Murphy	$10
4. Arnold Schwarznegger	$10
5. Michael Douglas	$9
6. Tom Cruise	$8
7. Mel Gibson	$7
Bruce Willis	$7
9. Dustin Hoffman	$5
10. Dennis Quaid	$3
Nick Nolte	$3

Actresses	Pay Per Film (Millions)
1. Julia Roberts	$7
2. Barbra Streisand	$6
3. Jane Fonda	$5
4. Meryl Streep	$5
5. Cher	$4
6. Sigourney Weaver	$4
7. Sally Field	$3
8. Michelle Pfeiffer	$3
9. Kim Basinger	$2

Source: "Best and Worst" original.

ADMIRALS
Best

Judging the "best" naval commanders is a difficult task and is open to much speculation and further discussion; in the following rating, the best commanders are judged not just by statistics, but by their stories as well. A great leader in any field tends to stand well above the rest for more than just racking up numbers. Factors in this assessment include relative force (offense vs. defense) in armament, ship number, men and guns available, weather conditions of battles, tactical planning and execution, and importantly, success. With this in mind, the best admiral is clearly Horatio Nelson.

Nelson, and the others who join him in this list, exhibit not only the technical skills of naval warfare; they have far and away the best characteristic of leadership — the ability to make men believe. The supporting characters that Nelson orchestrated all believed in him and would naturally follow where he led. Against impossible odds that meant certain defeat for other men, Nelson's contingent would overcome and win. His planning was excellent and his strategy well- thought out. Moreover, he possessed another intangible characteristic that all the leaders listed share: luck.

The following are the editors' selections for the greatest naval commanders of modern times.

Admiral	Significant Battle

1. Horatio Nelson   Nile, 1798
Defeats well-positioned French fleet despite overwhelming odds of 3 to 13, goes on to greater glory and fame.

2. Don John of Austria   Lepanto, 1570
Unites multi-national force, even numbers match, destroys Turkish foe.

3. Francis Drake   Spanish Armada, 1588
Facing much larger force, tough weather, deters foe; Drake's early daring raids delayed Spanish fleet departure.

4. Martin Tromp   The Downs, 1639
Takes initiative, attacks with 17 vs. 77 while rest of his fleet is elsewhere. Indecisive enemy + arrival of reinforcements = victory.

5. Chester Nimitz   Midway, 1942
Turning point in WWII in Pacific: Nimitz defeats Japanese fleet despite significant losses. Nimitz earns command of Pacific fleet, goes on to win control of entire Pacific. Father of "Nuclear" Navy.

6. George Monck   Four-day battle, 1666
Splits fleet, takes initiative anyway, attacks with less than 50 ships against an enemy of 90. Forces enemy to alter plan; reinforcements arrive — victory.

7. Edward Hawke   Quiberon Bay, 1759
Hawke makes bold move, pursues French fleet in a gale, defeats French in their own home waters, losing only two ships to seven for the French.

8. Heimachoro Togo   Tushima, 1905
Togo's well-planned and executed battle results in a massive victory over the slower but larger Russian fleet.

9. Pierre-Andre de Suffren   East Indies, 1782-83
This master tactician's excellent planning helped keep British away from French territory in the Caribbean until his departure.

10. David Farragut   Mobile, 1864
Strapped himself to the mast of his flagship to steady himself in battle. Loses one ship early to a sea mine, but gives famous order, "Damn the torpedoes, full speed ahead." Takes Mobile Bay from the hands of the Confederates.

Source: Great Sea Battles

ADMIRALS
Worst

After the greatest who controlled the seas, what of their opponents? The next rating is of the worst admirals — leaders who suffered an inordinate amount of bad luck, poor planning and execution, uninspired leadership. Some were simply incompetent (royal kindred appointed to the position by the reigning monarch; no experience, but excellent connections), while others made bad choices. The following worst admirals are rated by magnitude of their loss — the more lost in a single battle, the higher on the list.

1. Admiral Bruey   Nile, 1798
Has incredible superiority and position over Nelson, manages to lose entire fleet (only two ships escape), signals beginning of end for French empire.

2. Adm. Rojdestvensky   Tsushima, 1905
Commits gravest mistake a commander can make — goes into battle against Togo of Japan *expecting to lose!* Expectations realized — he loses entire, numerically superior, fleet.

3. Duke of Medina Spanish Armada, 1588

PEOPLE

Loses Spanish Armada. Deterred by Drake from attacking England, makes bad call to go to North Sea: six ships sink in battle, loses 64 more ships and 10,000 men to weather. Only 50% fleet returns to Spain.

4. Ali Pasha   **Lepanto, 1570**

Lost Turkish fleet to Don John of Austria: 300 ships, 3200 men, all previously captured European prisoners serving as rowers on Turkish ships are freed.

5. Admiral d'Oquendo   **The Downs, 1639**

Loses early initiative, his 77 ships are attacked by Adm. Tromp's 17 and Tromp wins encounter. Further bad planning, no tactics, allow Tromp to get reinforced. D'-Oquendo loses.

6. Admiral Buchanan   **Mobile Bay, 1864**

Poor planning, execution and equipment allow Farragut to take Mobile Bay easily.

7. Sir Richard Pearson
                Flamborough Head, 1779

Clear advantage over John Paul Jones in fight, bad maneuvering allows ships to grapple; subsequently British lose.

8. Comte de Toulouse   **Gibraltar, 1704**

Inexperienced commander (king's son) does not take initiative; first encounter a draw, next encounter, roundly defeated.

9. Prince of Denmark   **Copenhagen, 1801**

Foe of Nelson. Danes have harbor position, inflict much more damage against a stronger fleet under Nelson, but bad luck and weak will cause surrender of Danish fleet.

10. K.G. Wrangel   **The Sound, 1658**

Has numerical advantage, but loses wind. Bad luck in a fierce fight and Wrangle loses.

Source: Great Sea Battles

AMERICANS
Greatest, All-time

We scored Americans out of the history books from 1 to 10 in four categories: leadership, power or influence on his or her contemporaries, influence in changing the course of history, and lasting stature in history. According to our editors, Lincoln scores slightly higher than Washington in his influence on the course of history, because the editors felt that preserving the Union presented an even more challenging and, in the long run, historically significant, task than founding it. Washington gave birth to the country, but Lincoln saved it, and allowed it to become great. Edison scored highest in the contemporary influence and in the course of history categories — perfect 10s both — for the profound effects of his inventions on the daily lives not only of Americans but of people throughout the world.

1. Abraham Lincoln	36
2. George Washington	35
3. Franklin Roosevelt	31
4. Thomas Edison	27
5. Benjamin Franklin	24
6. Martin Luther King	21
7. Henry Ford	19
8. Theodore Roosevelt	18
9. Clara Barton	16
9. Eleanor Roosevelt	16

Source: "Best and Worst" original.

AMERICANS — WEALTH
The Wealthiest People
in America

According to *Forbes* magazine, John Kluge is the wealthiest individual in the United States, with more than $5.2 billion in net worth. That, friends, is more than the gross national product of Ethiopia or El Salvador. Kluge made his wad in the entertainment industry — he is 95% owner of Metromedia Co. — and from purchases of interest in cellular phone systems in New York and Philadelphia, the Ponderosa chain of restaurants, and Orion Pictures. Also making the list are financial wizards Warren Buffet and Ronald Perelman, youthful computer

3

PEOPLE

mogul Bill Gates, movie theater owner Sumner Redstone, and the members of the Walton clan, of Wal-Mart (not the TV family) fame.

Person/Source of Wealth	Net Worth
1. **John Kluge** Metromedia	**$5.2 billion**
2. **Warren Buffett** Stock Market	**$3.8 billion**
3. **Bill Gates** Microsoft	**$3.2 billion**
4. **Ronald Perelman** Leveraged Buyouts	**$2.8 billion**
5. **Sam Walton** Wal-Mart Stores	**$2.7 billion**
6. **Alice L. Walton** Inheritance	**$2.7 billion**
7. **Jim C. Walton** Inheritance	**$2.7 billion**
8. **John T. Walton** Inheritance	**$2.7 billion**
9. **S. Robson Walton** Inheritance	**$2.7 billion**
10. **Sumner Redstone** Movie Theaters	**$2.7 billion**

Source: *Forbes*.

ARCHITECTS
Most Popular Designers

Whilst few of us will ever afford the luxury of commissioning a building by a celebrated architect, at least some of us might be able to spare the cash to afford a Michael Graves tea kettle, Robert Venturi linen, a toothbrush by Phillipe Stark, or china by Frank Lloyd Wright or Robert Stern. Architects are big business for luxury essentials for the household. Purchased from that obligatory executive toy store found in every other major mall, the wares of today's high-flying architectural trendsetters are there for all to have and hold, serve coffee in or

tell the time with. No design-conscious bride should have fewer than three or four of these names on her register.

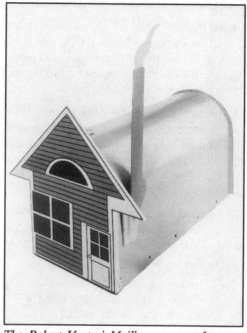

The Robert Venturi Mailbox, a must for every design-conscious home. Photo courtesy the Markuse Group.

The Top Ten

1. Michael Graves
2. Gwathmey Siegal
3. Robert Venturi
4. Richard Meier
5. Aldo Rossi
6. Robert Stern
7. Stanley Tigerman
8. Phillipe Stark
9. Ettore Sottsass
10. Frank Lloyd Wright

Source: "Best and Worst" original.

ARTISTS
Top Living Americans

The following rating of living American visual artists takes into account three factors: (1) the frequency and prestige of the

PEOPLE

artist's retrospective, one-man and group exhibitions; (2) the top dollar sale of the artist's work; and (3) the volume and distribution of the artist's work in major public collections. In the first category, five points were awarded for each retrospective exhibition, three for a one-person show, and one for participation in a group exhibit. Two extra points were awarded for each exhibit staged at one of the top-tier museums: the Museum of Modern Art, the Metropolitan Museum of Art, the Whitney Museum of American Art, and the Solomon R. Guggenheim Museum, all in New York, and the National Gallery in Washington; and an additional point was earned for shows at second-tier museums, such as the Art Institute of Chicago, the Los Angeles County Museum of Art and the Getty Museum. In category 2, artists were awarded from 2 to 30 points, the highest-grossing (De Kooning) receiving the full 30, and the lowest-grossing receiving 2. In the final category, we awarded two points for each work of art in the permanent collection of top-tier museums and one for each work in a second-tier institution. The overall winner, Willem De Kooning, was one of the founders of the Abstract Expressionist movement that dominated art after World War II.

The Top Ten	Total Score
1. Willem De Kooning	78
2. Jasper Johns	76
3. James Rosenquist	65
4. Roy Lichtenstein	62
5. Robert Rauschenburg	61
6. Frank Stella	58
7. Claes Oldenburg	51
8. Robert Motherwell	49
9. Julian Schnabel	44
10. Francesco Clemente	43

Source: "Best and Worst" original.

ASSOCIATIONS
America's Largest

We're a nation of joiners, but even more than that we're a nation of drivers. So it's not surprising that the largest association in the country is a driver's club. Triple-A provides road service to millions of stranded auto passengers each year, giving jump-starts on those freezing winter days or tows to the local service station when the radiator overheats. AAA is primarily a service association; not so with the American Association of Retired Persons. As the nation ages, AARP increasingly is seen as a political force for the elderly, mobilizing against cuts in Social Security, Medicare, retirement benefits and other issues affecting the aged. Look for its numbers to swell in the coming decade, as well as its influence.

Association Members (Millions)

1. Am. Automobile Association	29.0
2. Am. Assoc. of Retired Persons	28.0
3. YMCA of the U.S.A.	14.0
4. National Geographic Society	10.5
5. National Right to Life Committee	7.0
6. National PTA	6.1
7. National Wildlife Federation	5.1
8. Natl. Committee to Preserve Soc. Sec. & Medicare	5.0
9. 4-H Program	4.8
10. Boy Scouts of America	4.8

Source: American Society of Association Executives.

ATHLETES
Most Notable Sports Deaths

One of the most tragic events one can witness is a great athlete being struck down in the prime of his career by a debilitating illness or sudden fatal accident. The editors of this book have compiled a list of what we consider the most notable athletes' deaths of the century. Some of the deaths are the result of accidents or injuries caused by play on the field, while others are less related to athletics. But the saddest are those of Len Bias and Sonny Liston, whose succumbing to the temptations of drugs proved fatal.

1. Lou Gehrig
The Pride of the Yankees, a man who

PEOPLE

became known as the "Iron Horse" for his remarkable record of more than 2,100 consecutive games played, is forced to retire after being diagnosed with a mysterious muscle disorder. Gehrig succumbs two years later, in 1941, to the disease that now bears his name.

2. Len Bias

Drafted number two in the 1986 NBA draft by the Boston Celtics and projected as a huge NBA impact player, Bias parties the night he's drafted and dies of a cocaine overdose.

3. Roberto Clemente

While shuttling relief supplies to Nicaraguan earthquake victims on New Year's Eve, 1972, the Pittsburgh Pirate great— batting champ, 1971 World Series MVP, Puerto Rican national hero— is killed in a plane crash. Clemente's last hit of the '72 season, and the last of his career, was his 3000th.

4. Hank Gathers

Six-foot-seven, 210-pound forward for the runnin', gunnin' Loyola Marymount basketball team, the highest scoring college hoopsters of all time, Gathers faints on the court in a game against UC-Santa Barbara; diagnosed with an irregular heartbeat, Gathers gradually reduces his intake of the drugs to combat his condition. Three months after his first attack, in a game against the University of Portland, Gathers collapses on the court after a slam dunk; he dies a short time later.

5. Lyman Bostock

The California Angels star is mistaken for someone else and killed by a shotgun blast while sitting in his car.

6. Knute Rockne

The legendary Notre Dame football coach is killed in a plane crash.

7. Thurman Munson

The Yankee catcher is killed when the plane he is piloting crashes in Ohio during the 1979 season.

8. Spider Savage

Skiing star Savage is shot to death in a lover's tiff by Claudine Longet.

9. Sonny Liston

The former heavyweight champ, once considered the strongest and meanest man alive, dies of a heroin overdose shortly after losing his second heavyweight championship bout with Cassius Clay (Muhammad Ali).

10. Flo Hyman

Star of the U.S. women's gold medal volleyball team in the 1984 Olympics, Hyman succumbs on the court shortly after the Games to Marfan's Syndrome, a disease that strikes unusually tall persons.

Source: "Best and Worst" original.

BASEBALL CARDS
Most Valuable Baseball Card

Back in the good old days, before tobacco companies began to feel the heat for the questionable merit of their products, you used to get baseball cards along with your chew or smokes. Later on, the cards came in pack of bubble gum. Soon the gum became little more than a nuisance, a hard, cardboard-textured insert in the pack of cards, which became the real attraction. Little did the kids who traded those cards realize the incredible investment potential those cards would become. In fact, even people who work at baseball memorabilia shops sometimes find it hard to believe the mementos are worth so much: a sales clerk at a shop in the Chicago suburbs recently sold a Nolan Ryan rookie card to a young collector for $12.00, misreading the price tag of $1200; the error lead to litigation. Baseball cards have now become a multimillion dollar industry. The great Pittsburgh Pirates shortstop Honus Wagner's card from 1910 sold at auction in March, 1991, for an astounding $451,000! The incredibly rare card, of which only two have been found, are

PEOPLE

valuable because Wagner opposed youngsters smoking or chewing tobacco and had the cards withdrawn when he learned of the tobacco advertising tie-in. Wagner's cards from the American Tobacco Company Set 206 also are worth more than $100,000. In general, after such rarities as the Wagner cards, rookie cards of great players are the most valuable. Mickey Mantle's 1951 rookie card lists at almost $9,000; Jose Canseco's 1986 rookie card is already worth $125. Error cards — cards with some sort of mistake, such as a misspelled name or even the wrong player depicted — also command high prices. Who knows how much the recent Billy Ripken card — the one in which he unknowingly holds a bat on which the words "F___ Face" are inscribed — will be worth fifty years from now? Below are the most valuable baseball cards around, with their current value or most recent sale price, and the card company and year.

Player	Card Value
1. Honus Wagner Piedmont, 1910	$451,000
2. Honus Wagner T206, 1909-11	$110,000
3. Napoleon Lajoie Goudey, 1933	$25,000
4. Joe Doyle T-206, 1909-11	$18,000
5. Eddie Plank T-206, 1909-11	$15,000
6. Sherry Magie T206, 1909-11	$12,000
7. Mickey Mantle Topps, 1952	$8,700
8. Mickey Mantle Bowman, 1951	$5,000
9. Babe Ruth Goudey, 1933 (Card 181)	$4,800
10. Babe Ruth	$4,000

Goudey, 1933 (Cards 53, 144, 149)

Source: Sports Card Trader, May, 1991.

BASEBALL PLAYERS
Most Stolen Bases

Stolen base kings are the fleet-footed wonders of the baseball world. Thieves with fast feet and the instinctive ability to read the pitchers moves, these denizens of the base paths can take a simple single or a walk and turn it into a quick run. Many a game with Rickey Henderson involved has led off with Henderson walking, stealing second, advancing to third on an infield out and scoring on a sacrifice fly. Thus the pitcher, untouched in the hit column, already finds himself down in where in counts, in the score. The following totals for stolen bases are through May 2, 1991, the day following Henderson's historic steal that pushed him past Lou Brock on the list of all-time stolen base leaders.

Player	Steals
1. Rickey Henderson	939
2. Lou Brock	938
3. Ty Cobb	892
4. Eddie Collins	743
5. Max Carey	738
6. Honus Wagner	722
7. Joe Morgan	689
8. Bert Campaneris	649
9. Tim Raines	637
10. Willie Wilson	615

BASEBALL PLAYERS
Best Base-Stealers

We ranked base stealers on several factors. Most important was the player's success rate. This was followed by total stolen bases, runs resulting from stolen bases and wins resulting from stolen bases, all of which were rated equally. While we are confident of our ranking, readers will do well to remember the important but unquantifiable qualities of good base runners. For instance crafty base-stealers distract pitchers and may cause

PEOPLE

balks. A good example would be Joe Morgan's performance during the Boston Red Sox-Cincinnatti Reds World Series of the mid-1970s. Here then are the craftiest and the fleetest of foot the major leagues have seen.

Tim Raines, top base-stealer.

The Top Ten	Base-stealing Score
1. Tim Raines	1056.40
2. Rickey Henderson	1027.00
3. Willie Wilson	1015.90
4. Joe Morgan	1000.40
5. Davey Lopes	994.90
6. Lou Brock	954.00
7. Luis Aparicio	915.90
8. Ozzie Smith	912.80
Bert Campanaris	912.80
10. Julio Cruz	910.90

Source: "Best and Worst" original.

BASEBALL PLAYERS
Highest Career Batting Average

A ball no larger than a fist speeds at a man holding what looks like a dowel. In a fraction of a second the man pivots and brings the wood into contact with the ball. The collision of bat and ball resounds in the park immediately followed by a roar of from the crowd. A rush of activity follows and within moments the batter is standing on base brushing the dust from his uniform. Some say hitting a baseball ball is the most difficult feat in all of sports. Even the most accomplished baseball players can scarcely get a hit more than once in three chances, and fewer still can retain that average over the course of an entire career. These are the players with the highest lifetime batting averages. Only one, Wade Boggs, is an active player.

1. Ty Cobb	.366
2. Rogers Hornsby	.358
3. Joe Jackson	.356
Wade Boggs	.356
5. Ed Delahanty	.346
6. Ted Williams	.344
Billy Hamilton	.344
Tris Speaker	.344
9. Dan Brouthers	.342
Babe Ruth	.342
Harry Heilmann	.342

BASEBALL PLAYERS
All-time Greatest Hitters

Perhaps no topic is more endlessly debated in baseball circles than that of the all-time greatest player. One problem in creating an all-time rating is trying to match players from one era with that of another. The editors of *Total Baseball* have compiled their ratings from a plethora of statistical material — 95 statistics in all — meant to even out as much as possible the alleged differences between baseball eras. Thus we have judged it to be the most authoritative and comprehensive rating of ball players. Not surprisingly, Babe Ruth, the man who did more than any other player to make baseball America's national pastime, outscores the second greatest player, Ty Cobb, by a whopping 15 points, a much greater margin than separates any other two players in *Total*

PEOPLE

Baseball's entire listing of 500.

The Top Ten	Score
1. Babe Ruth	105.1
2. Ty Cobb	90.6
3. Hank Aaron	90.1
4. Ted Williams	89.8
5. Willie Mays	86.2
6. Nap Lajoie	85.2
7. Tris Speaker	79.9
8. Mike Schmidt	77.9
9. Rogers Hornsby	77.2
10. Honus Wagner	75.6

Source: *Total Baseball.*

BASEBALL PLAYERS
Most Bases Produced

There are innumerable measures of a baseball player's offensive performance — the traditional batting average, runs batted in and home runs, as well as more elaborate statistics — slugging percentage, ratio of bases to outs, runs produced, and ever more intricate manipulations of the available statistical information. Want to know how many times a particular batter has knocked in a runner from second with two outs after the seventh inning against a left-handed pitcher on astroturf in his home stadium? Some number-cruncher somewhere can tell you. The following is an interesting measure of an player's offensive productivity. The formula used to derive the list below adds together a player's total number of bases gained through hits, walks and steals over his career, then divides that number by the total number of games played. The result yields the average number of bases gained per game for each player, and multiplying that number by 150 gives an index of the offensive productivity of a player over the course of a regular season. The statistic favors powerful home run hitters, since a homer earns four bases for every swing of the bat, while a single accounts for only one base. The list is led by three power hitters — Ruth, Gehrig and Williams — but the interesting members of this top ten club are Rickey Henderson

and Ty Cobb, players shorter on power but longer on speed. The prowess of Henderson and Cobb in swiping bases adds greatly to their offensive threat.

The Top Ten	Bases Produced/150 Games
1. Babe Ruth	478
2. Lou Gehrig	462
3. Ted Williams	453
4. Rickey Henderson	436
5. Jimmy Foxx	421
6. Mickey Mantle	400
7. Ty Cobb	396
8. Willie Mays	394
9. Stan Musial	387
10. Hank Aaron	387

Source: *New York Times.*

BASEBALL PLAYERS
Greatest Pinch Hitters

Pinch hitting is one of those hard-to-understand baseball vagaries which leave many observers confused. Pinch hitters sit on the bench for almost the entire game. Then, when their team desperately needs a run, they are called upon to replace batters whose averages are often little lower than their own. Pinch hitting specialists are often older players who can still connect with the ball but whose legs are not quick enough to compete with their younger teammates — Manny Mota, for instance, extended his career by years through his ability to come off the bench and whack a base hit. In creating this ranking, the editors took into consideration both the player's total number of pinch hits and his pinch hitting average. The following are the top ten pinch hitters of all time. Note that none are Hall-of-Famers — the pinch hitter's art is as yet still unrecognized in that hall of immortals.

The Top Ten	Pinch Hit Score
1. Tommy Davis	332.6
2. Manny Mota	327.0
3. Frenchy Bordagray	322.0
4. Dave Philley	317.6
5. Frankie Baumholtz	316.4

PEOPLE

6. Bob Fothergill	315.2
7. Smokey Burgess	315.0
8. Red Schoendienst	314.2
9. Harvey Hendrick	305.2
10.Ted Easterly	305.0

Source: "Best and Worst" original.

BASEBALL PLAYERS

Best Hitters in the Clutch, Active

When the game's on the line, who would major league managers most like to see at the plate? According to the numbers, Will Clark of the San Francisco Giants is the best clutch hitter in baseball. Clark has batted .380 with runners in scoring position and two outs over the past three seasons. That figure is phenomenal, considering the next closest batters, Kirby Puckett and Barry Larkin, are 64 points below Clark's numbers. Teammates remark on the "sneer" Clark gets on his face in tight situations, "the Clint Eastwood look." This is the "controlled aggression" managers are looking for, concentration rather than wildness. Other factors that make up a great clutch hitter include competitive spirit, the ability to intimidate a pitcher, and the flair for the dramatic. Some players have it, some don't, and that's what distinguishes guys like Will Clark, George Brett and Rickey Henderson from able stickmen or 100-RBI hitters who don't seem to perform when it counts. Seems Clark has always had that intensity—his first major league at bat was a home run off of Nolan Ryan. The following list represents the top ten batters with runners in scoring position and two outs from 1988 to 1990.

Player	Average	RBI
1. Will Clark S.F. Giants	.380	89
2. Kirby Puckett Minnesota Twins	.316	72
3. Barry Larkin	.316	65
Cincinnati Reds		
4. Tim Raines Montreal Expos	.315	52
5. Pedro Guerrero Dodgers, Cardinals	.314	79
6. Eric Davis Cincinnati Reds	.314	78
7. Paul Molitor Milwaukeee Brewers	.310	55
8. Steve Sax Dodgers, Yankees	.305	67
9. Alvin Davis Seattle Mariners	.301	60
10. Andre Dawson Chicago Cubs	.298	66

Source: STATS, Inc.

Will Clark is the top hitter in the clutch, with a batting average of .380 with runners in scoring position. Photo courtesy S.F. Giants.

10

PEOPLE

BASEBALL PLAYERS

Greatest Pitchers, All-time

Like rating hitting, rating pitching is fraught with obstacles. How do you compare the iron men of the 1890s with the thoroughbreds of the 1990s? How do you weigh one great season, let's say Denny McClain's 31-game-winner against Nolan Ryan's career of excellence? The editors of *Total Baseball* have come up with a formula that takes into account more than 24 statistics including: earned run average, opponents' batting average, wins, walks, strike-outs, strike-outs per game, innings pitched, runs allowed, shutouts and saves. The following are the top ten pitchers according to that standard. The greatest all-time is Walter "Big Train" Johnson, who lobbed for the Washington Senators in the first half of the 1900s.

The Top Ten	Pitching Score
1. Walter Johnson	81.5
2. Cy Young	81.0
3. Kid Nichol	65.3
4. Pete Alexander	64.8
5. Lefty Grove	59.9
6. Christy Mathewson	54.6
7. John Clarkson	52.6
8. Tom Seaver	51.2
9. Bob Gibson	46.3
10. Warren Spahn	43.1

Source: *Total Baseball*.

BASEBALL PLAYERS

Highest Paid, 1990

Big money in baseball follows around winners. Jose Canseco, one of the Oakland Athletics' feared "bash brothers," has led his team to the American League West title the last three years and to a World Series victory in one of those years. His reward for his monster home runs was the highest salary in the major leagues in 1990, a whopping $4,700,000. This however, was eclipsed in the days leading up to the beginning of the 1991 season by Boston pitcher Roger Clemens new contract, which will reportedly pay him more than $5 million a year over the next several years. Joining Canseco in the upper stratosphere of baseball salaries are his Oakland teammates, Bob Welch and Dave Stewart. But money doesn't just follow winners — it follows big stars in big markets as well. All of the players in the list of the ten highest paid baseball stars for 1990 reside in mega-markets — Los Angeles, Chicago, New York and the Bay Area. Players in lesser baseball domains such as Cleveland, Milwaukee and Seattle often suffer salary-wise not from their play on the field but from geography — there simply aren't as many people in those markets to buy tickets and watch the games on television, thus generating the big bucks for teams in the major metropolitan areas.

Player	1990 Salary
1. Jose Canseco Oakland Athletics	$4,700,000
2. Darryl Strawberry Los Angeles Dodgers	$4,050,000
3. Don Mattingly New York Yankees	$3,860,000
4. Will Clark San Francisco Giants	$3,750,000
4. Kevin Mitchell San Francicso Giants	$3,750,000
6. Dave Winfield California Angels	$3,675,000
7. Andre Dawson Chicago Cubs	$3,700,000
8. Dave Stewart Oakland Athletics	$3,500,000
9. Bob Welch Oakland Athletics	$3,450,000
10. Tim Raines Chicago White Sox	$3,400,000

PEOPLE

BASEBALL TEAMS
Highest Payroll

Baseball players' salaries continue to rise, even while many fans bemoan the loss of innocence this phenomenon seems to impart to the game. Nowadays, baseball, like other sports (not including the World League of American Football) is big business, with many players more concerned with the bottom line on their paycheck than the bottom line in the box score. Players complain they're not paid enough and that the owners are in collusion in restricting salaries; they want a bigger piece of the lucrative, multi-billion dollar Major League television contract. Owners complain that despite record attendance every year and that megabucks TV contract, they're actually *losing* money. In fact, many teams do lose money, but not because of the players. The owners in many cases are victims of their own greed and pride. It's a blow to the owner's machismo to lose a player like Kevin Mitchell or Jose Canseco because you can't pay him enough; so you do. Like a horse owner collecting thoroughbreds, deep-pockets owners of teams such as the Oakland A's, the Boston Red Sox, the Los Angeles Dodgers and the San Francisco Giants collect highly paid baseball players. Meanwhile, it's the fans who really pay — in higher ticket and concession prices, in cable television costs, and, coming soon, in games televised only on a pay-per-view basis.

Team	Payroll (mill.)	Avg. Sal.
1. Oakland	$23.3	$806,554
2. Boston	$22.5	$777,683
3. Kansas City	$22.2	$692,973
4. N.Y. Mets	$22.0	$758,575
5. California	$21.5	$695,070
6. S. F.	$20.7	$666,927
7. L.A.	$20.6	$685,780
8. N.Y. Yankees	$20.3	$725,872
9. St. Louis	$19.7	$636,794
10. Milwaukee	$18.3	$678,581

Tightest Wads

1. Baltimore	$8.1	$279,326
2. White Sox	$11.0	$422,199
3. Atlanta	$11.6	$414,443
4. Seattle	$11.7	$388,649
5. Texas	$13.0	$481,290
6. Minnesota	$13.4	$495,270
7. Cubs	$14.0	$518,050
8. Philadelphia	$14.3	$461,484
9. Cleveland	$14.8	$508,756
10. Pittsburgh	$14.8	$592,390

Source: Major League Baseball Players Association.

BASEBALL TEAMS
Biggest Bang for the Buck, 1990

Previously we saw the baseball teams with the largest and smallest payrolls. But who really gets the most for their baseball dollar — the teams with the exorbitant payrolls or the penny pinchers? One can determine this by taking the average cost of a win and comparing it to what various teams actually paid for each of their wins in 1990. The average team's 1990 payroll was $17,270,420, and the average number of wins was, of course, 81, given the 162 game season. Thus, on average, a major league team paid $213,229 for each victory. If you divide the actual payroll of each team by the league average cost per victory of $213,229, you can project the number of games the team should have won, given its payroll. A comparison of this projected-win total with the actual-win total then yields the win differential, the number of games the team won above its projected number of wins. As the results reveal, the Chicago White Sox were the biggest overachievers of the 1990 season, getting 42 more wins for their money than the average team and finishing second to the well-compensated Oakland A's in their division. But caveat emptor. Of the top ten overachieving teams in 1990, only one won its division, the Pirates. Seems as soon as a team wins some games, the players start getting cocky and asking for more money.

PEOPLE

What nerve. The Oakland A's were closest to their projected total, winning only one fewer game than what their payroll would have dictated. On the other hand, perhaps the owners of the lowly Kansas City Royals, which, even with the third highest payroll in the majors, finished 36 games below their projected totals, will ask for some of that big free-agent money back. Indeed, their first move in the spring was to cut the injured Bo Jackson. Who picked up his contract? You guessed it. The White Sox.

Best	Projected	Actual	Diff.
1. White Sox	52	94	+ 42
2. Orioles	38	76	+ 38
3. Rangers	60	83	+ 23
4. Pirates	73	95	+ 22
5. Mariners	59	77	+ 18
6. Reds	74	91	+ 17
7. Cubs	65	77	+ 12
8. Phillies	66	77	+ 11
9. Twins	66	74	+ 8
9. Expos	77	85	+ 8
10. Indians	72	77	+ 5

Worst Bang for the Buck

1. Royals	111	75	-36
2. Yankees	97	67	-30
3. Angels	103	80	-23
4. Cardinals	92	70	-22
5. Giants	105	85	-20
6. Red Sox	107	88	-19
7. Mets	104	91	-13
8. Brewers	87	74	-13
9. Dodgers	96	86	-10
10. Astros	85	75	-10

Source: Inside Sports, April, 1991.

BASEBALL TEAMS
Who Spent What to Win

Big baseball payrolls are fine if the team is winning. But it's much harder to justify those big salaries if the players aren't producing on the field. The average team paid $213,229 for a victory in 1990. But the Kansas City Royals went after a bunch of high-priced free-agents before the 1990 season only to see them wash out when the money was on the line. They ended up paying 47 percent more per victory than average, and more than two and a half times as much as their division-mates the Chicago White Sox, who ended up in second place. The New York Yankees suffer from the legacy of the now-departed George Steinbrenner, whose luck with free agents was no better than his luck with managers (or judges). The Yankees are probably still paying the salary of the immortal Steve Kemp. Only one team in the top ten in dollars per win has a 1990 division title to show for their money, the Boston Red Sox.

Most Expensive Wins	Amount per win
1. Kansas City Royals	$314,894
2. New York Yankees	$307,193
3. St. Louis Cardinals	$279,964
4. California Angels	$274,192
5. San Francisco Giants	$264,190
6. Boston Red Sox	$258,110
7. Milwaukee Brewers	$249,378
8. New York Mets	$243,254
9. Houston Astros	$243,063
10. Los Angeles Dodgers	$236,851

Cheapest Wins	
1. Baltimore Orioles	$106,417
2. Chicago White Sox	$118,285
3. Texas Rangers	$153,651
4. Pittsburgh Pirates	$163,052
5. Seattle Mariners	$163,522
6. Cincinnati Reds	$173,092
7. Chicago Cubs	$178,983
8. Philadelphia Phillies	$183,844
9. Minnesota Twins	$191,382
10. Montreal Expos	$197,790

BASKETBALL CARDS
Most Valuable

Who's the top player in the NBA? It's in the cards—trading cards, to be exact. Michael Jordan is the only active player in basketball whose card is one of the top ten most valuable (Wayne Gretzky is the only other athlete who compares to Jordan in this regard). In fact, of the top 13 most valuable basket-

PEOPLE

ball cards, no less than *five* are those of Air Jordan. Amazingly, Jordan's appeal stretches beyond basketball: he even has a baseball card in the 1991 Upper Deck series which depicts him posing in a Chicago White Sox uniform. The card already goes for $8.00. Unlike baseball cards, the top ten list here contains few surprises. The list is amply supplied with great names. Watch for Bill Bradley's card to increase in value if he declares for the Presidency in 1992.

Player	Card Value
1. **George Mikan** Bowman, 1948	**$2,200**
2. **Bill Russel** Topps, 1957-58	**$2,000**
3. **Wilt Chamberlain** Fleer, 1961-62 (Card 8)	**$1,800**
4. **Lew Alcindor (R)** Topps, 1969-70	**$1,200**
5. **Michael Jordan (R)** Star NBA Reg., 1984-85 (Card 101)	**$900**
6. **Oscar Robertson (R)** Fleer, 1961-62	**$450**
7. **Michael Jordan** Star NBA Reg., 1984-85 (Card 195)	**$400**
8. **Julius Irving (R)** Topps, 1972-73	**$375**
9. **Michael Jordan** Fleer, 1986-87	**$350**
9. **Michael Jordan** Star NBA Reg., 1984-85 (Card 288)	**$350**
10. **Bob Cousy** Topps, 1957-58	**$325**
10. **Bill Bradley (R)** Topps, 1969-70	**$325**
10. **Michael Jordan** Star NBA Reg., 1985-86	**$325**

Source: Sports Card Trader, May 1991.

BASKETBALL COACHES
Most NBA Wins

These days, one National Basketball Association championship for a team is enough to make players weep. One championship ring can mitigate years of frustration on struggling teams or can allow a player to coast through the remainder of his career proudly flashing his championship jewelry. *Two* consecutive championships and the team enters the pantheon of NBA immortals. Talk of "three-peat" fills the air, until, like an old clock, the once-mighty champions succumb to age, trades or simple lethargy. How, then, to account for the amazing championship streak of the Boston Celtics, who, from 1959 to 1969 won *ten* NBA championships, including eight in a row from 1959 to 1966? Many things account for this incredible run, but most important was the man at the helm, Celtics coach Red Auerbach. Like Knute Rockne before him, Auerbach revolutionized the game to such an extent that teams took ten years to catch up with his strategy. Certainly the level of competition in NBA then wasn't what it was today, with an extremely sophisticated training system in the colleges and more and more talented athletes available to the highest bidding teams through free agency. Thus it's all the more uneven when a great coach can mold the team in his own image, like Auerbach did with the Celtics. It is probably safe to say that, as in baseball with the New York Yankees of old, there will never be another basketball dynasty like the Boston Celtics of the 1960s. The following are the ten winningest coaches in NBA history.

The Top Ten	Wins
1. **Red Auerbach**	938
2. **Jack Ramsay**	864
3. **Dick Motta**	849
4. **Bill Fitch**	805
5. **Gene Shue**	784
6. **Lenny Wilkens**	758
7. **Cotton Fitzsimmons**	752

PEOPLE

8. John MacLeod	707
9. Red Holzman	694
10. Don Nelson	664

Source: N.B.A.

BASKETBALL COACHES
Best NBA Winning Percentage

Winning percentage, like total NBA victories, can be a misleading statistic. A coach with the a high number of wins may simply be benefiting from longevity, as he shuffles from team to team every few seasons, picking up wins along the way. In most sports, coaching, especially these days, is a treadmill. Coaches with lifetime winning percentages below .500 continuously find employment at the helms of teams, proving once again the old adage that "winning isn't everything." In fact, of the top ten winningest coaches of all time, only two, Red Auerbach and Don Nelson, are in the top ten in winning percentage as well, and only one other, Red Holzman, places in the top 15. On the other hand, a high winning percentage doesn't tell the whole story. Take the case of the top dog on this list, the well-coiffed Pat Riley. Riley signed on with the Los Angeles Lakers in early 1980s, just as the Lakers began to flourish. With such stars as Magic Johnson and Kareem Abdul Jabbar, Riley wasn't inheriting a team requiring major rebuilding but stepping into championship shoes but rather a winner needed just some fine tuning. Certainly, Riley's four championships with the Lakers is impressive, but it will be interesting to see what he can do with a more troubled team as he takes the helm of the New York Knicks. As for the other coaches, three of the top five in winning percentage coached the Boston Celtics—Jones, Auerbach and Heinsohn.

The Ten Best	Winning %
1. Pat Riley	.733
2. Billy Cunningham	.698
3. K.C. Jones	.682
4. Red Auerbach	.662
5. Tommy Heinsohn	.619
6. Chuck Daly	.614
7. Larry Costello	.589
8. Don Nelson	.588
9. John Kundla	.583
10. Larry Brown	.562

Source: N.B.A.

BASKETBALL COACHES
Top Active College Basketball Coach

Like chess masters, today's college coaches have to be aware of all their options. Here are the best. Our criteria for ranking active college coaches was essentially the same as that for ranking all college coaches (see). However, since all four Coach of the Year awards (U.P.I., A.P., U.S. Basketball Writers Association, National Association of Basketball Coaches) have been in existence during the entire careers of virtually all coaches considered, we have given these honors slightly greater weight than in our ranking of the all-time greatest college basketball coaches.

The Top Ten	Score
1. Jerry Tarkanian	897.00
2. Dean Smith	866.70
3. Bobby Knight	851.40
4. Denny Crum	830.60
5. John Chaney	829.70
6. John Thompson	808.90
7. Jim Boeheim	789.70
8. Lou Carnesecca	780.00
9. Don Haskins	774.00
10. Bruce Stewart	758.20

Source: "Best and Worst" original.

BASKETBALL COACHES
All-Time Greatest College Basketball Coaches

We all remember the scenes of ecstatic basketball players cutting the nets from the baskets after the big game. But who were the great minds who guided them there? Compiled by Almanac staffers, our ranking of the all-time greatest college basketball coaches

PEOPLE

gives greatest weight to lifetime winning percentages, equal weight to total number of wins and number of championships and tie-breaking weight to coach of the year awards. The statistics were adjusted for contenders who coached before either the N.I.T. or N.C.A.A. held championships.

Best College Coaches	Score
1. John Wooden	1077.45
2. Adolph Rupp	990.25
3. Jerry Tarkanian	896.25
4. Clar Bee	868.00
5. F.C. "Phog" Allen	865.00
6. Dean Smith	864.70
7. Bobby Knight	846.15
8. Denny Crum	830.60

Source: "Best and Worst" original.

BASKETBALL PLAYERS
Greatest College Scorers

Great play in college basketball does not necessarily indicate a great future in the National Basketball Association. Many college superstars, fresh out of college programs in which they excelled, are shocked to find the level of competition so much higher in the NBA than that which they had to face in such conferences as the Missouri Valley, the Mid-American, the Metro-Atlantic, and even the Big Ten, Big East and Pac 10. Some of the top ten all-time collegiate scorers indeed went on to pro stardom — Maravich, Robertson, Elvin Hayes, Larry Bird — and Hersey Hawkins certainly has a bright future. But other top college scorers are destined to struggle for a few years on an NBA bench, in the Continental Basketball Association, or even in Europe before the realization that there's more to life than throwing a ball through a hoop.

Player/School	Total Points
1. Pete Maravich, LSU	3,667
2. Freeman Williams, Portland St.	3,249
3. Lionel Simmons, La Salle	3,217
4. Harry Kelly, Texas Southern	3,066
5. Hersey Hawkins, Bradley	3,008

6. Oscar Robertson, Cincinnati	2,973
7. Danny Manning, Kansas	2,951
8. Alfredrick Hughes, Loyola	2,914
9. Elvin Hayes, Houston	2,884
10. Larry Bird, Indiana St.	2,850

BASKETBALL PLAYERS
All-time Greatest Players

This rating, prepared by the Almanac editors, is based on lifetime averages per game for points, rebounds and assists; number of league Most Valuable Player awards; number of All-Star appearances; and number of championship teams played on. We used per-game averages for the first three categories instead of career totals in order not to penalize players like Michael Jordan and Larry Bird, who are in mid-career. Scoring was weighted twice that of rebounds and assists, the rationale being that a rebound gives the team the *opportunity* to score, and most teams average about 50% shooting — so a rebound will result in a two-point basket about 50% of the time. Thus a rebound is "worth" one point. Similarly with assists, about 50% of "assist attempts" will result in a two-point basket. The latter three categories take into account awards over an entire career, thereby benefiting players with longevity, such as Jabbar and Chamberlain. Most Valuable Player awards were weighted twice those of All-Star appearances and championships. Because we didn't want to overly reward players who spent their careers on good teams or penalize those who played with bad teams, the most difficult statistic to factor in is the championships. A player's statistics are certainly enhanced by the quality of his teammates. For example, he'll get more assists if the players he's passing to are good scorers. On the other hand, a good player will contribute much to the winning of championships, so we did allow one point for each championship won. The final figures are the sum of career per-game points (2x), rebounds and assists, and career MVP's (2x), All-Star appearances, and championships.

16

PEOPLE

Larry Bird, the top active NBA basketball player. Photo: Boston Tourist Bureau.

The Top Ten	Score
1. Wilt Chamberlain	108.7
2. Kareem Abdul-Jabbar	101.7
3. Larry Bird	98.3
4. Bill Russel	90.5
5. Michael Jordan	88.8
6. Bob Pettit	87.7
7. Elgin Baylor	83.4
8. Oscar Robertson	82.7
9. Jerry West	81.9
10. Julius Irving	80.1

Source: "Best and Worst" original.

BASKETBALL PLAYERS
Best Rookies, All-time

More often than not, an NBA player needs time to mature and develop — at least a season, sometimes several — before he becomes a real contributor to his team. But on occasion, all a basketball team needs is one missing ingredient to propel them from the also-rans into championship contention, and a rookie provides that ingredient. Below is a list of the rookies who made the biggest impacts in the NBA in their first year, as demonstrated by the difference between the number of wins the team posted the year prior to the rookie's arrival and the number of wins in the rookie's first season. The biggest-impact rookie of all time in the NBA is David Robinson, the center from the Naval Academy. But Robinson's case is special: between leaving college and joining the NBA, he spent a year maturing in the U.S. Navy. Some say this maturation was key to his ability to make a sudden and forceful impact in pro basketball, especially as his stock was down following a disappointing performance in the 1988 Olympics in Seoul. Robinson's team, the San Antonio Spurs, made him the first pick in the 1988 draft, but were willing to wait the extra year for the ensign to complete his military obligation. That wait paid off upon the arrival of Mr. Robinson to his neighborhood, when the Spurs improved their record from 21-61 in 1988-89 to 56-26 in Robinson's first season, 1989-90. Larry Bird is another rookie success story, the player who single-handedly restored the Boston Celtics to their former greatness from the doldrums of the late '70s, after the Celtics had lost such stars as Dave Cowens, John Havlicek and Jo Jo White to retirement. Indeed, save for the spotty career of Ralph Sampson, the list below is replete with current and future hall-of-famers. But the draft is a tough business, and for every Robinson and every Bird, there are dozens of players who shuffle from team to team, collecting splinters from their time on the bench, before unceremoniously departing professional basketball.

Rookie/Team

Year Before/ Rookie Year/ Diff.

1. **David Robinson, San Antonio, 1989-90**
   21-61   56-26   +35
2. **Larry Bird, Boston, 1979-80**
   29-53   61-21   +32

3. K. Abdul-Jabbar, Milwaukee, 1969-70
27-55	56-26	+ 29

4. Elvin Hayes, San Diego, 1968-69
15-67	37-45	+ 22

5. Wes Unseld, Baltimore, 1968-69
36-46	57-25	+ 21

6. Wilt Chamberlain, Phila., 1959-60
30-42	49-26	+ 19

7. Hakeem Olajuwon, Houston, 1984-85
29-53	48-34	+ 19

8. Rick Barry, San Francisco
17-63	35-45	+ 18

9. Ralph Sampson, Houston, 1983-84
14-68	29-53	+ 15

10. Oscar Robertson, Cincinnati, 1960-61
19-56	33-46	+ 14

BASKETBALL PLAYERS
Top Paid, 1990

Unless he really turns his game up a couple notches, John "Hot Rod" Williams probably won't be making anybody's list of basketball immortals. Yet, evidence of the free-spending ways of NBA owners and the desperation with which some teams deal with even players of moderate talent, Williams, a sometime-starting forward for the Cleveland Cavaliers, commanded a salary of $5,000,000 from Cleveland for the 1990 season. Williams had been offered that by one of the expansion teams, and in order to keep their player, the Cavs were forced to match the offer; they did. The inequities of athletic pay systems are such that rookie players like Danny Ferry and Derrick Coleman can command multimillion-dollar deals including big signing bonuses long before they prove their mettle on the court. On the other hand, big-name players, most notably Michael Jordan, earn huge sums from product endorsements. Already the most valuable commercial endorser in the pantheon of sports, Jordan's stock has risen even further with the NBA championship he and the Bulls won in 1991.

Player/Team	Salary
1. John "Hot Rod" Williams	$5,000,000

Cleveland Cavaliers

Player/Team	Salary
2. Patrick Ewing	$4,257,500
New York Knicks	
3. Akeem Olajuwon	$4,062,450
Houston Rockets	
4. Karl Malone	$3,300,000
Utah Jazz	
5. Danny Ferry	$3,000,000
Cleveland Cavaliers	
5. Sam Perkins	$3,000,000
Los Angeles Lakers	
7. Charles Barkley	$2,900,000
Philadelphia 76ers	
8. Earvin "Magic" Johnson	$2,892,860
Los Angeles Lakers	
9. Derrick Coleman	$2,700,000
New Jersey Nets	
10. Michael Jordan	$2,550,000
Chicago Bulls	
10. Chris Mullin	$2,550,000
Golden State Warriors	

BOXERS
Top Gross Purses, 1990

In the bad old days of big-time fisticuffs, the grand-daddy bruisers usually took a helluva beating, and got precious little to show for it, at the end of their too-long, punched-out, punch-drunk careers. With big-time heavies like Don King still running things on the financial end, the Sweet Science still has not caught the smell of the rose. The purses, however, have swelled considerably, and the publicity attending the sport has created a somewhat more equitable situation for the fighters. In fact, in one lucky night — catching Mike Tyson in the midst of lethargic funk — the relative unknown James "Buster" Douglass took the heavyweight crown, and wisely parlayed it into a fight with top contender Evander Holyfield for a purse of more than $24 million. Indeed, at press time, Evander Holyfield had lifetime winnings of

PEOPLE

$60 million.

The Top Ten	1990 Earnings
1. Buster Douglass Heavyweight	$25,400,000
2. Mike Tyson Heavyweight	$18,500,000
3. Evander Holyfield Heavyweight	$9,500,000
4. George Foreman Heavyweight	$3,025,000
5. Nigell Benn Middleweight	$2,760,000
6. Gerry Cooney Heavyweight	$2,500,000
7. Julio Cesar Chavez Jr. Welterweight	$2,225,000
8. Hector "Macho" Camacho Jr. Welterweight	$2,000,000
9. Michael Nunn Middleweight	$1,888,250
10. Thomas "Hit Man" Hearns Super Middleweight	$1,500,000

CELEBRITIES
Highest Profile

A few years back, a professor named E.D. Hirsch wrote a book called *Cultural Literacy*, in which he described the ideas, events, and historical personages with which a person must be familiar in order to be "culturally literate." But we think Hirsch didn't go far enough, limiting himself to the stuff of history, philosophy and culture. We, the Almanac editors, wanted to know what *celebrities* every person should be familiar with in order to call him or herself "pop-culturally literate." So we developed a "pop-culture index" of the highest-profile, most important, most media-genic celebrity icons. In order to do so, Almanac staffers searched the periodicals in the Magazine Database, a full-text, on-line service offering articles from 86 magazines for the period

from 1986 to 1991. We wanted to see how often each celebrity was mentioned, in magazincs ranging from *The Atlantic* and *Cosmopolitan* to *Playboy* and *Working Woman*. The final score is the overall number of articles in the database in which the celebrity is mentioned. *And the survey says* (yes, that too is a pop-culture reference): Madonna, the Material Girl, is the highest-profile celebrity in the country, garnering a whopping 383 on the Almanac profile-ometer. Next highest, with a score of 281, is the schlemiel-turned-auteur Woody Allen, followed by the sexually ambiguous, facially reconstructed anomaly, Michael Jackson. Five of the top ten celebrities were musicians (we hesitate to grant Madonna the status of actress after *Who's That Girl?*), while three were movie stars and two were television personalities. Other celebrities scoring high include Sting with 164 mentions, Cher (146), Jack Nicholson (143) and Steven Spielberg (141). Some of the scores may cause celebrities a bit of concern. Is Oprah worried that she's got the same index score as Vanilla Ice? Cher is somewhat more important on the celebrity scale than Jack Nicholson, but not nearly as hot as Jane Fonda or Madonna. If nothing else, our rankings should help out the people who make up the seating arrangements at celebrity benefits. And who should be consigned to the tables furthest from the stage and closest to the rest rooms? Some of the celebrities who have dropped a bit from the public eye include Tony Curtis (18), William Shatner (15), Gene Wilder (9), and the lowly Liza Minelli (4). In order to be truly pop-culturally literate, you'd better bone up on *Vogue*, *Manhattan* and *Thriller*, but you can safely plead ignorance to *Rent-a-Cop*.

The Top Ten	Celebrity Index
1. Madonna	383
2. Woody Allen	281
3. Michael Jackson	256
4. Jane Fonda	221
5. Paul Simon	197

19

6. Bruce Springsteen   186
7. Frank Sinatra   181
8. Bill Cosby   171
9. Johnny Carson   169
10. Eddie Murphy   148

Source: "Best and Worst" original.

CELEBRITIES
Top Dead Celebrities

Elvis is alive! And he has been spotted, not at a supermarket in Michigan, but at the top of our list of the most popular dead celebrities. The king, in fact, is so big he scored second only to Madonna in overall stardom, although some *claim* he died of a heart attack in 1977. By comparison, the Duke, John Wayne, received less than half the point total of Elvis. Yes, Elvis may have left the metaphorical "building" of life, but his memory lives on — in fact, grows stronger with each year of his passing — in supermarket tabloids, late-night TV record offers, sales of ceramic figurines on home shopping channels, countless Elvis impersonators in countless hotel lounges and

roadhouses, and, of course, in the hearts of the faithful who congregate at Graceland every day to pay homage to their beloved hero with the nervous tick in his upper lip and the penchant for guns and peanut butter. America's Anglophilia also demonstrates itself in this rating, based, as is the previous celebrity rating, on the number of mentions a celebrity has received in the on-line Magazine Database over the last five years. Four of the top ten dead celebrities — Olivier, Lennon, Chaplin, and Cary Grant — are British. Others who scored high include James Dean (69), who trails Bogie by only one point for the last spot in the list, Gary Cooper (67), and, in a surprise, Frank Capra (52), the director of the ubiquitous Christmas classic *It's a Wonderful Life*. Capra outscored such highly regarded auteurs as Alfred Hitchcock and John Ford.

The Top Ten	Celebrity Index
1. Elvis Presley	362
2. John Wayne	168
3. Laurence Olivier	157
4. Marilyn Monroe	156
5. John Lennon	126
6. Charlie Chaplin	103
7. Fred Astaire	97
8. Cary Grant	81
9. Orson Welles	79
10. Humphrey Bogart	70

Source: "Best and Worst" original.

CELEBRITIES
Top Female

When Madonna starts showing up on the normally stodgy *Nightline* to defend freedom of speech, you know she's made it. To some she may be just a tramp from Detroit, but to others, in the way she exploits her sexuality for her own ends, she's the ultimate feminist. Maybe Madonna doesn't sing as well as Whitney Houston (or your little sister, for that matter), maybe she has the dance moves of a high-school cheerleader, and maybe she can't act her way convincingly through a laundry detergent

He Lives! The King is tops among stiff stars. Photo courtesy Rogers & Beckwith.

commercial, but no one can deny that she's got one thing going for her — sex appeal. And the way she uses that sexuality to confront societal, religious and sexual traditions makes one stand up and take notice. The list below reflects the relative degree of media exposure for female celebrities, as indicated by the number of articles in which the celebrity received mention in the on-line Magazine Database. In addition to these ten, other high scorers included Whoopi Goldberg and Michelle Pfeiffer (61), Roseanne Barr (57), Katharine Hepburn (56) and Whitney Houston (53). Low scorers included Geena Davis (16), Kirstie Alley (15) and, surprisingly, supermodel Paulina, with a scant 9 mentions.

The Top Ten	Celebrity Index
1. Madonna	383
2. Jane Fonda	221
3. Marilyn Monroe	156
4. Cher	146
5. Meryl Streep	137
6. Elizabeth Taylor	135
7. Oprah Winfrey	104
8. Bette Midler	83
9. Barbra Streisand	78
10. Shirley MacLaine	75

Source: Almanac Original.

CELEBRITIES
Top Male Stars

Hollywood may be where most of the super-celebrity action, but New York is still the home of our top-rated male celebrity. Seemingly alone among popular entertainers, Woody Allen — comedian, actor, director — staunchly refuses to abandon his Upper East Side stomping grounds for the more serene and sunny climes of California. When Johnny Carson moved the *Tonight Show* from New York to beautiful Burbank, he heralded a trend in the entertainment industry that has gone unchecked for the past 25 years. Sure, Hollywood is the movie capital, but nowadays, musicians, comedians and television stars also migrate west at the

first sign of success. Consider the others on our top-ten male celebrity list — Michael Jackson from Gary, Indiana, Bruce Springsteen from the Jersey Shore to a bungalow in the Hollywood Hills, Paul Simon from Greenwich Village clubs, Eddie Murphy from Queens; even the paragon of New-Yorkitude, Frank Sinatra, now rarely spends his time in the Big Apple. If you can make it there, the saying goes, you'll make it anywhere — so why not make it somewhere else instead, Woody? The rating below indicates the degree of public exposure for male celebrities, based on the number of articles in which the celebrities were mentioned in 86 different magazines over the last five years.

The Top Ten	Celebrity Index
1. Woody Allen	281
2. Michael Jackson	256
3. Paul Simon	197
4. Bruce Springsteen	186
5. Frank Sinatra	181
6. Bill Cosby	171
7. Johnny Carson	169
8. Eddie Murphy	148
9. Jack Nicholson	143
10. Steven Spielberg	141

Source: "Best and Worst" original.

CELEBRITIES —
AUTOGRAPHS
Most Valuable

What's in a name? A lot of dough, it seems, if it's from a Hollywood film star and is attached to an 8x10 glossy. Greta Garbo "vanted to be alone" — thus the value of one of her rare autographed pictures tops the list here. The big surprise? The Three Stooges. The appeal of these proletarian knuckleheads — Larry, Curly and Moe — spans the ages. Long after their last movie was made, millions of late-night TV fans still do the Curly Shuffle, "nyuk, nyuk" to violent practical jokes, and perform the infamous Moe Howard Double-Eye Poke. These pranksters never were great lovers like Valentino, tight-lipped tough-guys like Bogie, or cool rebels like James Dean. Rather, they represented the sad-sack, the Everyman, influencing a generation even more than their more respected Hollywood counterparts.

Celebrity	Signed	Alone
1. Greta Garbo	$3,000	$1,000
2. Lon Chaney, Sr.	$2,500	$1,000
3. Marilyn Monroe	$2,000	$750
4. The Three Stooges	$1,500	$750
5. Humphrey Bogart	$1,500	$650
6. Jean Harlow	$1,500	$500
7. Rudolph Valentino	$1,200	$500
8. James Dean	$1,000	$350
9. W.C. Fields	$750	$300
10. Bruce Lee	$750	$250

CHIEF EXECUTIVE OFFICERS
Highest Paid Executives of the Last Ten Years

The men who claim the astronomical fees listed below are more than pretty-boy pitchmen presiding over boardroom tables. These fellows changed the course of entire industries. Charles Lazarus invented the supermarket of toy-stores. Frederick Smith pioneered overnight delivery. Steve Ross welded a diverse group of businesses (including undertakers and parking lots) into Warner Communications and then merged with Time Inc., creating the world's largest media conglomerate. Others were just as influential. The figures presented below reflect the value of stocks and other incentives at the time they were issued. No attempt has been made to adjust for inflation or stock price fluctuation.

CEO/Company	Total Pay, 1980-1990
1. Charles Lazarus Toys 'R' Us	$156.2 million
2. Steven J. Ross Time Warner	$84.6 million

3. Craig O. McCaw McCaw Cellular	$76.9 million
4. Lee A. Iacocca Chrysler	$65.9 million
5. Michael D. Eisner Walt Disney	$61.9 million
6. T. Boone Pickens, Jr. Mesa Petroleum	$56.9 million
7. Frederick W. Smith Federal Express	$55.9 million
8. Paul Fireman Reebok International	$54.5 million
9. Donald A. Pels Lin Broadcasting	$49.8 million
10. Jim P. Manzi Lotus Development	$47.9 million

Source: *Business Week*.

CHIEF EXECUTIVE OFFICERS
Highest Paid CEOs

America's highest paid chief executive officers run our leisure, luxury and entertainment businesses. Some, like Craig McCaw and August Busch, are the latest in long-running family dynasties. Others reached the top without family influence. Steve Ross, Martin Davis and Michael Eisner are three strong personalities who run three of America's biggest movie, publishing and leisure concerns. Of the chief executive officers listed, most are paid through a combination of salaries, stock options, incentive plans and deferred payments. Often their compensation varies according to how well or poorly the company and its stockholders are doing.

CEO/Company	Annual Pay
1. Craig O. McCaw McCaw Cellular	$53.9 million
2. Steven J. Ross Time Warner	$34.2 million

PEOPLE

August Busch III heads up the nation's top beer producer. And he seems to like his product, too!

CHIEF EXECUTIVE OFFICERS

Who's Earning The Money?

Because a chief executive officer's primary obligation is to make money for his shareholders, some people rate corporate heads on the rise and fall of stock prices. To find out if companies were getting their money's worth, *Business Week* factored salary into the rating and ranked executives on a ratio of pay to stock price. Honors for best value went to Albert L. Ueltschi and Flight Safety International. Ueltschi came in first because his income was low (averaging $245,000 a year while) while Flight Safety international stock increased 222%. Lee Iacocca and Chrysler came in last because Iacocca made about $8.4 million a year while Chrysler stock fell 10%.

Top Performers	Ratio
1. **Albert L. Ueltschi** Flight Safety International	437
2. **George L. Lindemann** Metro Mobile CTS	329
3. **Lawrence J. Ellison** Oracle Systems	326
4. **Angelo J. Bruno** Bruno's	227
5. **Robert E. Price**	206

Bottom Performers	Ratio
1. **Lee A. Iacocca Chrysler** Chrysler	3.6
2. **Paul Fireman** Reebok International	4.1
3. **Michael D. Eisner** Walt Disney	4.6
4. **W. Michael Blumenthal** Unisys	5.3
5. **William P. Stiritz** Ralston Purina	6.4

3. **Donald A. Pels** Lin Broadcasting	$22.8 million
4. **Jim P. Manzi** Lotus Development	$16.4 million
5. **Paul Fireman** Reebok International	$14.6 million
6. **Ronald K. Richey** Torchmark	$12.7 million
7. **Martin S. Davis** Paramount	$11.6 million
8. **Robert C. Goizueta** Coca-Cola	$10.7 million
9. **Michael D. Eisner** Walt Disney	$9.6 million
10. **August A. Busch III** Anheuser-Busch	$8.7 million

Source: *Business Week*.

Source: *Business Week*.

PEOPLE

COMPOSERS
Greatest All-time

Who's the most influential composer of all time? We used to bandy about the phrase "the three B's" — Bach, Beethoven and Brahms — which seemed to be based on an outmoded sense of popular recognition. But a more telling indication of influence is the sheer number of recordings of a composer's works, as well as the amount of scholarly and popular writing about the life and works of the composer. One way of determining this number is to check the number of records under a given composer in the Online Computer Library Center database, the most comprehensive information science database available on published and recorded material. As it turns out, those "three B's" should really be "two B's and an M," since the top three composers of all-time as judged by OCLC method are Bach, Mozart and Beethoven. In fact, the two top composers led the list by a wide margin over their nearest rival. Bach checked in with approximately 17,640 database records, and Mozart came in a close second with 17,150 records. Beethoven dropped a relatively distant third with 13,622, while that pretender to the third spot, Brahms, tallied a a mere 8,133. No rock stars came close, so Beethoven has no reason to roll over.

The Top Ten

1. Johann Sebastian Bach
2. Wolfgang Amadeus Mozart
3. Ludwig van Beethoven
4. Johannes Brahms
5. Josephy Haydn
6. Franz Schubert
7. George Handel
8. Peter Tchaikovsky
9. Robert Schumann
10. Richard Wagner

Source: "A Guide to Special Collections in the OCLC Database," OCLC Online Computer Library Center, Dublin, Ohio.

CONGRESSMEN
Most Conservative

Although the Democratic party still controls the House of Representatives, the conservative block of voters in the House and Senate still swing a mighty bat. These free marketeers, (not to be confused with three musketeers, or Mickey Mousketeers for that matter) had their heyday under the first Reagan administration. Now characterized by the superannuated likes of Jesse Helms and Strom Thurmond, the younger members of this set still get together to stop abortion, tear the guts out of the NEA and go on buying sprees for the military. Compiled by the American Conservative Union (ACU), these statistics represent the percentage of times each representative voted with the ACU position on 25 selected votes in 1989. Failure to vote did not lower scores. Intriguing names in this right-wing pantheon include new-comer Ileana Ros-Lehtinen from Miami, the first Cuban-American to serve in Congress.

Representatives	Cons. Voting Record
1. Wally Herger, California	100%
William E. Dannemeyer, Calif.	100%
Ileana Ros-Lehtinen, Florida	100%
Phillip Crane, Illinois	100%
John Hiler, Indiana	100%
Gene Taylor, Mississippi	100%
Clarence Miller, Ohio	100%
John Kasich, Ohio	100%
Don Ritter, Pennsylvania	100%
10. 22 Representatives	96%

Senators	Cons. Voting Record
1. William Armstrong, Colorado	100%
Jesse Helms, North Carolina	100%
Malcom Wallop, Wyoming	100%
4. Connie Mack, Florida	96%
Steve Symms, Idaho	96%
Trent Lott, Mississippi	96%
Gordon Humphrey, N.H.	96%
Don Nickles, Oklahoma	96%
Strom Thurmond, South Carolina	96%
Phil Gramm, Texas	96%

PEOPLE

Jake Garn, Utah   96%

Source: *1990 Congressional Quarterly Almanac.*

CONGRESSMEN
Best Second Jobs

Most senators and representatives earn extra money through public speaking. Some confine their oratorical activities to schools, churches and auditoriums within their states or districts. Others jet around the country and sometimes around the world speaking to distinguished gatherings of business people and politicians. But unlike in the past, when members of Congress could pad their paltry federal salaries or fill their re-election coffers with tens of thousands of outside dollars, nowadays, they're working mostly for charity. In exchange for the recent pay raise they voted themselves, both houses of Congress have limited the amount of money members can keep from outside sources. Of the payment they receive, Senators can keep up to $35,800, House members up to $26,850. The rest must be donated to charity. Interestingly, the top four earners were members of the House. They include Dan Rostenkowski, chairman of the powerful House Ways and Means Committee and Patricia Schroeder, an outspoken voice for women's and minority interests and military reform whose unsuccessful 1988 presidential campaign rocketed her to national prominence. Among senators, Fritz Hollings of South Carolina, chairman of the Commerce Committee, received the most honoraria.

Senators	Honoraria, 1990
1. Ernest F. Hollings, D-S.C.	$82,200
2. Alan K. Simpson, R-Wyo.	$78,900
3. Bob Dole, R-Kan.	$78,100
4. Orrin G. Hatch, R-Utah	$69,900
5. John B. Breaux, D-La.	$60,000
6. David L. Boren, D-Okla.	$59,600
7. Daniel P. Moynihan, D-N.Y.	$48,900
8. Conrad R. Burns, R-Mont.	$45,400
9. Bob Packwood, R-Ore.	$45,000
10. Pete V. Domenici, R-N.M.	$42,550

Representatives	
1. Dan Rostenkowski, D-Ill.	$309,850
2. Pat Schroeder, D-Colo.	$157,696
3. Willis Gradison, R-Ohio	$93,600
4. John J. LaFalce, D-N.Y.	$93,350
5. William H. Gray 3d, D-Pa.	$75,000
6. Henry Waxman, D-Calif.	$70,123
7. Norman Lent, R-N.Y.	$62,000
8. Newt Gingrich, R-Ga.	$61,234
9. Bob Michel, R-Ill.	$56,650
10. Les AuCoin, D-Ore.	$50,650

Source: New York Times.

CRIMINALS
The F.B.I's Ten Most-Wanted Fugitives From Justice

Fox television's landmark program, *America's Most Wanted*, has done much to renew interest in the dastardly doings of the nation's most notorious felons. Not only has the show chronicled the heinous — often grizzly — deeds of the maximum-security set, but it has also directly led to the capture of dozens of fugitives, making way for new faces on the honor roll of American crime. These are the ten most-wanted fugitives in America — keep your eyes and ears open for them.

Fugitive/Crime(s)

1. **Armando Garcia**
   Racketeering, narcotics violations

2. **Victor Manuel Gerena**
   Armed Robbery

3. **Leo Joseph Koury**
   Racketeering, murder, extortion

4. **Claude Daniel Marks**
   Firearms and Explosives violations

5. **Melvin Edward Mays**
   Terrorist

6. **Patrick Michael Mitchell**
   Armed Robbery

7. **Leslie Isben Rogge**

Robbery, wire fraud

8. Arthur Lee Washington, Jr.
Attempted murder

9. Donald Eugene Webb
Murder

10. Donna Jean Willmont
Terrorist

Source: F.B.I.

EDUCATORS
Most Influential Educators

The pragmatic philosophy of John Dewey, itself an outgrowth of the thinking of 19th-century American philosophers C.S. Pierce and William James, had reverberations not only in philosophic discourse but in wide-ranging fields, including psychology, sociology, and perhaps most forcefully, education. His doctrine that experience is the most effective tool in education—"learn by doing"—continues to play an integral in educational theory up to the present day. The three most influential living educators on our list—William Bennett, E.D. Hirsch and Allan Bloom—all are proponents of a traditional education stressing a fundamental core of knowledge basic to an informed and enlightened citizenry. Bennett made his influence felt most strongly while Secretary of Education under Reagan; Hirsch published a widely discussed book entitled *Cultural Literacy*; while Bloom expounded on what he thought was wrong with modern post-secondary education in his controversial book *The Closing of the American Mind*. In order to rate the relative influence of educators, the editors searched for references to each individual in the Educational Research Information Center (ERIC) database, a CD-ROM service offering abstracts from tens of thousands of articles, surveys and other education research sources; educators received one point for each reference to them, the final score being the total number of references for each educator.

Educator	Score
1. John Dewey	380
2. Thomas Hopkins Gallaudet	238
3. Carl Rogers	115
4. William Bennett	114
5. E.D. Hirsch	85
6. Horace Mann	64
7. Allan Bloom	40
8. Marshall McLuhan	40
9. Maria Montessori	39
10. Friedrich Wilhelm Froebel	38

Source: "Best and Worst" original.

ENTERTAINERS
Most Lucrative Concert Tours, 1990

The bodacious bucks in bigtime rock are yesterday's news, but the lucre loads scored on some recent outings may raise even the most seasoned eyebrows. Although the classic acts like the Rolling Stones and the Grateful Dead finished the touring season high indeed on the hog, top honors and honoraria go to the the wish-washily-winsome New Kids on the Block.

Act	Gross Receipts
1. New Kids on the Block	$58,584,801
2. Paul McCartney	$44,930,681
3. Billy Joel	$41,670,036
4. The Grateful Dead	$27,923,513
5. Motley Crue	$25,521,888
6. Janet Jackson	$23,556,881
7. Aerosmith	$23,383,600
8. Madonna	$19,144,624
9. Phil Collins	$19,144,510
10. The Rolling Stones	$18,837,313

Source: *Amusement Business Magazine.*

ENTERTAINERS
Highest-Earning Entertainment Acts

For the last two decades, the dollars in the upper echelons of the entertainment world have been unmistakably grand. In the last two years, however, the pot has sweetened

PEOPLE

to an almost saccharine consistency. The top three winners in these breakthrough times are not newcomers, but rather some of the most stage- and studio-worn of our superstar survivors. Bill Cosby has been plugging away with his jokes and chomping his cigars since the mid-60s; Michael Jackson's days in the limelight began as Lilliputian front-man for his brotherly singing group; the crusty Rolling Stones can still bring home the bacon after nearly thirty years of musical ups and downs. To the New Kids: If history forgets you, the elephants at least shall always remember. Let's hope they've got their trust funds set up.

Act	Earnings 89-90 (millions)
1. Bill Cosby	$115
2. Michael Jackson	$100
3. The Rolling Stones	$88
4. Steven Spielberg	$87
5. The New Kids on the Block	$78
6. Oprah Winfrey	$68
7. Sylvester Stallone	$63
8. Madonna	$62
9. Arnold Schwarzenegger	$55
10. Charles M. Schulz	$54

Source: Forbes.

FAMILIES
The Wealthiest in America

Old money, indeed. The wealthiest family in the United States, the Du Ponts, have known wealth in the state of Delaware since the Revolutionary War years, building a textile mill in the small town of Rockdale, Delaware, into one of the largest and most valuable companies in the world, the chemical giant E.I. Du Pont de Nemours. Others of the wealthiest families have also enjoyed their money over many generations—the Hearsts from newspapers in the early 1900s, the Mellons from banking in the gilded age of the late 1800s.

The Top Ten	Value
1. Du Pont	$10.0 billion
2. Cargill/MacMillan	$4.8 billion
3. Hearst	$4.4 billion
4. Mellon	$4.2 billion
5. Dorrance	$3.8 billion
6. Milliken	$2.8 billion
7. Lilly	$2.3 billion
8. Busch	$2.0 billion
9. Phipps	$1.9 billion
10. Upjohn	$1.9 billion

Source: Forbes.

FOOTBALL CARDS
Most Valuable

Unlike baseball cards, trading cards for football players have yet to become an investment opportunity equal to real estate or Old Masters paintings. But you still can make a pretty penny out there by rooting through the attic in search of your old football card collection. The highest-priced cards are the oldies from the early years of football, featuring the true immortals of the gridiron like Bronco Nagurski (who played both ends—offense and defense) and fabled Notre Dame coach Knute Rockne. But surprisingly valuable is Joe Namath's 1965 AFL rookie card with the New York Jets. Also high on the list are rookie cards for Frank Gifford, Johnny Unitas, Bart Starr, Tom Landry, Paul Hornung, and Otto Graham, each of whom went on to stardom either as a player or coach. Joe Montana's rookie card from 1981 is already worth $250; Mark Gastineau's rookie card from the same year is worth only a buck. These rookie cards appeal because they symbolize a potential not yet achieved, a time when every player, and by extension, every man, is equal—the level playing field, so to speak. Equating ourselves with these players, then, allows us to appropriate their achievements as our own. Their touchdowns are our touchdowns, their trophies our own. Unfortunately, their salaries are not.

Player/Card/Year	Value
1. Nagurski (R)	$6,500
National Chicle, 1935	

2. Landsford	$3,300
Bowman Large, 1952	
3. Rockne	$3,000
National Chicle, 1935	
4. Namath (R)	$1,700
Topps, 1965	
5. Clark (R)	$1,000
National Chicle, 1935	
5. Masterson	$1,000
National Chicle, 1935	
6. Unitas (R)	$650
Topps, 1957	
7. Gifford (R)	$600
Bowman Large, 1952	
8. Brown (R)	$500
Topps, 1958	
8. Landry	$500
Bowman, 1951	
8. Starr (R)	$500
Topps, 1957	
9. Gifford (R)	$475
Bowman Small, 1952	
10. Ray	$450
Bowman, 1948	
10. Graham (R)	$450
Bowman, 1950	
10. Hornung (R)	$450
Topps, 1957	

Source: Sports Card Trader, May 1991.

FOOTBALL COACHES
Best College Coaching
Record, Active

Nebraska coach Tom Osborne is the only active coach with a spot among the top ten on the all-time winning percentage list. But the man right behind him, Joe Paterno of Penn State, begins the 1991-92 season within striking distance of both spots. Paterno has won two national championships and has been named Coach of the Year by the American Football Coaches Association four times, awards that have thus far eluded Osborne. Paterno is number six among all coaches in terms of total victories. The other coach who bears watching is the last name on the list, Dennis Erickson, who took over the program at Miami and guided the Hurricanes to a third national title in his first season at the school, then finished ranked number three in the country on his second go-round. At least one-hundred games were needed to qualify.

Name, School	Winning Pct.
1. Tom Osborne, Nebraska	.809
2. Joe Paterno, Penn State	.789
3. LaVell Edwards, BYU	.747
4. Pat Dye, Auburn	.732
5. Bobby Bowden, Florida St.	.732
6. Jackie Sherrill, Miss. St.	.697
7. Dick Sheridan, N.C. State	.686
8. Terry Donahue, UCLA	.686
9. Herb Deromedi, Cent. Mich.	.683
10. Dennis Erickson, Miami (Fla.)	.675

FOOTBALL COACHES
Best College Coaching Record,
All-time

Winning percentage is the best measure of success, but Knute Rockne's position atop the rankings is secured by more than that. Notre Dame's domination of the college game during most of this century traces directly to the pioneering efforts of Rockne and those of his disciple, Frank Leahy, who played tackle on Rockne's last three teams at South Bend. The Fighting Irish won six national championships and put together five unbeaten and untied seasons under "Rock." He not only helped popularize the sport by making Notre Dame's the first program to play a national schedule, but he also helped change the way it was played. Rockne often used his so-called "shock troops," a full team of second stringers, at the start of games, presaging the day of two-platoon systems. Imitating the precision and

PEOPLE

timing of a chorus line, he put his backfield in motion before the snap of the ball, a scheme that would be outlawed by the rules-makers of his day but eventually accepted and employed by just about every team, college and pro, playing the game today. He recognized the potential of the forward pass, then in its infancy, and used it to great advantage while most of his counterparts stubbornly kept the ball on the ground. Rockne was inducted into the National Football Foundation Hall of Fame in 1952, the first year of induction. For all their fame, none of the first five names on the all-time coaching victories list — Paul "Bear" Bryant (323 wins), Amos Alonzo Stagg (314); Glenn "Pop" Warner, 313; Wayne "Woody" Hayes (238); and Glenn "Bo" Schembechler (234) — managed to crack the list of top winning percentages.

Coach	Winning Pct.
1. Knute Rockne	.881
2. Frank Leahy	.864
3. George Woodruff	.846
4. Barry Switzer	.837
5. Percy Haughton	.832
6. Robert Neyland	.829
7. Fielding Yost	.828
8. Bud Wilkinson	.826
9. John Sutherland	.812
10. Tom Osborne	.809

FOOTBALL PLAYERS
Highest Paid

Clarity in life is so important. A great many of us are sandbagged by lack of focus — singularity of vision. A few others among us, in the most literal sense, take the ball and run with it. And these giant men are rewarded for their hard-charging efforts, in spades. Noticeable from the list of highest-paid pigskin playmates is the preponderance of unproven young pros. Sure, Jim Kelly and Joe Montana have earned their keep through conference championships and Super Bowl appearances, but the likes of first-year Indianapolis quarterback Jeff

Knute Rockne, the college football coach with the highest winning percentage of all time. Photo courtesy Notre Dame University.

George, Seattle's Cortez Kennedy and Detroit third-stringer Andre Ware have yet to make NFL names for themselves anywhere but at the bank.

Player/Team Salary

1. Jim Kelly Buffalo Bills	$4,800,000
2. Joe Montana San Francisco 49ers	$4,000,000
3. Jeff George Indianapolis Colts	$3,650,000
4. Cortez Kennedy Seattle Seahawks	$3,100,000
5. Keith McCants Tampa Bay Buccaneers	$2,950,000
6. Blair Thomas New York Jets	$2,800,000
7. Andre Ware Detroit Lions	$2,500,000
8. Jim Everett Los Angeles Rams	$2,400,000

PEOPLE

9. **Herschel Walker**	**$2,200,000**
Minnesota Vikings	
10. **Neal Anderson**	**$2,200,000**
Chicago Bears	
10. **Eric Dickerson**	**$2,200,000**
Indianapolis Colts	

Source: National Football League.

FOOTBALL PLAYERS
Dads, Train Them to Toss:
Pay By Position

In football, the offense more often than not gets all the glory. The vast majority of Heismann trophies and Most Valuable Player awards in the past two decades have gone to quarterbacks or running backs. The quarterback is seen as the team leader, the general on and off the field. It should come as no surprise that the list of Super Bowl champion quarterbacks reads like a hall-of-fame roster—Starr, Bradshaw, Staubach, Griese, Montana—while the Super Bowl also-rans contain some truly forgettable names—Ferragamo, Morton, Eason, Jaworski. Let's face it—quarterbacks make the team what it is. Even superstar running backs don't compare in importance. O.J. Simpson never played on a Super Bowl team; Walter Payton had to wait almost his entire career until the Bears got a quarterback of some competence (Jim McMahon) to lead them to the big show. Thus the discrepancy in quarterback salaries—their average salary is twice that of running backs, almost three times that of defensive linemen, and five times that of placekickers and punters—is justified. Below are the average salaries, by position for NFL starters in 1990. The average for all starters is $460,000.

Position	Avg. Salary (Starters)
1. Quarterback	$1,250,000
2. Running Back	$667,000
3. Wide Receiver	$494,000
4. Linebacker	$494,000

5. **Defensive Lineman**	**$444,000**
6. **Defensive Back**	**$395,000**
7. **Offensive Linemen**	**$387,000**
8. **Tight End**	**$345,000**
9. **Placekicker**	**$252,000**
10. **Punter**	**$233,000**

Source: Inside Sports, April 1991.

FOOTBALL TEAMS
Best College Team in the
1991 Draft

Who's the best in college football? The 1990-91 season turned out to be a particularly strange one, with three different rankings selecting three different teams. The Associated Press poll of writers chose Colorado, while the UPI Poll of Coaches thought Georgia Tech deserved the nod for its unbeaten season, and the New York Times's computer ranking said Miami was the best team. Controversy aside, one way to judge the pure talent on a team is to see how its senior players do in the draft. The following rating of college football programs is derived from a formula that grants points for the overall position of a school's players in the 1991 college draft. Each of the 334 selections in the draft received a point value—the formula being 334 minus the actual number of the selection. Thus the number one pick overall receives 333 points, the number two pick 332 points, and so on, the last pick receiving no points. But even this fairly straightforward, objective system is not immune to controversy. Who was the real number one selection—Russell Maryland of Miami University, or Raghib Ismael of Notre Dame, the consensus number one if he hadn't at the last minute chosen to sign a huge deal with the Toronto Argonauts of the Canadian Football League? After much debate among the editors of the Almanac, we decided that since Ismael would most assuredly have gone to the Dallas Cowboys as the first selection (Dallas had done much pre-draft maneuvering in order to be in the position to draft the Rocket), and since his

PEOPLE

contract with Toronto contains some truly astounding, unprecedented sums of money (even if it is Canadian), we gave the top point score to Ismael, thus shoving Notre Dame over Miami as the top school in the 1991 draft. (If Ismael is assigned his score for his actual selection in the NFL draft by the Los Angeles Raiders—234 points for the 100th selection—Miami comes out on top). The relatively youthful Georgia Tech team had only two players drafted, for a paltry overall score of 226.

The Top Ten	Total Points
1. Notre Dame	2130
2. Miami	2092
3. Colorado	2081
4. Tennessee	1905
5. Clemson	1634
6. Michigan St.	1605
7. USC	1466
8. Auburn	1287
9. Texas A&M	1246
10. Texas	1262

Source: Almanac Original.

FOOTBALL TEAMS
Best College Winning Percentage, All-Time

Since the Associated Press began certifying the national champion by virtue of a poll of sportswriters and broadcasters in 1936, Notre Dame has won more titles—eight, the most recent awarded after the 1988 season—than any other team in the country. Additionally, the Irish were recognized as the nation's best six times during Knute Rockne's tenure (1919-1930) by at least one of the several ratings systems of the day. But some of the other programs on the list claim some notable achievements. Oklahoma won a record 47 straight games under Bud Wilkinson from 1953 to 1957, and Penn State went 49 seasons, from 1939 until 1987, without a losing one.

The Top Ten	Winning Percentage
1. Notre Dame	.759
2. Michigan	.743
3. Alabam	.722
4. Oklahoma	.722
5. Texas	.716
6. USC	.709
7. Ohio State	.700
8. Penn State	.688
9. Nebraska	.686
10. Tennessee	.684

FOOTBALL TEAMS
Worst College Winning Percentage, All-time

Measuring futility is never easy, but most of the teams on this list can find more than a miserable winning percentage to be ashamed of. Kansas State, for instance, has had losing records in 65 of the 95 seasons it has fielded a program. The school also shared the record for most consecutive games lost (28) with Virginia through 1981, only to have Big Ten doormat Northwestern come along and extend the standard to 34 before defeating Northern Illinois early the next year. And by failing to make a two-point conversion against Baylor in the last game of the 1990 season, Rice kept hold of the dubious distinction of having gone a record 27 consecutive seasons without a winning one. Ties were broken by the team with the most all-time losses (UTEP has 329 to Cal. State-Fullerton's 132).

The Bottom Ten	Winning Percentage
1. Kansas St.	.374
2. Wake Forest	.405
3. Northwestern	.425
4. Indiana	.436
5. UTEP	.437
6. Kent State	.439
7. Cal. State-Fullerton	.439
8. Rice	.443
9. Colorado State	.456
10. New Mexico St.	.463

PEOPLE

GENERALS
Best

The best generals through history proved to be not only masters of war, but of politics as well. Rising from the origins of humanity was the idea of safety and prosperity for one's tribe. The art of generalship stems from this very principal, with the strongest individual rising to the leadership position. Soon after civilization entered the domain of mankind, strength of flesh no longer was enough for a leader but strength of mind as well. The men that are rated in this list exhibit the extraordinary ability to lead, they are masters of military planning and masters of politics which led the best to rule kingdoms. The criteria used in judgment is as follows: winning battles, capturing and securing territory; and the legacy that was left in place following the individual career. Alexander the Great emerges as the best general. Carrying the society and culture of Greece, he captured great swaths of territory and securely established them so they did not immediately return to enemy hands when the soldiers were reduced to guardians-only levels. Sweeping into the Persian empire, Alexander took over much of Egypt and India. The stamp he left has reverberated through history and still affects us today (is there not a current debate about "core" curriculums which still employ texts on Greek philosophy and the ideas put forth then? Not to mention our system of democratic government which also finds its origins in Greek culture). Alexander, by conquering other cultures and assimilating them (rather than attempting to subjugate), let his influence not only affect his immediate subjects (he did become king) but on history itself.

General/Major Accomplishment

1. Alexander the Great

Defeats Persian Forces, assimilates populations, fundamental in the spread and persistence of Greek cultural and political traditions.

2. Napoleon Bonaparte

Gains control of France after leading revolutionary armies against rest of Europe; masterful tactics in Battle of Austerlitz leaves him de facto ruler of Europe; only his own ego defeats him in vain attack on Russia. Nearly regains European dominion at Waterloo.

3. Ulysses Grant

First "modern" general. Created the "American way of war" — destruction of enemy's warmaking capacity. Realized the power of the Union's industrial and manpower resources. Eschewed nonsense of "accepted" theories. Hard-headed refusal to accept or admit defeat results in victory over Lee's armies.

4. Duke of Wellington

Defeats Napoleonic forces in Spain. At Waterloo, maintains cool head and defeats Napoleon himself. Claims "the Battle of Waterloo was won on the playing fields of Eton."

5. Hannibal

Master tactician in the mold of Alexander. Pincers envelopment of enemy at Cannae achieved one of the most remarkable victories in the history of warfare. Greatest achievement of any general to this day is to win his own "Cannae."

6. King Henry V

Victor at Battle of Agincourt, stunning defeat over French. Henry forces French into ill-conceived attack for which English forces, a mere one-fifth the size of the French, are well-prepared and entrenched. Casualties: several dozen English, several thousand French.

7. George Washington

Against great odds, unites colonies and inspires American Revolutionary forces to victory over British. First American President.

8. Erwin Rommel

First, and perhaps greatest, master of

tank warfare. Daunted Allies throughout Second World War. Lead German spearhead through France; commanded vaunted "Afrika Korps." Respected even by foes.

9. George S. Patton

Charismatic American General in WWII. Disengages entire army in midst of major battle, turns 90 degrees and travels 100 miles in 48 hours to relieve besieged Bastogne during Battle of Bulge.

10. Robert E. Lee

A great leader of men, even in defeat by the better equipped North. Consistent victories over numerically superior Northern forces include Chancellorsville, where he divides his forces, and, with Stonewall Jackson, rolls up the staggered Union General Hooker's right.

Source: "Best and Worst" original.

GENERALS
Worst

A bad commander is the worst possible thing to inflict on a corps of soldiers. It is said that some men are born mediocre, some men rise to mediocrity and other men have mediocrity thrust upon them. The following generals have gone down in history as the worst figures at the head of an army. Not only are all of them losers of battles, many either died (some by their own hands) or were relieved of command so they could not inflict further damage on their own forces.

1. Marcus L. Crassus (115?-53 B.C.)

Lost two-fifths of force of 50,000 and was himself killed in a single battle in the Roman-Parthian War.

2. Philip VI of France (1293-1350)

Battle of Crecy, terrible commander, loses 4,000 (one-third of his force) to a mere 100 English.

3. Horatio Gates (1728?-1806)

More concerned with politics than command. Ineffective leader, his underlings took charge (luckily), later relieved of command.

4. William H. Winder (1775-1824)

Battle of Stony Creek, snatches failure from the jaws of victory, loses battle with 3 to 1 advantage over foe.

5. A. Lopez de Santa Anna (1795-1876)

Lost two wars for Mexico. In Mexican-American war, lost every battle he waged.

6. George McClellan (1826-1885)

Diminutive commander of Union Army for first two years of Civil War. "Little Napoleon" turns out to be Big Chicken, continually overestimating opposing Confederate forces by factors of 2 to 3. Indecisiveness and inability to take risks led to decisive defeat to Lee in Peninsular Campaign and draw at Antietam; does not pursue weak and vulnerable Southern forces after that battle; relieved of command by Lincoln.

7. Sir Ian Hamilton (1853-1947)

Losing commander at one of the bloodiest battles, Gallipoli, in WWI; 250,000 dead/wounded.

8. Robert Nivelle (1856-1924)

Continues to order fruitless attacks in WWI. Relieved of command.

9. Aleksander Samsonov (1859-1914)

Beaureaucrat thrust into command. Hopelessly confused, loses battle of Tannenberg and commits suicide.

10. Maurice Gamelin (1872-1958)

Held Maginot line believing the Blitzkrieg was a "diversion." Bad call, Germany over-runs France.

Source: Book of Lists.

GOLFERS
Highest Paid Men, 1990

The 1990 golf season was a good one for the ever-popular Australian Greg Norman. The "Shark" successfully shed the image he had built up over the past several seasons of a hard-luck golfer, always the bridesmaid never the bride. Seemed in every major tournament Norman would be in contention, only to see his luck turn into disaster. And it appeared that would be the sad situation again in 1990—Norman shot blistering, back-to-back 66's in the first two rounds of the British Open at St. Andrews, only to stumble badly with a 79 in the third round and finish a disappointing fourth. But Norman's luck changed, and by the end of the season he had two PGA tournaments under his belt.These winnings led Norman to the top post on the money chart for 1990.

Player	Earnings
1. Greg Norman	$907,977
2. Payne Stewart	$856,393
3. Paul Azinger	$790,231
4. Wayne Levi	$772,397
5. Hale Irwin	$753,749
6. Mark Calcavecchia	$744,021
7. Fred Couples	$682,499
8. Gil Morgan	$616,964
9. Lanny Wadkins	$604,433
10. Larry Mize	$603,448

Source: PGA.

GOLFERS
Highest Paid Women, 1990

After eleven years on the Ladies PGA tour, Beth Daniel finally got her due, winning the LPGA Championship at Bethesda, Maryland, and finishing among the leaders in the Women's U.S. Open, the du Maurier Classic and the Nabisco Dinah Shore. Her torrid golfing wasn't limited to the major tournaments, though. She won an astounding five more tournament victories: The Hawaiian Open, the Kemper Open, the Youngstown Classic, the Northgate Classic and the Rail Classic, making her season one of the most remarkable of any woman golfer in the history of the LPGA.

Player	Earnings
1. Beth Daniel	$863,578
2. Patty Sheehan	$725,418
3. Betsy King	$520,101

Beth Daniel, top women's golfer. Photo courtesy LPGA.

4. Pat Bradley	$471,443
5. Cathy Gerring	$463,493
6. Rosie Jones	$338,570
7. Nancy Lopez	$301,262
8. Ayako Okamoto	$298,073
9. Danielle Ammaccapane	$256,231
10. Cindy Rarick	$252,788

Source: LPGA.

HOCKEY CARDS
Most Valuable

These days, people will buy just about anything as an investment, and that includes Hockey trading cards. Even the most avid sports fan might be unaware of the lucrative market in this commodity. One interesting note among our list of the most valuable hockey cards is the inordinate preponderance of Americans among the list, —Gordie Howe, Bobbie Orr and Bobbie Hull dominate the top spots, although it is Canadians, not Americans, who truly dominate on the ice in the NHL. Do we sense a bit of national prejudice against our neighbors to the north, or is it just that a good American hockey players are indeed so rare as to justify the high price of their trading icons?

Player/Card	Value
1. Gordie Howe (R) Parkhurst, 1951-52	$2,500
2. Gordie Howe Topps, 1954-55	$2,100
3. Gordie Howe Parkhurst, 1952-53	$1,900
4. Bobbie Orr Topps, 1966-67	$1,750
5. Bobbie Hull (R) Topps, 1958-59	$1,450
6. Gordie Howe Parkhurst 1953-54	$1,000
7. Maurice Richard (R) Parkhurst, 1951-52	$875
8. Wayne Gretzky (R) O-Pee-Chee, 1979-80	$750
9. T. Sawchuck (R) Parkhurst, 1951-52	$700
10. Gordie Howe Topps, 1957-58	$650

Source: Sports Card Trader, May 1991.

HOCKEY PLAYERS
Highest Paid

With the coming of the Great One, Wayne Gretzky, the image and popularity of professional hockey has improved almost miraculously, and as the green has begun to flow to the owners, promoters and telecasters, so to has some small remittance flown to icy, dashing dudes on skates. Since Gretzky's arrival in Los Angeles from the frozen wastelands of Edmonton, even the jaded fans of Tinsel Town have taken the Kings, and their sport, heart, though it's hard to tell what about the Kings is more appealing—their play on the ice or their cool silver-and-black color scheme appropriated by inner-city youths across the country.

Player/Team	Salary
1. Wayne Gretzky Los Angeles Kings	$3,000,000
2. Mario Lemieux Pittsburgh Penguins	$2,200,000
3. Brett Hull St. Louis Blues	$1,600,000
4. Steve Yzerman Detroit Red Wings	$1,400,000
4. Patrick Roy Montreal Canadiens	$1,400,000
6. Scott Stevens St. Louis Blues	$1,300,000
7. Denis Savard Montreal Canadiens	$1,250,000
7. Ray Bourque Boston Bruins	$1,250,000
9. Chris Chelios Chicago Blackhawks	$1,200,000
10. Paul Coffey Pittsburgh Penguins	$1,100,000
10. Mark Messier Edmonton Oilers	$1,100,000

JOCKEYS
Highest Earning, 1990

The highest profile competitions in horse racing are the triple crown races—the Kentucky Derby, the Preakness and the Belmont Stakes. But a jockey knows he can't rely on those races alone for the big purses. In fact, the winningest jockey in 1990, Gary Stevens, finished in the money in only one of the three triple crown races—a third-place finish on Mr. Frisky in the Preakness. Stevens won most of his money riding winners in lesser-known handicap races—the Hollywood

PEOPLE

Park Breeders Cup, the Santa Monica Handicap, the Swaps, the Santa Anita Handicap — on a number of different horses whose names will be remembered only by their owners and some die-hard bettors — Stormy But Valid, Ruhlmann, Jovial, Frost Free. On the other hand, jockeys like Craig Perret and Pat Day who hook up with a major triple crown competitor like 1990's Unbridled and Summer Squall (one-two finishers in the Kentucky Derby and Preakness) can get big bucks from just one horse. Below are the total winnings for the top ten jockeys in 1990.

Jockey	Total Winnings
1. Gary Stevens	$12,146,703
2. Jose Santos	$11,329,411
3. Craig Perret	$10,003,351
4. Pat Day	$9,439,516
5. Angel Cordero	$7,741,077
6. J.D. Bailey	$7,562,560
7. Pat Valenzuela	$7,097,412
8. Eddie Delahoussaye	$6,998,205
9. Mike Smith	$6,893,141
10. Chris Antley	$6,193,416

LAWYERS
Most Influential Male Lawyers

The following list is derived from the *National Law Journal*'s annual "Profiles in Power: The 100 Most Influential Lawyers in America." From those 100, the editors of the Almanac have chosen what we consider the pre-eminent ten — those with the highest profiles and the most influence over the widest range of governmental, legal and institutional entities. The ten below are listed in alphabetical order.

1. Robert Cox
Full-time chairman of Baker and McKenzie, the country's largest firm, with 1600 lawyers in 51 offices worldwide.

2. Alan Dershowitz
Harvard professor; media darling; subject of film *Reversal of Fortune*.

Geoffrey R. Stone, Dean and Professor in the Law School at the University of Chicago.

3. Joseph Flom
Partner in Skadden, Arps, Slate, Meagher and Flom; top lawyer for big corporate takeovers of the 1980s.

4. C. Boyden Gray
White House counsel; close advisor to President Bush.

5. Arthur Liman
Nation's premier litigator; Senate Iran-Contra counsel; clients include Michael Milken.

6. Arthur Miller
Harvard professor; competes with Dershowitz for most media appearances; author of more than 30 books on procedure, including seminal *Federal Practice and Procedure*; syndicated television programs bring simulated courtroom episodes to public.

7. Robert Morgenthau
Manhattan District Attorney for more than 15 years, office is "a major training ground for trial lawyers in New York," according to the *National Law Journal*.

PEOPLE

8. Geoffrey Stone
Dean of University of Chicago Law School, the top-rated law school in the country; young, dynamic, "a force within American law schools."

9. Robert Strauss
Former chair of Democratic National Committee; the "ultimate Washington insider."

10. Richard L. Thornburgh
U.S. Attorney General; possible successor to late Sen. Heinz from Pennsylvania.

LAWYERS
Most Influential Female Lawyers
Women have made great strides in the practice of law, but the bar is still very much a boys club—only 18% of all lawyers and judges are women (despite Susan Dey's winning turns on *L.A. Law*). Further evidence is apparent in the *National Law Journal's* list of the 100 most influential lawyers in America: only six of those are women. We have listed those six below, in alphabetical order.

1. Judith Areen
Dean of Georgetown University Law Center; noted family law and biomedical law scholar.

2. Sheila Birnbaum
Head of products liability department at New York's Skadden, Arps, Slate, Meagher & Flom.

3. Hilary Rodham Clinton
Chair of American Bar Association's Commission on Women in the Profession.

4. Roxanne Conlin
Soon-to-be President of Association of Trial Lawyers of America (running unopposed); former president of NOW Legal Defense and Education fund; prominent plaintiff's personal injury lawyer.

5. Elizabeth Rindskopf
General counsel for Central Intel-

Judith Areen, Dean of the Georgetown University Law Center.

ligence Agency; primary advisor to U.S. intelligence community.

6. Nadine Strossen
New York University law professor; president of the American Civil Liberties Union; leading theorist on free speech.

PHILOSOPHERS
Top Living Philosophers
For all its dubious merit, the literary-philosophical theory of deconstruction, developed by the French philosopher Jacques Derrida, has been perhaps the most influential philosophical idea of the postwar era. Derrida's conception that a reader's response to a text, as opposed to the author's intentions when writing the text, is the real element for philosophical analysis has been expanded to a wide range of other critical fields, from literature, art and architecture to political science and law. Thus, though Anglo-American academic

PEOPLE

philosophers would hesitate even to count Derrida as a colleague among their ranks, he is in fact the most influential living philosopher in the world. Our method of rating philosophers is a citation analysis in the Arts and Humanities citation index for the first six months of 1990. Interestingly, accompanying Derrida at the top of the list are two more philosophical gadflies — Noam Chomsky and Richard Rorty. We hesitate to include Chomsky on this list, since his philosophical output in the last decade has declined considerably, while he pursues more and more entrenched left-wing political causes. Yet, as it is beyond our capacity to judge exactly what a particular author is being cited for — in Chomsky's case, whether it be his political or his philosophical-linguistic writings — and since Chomsky has written some of the most influential treatises on philosophy and linguistics, the final decision was for inclusion on this list of philosophers. Of the Anglo-American philosophers working within the traditions of 20th-century mathematico-linguistic philosophy, the leader is David Lewis, whose main tenet is that of modal realism: the idea that our world and its inhabitants are only one of an infinite plurality of worlds containing an infinite number of conceivable objects that actually exist, or, as Lewis puts it, "There are so many worlds, in fact, that absolutely *every* way that a world could possibly be is a way that some world in fact *is*.

Philosopher	Score
1. Jacques Derrida	405
2. Noam Chomsky	284
3. Richard Rorty	178
4. David Lewis	118
5. Paul Ricouer	108
6. John Rawls	104
7. Donald Davidson	99
8. Nelson Goodman	83
9. Thomas Nagel	76
10. Bernard Williams	74

Source: "Best and Worst" original.

PLAYBOY PLAYMATES
Ambitious Women

It's a tough job, but somebody had to do it. New York's iconoclastic *Spy* magazine recently took it upon itself to analyze the 160 Playboy Playmate data sheets from July 1977 to September 1990 to see what really makes a Playmate tick. The average All-American playmate, *Spy* found, is 5'6" tall, weighs 113 lbs. and stacks out at 35-23-34. Of the 160 Playmates during that period, 20, or one-eighth, had first names that begin with K. Five were African-American, four Asian-American. But these women are not just figures on a data sheet (or an air-brushed centerfold). They have hopes, dreams, desires — in a word, *ambitions*. Below are the top ten of these ambitions. Fully 36, or one-fifth, of all Playmates hope to become actresses some day — but even they should know that Hollywood just ain't big enough for all those ambitious Playmates. According to *Spy*, only two Playboy centerfolds actually went on to become famous actresses, the late Dorothy Stratten and Julie Mc-Cullough, late of *Growing Pains*. Appearances in ZZ-Top music videos doesn't count.

Ambitions	# of Playmates
1. Acting	36
2. Happiness	29
3. Modeling	23
4. Success	21
5. Travel	15
6. Personal Growth	12
7. Help Others/Do Good	11
Lasting Relationship/Marriage (tie)	11
8. Family	10
Live Life to the Fullest (tie)	10

Source: *Spy*.

PLAYBOY PLAYMATES
Top Turn-ons and Turn-offs

Want to know what really turns a girl on? Want to know what to avoid on your first date with the 5'6", 113 lb., 35-23-34, 22-year-old ambitious future actress? Forget those

PEOPLE

Lisa Matthews, Playmate of the Year, 1991. Favorite Book: The Best and Worst of Everything? Photo: Playboy 1991.

"How to Make a Woman Love You" books and tapes. *Spy* magazine has taken care of your concerns, by compiling the top turn-ons and turn-offs of Playboy centerfolds over the past 13 years. Your best bet is to pick her up in your car with your dog, turn on the stereo, drive to the beach (in your clothes), pick some flowers (naturally somewhat hard to do on the beach), watch the sunset, then do some dancing in the rain. Whatever you do, don't rudely light up a cigarette, be jealous of her old boyfriends (or the guys ogling her on the beach), and don't get stuck in traffic.

Top Turn-ons	Number of votes
1. Music	34
2. Cars	28
3. Animals	27
4. Beach and Ocean	22
5. Clothes	21
6. Flowers	18
7. Sun and Sunset	17
8. Outdoors and Nature	16
9. Dancing	15
Rain, thunder, lightning	15

Top Turn-offs	
1. Tobacco and smoke	24
2. Rude or pushy people	23
3. Jealousy	21
4. Traffic	16
Waiting	16
6. Pessimists or Naysayers	15
7. Phony People	11
8. Egomaniacs and egoists	10
Judgmental people	10
Liars	10
Pollution and litter	10
Waking up early	10

Source: *Spy.*

PRESIDENTS
Biggest Presidential Victories

Most presidential elections are fairly close, with a few million swing voters deciding the outcome. Sometimes however, the public gets enthusiastically behind one candidate and gives him a mandate of 60% or more. Other times voters instinctively distrust a candidate and leave him high and dry in the voting booth. Recent examples of this were Ronald Reagan's 1984 blow-out of Walter Mondale and the election of 1980 when people voted for John Anderson, an obvious spoiler, rather than voting for then-president Jimmy Carter. Most of the really spectacular wins have come in this century when political parties have become more settled than they were in the 1800s. What is interesting in this list of presidential landslides is the prevalence of truly mediocre, even downright terrible, presidents on the winning end of some of the biggest landslides in American history—Warren Harding, who ran one of the most corrupt administrations ever and who died ignominiously in office; Richard Nixon, who even while celebrating his crushing of McGovern was plotting the cover-up of the Watergate break-in that

PEOPLE

eventually led to his downfall; Herbert Hoover, who in 1932, four years after his large mandate from the people, received an even smaller percentage of the votes than the man he defeated in 1928; James Buchanan, who did nothing during his term to prevent the country's plunging into civil war; Lyndon Johnson, who, four years after his overwhelming defeat of Barry Goldwater, was driven from office by the tragedy of Vietnam; and even Ronald Reagan, who, despite all the good times America seemed to be having, left office under the cloud of the Iran-Contra affair and a general feeling that the country would soon have to start paying for the high-flying, free-spending, fun-filled '80s.

Year/Race/Differential

1. 1920
Warren Harding beats James Cox, 63.8% to 36.2%

2. 1936
Franklin Roosevelt beats Alf Landon, 62.5% to 37.5%

3. 1972
Richard Nixon beats George Mc-Govern, 61.8% to 38.2%

4. 1964
Lyndon Johnson beats Barry Goldwater, 61.3% to 38.7%

5. 1904
Theodore Roosevelt beats Alton Parker, 60% to 40%

6. 1984
Ronald Reagan beats Walter Mondale, 59.2% to 40.8%

7. 1928
Herbert Hoover beats Al Smith, 58.8% to 41.2%

8. 1836
Martin Van Buren beats William Harrison, 58.2% to 41.8%

9. 1856
James Buchanan beats John Fremont, 58.1% to 41.9%

10. 1932
Franklin Roosevelt beats Herbert Hoover and Socialist Norman Thomas, 57.8% to 39.9% and 2.3% respectively.

Source: Federal Election Board.

PROFESSIONALS
Most Trusted People
O, Dear Lord, who can we trust in these hazy times? If the Gallup organization is to be believed, the corner druggist is our best bet. Funeral directors, bankers and journalists also earned high marks for honesty. Clergyman did well, but they were edged out by M.D.'s and dentists. The following are the most trusted professions in America, measured by the percentage of the population expressing "high" faith in the ethical standards of the occupation

Occupation	% "High" faith
1. Druggist	52
2. College Teachers	44
3. Dentists	41
4. Medical Doctors	40
5. Clergymen	38
6. Policeman	37
7. Bankers	23
8. Funeral Directors	20
8. Journalists	20
10. TV Reporters	19

Source: The Gallup Report, #279, 1988

PROFESSIONALS
Least Trusted People
While it is unrealistic and inequitable to judge a person solely by his occupation (particularly if that occupation is a putatively legal one), some jobs have been stigmatized by the actions of their traditional practitioners. In occupations like car salesman, the economic temptation to distort or dispense with hard truths is enormous. Similar forces come to bear on our elected officials from lobbyists, co-opting opponents and vo-

cally gifted constituents. Below are the least trusted professionals, measured by the percentage of those surveyed who expressed "high" faith in the ethical standards of the occupation

Occupation	% "High" faith
1. Car Salesman	1
2. Advertising Practitioners	1
3. State Officeholders	1
4. Insurance Salesmen	2
5. Stockbrokers	2
6. Business Executives	2
7. Congressman	2
8. Local Office-holders	2
8. Labor Union Leaders	3
10. Real Estate Agents	3

Source: The Gallup Report, #279, 1988

RACE CAR DRIVERS
Highest Paid, NASCAR, 1990

Without a doubt Dale Earnhardt's got the heaviest leadfoot on the NASCAR stock car circuit. In 1990, Earnhardt strung together victories in such major races as the Winston 500, the Talladega 500 and the Southern 500, as well as another four minor races—the Motorcraft 500, TranSouth 500, Miller 400, and Pepsi 400. In fact, Earnhardt was well on his way to a victory in the granddaddy of stock car races, the Daytona 500, when he ran over debris and blew a tire on the last lap in one of the most dramatic finishes in Daytona history. Derrick Cope passed Earnhardt to notch his first career victory, and three other racers passed Earnhardt before he limped home in his Chevy Lumina to take the fifth spot. But judging from his winnings elsewhere in 1990, Dale probably couldn't have been too upset by the finish.

Driver	Winnings
1. Dale Earnhardt	$1,614,280
2. Mark Martin	$834,170
3. Bill Elliott	$789,890
4. Rusty Wallace	$771,764
5. Geoff Bodine	$719,020
6. Kyle Petty	$662,040
7. Ken Schrader	$636,800
8. Davey Allison	$552,505
9. Derrike Cope	$504,830
10. Ricky Rudd	$440,407

RACE CAR DRIVERS
Highest Paid, CART, 1990

By dint of his victory in the 1990 Indianapolis 500, Arie Luyendyk took home about two-thirds of his total winnings for the year—over $1,000,000 in the largest Indy winner's purse ever. The other star on the Indy circuit was Al Unser, Jr., who broke an eight-year drought in 500-mile races by winning the Marlboro 500, then proceeded to take the checkered flag in the Miller Genuine Draft 200, the Molson Indy Toronto, the Molson Indy Vancouver, and the Grand Prix of Denver, as well as the Formula One Grand Prix of Long Beach, capping off a fine racing season. At press time, Ayrton Senna was top earner with $12 million.

Racer	Winnings
1. Arie Luyendyk	$1,666,076
2. Al Unser Jr.	$1,443,025
3. Emerson Fittipaldi	$1,368,276
4. Bobby Rahal	$1,276,450
5. Rick Mears	$1,190,086
6. Michael Andretti	$999,172
7. Mario Andretti	$891,613
8. Danny Sullivan	$800,253
9. Eddie Cheever	$748,492
10. Teo Fabi	$565,627

REPRESENTATIVES
Attendance Record

"I slept late!" is a favorite excuse for not going to work. What's yours? Here is a list of our government representatives who seemed to go to work less often than their counterparts. To be fair, Hyde, Collins, Yatron and Brooks all owed at least some of their absences to illnesses or deaths in the family. Similarly, both Florio and Garcia switched jobs in the middle of their terms. Florio was elected governor of New Jersey and Molinari took the job of Staten Island Borough President. Finally, poor Robert Garcia of New York owed at least some of his absences to his trial and conviction on charges of extortion and conspiracy. The following is a list of the members who were absent the most for votes in the House of Representatives, and those whose attendance was perfect.

Worst House Attendance

1. James Florio, New Jersey	19%
2. Jim Courter, New Jersey	24%
3. Robert Garcia, New York	49%
4. Cardiss Collins, Illinois	52%
5. Guy Molinari, New York	64%
6. John Conyers, Michigan	68%
7. Henry Hyde, Illinois	72%
Gus Yatron, Pennsylvania	72%
John Bryant, Texas	72%
Jack Brooks, Texas	72%

Perfect House Attendance

Charles Bennet, Florida	100%
Larry Combest, Texas	100%
Dale Kildee, Michigan	100%
Sander Levin, Michigan	100%
Tom McMillen, Maryland	100%
William Natch, Kentucky	100%
Timothy Penny, Minnesota	100%
Thomas Petri, Wisconsin	100%
Christopher Shays, Connecticut	100%
Gene Taylor, Mississippi	100%
James Traficant, Ohio	100%
Harold Volkmer, Missouri	100%

Source: *Congressional Quarterly 1990 Almanac.*

REPRESENTATIVES
Top PAC Congressional Contribution Recipients

To take, it must be noted, is not necessarily to be taken. It is quite conceivable than most politicians who accept large donations from self-interested PAC's and lobbyists main-

tain their integrity and objectivity. Others, however, most assuredly, are unduly influenced by the wants and wishes of their largest campaign contributors and ultimately the public interest is compromised. Below are the House members who have received the most in campaign contributions from political action committees. Despite their griping about the Republicans as the party in which money talks most powerfully, the list of well-financed House members is dominated by Democrats.

Congressman	Receipts
1. Robert Michel (R)	$523,466
2. Jim Moody (D)	$482,403
3. Thomas Foley (D)	$456,248
4. James Jontz (D)	$440,604
5. Robert Matsui (D)	$435,191
6. Byron Dorgan (D)	$430,796
7. John Dingell (D)	$425,642
8. David Price (D)	$403,195
9. Ronnie Flippo (D)	$392,048
10. Dan Rostenkowski (D)	$382,048

Source: Federal Election Committee

REPRESENTATIVES
Fewest Defense-related Contributions

Despite the voters' suspicions to the contrary, not all members of Congress reside within the pockets of defense contractors. Indeed, many receive little or no monetary support from defense-related political action committees. All of the members of this club of U.S. Representatives with low amounts of defense-related political action committee contributions are Democrats.

Rep /State	Defense Cont.
1. Atkins, Chester, Mass.	225
2. Jontz, James, Ind.	250
3. Sunia, Fofo, Amer. Samoa	250
4. Synar, Mike, Okla.	340
5. De Lugo, Ron Virg. Is.	250
6. Weiss, Ted, N.Y.	363
7. Markey, Edward, Mass.	450
8. Mfume, Kweisi, Md.	490

PEOPLE

9. Studds, Gerry, Mass.   500
9. Ackerman, Gary, N.Y.   500
10. Skaggs, David, Colo.   550

Source: *Congress and Defense*.

ROCK MUSICIANS
Most Influential

The first thing any kid who ever picks up an electric guitar learns is the opening riff from Chuck Berry's classic "Johnny B. Goode," and for that alone, Berry merits top honors as rock 'n' roll's most influential figure. Every rock guitar player from John Lennon and Keith Richards to Eddie Van Halen and U2's The Edge owe a deep debt to Berry's style, which gave an electric jump-start to rock music and placed the guitar squarely at front and center as *the* instrument of the rock era. The following are the ten most influential rock musicians of all time, as determined by the "Best and Worst" editorial staff.

The Top Ten

1. Chuck Berry
2. John Lennon
3. Buddy Holly
4. Bob Dylan
5. Jimi Hendrix
6. Eric Clapton
7. Jimmy Page
8. Keith Moon
9. Joey/Dee Dee Ramone
10. Jim Morrison

Source: "Best and Worst" original.

SENATORS
Most Defense Contributions

Below are the senators receiving the most in campaign contributions from defense-related political action committees in the 1986 senate campaign, the most recent campaign for which figures are available. It should come as no surprise that nine of the top ten in this list are hawkish Republicans (including John McCain, the former Vietnam prisoner of war), or that the majority of the bottom ten senators in terms of defense campaign contributions are Democrats.

The Top Ten	Defense Cont.
1. Symms, Steve (R), Id.	$260,960
2. Bond, Christopher (R), Mo.	$252,475
3. Kasten, Bob (R), Wisc.	$220,441
4. Specter, Arlen (R), Penn.	$217,300
5. McCain, John (R), Ariz.	$208,045
6. Nickles, Donald (R), Okla.	$207,464
7. Dole, Robert (R), Kan.	$180,435
8. D'Amato, Alfonse (R), N.Y.	$179,462
9. Dixon, Alan (D), Ill.	$163,788
10. Packwood, Bob (R), Ore.	$148,969

Note: Vice President Dan Quayle received $247,602 from defense-connected political action committees in his successful 1986 campaign for the Senate, which placed him third.

The Bottom Ten	Defense Cont.
1. Johnston, J. Bennett (D), La.	$50
2. McClure, James (R), Id.	$100
3. Boschwitz, Rudy (R), Minn.	$200
4. Heflin, Howell (D), Ala.	$250
5. Exon, J. James (D), Neb.	$325
6. Pressler, Larry (R), S.D.	$500
7. Biden, Joe (D), Del.	$600
8. Evans, Daniel (R), Wash.	$700
9. Baucus, Max (D), Mont.	$1,000
10. Pryor, David (D), Ark.	$1,000

Note: Fourteen senators received no money from defense-related politial action committees.

Source: *Congress and Defense*.

SENATORS
Top PAC Congressional Contribution Recipients

The PAC's are generous to Congressmen, but they positively dote on Senators. While Robert Michel of the House received a little in excess of half a million dollars from his PAC angels, opposite number Lloyd Bentsen took home a whopping $2,144,016, for his war chest.

PEOPLE

Senator	Receipts
1. Lloyd Bentsen (D)	$2,144,016
2. Pete Wilson (R)	$1,598,290
3. James Sasser (D)	$1,287,027
4. Frank Lautenberg (D)	$1,272,471
5. Dave Durenberger (R)	$1,239,932
6. John Heinz (R)	$1,213,513
7. Donald Riegle, Jr. (D)	$1,191,791
8. Orrin Hatch (R)	$1,054,213
9. John C. Danforth (R)	$1,051,557
10. Jeff Bingaman (D)	$1,007,630

Source: Federal Election Committee

SENATORS
Best Attendance Record

While it might be fun to blame all our nation's troubles on absentee senators who vote when they please and spend most of their time on yachts with pin-up girls in their laps, the fact is that attendance in the Senate is extraordinarily high. A study of 310 votes conducted by *Congressional Quarterly* showed a 98% participation rate in the 101st Congress. The study counted the number of roll-call votes in which a member voted "yea" or "nay." Votes of "present" or live pairs were not counted. Among active senators, only Al Gore of Tennessee, who was called away by an illness in the family, had a score below 90%. His score was 89%.

Perfect Senate Attendance

Robert Byrd, West Virginia
John Chaffee, Rhode Island
William Cohen, Maine
Kent Conrad, North Dakota
Alan Dixon, Illinois
Slade Gorton, Washington
Charles Grassley, Iowa
Howell Heflin, Alabama
Earnest Hollings, South Carolina
J. Bennett Johnston, Louisiana
John Kerry, Massachussets
Bob Kerrey, Nebraska
Joseph Lieberman, Connecticut
Mitch McConnell, Kentucky
George Mitchell, Maine

Rhode Island Senator John Chaffee is among a number of senators with perfect attendance.

Larry Pressler, South Dakota
Charles Robb, Virginia
Richard Shelby, Alabama
Arlen Specter, Pennsylvania
Strom Thurmond, South Carolina

Source: *1990 Congressional Quarterly Almanac.*

SENATORS
Lefties: Most Liberal Senators

Right on! Power to the people! Well, not exactly. These liberal senators wear white shirts and bow ties. When they run for office they make a lot of speeches about care for the down-trodden, national health insurance, funding education and cutting the defense budget. When they are in the Senate they vote for these things. If the 1988 Presidential campaign proved one thing, it was that the nation was not yet ready for a bow-tied, flop-eared, slow-talking liberal

PEOPLE

from farm country to lead it. But the people of Illinois are, sending ultra-liberal Paul Simon back to the Senate in 1990 after his unsuccessful bid for the Democratic Presidential nomination in 1988. Compiled by the liberal interest group Americans for Democratic Action, this ranking represents the percentage of times each senator voted in accordance with the ADA position on 20 selected votes during the 101st Congress. Space prohibits us from listing the large number of Representatives who scored a perfect 100% on the liberal voting scale.

Senator	Liberal Voting Record
1. Paul Simon, Illinois	100%
Patrick Leahy, Vermont	100%
3. Tim Wirth, Colorado	95%
Tom Harkin, Iowa	95%
John Karry, Massachussetts	95%
Howard Metzenbaum, Ohio	95%
Brock Adams, Washington	95%
Herb Kohl, Wisconsin	95%
9. Dale Bumpers, Arkansas	90%
Joseph Biden, Delaware	90%
Barbara Mikulski, Maryland	90%

Source: *Congressional Quarterly Almanac*.

SENATORS
Biggest Winners in the '90 Senate Race

The U.S. Senate has often been called a millionaire's club and a men's club. Both are still fairly apt nicknames. Many in the upper house are still wealthy, and while this ranking shows that Nancy Kassebaum of Kansas is one of the country's most popular elected officials, a total of eight women lost their 1990 bids to enter the senate. Among winners, the one with the smallest margin of victory was Bill Bradley of New Jersey. The former New York Knicks basketball star and a man who is regarded as one of the great minds of the Senate received just 51% of the vote as compared with his challenger Christine Todd Whitman's 49% of the vote. We shall see just how this surprisingly small

majority in his home state affects Bradley's future presidential considerations.

Senator	Percent of Votes
1. David L. Boren (D-Okla.)	83%
2. John W. Warner (R-Va.)	82%
3. Nancy Kassebaum (R-Kan.)	74%
4. Pete V. Domenici (R-N.M.)	73%
5. Max Baucus (D-Mont.)	70%
6. Al Gore (D-Tenn.)	70%
7. John D. Rockefeller IV (D-W.V.)	69%
8. Ted Stevens (R-Ak.)	67%
9. Robert C. Smith (R-N.H.)	67%
10. Strom Thurmond (R-S.C.)	66%

Source: *Congressional Quarterly*.

TELEVISION VIEWERS
Most Hooked

Over two decades we weathered innumerable warnings of the corrosive effects of TV saturation on developing and (purportedly) mature minds. In the fullness of time, however, these warnings began to ring hollow. Although a substantial group of once-dependent viewers have forsaken their prime-time rituals for vegetarianism and a host of other New Age pastimes/retreats, those who have stayed tight with their high-voltage oracles are watching more than ever. Surprisingly, despite the constant complaints from parents that "kids are watching to much TV," it is in fact the older generations that are most glued to the tube. Teenagers, it seems, have other things on their agendas, like the telephone.

Group	Viewing Time Per Week
1. Women 55 and over	38 h 53 min
2. Men 55 and over	37 h 32 min
3. Women 35-54	32 h 14 min
4. Women 18-34	28 h 43 min
5. Men 35-54	27 h 01 min
6. Men 18-34	25 h 44 min
7. Children 2-5	25 h 43 min
8. Children 6-11	23 h 17 min
9. Male Teens	22 h 36 min
10. Female Teens	21 h 18 min

Source: Nielsen Media Research, Nielsen

PEOPLE

Report on Television

TENNIS PLAYERS
Million Dollar Babies

Tennis has always had the image of the rich man's game—strawberries and cream at Wimbledon, don't you know—and the list below goes a long way toward confirming that image. Here are the winningest players on the men's tennis circuit for the 1990 season. The pleasant surprise in men's tennis in the last several years has been the resurgence of the American tennis program. Young players like Andre Agassi, Pete Sampras and Brad Gilbert are budding stars who hope to carry the mantle of American tennis for the coming years. At press time, Edberg's winnings for 1991 were $1.4 million.

Player	Winnings
1. Stefan Edberg	$1,251,991
2. Boris Becker	$1,102,332
3. Ivan Lendl	$973,182
4. Andres Gomez	$800,890
5. Andre Agassi	$785,212
6. Pete Sampras	$732,697
7. Goran Ivanisevic	$641,510
8. Emilio Sanchez	$542,324
9. Brad Gilbert	$511,803
10. Thomas Muster	$492,597

TENNIS PLAYERS
Million Dollar Babies, Part II

Women's tennis used to be assigned a back seat to the men's version of the game, but no more. In fact, the top women players now earn just about the same amount on the professional circuit as their male counterparts, as can be seen from the following list of the top female money winners for 1990. Missing from this list is the 13-year-old American phenomenon Jennifer Capriati, who burst on the tennis scene to much fanfare and some success as perhaps the youngest major professional athlete ever. She'll certainly be among the top money

winners in the next couple of years, barring a serious injury or other setbacks. At press time, Monica Seles was 1991's top earner with $1.6 million.

Player	Winnings
1. Steffi Graf	$1,114,070
2. Martina Navratilova	$1,041,380
3. Monica Seles	$885,924
4. Gabriela Sabatini	$681,783
5. Jana Novotna	$532,732
6. Zina Garrison	$487,193
7. Helena Sukova	$422,184
8. Arantxa Sanchez Vicario	$420,749
9. Natalia Zvereva	$393,363
10. Mary Joe Fernandez	$362,116

WOMEN
Highest Paid American Women in Business

American business is still very much a boys club—just take a look at the pictures in *BusinessWeek's* annual issue on the CEOs of the top 1,000 companies for a profile of the classic white, middle-aged business executive, male by a vast majority. But some women have made their way to the top of the male-dominated corporate ladder. Here are the ten women who earn the most in American business.

Woman/Salary/Position	Salary
1. Margaret Hunt Hill	$55 Million

Owns and operates oil and real estate interests in Dallas, Texas. Eldest child of tycoon H.L. Hunt.

2. Helen Kinney Copley	$40 Million

Chairman and CEO of Copley Press in La Jolla, California.

3. Estee Lauder	$35 Million

Chairman and owner of controlling interest in Estee Lauder Cosmetics Company.

4. Caroline Rose Hunt	$30 Million

Operates own real estate company, Rosewood, and holds oil and finance interest in Dallas, Texas.

5. Oveta Culp Hobby $17 Million
Chariman of H&C Communications (vast broadcasting holdings) in Houston, Texas.

6. Donna Steigerwaldt $15 Million
Chairman and CEO of Jockey International (underwear manufacturer) in Kenosha, Wisconsin.

7. Priscilla ("Patsy") Collins $13 Million
Chairman of King Braodcasting in Seattle, Washington.

8. Beatrice Coleman $8 Million
President and CEO of Maidenform (sleepwear) in New York City.

9. Katherine Graham $4.5 Million
Chairman of Washington Post Company (newspapers, magazines, broadcasting).

10. Debbi Fields $4 Million
President and CEO of Mrs. Fields, Inc. (cookies) in Park City, Utah.

Source: *Good Housekeeping.*

WRITERS
Most Published

The author with the all-time record for the most titles published is the ubiquitous William Shakespeare, with more than 15,000 titles in a computer survey of authors in the Online Computer Center Library database. Shakespeare had almost twice as many titles as his next closest rival, Charles Dickens, who had just under 8,000 titles. The list of the top one-hundred authors contains only five women: Agatha Christie, George Eliot, Ellen G. White, Jane Austen and George Sand (two of whom, strangely enough, took identical male monikers). Compare this list with our list of the greatest writers of all time to see whether there is any correlation between the sheer volume of publication and an author's lasting influence.

The Top Ten

1. William Shakespeare

2. Charles Dickens
3. Sir Walter Scott
4. Johann Goethe
5. Aristotle
6. Alexandre Dumas (pere)
7. Robert Louis Stevenson
8. Mark Twain
9. Marcus Cicero
10. Honore de Balzac

Source: "A Guide to Special Collections in the OCLC Database," OCLC Online Computer Center, Dublin, Ohio.

WRITERS
Greatest Writers, All-time

Our list of the greatest writers of all time is topped, of course, by Shakespeare — also the most published author the world has ever known. The rating is derived from an analysis of citations in the Modern Language Association International Bibliography; the score reflects the number of scholarly articles written about a particular author during the period from 1981 to 1990 (for a complete description of the methodology, see "Writers, Greatest American, All-time"). Eight of the top ten writers are English or American — including T.S. Eliot, who, one might say, is both, having been born in St. Louis but adopting England as his home. This preponderance reflects not only the influence of writers in English but of Anglo-American academia in the field of literature. Nevertheless, the list is an accurate reflection of the influence of various writers on the literary world.

The Top Ten	Score
1. William Shakespeare	5848
2. James Joyce	1943
3. Johann Wolfgang von Goethe	1802
4. Geoffrey Chaucer	1593
5. John Milton	1445
6. Dante	1330
7. William Faulkner	1324
8. Henry James	1210
9. Charles Dickens	1080
10. T.S. Eliot	1057

PEOPLE

Source: "Best and Worst" original.

WRITERS
Top Living Writers

The top living writer in the world, according to our ranking system, is the Colombian Nobel Laureate Gabriel Garcia Marquez, a writer who exemplifies the Latin American literary style that blends fantasy and reality and whose origins can be traced through Jose Luis Borges back to Cervantes. The list is rounded out by three American writers, Pynchon, Bellow and Welty, three British writers, Lessing, Fowles and Pinter, one other Latin American writer, Carlos Fuentes, and the African novelist Wole Soyinka (for a complete description of the methodology, see "Writers, American, Greatest").

Writer/Notable Work	Score
1. Gabriel Garcia Marquez *One Hundred Years of Solitude*	502
2. Thomas Pynchon *Vineland*	364
3. Saul Bellow *Herzog*	362
4. Carlos Fuentes *Our Land*	335
5. Doris Lessing *The Summer Before the Dark*	274
6. Eudora Welty *The Golden Apples*	254
7. Wole Soyinka *Aké: The Years of Childhood*	242
8. Marguerite Duras *The Lover*	196
9. John Fowles *Mantissa*	191
10. Harold Pinter *The Birthday Party*	176

Source: "Best and Worst" original.

WRITERS
Greatest Novelists, All-time

The novel is the most popular and accessible of literary forms, but the greatest novelist of all time, according to our rankings, is responsible in part for turning the novel into a less accessible, more esoteric art form. James Joyce is commonly credited with creating the modern novel form, with his extensive use of stream of consciousness and other experimental techniques in his great work, *Ulysses*, the narrative of which takes place in a single day, June 16, 1904. His last novel, *Finnegan's Wake*, is an even more difficult work, for in it Joyce employs an idiosyncratic language in which he uses invented words, plays on words and obscure allusions. The study of Joyce, especially of this last work, is a cottage industry among academics; indeed, the imposing *Finnegan's Wake* is rarely approached by the lay reader. Many of Joyce's techniques were adopted by the second writer on our list, the American William Faulkner. For the common reader, though, it is good to see the populist Charles Dickens high up on out scale. The following are the ten greatest novelists of all time, as measured by the number of scholarly articles written about their work in the ten-year period from 1981 to 1990.

Writer/Notable Work(s)	Score
1. James Joyce *Ulysses*	1943
2. William Faulkner *As I Lay Dying*; *Absalom, Absalom*	1324
3. Henry James *The Ambassadors*	1210
4. Charles Dickens *Nicholas Nickleby*	1080
5. Miguel de Cervantes *Don Quixote*	1038
6. Herman Melville *Moby Dick*	996
7. D. H. Lawrence	919

PEOPLE

Women in Love

8. Fyodor Dostoevsky   901
The Brothers Karamazov

9. Franz Kafka   844
The Trial; The Castle

10. Nathaniel Hawthorne   817
The House of the Seven Gables

Source: "Best and Worst" original.

WRITERS
Greatest Playwrights, All-time

As with the ranking of all-time greatest writers, William Shakespeare leads the list of greatest playwrights—by a wide margin indeed. But following him on the list are two twentieth- century writers known for their iconoclasm. The second greatest playwright, Bertolt Brecht, was known for his fervent commitment to Marxism, most obvious in his *Threepenny Opera* and *Rise and Fall of the City of Mahogonny*. Number three on the list is Samuel Beckett, whose *Waiting for Godot* shattered all accepted theatrical traditions, with its quintessential line that sums up the story and is Beckett's comment on life: "It's terrible. Nothing happens." (Indeed, at least one critic, not recognizing the genius of the work, used that line as his brief review of the play—something Beckett would have admired). The following are the greatest playwrights of all time, measured by the amount of influence they have had on the scholarly world (for a complete description of the methodology, see "Writers, American, Greatest").

Writer/Notable Work(s)	Score
1. William Shakespeare	**5848**
The Tempest; A Midsummer Night's Dream	
2. Bertolt Brecht	835
Rise and Fall of the City of Mahogonny	
3. Samuel Beckett	766
Waiting for Godot; Endgame	
4. Lope de Vega	509

Punishment without Revenge

5. Ben Jonson   460
The Alchemist

6. Friedrich von Schiller   438
The Gods of Greece

7. Pierre Corneille   431
Horace; Le Menteur

8. Moliere   414
Tartuffe; Le misanthrope

9. Gotthold Ephraim Lessing   396
Emilia Galotti

10. Eugene O'Neill   394
Mourning Becomes Electra; The Iceman Cometh

Source: "Best and Worst" original.

WRITERS
Greatest Poets, All-Time

The influence of Goethe on the German-speaking world is hard to overestimate. He is, far and away, the first man of German letters, the leading figure of the important *Sturm und Drang* movement of the late 18th century and the German Romanticism of the early 19th. Not a poet only, Goethe, with Voltaire and Kant, was a true giants of the Enlightenment and a master of many forms—epic poetry, epistolary novel, drama. In addition, he wrote numerous scientific tracts, most notably on plant biology and optics. His works, read by every German schoolchild to this day, created a uniquely German literary style and influenced most every subsequent German author, from Karl Marx to Thomas Mann. Other poets on our list of greats include those two banes of high school English students, Chaucer and Milton.

Poet	Score
1. Johann Wolfgang von Goethe	1802
2. Geoffrey Chaucer	1593
3. John Milton	1445
4. Dante Alighieri	1330
5. T. S. Eliot	1057

PEOPLE

6. William Wordsworth 969
7. Ezra Pound 907
8. William Butler Yeats 791
9. William Blake 732
10. Alexander Pushkin 710

Source: "Best and Worst" original.

WRITERS — AMERICAN
Greatest, All-time

Who is America's greatest writer? Some say it's simply a matter of taste. Do you prefer the vernacular of Mark Twain or the esoteric intellectualism of William James? The strong, spare prose of Ernest Hemingway or the gothic grotesquery of Poe? Certainly no one can quantify preference, or, more importantly, greatness, in literature. But it is possible at least to judge the overall influence of a writer on his generation and on ours. The editors of the Almanac have developed a method that allows us to give a quantitative score which we feel successfully reflects the overall importance of a writer across time and throughout the world. The Modern Language Association International Bibliography contains citations from articles in more than 3,000 journals and series published worldwide on literature and language. The citations include monographs, collections, working papers, proceedings of conferences, dissertations and reference works, in all modern languages. We feel that it is the most comprehensive and authoritative guide to literature in existence. Using the MLA International Bibliography, available on CD-ROM from the Wilsonline Information System, we compiled a numerical score reflecting the number of articles about a particular author that appeared in print over a ten year period from 1981 to 1990.

Based on this method, the following list represents the ten most influential American writers of all time, together with one or more of their most notable works. The list includes three 20th-century writers, including the top-rated writer overall, as well as three

poets, but only one woman, the tenth-rated Emily Dickinson. Interestingly, two of the top ten American writers became expatriates. Henry James of the illustrious James family (father Henry was a noted 19th-century historian and brother William the first great American psychologist) eventually took British citizenship. The poet Ezra Pound spent a good deal of time with the American literary crowd in Paris in the 1920s; he then moved to Rome, and, in perhaps the most bizarre episode in the annals of American literature, became an avid propagandist for Mussolini. His family is still seeking the right to bury him the United States.

Our method seems a real indicator of literary greatness, unlike, say, the strange machinations of the Nobel Prize committee. Only two of our top ten American writers were awarded the Nobel Prize in their lifetimes; but no one reads some of the other American winners of that dubious prize. The best indication of this is Pearl Buck, whose literary fame has all but vanished since being awarded the Nobel in 1932, as indicated by her score of a mere 6 in the MLA Bibliography.

Writer/Notable Work(s)	Score
1. William Faulkner *The Sound and the Fury*	1324
2. Henry James *Portrait of a Lady*	1210
3. Herman Melville *Moby Dick*	996
4. Ezra Pound *Cantos*	907
5. Nathaniel Hawthorne *The Scarlet Letter*	817
6. Ernest Hemingway *A Farewell to Arms*	810
7. Mark Twain *The Adventures of Huckleberry Finn*	744
8. Edgar Allan Poe	658

The Raven, The Tell-Tale Heart

9. Walt Whitman	**607**
Leaves of Grass	
10. Emily Dickinson	**554**
Collected Poems	

Source: "Best and Worst" original.

WRITERS — AMERICAN
Greatest American Novelists, All-time

The greatest American novelist of all time is best known for creating the imaginary Mississippi county of Yoknapatawpha, complete with its own idiosyncratic characters and social structure that examined the burdens of Southern history, race relations, class conflict and a way of life in conflict with the progress of the twentieth century. Second on the list is a writer much different from Faulkner in background and in subject matter; where Faulkner was intrigued by the people of the American South, the anglophilic James explored the confrontation between American and European cultures and deeply probed the psychology of his characters. The list of the ten greatest American novelists contains two living authors, Thomas Pynchon and Saul Bellow, and one woman, Willa Cather.

Writer/Notable Work	Score
1. William Faulkner	**1324**
Light in August	
2. Henry James	**1210**
The Turn of the Screw	
3. Herman Melville	**996**
Billy Budd	
4. Nathaniel Hawthorne	**817**
Twice-Told Tales	
5. Ernest Hemingway	**810**
For Whom the Bell Tolls	
6. Mark Twain	**744**
Life on the Mississippi	
7. Vladimir Nabakov	**465**

Lolita

8. Thomas Pynchon	**364**
V	
9. Willa Cather	**363**
O Pioneers!	
10. Saul Bellow	**362**
Henderson the Rain King	

Source: "Best and Worst" original.

WRITERS
Greatest American Playwrights, All-time

The figure of Eugene O'Neill towers above the realm of American drama. Commonly considered the founder of the modern American theater, O'Neill is one of a very few — perhaps the only other is Tennessee Williams — whose works are consistently produced in Europe and who has become a part of the international dramatic canon. O'Neill, whose parents were both actors, expressed in his work a profound interest in classical Greek drama, as seen in his trilogy *Mourning Becomes Electra*. O'Neill's works covered a wide range of topics; his early works were based on his life as a seaman, while his later works became progressively more involved psychologically. The ideas of Freud and Nietzsche played an important role in these later works, culminating in the autobiographical *Long Day's Journey Into Night*, an emotional and psychological tour de force probing the conflicts in the playwright's own family. The work, written in 1941, was so disturbing that O'Neill did not allow it to be produced in his lifetime. The following are the ten most influential American playwrights of all time, based on the number of citations of their works in the MLA International Bibliography.

Playwright/Notable Work	Score
1. Eugene O'Neill	**394**
Long Day's Journey Into Night	
2. Tennessee Williams	**159**

PEOPLE

A Streetcar Named Desire

3. Edward Albee	**107**
Who's Afraid of Virginia Woolf?	
Sam Shepard (tie)	**107**
Buried Child	
4. Arthur Miller	**99**
Death of a Salesman	
5. Thornton Wilder	**47**
Our Town	
6. David Mamet	**31**
American Buffalo	
7. Lorraine Hansberry	**19**
Raisin in the Sun	
8. William Saroyan	**16**
The Human Comedy	
9. Lanford Wilson	**15**
Talley's Folly	
10. Clifford Odets	**11**
Waiting for Lefty	

Source: "Best and Worst" original.

WRITERS — AMERICAN
Greatest American Poets, All-time

The greatest American poet of all time died in Italy, an outcast from his own country for his strange, outspoken support of Mussolini and his perceived acceptance of fascism. Arrested in May of 1945 in Italy for his fascist propaganda broadcasts during the war, Pound was tried in the U.S. and judged insane. He spent 12 years in St. Elizabeth's hospital in Washington, D.C. before being released and allowed to return finally to Italy—a parable, perhaps, of how America treats its artists. However, Pound's influence as poet, critic, essayist and scholar cannot be understated, and his epic *Cantos* mark a watershed in the poetic form.

Poet	Score
1. Ezra Pound	**907**
2. Edgar Allan Poe	**658**
3. Walt Whitman	**607**

4. Emily Dickinson	**554**
5. William Carlos Williams	**486**
6. Wallace Stevens	**427**
7. Robert Frost	**304**
8. H.D. (Hilda Doolittle)	**196**
9. Marianne Moore	**165**
10. Robert Penn Warren	**145**

Source: "Best and Worst" original.

WRITERS — AMERICAN
Greatest Black Americans, All-time

The struggle for acceptance and for civil rights is reflected in the often angry works that comprise the oevre of American Black literature. The impassioned novels and essays of Richard Wright, Ralph Ellison and James Baldwin, and the poetry of Langston Hughes, Toni Morrison, Amiri Baraka, and the works of other African-American writers gives voice to a people's continuing quest for their fair share of the American dream, or, for those more disillusioned writers, to a rejection of that dream. The following list gives the ten most influential African-American writers, as reflected in the total number of citations under their name in the MLA International Bibliography.

Writer/Notable Work(s)	Score
1. Richard Wright	**187**
Native Son	
2. Toni Morrison	**170**
Beloved	
3. Alice Walker	**124**
The Color Purple	
4. Ralph Ellison	**120**
The Invisible Man	
5. Langston Hughes	**105**
Shakespeare in Harlem	
6. Zora Neale Hurston	**89**
Their Eyes Were Watching God	
7. James Baldwin	**71**
Go Tell It on the Mountain	

PEOPLE

8. **Gwendolyn Brooks** 57
   The World of Gwendolyn Brooks

9. **Imanu Amiri Baraka** 39
   The Slave

10. **Charles Chesnutt** 37
    Conjure Woman

Source: "Best and Worst" original.

WRITERS — AMERICAN
Greatest Female American Writers, All-time

The greatest American woman writer never published a word of her work in her lifetime. Emily Dickinson wrote more than 1,000 poems in her lifetime, but the reclusive poet withdrew entirely from society before the age of thirty. Her works, typified by spare lyricism in an idiosyncratic diction and meter, were discovered in only after her death. Below are the ten most important female American writers of all time, as determined by the number of citations in the MLA International Bibliography (for a complete description of the scoring methodology, see the description under "Writers, American: Greatest, All-time"). Other women writers scoring highly include the poets Alice Walker with 124 citations, Sylvia Plath (115), and Anne Sexton (90), and the novelist, short story writer and essayist Joyce Carol Oates (82).

Writer/Notable Work(s)	Score
1. **Emily Dickinson** *Collected Poems*	554
2. **Willa Cather** *One of Ours*	363
3. **Flannery O'Connor** *A Good Man is Hard to Find and Other Stories*	338
4. **Eudora Welty** *The Optimist's Daughter*	254
5. **Edith Wharton** *House of Mirth*	209

6. **H.D. (Hilda Doolittle)** 196
   Red Shores for Bronze (poetry)

7. **Toni Morrison** 170
   Beloved

8. **Gertrude Stein** 166
   The Autobiography of Alice B. Toklas

9. **Marianne Moore** 165
   Collected Poems

10. **Kate Chopin** 126
    The Awakening

Source: "Best and Worst" original.

WRITERS — AMERICAN
Top Living Americans

America is a melting pot, and so it's not surprising that diversity is the main element apparent in the list of the top living American writers. Three black writers are included on the list, as are three women. The top ten are predominantly novelists — poetry being, it seems, not entirely acceptable to Americans with their demand for practicality and immediate payoff. The top American on our list, Thomas Pynchon, has authored two highly experimental, darkly comic novels, *Gravity's Rainbow* and *V*, as well as a novella, *The Crying of Lot 49*. After years of silence and seclusion, in 1989 Pynchon published *Vineland*, to mixed reviews. Time will only tell whether this most recent work will ultimately reside in the pantheon of great American literature along with his previous output. Others scoring just below the top ten include playwrights Edward Albee and Sam Shepard with 107 citations and Arthur Miller (99), and novelists William Styron (110), Norman Mailer (104), John Hawkes (91) and Kurt Vonnegut (91). (For a complete description of the scoring methodology, see the description under "Writers, American: Greatest, All-time").

Writer/Notable Work(s)	Score
1. **Thomas Pynchon** *Gravity's Rainbow*	364

PEOPLE

2. Saul Bellow *Humboldt's Gift*	362
3. Eudora Welty *A Curtain of Green*	254
4. John Barth *Giles Goat-Boy*	171
5. Toni Morrison *The Bluest Eye*	170
6. John Updike *Rabbit at Rest*	126
7. Alice Walker *Once*	124
8. Philip Roth *The Zukerman Trilogy*	122
9. Ralph Ellison *Shadow and Act*	120

Source: "Best and Worst" original.

John Updike, the top American writer of the last decade.

WRITERS—AMERICAN
Top American Writers, 1980-1990

John Updike, whose novels deal with the superficial materialism of middle class life (just think of the Reagan years), is the clear winner in this category. His novels about the life of Harry "Rabbit" Angstrom—including *Rabbit is Rich*, about the Seventies, and *Rabbit Redux*, about the Eighties, have attained the unlikely status of both popular and critical success, the former being not only a best-seller but the winner of the Pulitzer Prize and the National Book Award. However, a writer did not have to win one of those prized to make in on the list; two novelists who didn't were Stephen King and James Michener. They earned "top writer" status because of the enormous popularity of their books—eight best-sellers each in ten years. The selections were made according to three factors: (1) Pulitzer Prize awards; (2) National Book Award; and (3) best sellers. In the first category, 50 points were awarded for a Pulitzer Prize. In category two, 40 points were awarded for a National Book Award. In category three, 30 points were awarded for a best seller that won a Pulitzer Prize, 25 points was awarded for a best seller whose author won a Pulitzer Prize for another book; and 8 points were awarded for best sellers that didn't win any prizes.

Writer Total Points

1. John Updike	120
2. Alice Walker	90
3. Larry McMurtry	80
4. Anne Tyler	75
5. Louis L'Amour	72
6. Stephen King	64
James Michener	64
8. Tom Wolfe	56
John Irving	56
10. E.L. Doctorow	48

Source: "Best and Worst" original.

WRITERS—BRITISH
Greatest, All-time

Although not really considered a poetic people, the list of the ten greatest English writers contains five poets, while there are four novelists and only one playwright, the ubiquitous Shakespeare, on the list. Other interesting aspects of this compendium of British writers is that two—T.S. Eliot and Joseph Conrad—were not English-born. Eliot hailed from the mundane American Midwestern town of St. Louis, while Conrad's native tongue was Polish. The scores here reflect the amount of scholarly work produced on a particular author's work in the period from 1981 to 1990, as measured by the number of citations in the MLA International Bibliography.

Writer/Notable Work(s)	Score
1. **William Shakespeare** *Hamlet, Macbeth*	5848
2. **Geoffrey Chaucer** *The Canterbury Tales*	1593
3. **John Milton** *Paradise Lost*	1445
4. **Charles Dickens** *A Tale of Two Cities*	1080
5. **T.S. Eliot** *The Waste Land*	1057
6. **William Wordsworth** *The Prelude*	969
7. **D.H. Lawrence** *Lady Chatterly's Lover*	919
8. **Joseph Conrad** *Heart of Darkness*	771
9. **William Blake** *Songs of Innocence*	732
10. **Virginia Woolf** *To the Lighthouse*	673

Source: "Best and Worst" original.

WRITERS — CLASSICAL
Greatest Classical Writers

Although the Greek poet Homer is widely regarded as the first true literary figure, his Roman counterpart Vergil is seen here as the writer from classical antiquity with the most influence on modern-day literary forms. Vergil employed Homer's style of epic poetry in his *Aeneid*, but, unlike Homer, mastered other poetic forms as well, as can be seen in his *Bucolics* and *Georgics*. His acceptance by the early Christians, moreover, made him extremely popular during the Middle Ages. Whereas Homer gave life to the classic literary form, Vergil was its greatest proponent and greatest practitioner. The following are the ten most influential Greek and Roman writers, measured by the amount of scholarship on their works written in the ten year period from 1981 to 1990.

Writer/Notable Work	Score
1. **Vergil** *The Aeneid*	402
2. **Ovid** *Metamorphoses*	344
3. **Homer** *The Iliad; The Odyssey*	309
4. **Horace** *Odes*	158
5. **Sophocles** *Oedipus Rex*	114
6. **Euripedes** *Medea*	83
7. **Aeschylus** *The Oresteia*	46
8. **Catullus** *Attis*	44
9. **Lucretius** *De rerum natura*	43
10. **Plautus** *Amphitruo*	41

Source: "Best and Worst" original.

WRITERS — DETECTIVE/MYSTERY
Greatest Detective/Mystery Writers

Although Agatha Christie is one of the most

successful writers in history—her books have sold over 100,000,000 copies worldwide— she has not met with the critical success and acclaim of some other detective writers, most notably Arthur Conan Doyle, creator of Sherlock Holmes. The following are the top detective and mystery writers as measured by the number of citations for each author in the MLA International Bibliography.

Writer/Notable Charcter or Work	Score
1. Sir Arthur Conan Doyle Sherlock Holmes	270
2. G.K. Chesterton Father Brown	193
3. Raymond Chandler Philip Marlowe	79
4. Wilkie Collins *The Woman in White*, first detective novels in English	72
5. Dashiell Hammett Sam Spade; Nick and Nora Charles	66
6. Dorothy Sayers Lord Peter Wimsey	71
7. Agatha Christie Hercule Poirot; Jane Marple	37
8. Georges Simenon Inspector Maigret	34
9. John D. MacDonald Travis McGee	29
Ross MacDonald (tie) Lew Archer	29
10. P.D. James Adam Dalgleish	22

Source: "Best and Worst" original.

WRITERS—FRENCH
Greatest, All-time

Gustave Flaubert edges out Marcel Proust by a scant two points in our ranking of the greatest French writers of all time. Flaubert was master of the naturalist style, of depicted object and event in a precise, impersonal way; but his dedication to an artistic ideal in the depiction of reality was intense. A highly disciplined writer, he is legendary for spending hours contemplating the sound of a particular phrase or searching for the *mot juste*, the right word. Proust, too, was a literary perfectionist, and the last years of his life were spent in the cork-lined bedroom of his Parisian apartment, writing and revising his monumental *Remembrance of Things Past*, an ode to memory, thought and emotion.

Writer/Notable Work	Score
1. Gustave Flaubert *Madame Bovary*	720
2. Marcel Proust *Remembrance of Things Past*	718
3. Stendahl *The Red and the Black*	668
4. Honore de Balzac *The Human Comedy*	628
5. Charles Baudelaire *Flowers of Evil*	615
6. Michel de Montaigne *Essays*	604
7. Victor Hugo *Les Miserables*	534
8. Emile Zola *Les Rougon-macquart*; "J'accuse"	504
9. Andre Gide *The Immortals*	434
10. Pierre Corneille *Le Cid*	431

Source: "Best and Worst" original.

WRITERS—GERMAN
Greatest, All-time

As we said before, Johann Wolfgang von Goethe is the towering figure of German literature; indeed, of the nine other writers on the list of greatest German authors, none preceded Goethe, and only one, Schiller, was his contemporary. The two were fundamental in founding Weimar Classicism, which led eventually to the German Romantic movement, whose influence spread from music to philosophy. We include in this list authors and poets who wrote in German, and thus the Czech writers Franz Kafka and Rainer Maria Rilke appear here. The following are the ten greatest practitioners of the German language; the score reflects the number of scholarly articles about the author's works in a ten year period from 1981 to 1990.

1. Johann Wolfgang von Goethe		**1802**
The Sorrows of Young Werther		
2. Franz Kafka		**844**
The Metamorphosis		
3. Bertolt Brecht		**835**
The Caucasian Chalk Circle		
4. Thomas Mann		**572**
The Magic Mountain		
5. Friedrich von Schiller		**438**
The Robbers		
6. Gotthold Ephraim Lessing		**396**
Nathan the Wise		
7. Heinrich von Kleist		**358**
The Prince of Homburg		
8. Hugo von Hoffmannsthal		**342**
Der Rosenklavier		
9. Rainer Maria Rilke		**340**
Duino Elegies		
10. Heinrich Heine		**330**
Reisebilder		

Source: "Best and Worst" original.

WRITERS — HORROR
Greatest Horror Writers

Edgar Allan Poe was many things — a great short story writer, a great poet, and the inventor of the detective story — but above all, he was a great horror writer. His short stories and poems — "The Tell-Tale Heart," "The Fall of the House of Usher," "The Raven," "Annabel Lee" — are infused with a gothic melancholy and psychological torment that established the standards for the popular exploitation of fear we see in such contemporary writers as Stephen King. Other greats on the horror hit parade include Mary Wollstonecraft Shelley, the creator of Frankenstein's monster, and Bram Stoker, the father of Dracula. The following list represents the top five horror writers of all time, as measured by the number of citations for each writer in the MLA International Bibliography.

Writer	Score
1. Edgar Allan Poe	658
2. Mary Wollstonecraft Shelley	127
3. H.P. Lovecraft	77
4. Stephen King	69
5. Bram Stoker	60

Source: "Best and Worst" original.

WRITERS — IRISH
Greatest, All-time

The Irish literary voice has long struggled to distinguish itself from that of English literature as a whole, and the list below of greatest Irish writers presents a variety of authors who either entered into the mainstream of English literature — such as Oscar Wilde — or who held out for a more purely Irish literature, as exemplified by the proponents of the Irish Renaissance such as W.B. Yeats and John Millington Synge. Indeed, something about the conflict in the Irish soul between the English language and that of Irish Gaelic seems to make Irish writers something of linguistic basket-cases: Joyce's *Finnegan's Wake* is written in a highly idiosyncratic, invented language; and his early apostle Samuel Beckett abandoned English after his first several novels to write mainly in French. The list below represents the ten greatest Irish writers of all time, as measured by the number of citiations in the MLA International Bibliography.

PEOPLE

Writer/Notable Work	Score	Writer/Notable Work	Score
1. James Joyce *Finnegan's Wake*	1943	1. Dante Alighieri *The Divine Comedy*	1330
2. William Butler Yeats *The Wild Swans at Coole*	791	2. Petrarch *Ecologues*	479
3. Samuel Beckett *Waiting for Godot*	766	3. Giovanni Boccaccio *Decameron*	390
4. Jonathan Swift *Gulliver's Travels*	557	4. Allesandro Manzoni *The Betrothed*	298
5. Oscar Wilde *The Importance of Being Earnest*	214	5. Luigi Pirandello *Six Characters in Search of an Author*	293
6. John Millington Synge *The Playboy of the Western World*	117	6. Giacomo Conte Leopardi *Canzoni*	233
7. Sean O'Casey *Juno and the Paycock*	112	7. Italo Calvino *Italian Fables*	205
8. Oliver Goldsmith *The Vicar of Wakefield*	105	8. Ludovico Ariosto *Roland Mad*	196
9. Isabella Augusta Gregory *The Rising of the Moon*	36	9. Torquato Tasso *Jerusalem Liberated*	193
10. Richard Brinsley Sheridan *The Rivals*	32	10. Eugenio Montale *The Offender*	186

Source: "Best and Worst" original.

Source: "Best and Worst" original.

WRITERS — ITALIAN
Greatest, All-time

As Shakespeare is the guiding force in English literature and Goethe in German, so Dante is the great figure of Italian literature. His *Divine Comedy*, completed in 1321, is based firmly on the theological writings of St. Thomas Aquinas and is an allegory of the journey of the human soul toward God, beginning in the *Inferno* to free the soul from temptation, progressing to *Purgatorio* to purge man of error, and finally to *Paradisio*, where Dante meets his Beatrice, who represents perfection and divine revelation. In its highly religious content, and in its allusions to the political and social climate of his times, Dante's masterwork is a detailed evocation of the late Middle Ages and the signal literary epic of the early Renaissance.

WRITERS — LATIN AMERICAN
Greatest Latin American Writers

The top Latin American writer, the Argentine Jorge Luis Borges, was the master of the style of fantastic, metaphysical literature that so marks modern Latin American writing. Intrigued by the creation of philosophical and linguistic systems and a prolific reader of sometimes obscure writers in a wide range of fields, Borges brought a distinctly philosophical approach to the art of literature, creating in his short, fictional narratives strange episodes evoking Kafka and Poe. Hard to characterize, his writings contain elements of horror, fantasy, science fiction and pure narrative. His legacy is obvious, in the works of Latin American writers from Gabriel Garcia Marquez and

PEOPLE

Carlos Fuentes to Eduardo Galeano.

Source: "Best and Worst" original.

WRITERS — RUSSIAN
Greatest, All-time

Although Tolstoy is considered to have created the greatest novel of all time in *War and Peace*, the literary output of Dostoevsky places him at the top of the list of greatest Russian writers. In part, this reflects the different subject matter that the two approached, and their styles. Tolstoy, though master at evoking a complete universe of characters and events in his larger works, still wrote in a traditional, even at time romantic, style, characterized by a deep commitment to spirituality. Dostoevsky, on the other hand, explored the darker psychological motivations of his characters—the "Grand Inquisitor" passage from *The Brothers Karamazov* is felt to be one of the main precursors to 20th-century existen-tialism. The yin and yang of Russian literature, Tolstoy and Dostoevsky represent, perhaps, the dividing line between the Romantic and the Modern eras. These, then, are the greatest Russian writers of all time, measured by their citation score in the MLA International Bibliography.

Writer/Notable Work(s)	Score
1. Fyodor Dostoevsky *Notes from Underground*	901
2. Alexander Pushkin *The Prisoner in the Caucuses*	710
3. Leo Tolstoy *War and Peace; Anna Karenina*	550
4. Anton Chekhov *The Cherry Orchard*	371
5. Nikolai Gogol *Dead Souls*	328
6. Ivan Turgenev *Notes of a Hunter*	289
7. Boris Pasternak *Dr. Zhivago*	210
8. Mikhail Bulgakov *The Master and Margarita*	201
9. Aleksandr Blok *The Scythians*	185
10. Anna Akhmatova *Anno Domini MCMXXI*	178

Source: "Best and Worst" original.

WRITERS — SCIENCE FICTION
Greatest Science Fiction Writers

Science fiction is one of the more recent additions to the pantheon of literary genres, although its roots go back at least to Jonathan Swift's *Gulliver's Travels*. The first truly modern science fiction writer—the one who really used scientific principles and theories to look into the future or create fantastic alternative worlds—was the Frenchman Jules Verne. But, according to

PEOPLE

our rating, which measures SF writers by the number of scholarly articles about their work in the MLA International Bibliography, H.G. Wells ranks as the all-time master of the field, with his two early 20th-century masterpieces, *The Invisible Man* and *The Time Machine*. Taking a surprising fifth position in the ratings is the late American writer Philip K. Dick, whose fame seems to increasing as his works become better known. Dick's consistent theme is that of displacement; his characters never seem to be firmly entrenched in any one reality, but are always drifting, consciously or unconsciously, through different times, different universes. Dick is perhaps best known as the author of the works that were later made into the popular movies *Blade Runner* and *Total Recall*.

Writer/Notable Work(s)	Score
1. H.G. Wells *The Invisible Man*; *The Time Machine*	211
2. Jules Verne *Twenty Thousand Leagues Under the Sea*	128
3. Ursula Le Guin *Left Hand of Darkness*	96
4. Stanislaw Lem *Solaris*	62
5. Philip K. Dick *The Man in the High Castle*	58
6. Samuel Delany *Dahlgren*	30
7. J. G. Ballard *The Drowned World*	27
8. Arthur C. Clarke *Childhood's End*	26
9. Ray Bradbury *The Martian Chronicles*	23
10. Isaac Asimov *Foundation*	24

Source: "Best and Worst" original.

WRITERS — SPANISH
Greatest Spanish andPortuguese Writers

The greatest Iberian writer of all time is known almost entirely for his massive work *Don Quixote*, the images of which — a aging, nearly blind knight-errant, accompanied by his faithful, practical servant Sancho Panza, vainly jousting at windmills and other figments of the imagination — have become part of man's common literary heritage, as well as a vivid evocation of the Spanish character. For this, Cervantes' place atop the list of greatest Spanish and Portuguese writers is well-deserved. The ratings are based on the number of scholarly articles written about a particular author's work from 1981 to 1990 and degree of lasting influence of the author in scholarly and popular circles.

Writer/Notable Work	Score
1. Miguel de Cervantes *Don Quixote*	1038
2. Federico Garcia Lorca *Lament for the Death of a Bullfighter*	534
3. Lope de Vega *The Knight of Olmedo*	509
4. Miguel de Unamuno *Mist, A Tragicomic Novel*	326
5. Pedro Calderon de la Barca *El Gran Teatro del Mundo*	308
6. Francisco Gomez de Quevedo y Villegas *The Life of a Scoundrel*	285
7. Juan Ramon Jimenez *Diary of a Recently Married Poet*	272
8. Luis Vaz de Camoes *The Lusiads*	266
9. Antonio Machado y Ruiz *Campos de Castilla*	189
10. Luis de Gongora y Argote *Soledades*	153

Source: "Best and Worst" original.

PLACES

AIRPORTS — BUSIEST
Busiest U.S. Airports

It's easy to complain about the density of air traffic at major international hubs, and the frequency of delays, but solutions are not so easily forthcoming. In the main, major American cosmopolitan airports are hemmed in by residential neighbors and overzealous tax collectors. In most of the business world more is more. In the overheated airline industry, more is definitely too much. Chicago's O'Hare International Airport is the nation's busiest at the moment, but officials at the Federal Aviation Administration predict that O'Hare will be surpassed by Dallas in terms of hustle and bustle by the middle of the 1990s.

Airport	Passengers, 1989
1. Chicago-O'Hare	63,000,000
2. Dallas-Fort Worth	59,130,007
3. Los Angeles	47,579,046
4. Atlanta	44,967,221

Dallas-Ft. Worth Airport, shown here, will soon eclipse Chicago's O'Hare as the busiest airport in the world. Photo courtesy American Airlines.

Airport	Passengers
5. New York (JFK)	43,312,285
6. San Francisco	30,323,077
7. Denver	29,939,835
8. Miami	27,568,033
9. New York (LGA)	23,158,317
10. Honolulu	22,617,340

Source: Airport Operators Council

AIRPORTS — BUSIEST
Busiest Foreign Airports

The five busiest airports in the world are all in the United States, but things are far from sluggish at the globe's other major air centers. London's Heathrow, a traditional hub for passengers traveling to and from Europe and the United States, handles the most passengers of any airport outside America. Tokyo's bustling Haneda is a close second.

Airport	Passengers, 1989
1. Heathrow London, UK	45,000,000
2. Haneda Tokyo, Japan	39,905,200
3. Frankfurt Frankfurt, Germany	36,567,738
4. Orly Paris, France	26,006,900
5. Osaka Osaka, Japan	24,288,440
6. Gatwick London, U.K.	21,873,831
7. Charles De Gaulle Paris, France	21,293,200
8. Lester B. Pearson Toronto, Canada	20,669,542
9. Hong Kong Hong Kong	20,418,094
10. Narita New Tokyo	17,431,124

Source: Airport Operators Council.

PLACES

AIRPORTS — COMPLAINTS
Most Common Complaints
Against U.S. Airports

Since the demise of Peoples Express, the airline industry has lacked an identifiable archvillain, but the generic infamies of the other carriers have proven more than sufficient to stir consumer ire. First among complaints of commercial travelers in 1988 was the frequency and duration of flight delays resulting from technical difficulties. Problems with baggage, though still vexingly frequent, took a distant second place in the complaint box.

Complaint	Number Recorded, 1988
1. Flight Difficulties	8,831
2. Baggage	3,938
3. Refunds	2,120
4. Ticketing Problems	1,445
5. Overbooking	1,353
6. Smoking	546
7. Fares	455
8. Advertising	141
9. Credit	35
10. Tour Problems	39

Source: U.S. Department of Transportation, Air Travel Consumer Report

AIRPORTS — ON-TIME RECORDS
Worst On-time Records

The more crowded, overbuilt and underthought an airport is, the more time you are likely to spend there, on a trip-to-trip basis. Our biggest worries are of mid-air collisions in over-trafficked skies, but the perils in the hangar, at the gate and on the ticket line are also considerable. Here are the worst examples of the sluggish side of rapid transit.

Airport	% of departures on time
1. Philadelphia	76.0
2. Chicago-O'Hare	76.4
3. Denver	76.6
4. New York-Kennedy	77.0
5. Boston	78.4
6. Pittsburgh	78.9
7. Dallas–Fort-Worth	78.9
8. Atlanta	79.3
9. Newark	79.7
10. Seattle	80.2

Source: U.S. Department of Transportation

AQUARIUMS
Most Popular

We live in extremely touchy-feely times, where the environment needs saving and nature is Mother, King and Queen. Love for animals, and respect for their rights, is on the rise. Even at sea, species-to-species affection runs high. Americans love dolphins, killer whales and even giant squid. The stocks of aquariums everywhere are on the rise: from the mammoth new concrete ocean simulation at Chicago's Shedd, to the sold out marine shows at Sea Worlds throughout the temperate states. The following are attendance figures for the ten most visited aquariums in the country.

Aquarium	1990 Attendance (millions)
1. Sea World of Florida	4.0
2. Sea World of California	3.7
3. Sea World of Texas	2.5
4. Monterey Bay Aquarium	1.7
5. National Aquarium (D.C.)	1.5
6. Marine World Africa USA	1.4
7. Sea World of Ohio	1.3
8. New England Aquarium	1.2
9. John G. Shedd Aquarium (Chic.)	1.0
10. Mystic Marinelife Aquarium(CT)	.7

Source: American Association of Zoological Parks and Aquariums

ARCHITECTURAL ACHIEVEMENTS
Greatest in America

To list the "best building" in the U.S. is a daunting task; how does one judge such a contest? Architecture, considered by Vitruvius to be "the Mother of the Arts," is a very personal thing, much like painting or sculpture, although buildings influence our

PLACES

daily lives to a much greater extent whether we are aware of it or not. Distinguished practitioners of the American Institute of Architects chose not to name the "best buildings," but rather the "proudest achievements" of American Architecture. Their choices are varied in date, style, aesthetic and location. The campus of the University of Virginia, designed by Thomas Jefferson, was the most popular choice, undoubtedly for its Palladian beauty and its idyllic campus quality. The architect most represented in the top ten list is Frank Lloyd Wright, with Falling Water, Robie House and the Johnson Wax building. Wright, by both his own opinion and that of more impartial scholars, is considered the greatest American architect of the twentieth century.

Achievement/Location

1. **University of Virginia**
   Charlottesville, NY

2. **Rockefeller Center**
   New York, NY

3. **Dulles International Airport**
   Chantilly, VA

   Falling Water
   Mill Run, PA

5. **Carson Pirie Scott**
   Chicago, IL

6. **Seagram Building**
   New York, NY

   Phila. Savings Fund Soc. Building
   Philadelphia, PA

8. **Trinity Church,**
   Boston, MA

   Boston City Hall
   Boston, MA

10. **Robie House**
    Chicago, IL

    Ford Foundation
    New York, NY

    Johnson Wax

Racine, WI

Lever House
New York, NY

Source: American Institute of Architects.

ART MUSEUMS
Most Visits

Who says Americans are philistines? Overall, the top ten art museums in the country enjoy over 20 million visitors a year, feasting their eyes on the works of Picasso, Renoir, Michelangelo and ancient Greek statuary in the nation's great public collections. No doubt, the National Gallery benefits from its location in Washington, where each summer hosts of unwilling kids are subjected to a little "culture" on their family's vacation before being allowed to romp through the really neat stuff at the Smithsonian. What's more, admission is free.

Museum	Number of Visitors/Year
1. National Gallery of Art Washington, DC	7.5 million
2. Metropolitan Mus. of Art New York City	3.7 million
3. Art Institute of Chicago Chicago	1.8 million
4. Museum of Modern Art New York City	1.6 million
5. Hirshhorn Museum & Sculpture Garden Washington, DC	1.3 million
6. Detroit Institute of Art Detroit	1.0 million
7. Museum of Fine Arts Boston	894,000
8. L.A. County Museum of Art Los Angeles	880,000
9. Whitney Museum of Art New York City	837,000
10. Museum of Fine Arts Houston	631,000

PLACES

BEACHES

Best in Southern California

Heading for a vacation in sunny Southern California? Heard about the great surf, the sunny skies, the clean water, the uncrowded beaches? Well, be forewarned. All beaches are not equal, even in the home of the Beach Boys and Gidget. The place is also the home of off-shore oil refineries and the largest port on the West Coast. Santa Monica Bay sometimes seems like it serves as the sewer for the entire Los Angeles basin. And where do you think 17 million sun-worshipers go on their numerous days off? Not to Disneyland or Universal studios — they pack their beaches as tight as Coney Island. So take a look at the list below before heading off for your day in the sun. It rates Southern California's beaches from best to worst, taking into account, in descending order of importance, water quality, surf, sand quality, parking and access to the beach. Water quality was scored from 8 to 32 points, surf and sand from 5 to 15 points, and parking and access 2 to 6 points. The maximum score possible was 74, which was earned only by Zuma Beach, a beautiful enclave north of Los Angeles — far enough north to discourage the mere amateur beachgoer (for the exact location of these beaches, consult any map of the area). Zuma's ample parking, great surf and sand, pure water, and easy access make it the best of the Southland's many beaches. In the tie for ninth place, Cardiff has better surf, Windansea better sand. In the tie for tenth, Malibu has better surf and access, Corona Del Mar better sand and parking.

The Ten Best	Total Score
1. Zuma	74
2. San Buenaventura	64
3. El Pescador/El Matador	61
4. Leo Carillo	60
5. Crystal Cove	63
6. La Jolla Shores	62
7. San Clemente	61
8. Bolsa Chica	59
9. Cardiff	58
Windansea (tie)	58
10. Corona Del Mar	57
Malibu (tie)	57

The worst beaches on our list are, unfortunately, the ones that are easiest to get to for most vacationers and residents of the Los Angeles megalopolis. Santa Monica, Redondo, Temescal and Will Rogers are all located in the aforementioned Santa Monica Bay, with its frequent beach closings; the overall loser, Belmont Shore, suffers from the industrial output of Long Beach; Seal Beach is the home of a naval weapons facility.

The Ten Worst	Total Score
1. Belmont Shore	24
2. Imperial Beach	26
3. Santa Monica	28
4. Redondo Beach	29
5. Cabrillo Beach	31
Temescal Canyon (tie)	31
6. Will Rogers	35
7. Royal Palms	38
8. Pt. Mugu	39
9. Dockweiler	40
10. Seal Beach	41

Source: "Best and Worst" original, from information in the Los Angeles Times.

BEACHES

Dirtiest and Cleanest Beaches

Remember several summers ago when the airwaves and magazine covers were filled with of New York and New Jersey beaches polluted by medical debris — syringes, operating gloves, vials — that had washed up on shore? Well, it may be informative to know that East Coast beaches are not the dirtiest in the country. According to the Center for Marine Conservation, which details the amount of debris picked up on state beaches over the course of a year by volunteers, the worst beaches are in the South, although New York and New Jersey do rank right up there. Even the seemingly

PLACES

pristine shores of Hawaii suffer from a relatively high amount of junk piling up on shore. And don't get the impression that this junk is just plastic bottles, styrofoam cups or soda cans (though these items are the most prevalent). All manner of animal carcass find their way onto America's shores — from seagulls, turtles, seals, dolphins, whales and walruses to the odd deer and sheep. The lucky beach prospector will also come across products of foreign lands that have made their way across the seas much as the Pilgrims once did. Among the things the CMC's beach scourers turned up were a canister of "Hombres" deodorant from Cuba, lip balm from France, a lemon juice bottle from Greece, a plastic ladle from Brazil, and a condom wrapper from Spain. The following are the states with the most debris-strewn beaches.

Dirtiest	Debris /mile of beach (lbs.)
1. Georgia	4,000
2. Texas	3,549
3. Mississippi	3,000
4. Louisiana	2,338
5. New York	1,086
6. Hawaii	973
7. Puerto Rico	731
8. New Jersey	652
9. Virginia	651
10. North Carolina	627

Cleanest	
1. Connecticut	95
2. Delaware	112
3. Maine	133
4. Rhode Island	150
5. South Carolina	152
6. California	181
7. Maryland	208
8. Alabama	209
9. Oregon	237
10. Massachusetts	333

Source: "Trash on America's Beaches," Center for Marine Conservation, Washington, DC, 1989.

BOMB TARGETS

Combat Zones: Most Common Bomb Targets

One often hears of explosions in war-torn locales like Beirut and El Salvador, but we hardly think of our nation as a likely site for such explosive action. In point of fact, though, America is a highly incendiary culture, which saw more than 880 separate bombing incidents in 1989 alone.

Location	Bombings, 1989
1. Residential Properties	239
2. Cars	125
3. Other	91
4. Homes	86
5. Businesses	68
6. Schools	57
7. Individuals	48
8. Commercial Postal	35
9. Entertainment	27
10. Other Vehicles	23

Source: F.B.I. Uniform Crime Reports

CITIES — ACTIVITIES

Most Things to Do

We rated the most active cities in seven categories: sun, sea, surf, snow, nature, sports and culture. Each city was assigned a point total from 0 to 100 in each category to create an index of the amount of leisure and recreational activities are normally available to residents of each locale. The sun category is a relative score based on weather conditions — Los Angeles and San Diego topped the list with perfect scores of 100. Similarly, the sea category reflects water-based recreation such as boating; sand referred to beach activities; snow referred to winter activities, especially skiing, and scores were determined by the proximity of major ski resorts; nature was a subjective evaluation of the natural beauty of the area and the number of major national parks in the vicinity; sports referred to major sports

PLACES

franchises in the area and their success; and culture evaluated art museums, galleries, symphonies, dance and specialty museums. The good-times capital of the U.S., according to our ranking, is sunny Los Angeles, with its abundance of sun, sand, boating, desert and even skiing opportunities.

The Top Ten	Score
1. Los Angeles	596
2. San Diego	440
3. Miami	432
4. New York City	427
5. Washington	426
6. San Francisco	412
7. Boston	392
8. Seattle	387
9. Denver	358
10. Phoenix	291

Source: "Best and Worst" original.

CITIES — AGE
Oldest Populace

As we get on in years, if everything has gone psychologically right, we express our fondness for ourselves by erecting a life of greatest possible comfort. For many, this means a movement away from a long-time place of residence to a more accommodating, convenient or inexpensive locale. Some flock to family, others to the Sunbelt. Here's where the golden girls and boys have settled in greatest concentrations.

Metro Area	Median Age
1. Sarasota, Fl	51.1
2. Chicago	45.7
3. Detroit	43.1
4. New York	42.2
5. Philadelphia	42.1
6. Los Angeles	41.1
7. Dallas	40.9
8. Atlanta	40.5
9. New Orleans	39.9
10. Denver	38.7

Source: Sales and Marketing Magazine, Survey of Buying Power.

CITIES — AGE
Where the Boys and Girls Are:
Youngest American Cities

Some of the youngest cities, not surprisingly, are college towns — Pennsylvania State Univeristy in State College, Pennsylvania; Brigham Young University in Provo, Utah, the University of Illinois in Champaign-Urbana. Other young cities contain or are located near military bases; still others are border towns that see a good deal of immigration from Mexico, including children. The median age in the United States is a little over 32. Below are listed most youthful cities in the land, as measured by median age.

City	Median Age
1. Provo-Orem, UT	21.5
2. Jacksonville, NC	24.3
3. Laredo, TX	24.8
4. Bryan-College Station, TX	25.1
5. McAllen-Edinburg-Mission, TX	25.3
6. Salt Lake City-Ogden, UT	25.5
7. Brownsville-Harlingen, TX	25.7
8. State College, PA	26.4
9. Killeen-Temple, TX	26.5
10. Champaign-Urbana, IL	26.6

Source: Donnelley Marketing Information Service.

CITIES — AIDS
Largest Concentrations of
AIDS Victims

AIDS has simultaneously struck America deaf, dumb, dumb and blind. We listen but don't hear. We are told, but don't repeat. We see but don't understand. AIDS is an epidemic which must be quartered and destroyed, to fight it we will need all of our senses intact. Below are the cities where this epidemic has struck hardest.

Cities	Known cases of HIV infection
1. New York	25,595
2. Los Angeles	10,194
3. San Francisco	8,933

PLACES

4. Houston	4,481
5. Washington, D.C.	4,323
6. Newark	4,136
7. Miami	4,049
8. Chicago	3,722
9. Philadelphia	3,156
10. Atlanta	3,075

Source: HIV/AIDS Surveillance Report

CITIES — AIDS
Childhood AIDS Cases

AIDS, of course, is not limited to the gay community. In fact, reports now suggest that Acquired Immune Deficiency Syndrome is growing most rapidly not within the gay community, where awareness and education have brought about a change in behaviors that helped spread the disease, but among intravenous drug abusers, who may be less educated about the dangers of AIDS. Sadly, the legacy of this ignorance is a growing population of children infected with the virus — since a pregnant mother who is infected may be extremely likely to infect her fetus as well. Other childhood AIDS cases have resulted from blood transfusions with infected plasma. Below is a list of the states with the most incidences AIDS among children. Figures cover period from June, 1981 to September, 1988.

States	Childhood AIDS Cases
1. New York	364
2. New Jersey	163
3. Florida	141
4. California	93
5. Texas	43
6. Connecticut	33
7. Illinois	28
8. Maryland	28
9. Massachusetts	26
10. Pennsylvania	26

Source: Centers for Disease Control.

CITIES — ALCOHOL
Most Spending on Alcohol

Hard alcohol, we all know, has its quasi-medicinal, utilitarian purposes, the first of which is to make us feel a little warmer, when life tosses our fragile bodies into cold place. So when the occasional Anchorage Andy takes the occasional swig or icy shot, we are want to sympathize, forgive, even applaud the drinking deed. We are not, however, quite so sure that we can clap flesh for the Miamian who sips so frequently.

City	Yearly Spending on Alcohol
1. Miami	$546
2. Anchorage	$531
3. San Diego	$465
4. Seattle	$456
5. Boston	$441
6. Washington, D.C.	$422
7. San Francisco	$413
8. Baltimore	$405
9. Milwaukee	$390
10. Dallas-Ft. Worth	$377

Source: Consumer Expenditure Survey, U.S. Dept. of Commerce.

CITIES — ALCOHOLISM
Highest and Lowest Rates

Contrary to popular opinion, one does not find the highest incidences of alcoholism in the cold, bleak Rust Belt cities where one imagines unemployed auto workers drowning their sorrows at the local tavern. On the contrary, the ten cities with the highest rates of alcohol abuse among their citizenry are located in temperate climes — California, Florida, North Carolina and, most of all, Nevada. The top cities in the country for alcohol abuse are the two gambling capitals of Reno and Las Vegas. In these towns, where the wheels spin all day and all night, dreams of the big jackpot are fueled more often than not, by high-proof beverages. And although people are flocking to the Sun Belt with its promise of economic growth and moderate climate, the disruption such a

PLACES

The risk-taking and non-stop partying in the Nevada towns of Reno and Las Vegas fuel the highest incidence of alcoholism in the country.

move might have on the psyche could account for the high rates of alcoholism in those locales. A number of the cities with the lowest incidences of alcoholism are college towns — State College, Lawrence, Bloomington, Iowa City and Provo are all homes to large universities.

Highest Incidence

1. Reno, NV
2. Las Vegas, NV
3. Albuquerque, NM
4. Stockton, CA
5. Asheville, NC
6. Redding, CA
7. Winter Haven, FL
8. Fresno, CA
9. Pueblo, CO
10. Raleigh-Durham, NC

Lowest Incidence

1. State College, PA
2. Lawrence, KS
4. Bloomington, IN
   Iowa City, IA (tie)
5. Bismarck, ND
6. Rochester, MN
7. Green Bay, WI
8. Provo/Orem, UT
10. Lancaster, PA
    Sheboygen, WI (tie)

CITIES — ARCHITECTURE
Greatest Architecture Town

Since the late 1800s, Chicago has been America's first city of architecture. From the urban planning of Daniel Burnham, whose motto was "Make no small plans," to Louis Sullivan, Frank Lloyd Wright, Mies Van der Rohe and the architectural firm of Skidmore, Owings and Merrill, the city has been home to the country's most innovative and influential architects. An architectural competition in Chicago always manages to stip up big interest, both here and abroad, as was the case with the recent design of the city's new library. Our ratings are a subjective scoring by "Best and Worst" editors of cities in four different categories: number of important architectural works, diversity of architecture, indigenous architectural styles, and drama of skyline. Each city received a point score from 1 to 250 in these four categories. The top ten American architectural towns based on this formula are as follows:

The Top Ten	Score
1. Chicago	753
2. New York City	616
3. Los Angeles	605
4. Miami	423
5. San Francisco	395
6. Boston	382
7. Houston	344
8. Pittsburgh	317
9. Philadelphia	272
10. New Orleans	244

Source: "Best and Worst" original.

PLACES

New York City is tops in the arts. Photo of Metropolitan Museum of Art, © N.Y.S. Dept. of Economic Development, 1991

CITIES — ARTS
Top Towns in the Arts

These a ratings of cities are derived from the rating of overall activities, and reflect the cultural opportunities of the cities in the areas of art galleries and museums, dance, theater, orchestral music, and specialty museums. The scores are subjective evaluations from the editors of the "Best and Worst." New York City, of course, comes out on top for its plethora of art galleries and museums, its specialty museums catering to a variety of artistic and cultural interests, and its large arts community. New York is indeed still the place to be for the up-and-coming artist.

The Top Ten

1. New York City	97
2. Chicago	84
3. Washington, D.C.	82
4. San Francisco	77
5. Los Angeles	68
6. Boston	66
Philadelphia	66
7. Atlanta	56
8. Houston	44
9. Pittsburgh	42
10. Cleveland	37

Source: "Best and Worst" original.

CITIES — AUTOMOBILES
Most Cars

Americans love their cars. This is a culture in which the automobile has become such an integral part that it even generates it's own mythology. The appeal goes to a gut level — the car is a place that is an entirely self-contained environment, almost like an extension of the womb. Inside your car you can personalize it and seal yourself away from the outside world. A mobile, self-contained environment that can go anywhere the roads go, which in our case is anywhere in the country. Having a car, or at least access to one, is essential in our society and it is interesting to note where most of the cars are. The following are the top ten metropolitan areas by percent of households with at least one car and with at least three cars.

Cars per Household	1+	3+
1. Oklahoma City	93.3	20.5
2. Dallas	93.2	21.2
3. Phoenix	92.3	21.4

36% of New Yorkers do not own a car. Photo © N.Y.S. Dept. of Economic Development.

PLACES

4. Tucson	92.0	19.5
5. Denver	91.4	22.2
6. Sacramento	90.6	20.4
7. San Diego	90.2	20.3
8. San Antonio	89.1	18.2
9. Seattle	89.0	21.0
10. Kansas City	89.0	16.6

Fewest Cars

Living in a city makes it impractical as well as difficult to own a car. The costs of storage, insurance, etc. for city residents is much higher all around than for those in rural areas. And you might as well forget about parking, unless you're willing to pay for a spot what elsewhere you'd pay for a house. Moreover, with easy mass transit available, it is more cost effective to rent a car when the necessity arises, rather than meet the costs of ownership. The following cities have the fewest cars per household, with New York leading the way (anyone who's tried to drive in Manhattan can tell you the reasons why immediately).

Metropolitan Area	% Pop. with no cars
1. New York	36.1
2. Philadelphia	22.2
3. Chicago	21.1
4. Baltimore	20.9
5. Boston	20.8
6. Buffalo	19.0
7. Miami	18.4
8. Cincinnati	16.1
9. Milwaukee	16.1
10. San Francisco	15.8

CITIES—AUTOMOBILES
Car Spending

America is hell on wheels, and heaven as well. We drive here, we drive there, in point of fact, we drive just about everywhere. Of course, we can not sustain this gas-guzzling pace for long. But to the long lines of U.S. Joe's at the pumps, its fun while it lasts! Below are the metro areas that spend the most on automobile purchases annually.

Metro Area	Auto Sales Revenues (000)
1. Los Angeles-Long Beach	$14,461,889
2. Chicago	$8,853,426
3. Detroit	$8,142,088
4. Philadelphia	$8,015,528
5. Boston-Salem-Brockton	$7,036,905
6. Washington, D.C.	$6,830,874
7. New York	$6,110,423
8. Houston	$5,574,302
9. Dallas	$5,478,974
10. Nassau-Suffolk	$5,474,396

Source: Sales and Marketing Management.

CITIES—BARS AND RESTAURANTS
Wining and Dining Capitals

As one grows slightly older, having suffered almost innumerable frustrations, irritations and aches, the thought of toiling to prepare one's own food, drink and other sustenance becomes proportionately more loathsome at moments of weakness. It is in those times that many are magnetically drawn through the doors of our local pubs and cafes. On the other hand, some cities just tend to have a more happening nightlife than others. Below are the towns where folks spend the most on dining and drinking out.

City	Restaurant Tab/Household (yr.)
1. San Francisco	$3,354
2. Boston	$2,734
3. Anaheim-Santa Ana	$2,699
4. San Jose	$2,401
5. Atlanta	$2,259
6. Hartford	$2,210
7. Fort Lauderdale	$2,179
8. Seattle	$2,169
9. Washington, D.C.	$2,166
10. San Diego	$2,111

Source: Sales and Marketing Management.

CITIES—BIRTH RATE
Highest and Lowest

In the beginning, God said go forth and multiply, but these days, most of us are doing our procreation at or near home. And from these carnal conjurings come the young folk, who in turn stick close to the hearth for many years. In some of our cities, the blood runs hotter and heavy-petty-er than in others. Herewith, the birth capitals and backwoods of these United States, measured in births per 1,000 populations.

Highest	Birth Rate
1. Miami, FL	36.1
2. Sacramento, CA	31.5
3. Santa Ana, CA	30.7
4. Fresno, CA	27.4
5. Riverside, CA	25.4
6. Anchorage, AK	22.9
7. El Paso, TX	22.5
8. Aurora, CO	22.1
9. Houston, TX	22.1
10. Wichita, KS	22.0

Lowest	
1. San Francisco, CA	13.6
2. Pittsburgh, PA	13.6
3. Seattle, WA	13.7
4. St. Petersburg, FL	13.7
5. Louisville, KY	14.6
6. Boston, MA	14.9
7. Philadelphia, PA	15.2
8. Pittsburgh, PA	15.2
9. Charlotte, NC	15.2
10. New York, NY	15.3

Source: U.S. Census Bureau.

CITIES — BLACK POPULATION

African America: Metro Areas with Highest Percent Black Population

Populations of African Americans are most concentrated in urban areas, especially those of the South and industrial North. Large migrations of blacks from the South to such cities as New York, Chicago and Baltimore took place at the end of the 19th and beginning of the 20th century, as these oppressed populations sought economic opportunities and greater acceptance in the North. Jobs, they found, in the booming industrial heartland; the battle for civil rights is still being fought. Below are the ten metropolitan areas with the greatest percentage of black Americans.

Metro Area	% Black Population
1. Memphis	41.8
2. New Orleans	33.5
3. Norfolk-Va. Bch.-Newport News	28.6
4. Washington, D.C.	27.1
5. New York	26.3
6. Baltimore	26.1
7. Newark, NJ	24.3
8. Chicago	23.8
9. Atlanta	23.4
10. Charlotte-Rock Hill-NC-SC	21.7

Source: Sales and Marketing Magazine, Survey of Buying Power

CITIES — BUSINESS

Most Favored Business Locations

Each year the respected real estate firm Cushman & Wakefield conducts a survey of more than four hundred chief executive officers. Among the questions they ask is: What is your favorite business location? We have printed here the results of the latest survey. For the purpose of Cushman & Wakefield's survey, cities included surrounding suburbs. Places like Dallas/Fort Worth and Minneapolis/St. Paul were also considered as single metropolitan areas. Interestingly, the list came out quite differently when the question was: Where will you open new office space in the next twelve months? New York led that survey followed by Los Angeles, Chicago and Atlanta.

The Top Ten

1. Atlanta, Georgia
2. San Diego, California
3. Boston, Massachusetts
4. Chicago, Illinois
5. Dallas/Fort Worth, Texas
6. Los Angeles, California
7. Washington, D.C.

PLACES

Source: Cushman & Wakefield.

CITIES — CABLE TV
Top 20 Cable T.V. Markets

Once upon a time, it seemed that the networks were all but invincible, and a free, clear signal was thought of as a God-given right. But progress, and commercialism, can't be stopped, and the penetration of pay cable channels have made deep inroads into traditional broadcast markets. Although cable is still looked on by many as a low-level luxury, over the next decade, a battle will be played out for supremacy of the screen. The following are the towns where cable reigns most supreme.

Area	% of households serviced
1. Pittsburgh	51.1
2. San Francisco-Oakland	44.1
4. Philadelphia	42.0
5. Houston	36.3
6. Atlanta	33.3
7. Cleveland-Akron	32.8
8. Miami-Fort Lauderdale	30.4
9. Tampa-St, Pete.-Sarasosta	30.0
10. New York	29.9

Source: Nielsen.

CITIES — CLEANEST
Cleanest Inhabitants

What makes the people of Pittsburgh such cleanliness nuts? Perhaps it has something to do with the years during which the city had to cope with its image as a grimy, smoke-filled steel town. Now that the mills have mostly gone quiet, the folks who live where the Monangahela and the Allegheny meet to form the mighty Ohio still spend an average of more than $21 a year on soap. People in St. Louis, on the other hand, spend about than half that much. Is it compulsive cleanliness in Pittsburgh or mere slovenliness in St. Louis?

City	Yearly expenditures on soap
1. Pittsburgh	$21.66
2. San Antonio/Corpus Christi	$17.69
3. New York	$17.41
4. Philadelphia	$17.28
5. Grand Rapids/Kalamazoo	$16.59
6. El Paso/Albuquerque/Lubbock	$16.59
7. Hartford/Springfield/N. Haven	$16.18
8. Miami	$16.04
9. Portland, ME/Concord, NH	$15.77
10. Scranton/Wilkes-Barre	$15.36

Source: Arbitron/SAMI.

CITIES — COCAINE
Cocaine-Related Emergency Room Visits

For many years, cocaine was popularly regarded as a sophisticated, even luxurious recreational drug. In this decade, we have recognized the ugliness and enormity of the threat posed by this substance. Now it remains for us to reverse the stranglehold powdered and crystallized ("crack") cocaine have taken on the nation's health and pockets. Cocaine ravages not just its addicts, but the communities that must support them. The following list gives the cities with the worst cocaine epidemics in the country, as measured by the number of hospital emergency room visits in which cocaine was a contributing factor in the victim's debility.

City	1989 ER Visits
1. New York	5,615
2. Philadelphia	4,640
3. Washington, D.C.	4,508
4. Chicago	4,135
5. Detroit	4,000
6. New Orleans	3,101
7. Los Angeles	2,984
8. Atlanta	1,643
9. Baltimore	1,539
10. Boston	1,348

Source: "Overview of Selected Drug Trends," NIDA Drug Abuse Warning Network.

PLACES

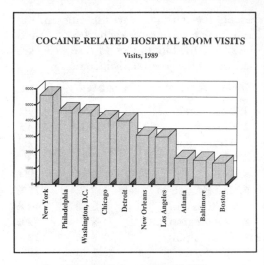

COCAINE-RELATED HOSPITAL ROOM VISITS
Visits, 1989

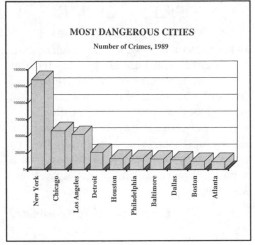

MOST DANGEROUS CITIES
Number of Crimes, 1989

CITIES — CRIME

Most Number of Dangerous Crimes, Total

The affluent folks of Wilmette, Illinois, a suburb of Chicago along the northern shore of Lake Michigan, enjoy a relatively crime free environment. But on occasion these sleepy towns are rocked by hideous crimes that reveal the dark underside of suburban life. In 1988 in the neighboring town of Winnetka, a troubled young woman named Laurie Dann went on a shooting spree at a local elementary school, killing one student and wounding several others before she finally took her own life. Such shooting rampages seemingly always occur in quiet, peaceful suburban communities — San Ysidro, Stockton, Winnetka. Perhaps some of the tensions that result in such a high number of murder in major cities are lying just below the surface of sylvan suburbs, exploding all the more violently for their suppression. From a database of cities with populations of 25,000 or more, we have compiled rankings of the ten cities with the most violent crime incidences, and those ten with the least incidence of violent crime. The data is drawn from Bureau of the Census population figures and the F.B.I.'s Uniform Crime Reports for 1989.

Fewest Crimes	Total
1. Wilmette, IL	6
2. Ridgewood, NJ	7
3. Upper Arlington, OH	10
4. Rockville, MD	11
Stowe, OH	11
5. Minot, ND	13
Northbrook, IL	13
State College, PA	13
6. Wheaton, IL	14
7. Garfield, NJ	15
7. Winona, MN	15
8. Strongsville, OH	16
Waukesha, WI	16
9. Biloxi, MS	17
Nutley, NJ	17
10. Kirkwood, MO	18
Menomonee Falls, WI	18

Most Crimes	Total
1. New York, NY	135,152
2. Chicago	58,446
3. Los Angeles	52,832
4. Detroit	25,904
5. Houston	16,461
6. Philadelphia	16,209
7. Baltimore	15,498
8. Dallas	14,364
9. Boston	11,887
10. Atlanta	11,610

Source: F.B.I.

PLACES

CITIES—CRIME
Most Dangerous Cities

In the previous rating, we saw which city has the highest total number of dangerous crimes in the country. In this rating, we present the most dangerous city—that which has the most number of dangerous crimes per capita. New York, which tops the list for most total crimes and is perceived by many across the country as crime-ridden, is seen here as relatively safe, comparatively speaking.

City	Crimes per 100,000 residents
1. Atlanta	1,919
2. Miami	1,645
3. Newark	1,437
4. St. Louis	1,386
5. Chicago	1,110
6. Los Angeles	1,074
7. New York	1,067
8. Detroit	1,038
9. Boston	993
10. Portland, Ore.	966

Source: Federal Bureau of Investigation; U.S. Census Bureau.

CITIES—DAY CARE
Most Expensive City for Child Day-Care

Remember Nanny and the Professor? Well, nowadays the poor professor probably couldn't afford the services of his British surrogate wife. The cost of a full-time babysitter can run several hundred dollars a week, per child—tough sledding on a professor's salary. Statistics indicate that more than half of all mothers now work—and that means finding someone to take care of the youngsters while mommy brings home some bacon. In New York City that can be a very expensive proposition indeed. The average day-care bill—$104 per week—eats up almost 20 percent of the yearly family income. In Ogden, Utah, on the other hand, the cost of day care is a mere six percent of the annual income. The following rating rep-resents the ten most expense cities in the country in terms of weekly health care, and the size of the bite that child care expenses take out of the year family income.

Most Expensive	Cost/Wk.	% Inc.
1. New York	$104	19%
2. Boston	$101	14%
3. Minneapolis	$ 86	11%
4. Manchester, NH	$ 84	13%
5. Anchorage	$ 84	9%
6. San Francisco	$ 82	11%
7. Portland, ME	$ 80	14%
8. Washington, DC	$ 77	9%
9. Philadelphia	$ 76	12%
10. Hartford	$ 76	10%

Least Expensive		
1. Ogden, UT	$39	6%
2. Jackson, MI	$43	8%
3. Columbia, SC	$45	8%
4. Huntington, WV	$45	10%
5. Mobile, AL	$46	10%
6. Tampa	$46	9%
7. New Orleans	$47	9%
8. Cheyenne, WY	$48	8%
9. Grand Isl., NE	$48	8%
10. Tucson	$49	9%

Source: Runzheimer International; Donnelley Marketing Information Services.

CITIES—DEATH
Highest and Lowest Death Rate

Death, funnily enough, is a fact of life. In the era of mass communication, with printed and broadcast obituaries and crime reports cascading at all times, mortality is everyday news. Being human, there is, horribly, no place to hide from eternity. Some spots, we see here though, are slightly safer than others. However, we wouldn't suggest moving to one of the lower death-rate cities in an attempt to escape the Grim Reaper; these death rates are more a matter of demographics than geography.

Highest	Deaths per 1,000 Pop.
1. St. Petersburg, FL	18.1

PLACES

2. Sacramento, CA	15.0
3. St. Louis, MO	14.5
4. Pittsburgh, PA	13.6
5. Buffalo, NY	13.5
6. Miami, FL	13.1
7. Louisville, KY	12.7
8. Baltimore, MD	12.6
9. Cleveland, OH	12.5
10. Cincinnati, OH	12.3

Lowest	Deaths per 1,000 Pop.
1. Anchorage, AK	3.1
2. Arlington, TX	4.1
3. Aurora, CO	4.4
4. Virginia Beach, VA	4.5
5. San Jose, CA	5.6
6. El Paso, TX	5.7
7. Austin, TX	6.0
8. Colorado Springs, CO	6.3
9. Santa Ana, CA	6.5
10. Anaheim, CA	6.8

Source: U.S. Census Bureau.

CITIES — DEFENSE
Defense Industry Mill Towns

The business of war is serious indeed, not only in deaths, but in dollars as well. America has been on a war footing (hot and cold) for the better part of a century now, and our civilian economy has come to depend largely on military-related revenues. The presence of a major military installation or defense manufacturer in an ailing metro can make all the difference, for better or for worse. But St. Louis will see a big drop in its military business if top defense contractor McDonnel-Douglas goes ahead with its planned move to the Washington, D.C. area. These are the top U.S. cities ranked by annual Department of Defense contract totals. Figures are for 1986.

City	Defense Dollars (000)
1. St. Louis	$5,089,872
2. Ft. Worth	$4,573,951
3. Los Angeles	$4,301,819
4. Bethpage, NY	$2,865,703
5. Cincinnati	$2,812,728
6. Sunnyvale, CA	$2,548,816
7. Marietta, GA	$2,129,421
8. Groton, CT	$2,056,579
9. El Segundo, CA	$1,983,658
10. Stratford, CT	$1,780,473

Source: Congress and Defense.

CITIES — DIVERSITY
Most Diverse Population

New York has always been a melting pot and the first glimpse of America for its newly-arrived immigrants. From the processing rooms of Ellis Island to the Customs Office at Kennedy Airport, New York holds out a somewhat dubious welcome for the tired, the poor and the huddled masses yearning to breathe free (or at least free-market). However, in recent years, such hot spots as Los Angeles and Miami have become major centers of immigration to the U.S., from Latin America and the Far East. Los Angeles, with its thriving Latino population, its strong Jewish community, and its large concentrations of Armenian-Americans and other Middle Eastern immigrants rates highly in terms of ethnic diversity, as does Miami, with thriving communities of Cubans, Haitians, Central Americans and African-Americans, and its older Jewish community. These, then, are the most ethnically diverse North American cities, based on editors' evaluations of Census information.

The Top Ten

1. New York City
2. Los Angeles
3. Miami
4. Chicago
5. Washington, D.C.
6. Toronto
7. Houston
8. San Diego
9. Seattle
10. Boston

Source: "Best and Worst" original, based on U.S. Census Bureau information.

75

PLACES

CITIES — EDUCATION
Educational Attainment
The following list ranks those cities in the top 75 in population by educational attainment, measured by the percentage of the population with 16 or more years of education. The list of big cities with the best-educated populace is lead by Austin, home of the University of Texas, and the West Coast meccas of San Francisco and Seattle. Washington, with its preponderance of white-collar workers — lawyers and bureaucrats, also scores high. The cities in which educational attainment is lowest primarily are Northeastern urban centers that also suffer from other blights — unemployment, high crime, an entrenched underclass. These factors are part of the continued cycle of poverty that keeps educational, and ultimately social, opportunity out of reach for many inner city residents. In Newark, a mere 6.3 percent of the population has reached a college-degree level of education.

Most Educated	16 Yrs. School (%)
1. Austin, TX	30.6
2. San Francisco, CA	28.2
3. Seattle, WA	28.1
4. Washington, DC	27.5
5. Arlington, TX	27.3
6. Lexington-Fayette, KY	25.6
7. Baton Rouge, LA	25.0
8. Aurora, CO	25.0
9. Albuquerque, NM	24.9
10. Denver, CO	24.8

Least Educated	
1. Newark, NJ	6.3
2. Cleveland, OH	6.4
3. Detroit, MI	8.3
4. St. Louis, MO	10.0
5. Philadelphia, PA	11.1
6. Buffalo, NY	11.1
7. Baltimore, MD	11.3
8. Jersey City, NJ	11.7
9. Santa Ana, CA	12.0
10. Toledo, OH	12.2

Source: U.S. Bureau of the Census.

CITIES — ELECTRICITY
Highest Electric Bills
Energy consumption has become an enormous issue over the last several decades, ever since the oil crisis and increasing again with every Persian Gulf crisis. A new environmental consciousness in the '80s and '90s will bring the issue even more to the forefront in the coming years. A large portion of America's energy consumption volume is generated from electricity. The following lists are rankings of the ten cities with the highest and those with the lowest electricity bills. The data is drawn from a field of the 75 largest cities in the U.S. and illustrate typical monthly residential electric bills.

City	Avg. Monthly Elec. Cost (750 kwh)
1. New York City	$86.37
2. Jersey City, NJ	$75.19
Newark, NJ	$75.19

Keeping that magnificent skyline lit up costs New Yorkers the highest electricity bills in the country. Photo © N.Y.S. Dept. of Economic Development.

PLACES

3. San Diego, CA	$74.98
4. Pittsburgh, PA	$73.98
5. Philadelphia, PA	$72.99
6. Riverside, CA	$72.66
7. Toledo, OH	$71.68
8. Miami, FL	$70.47
9. Boston, MA	$69.65
10. Wichita, KS	$69.48

Source: U.S. Bureau of the Census.

CITIES— ENTERTAINMENT
Entertainment Capitals

As with fun and sun, Los Angeles merits top honors for entertainment, based on the huge entertainment industry the city plays home to. Virtually all national network television programming is filmed in Los Angeles — it's funny how ever television setting, from the war-torn Korea of *M*A*S*H* to the Alabama backwoods of *The Dukes of Hazard*, resembles the scrubby brushland and semi-desert of the Los Angeles area. Hollywood is indeed still the home of the glitz and glamour of the entertainment world. Scores were determined by "Best and Worst" editors and are based on entertainment industry involvement in the community.

The Top Ten	Score
1. Los Angeles	145
2. New York City	46
3. Chicago	44
4. Toronto	42
5. Washington, D.C.	39
6. San Francisco	38
7. Boston	33
8. Miami	32
9. Houston	29
10. Philadelphia	27

Source: "Best and Worst" original.

CITIES—FANS
Best and Worst Sports Fans

Everybody likes a winner, but only a true sports maniac can embrace the futility generated by Chicago sports franchises. The Cubs haven't won a world championship in eighty years, but try getting a ticket to Wrigley Field on a Saturday in July and you'll realize what the phrase "Die-Hard Cub Fan" really means. Similarly, Chicago's NHL Black Hawks haven't brought home the Stanley Cup since the '60s, but they still sell out every game at the venerable old Chicago Stadium, as do the until-very-recently championshipless Chicago Bulls. Even the Bears, whose fan loyalty and rabidness equals that of the rowdy Hawks fan, have seen only two NFL championships in almost thirty years. And with the new Comiskey Park, the all-but-forgotten White Sox, who nearly left the city in 1988, are setting attendance records. With their attendance, perseverance, faithfulness, rowdiness and sheer ability to generate noise, Chicago's sports fans merit top honors for sports madness. Oh, yeah — and they *don't* do the wave at Wrigley. Ratings are subjective evaluations by editors of the "Best and Worst" based on observations and interviews with fans.

The Top Five

1. Chicago
2. Boston
3. Baltimore
4. Washington, D.C
5. San Francisco

The Bottom Five

1. Phoenix
2. San Diego
3. St. Louis
4. Atlanta
5. Los Angeles

Source: "Best and Worst" original.

CITIES—FIRE DEPARTMENTS
Busiest and Biggest

At some time in every boy's life, there is the dream to become a fireman. Of course, only

77

PLACES

a few of these fantasies are ever realized because the reality of such work tends to dissuade most people from pursuing such careers. According to ratings elsewhere, firefighters have the most stressful and most physically demanding jobs in the workforce. The stress is high, the life and death situations are frequent, and the "glory" quickly loses its luster. Regardless, it is vital that someone do this work and rise to the challenge on a daily basis. Although every situation is not necessarily extreme (some are false alarms, minor incidents or other easily resolved problems), the chance is always there for the handling of something major. The following engine companies (including both fire & EMT) are the busiest in the nation with the leading company responding to an average 13 calls a day, every day of the year!

Busiest Engine Companies

City	Company	Runs
1. New York	4P	4933
2. Phoenix	3	4753
3. Cincinnati	5	4620
4. Milwaukee	13	4294
5. Sacramento	6	3939
6. Denver	8	3745
7. Los Angeles	46	3671
8. Tucson	5	3587
9. Washington, D.C.	10	3555
10. Minneapolis	6	3533

Most Fire Alarms Answered

City	Alarms
1. New York	304,798
2. Chicago	293,421
3. Los Angeles	253,000
4. Washington, D.C.	156,912
5. Philadelphia	155,538
6. Houston	142,963
7. Baltimore	139,426
8. Detroit	139,030
9. Dallas	105,209
10. Phoenix	89,190

CITIES — GENTRIFICATION
Most Gentrified Metropolitan Areas

Even the poshest of cities have their own unsightly slices of life. Dwellings for servants, employees and other nuts-and-bolts service-oriented folks mar the most uppity and pretentious of urban landscapes. It is these ivoried walls that every marketer wants to breach, and every underclassman aspires to. The following list presents the ten areas with the highest percentage of their households earning over $50,000.

Metro Area	Percent Over $50,000
1. Nassau-Suffolk, NY	44.8
2. Stamford-Norwalk-Danbury, CT	43.4
3. Middlebury-Somerset, NJ	43.2
4. San Jose, CA	40.8
5. Washington, D.C.	40.4
6. Bergen-Passaic, NJ	39.7

Washington has the highest preponderance of government workers in the country. Here, Washingtonians load up on their new Metro.

PLACES

Source: Sales and Marketing Management, 1990 Survey of Buying Power.

CITIES – GOVERNMENT WORKERS

Most Government Employees

Nearly everyone complains about big government, but few in that teeming majority recognize the irony when they also complain of the scarcity of staff at public places (trains, schools, parks, prisons) and the sloth of service (at public-sector glamour spots like the departments of Motor Vehicles and Health). City workers, who engage the public mano-a-mano, are the closest link of 'us' (the citizens) with 'them' (the "leaders"). Power to those people-of-the-people! Here are the cities with the most public sector employees per 10,000 people.

City	Govt. Empl./10,000Pop.
1. Washington, DC	700.3
2. New York, NY	541.5
3. Richmond, VA	462.1
4. Jersey City, NJ	427.9
5. Baltimore, MD	417.4
6. Norfolk, VA	403.2
7. Anchorage, AK	391.6
8. Nashville-Davidson, TN	380.9
9. Buffalo, NY	370.1
10. Rochester, NY	367.4

Source: U.S. Bureau of the Census.

CITIES – HEROIN

Most Potentially Heroin-Related Deaths

Although the nation's attention is deservedly focused on the prevalence of crack and and other socially-corrosive cocaine derivatives, heroin still poses a deadly threat. In fact, the danger from this drug has now become a two-edged sword, with the very real

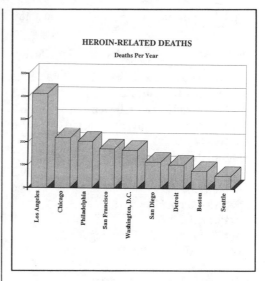

HEROIN-RELATED DEATHS
Deaths Per Year

threat of HIV infection that heroin injectors face from shared needles. The following figures are from coroners reports of deaths that mention heroin for the year 1989.

City	Potentially Heroin-Related Deaths
1. Los Angeles	412
2. Chicago	219
3. Philadelphia	204
4. San Francisco	172
5. Washington, D.C.	166
6. San Diego	115
7. Detroit	103
8. Boston	77
9. Seattle	56

Source: "Overview of Selected Drug Trends," NIDA Drug Abuse Warning Network.

CITIES – HISPANIC

Latin America: Most Hispanic Metro Areas

America has always prided itself on being a nation of immigrants. Such celebration should continue well into the forseeable future, for America remains a nation of new arrivees. Of course, many of these folks arrive without proper papers or legal pedigree, but in time even these less-than-

PLACES

legal immigrants are assimilated into the fabric of America.

Metro Area	% Hispanic Population
1. San Antonio, TX	52.2
2. Miami-Hialeah, FL	45.3
3. Los Angeles-Long Beach, CA	36.8
4. Riverside-San Bernadino, CA	22.6
5. New York, NY	21.9
6. San Jose, CA	21.7
7. Anaheim-Santa Ana, CA	19.3
8. Houston, TX	18.6
9. San Diego, CA	15.7
10. Phoenix, AZ	13.8

Source: Sales and Marketing Management, Survey of Buying Power.

CITIES — HISPANIC
Least Hispanic

The neo-Hispanic bent of American urban culture is unmistakable, but unbroken bastions of Caucasian exclusionism still abound. Most often, the sterile cultural purity of these metros has less to do with discriminatory attitudes of locals than with the remoteness or undesirability of their locales. These, then, are the toughest places in the U.S. in which to find a good burrito.

Metro Area	% Hispanic Population
1. Cincinnati, OH	0.6
2. Pittsburgh, PA	0.6
3. Columbus,OH	0.7
4. Nashville, TN	0.8
5. Indianapolis, IN	0.8
6. Charlotte-Rockhill-NC-SC	0.9
7. Memphis, TN	1.1
7. St. Louis, MO	1.1
7. Minneapolis-St. Paul, MN	1.1
7. Baltimore, MD	1.1

Source: Sales and Marketing Management, Survey of Buying Power.

CITIES — HOSPITAL CARE
Most Hospital Beds

Ready access to competent emergency care is probably the first medical priority for any community. But to augment the provision of initial care, those communities must marshal the beds and other hospital resources necessary to maintain those whose recovery is not immediate. Here are the metro areas which have proven most competent and most delinquent in this task. Rankings are based on the number of hospital beds available per 100,000 population in the top 75 metropolitan areas. Figures are from 1985, the most recent available.

The Top Ten	Beds/100,000 Pop.
1. Pittsburgh, PA	2,417
2. St. Louis, MO	2,261
3. Richmond, VA	2,173
4. Buffalo, NY	1,946
5. Birmingham, AL	1,865
6. Cincinnati, OH	1,826
7. Louisville, KY	1,727
8. Rochester, NY	1,719
9. Miami, FL	1,659
10. Minneapolis, MN	1,634

The Bottom Ten	Beds/100,000 Pop.
1. Virginia Beach, VA	161
2. San Jose, CA	253
3. Arlington, TX	260
4. Santa Ana, CA	313
5. Los Angeles, CA	340
6. Aurora, CO	347
7. Mesa, AZ	379
8. Anchorage, AK	417
9. San Diego, CA	440
10. El Paso, TX	480

Source: U.S. Bureau of the Census.

CITIES — HOUSING
Most Costly New Home

Statistics generated from a wide variety of fields suggest that the generation that is now approaching "adulthood" and its accompanying responsibilities will have a much more difficult time attaining the lifestyle that their parents enjoyed. The federal deficit, the strain on services, increased costs of health care both for the young and for the

PLACES

elderly, the costs of fighting social ills such as drugs, crime and homelessness, a declining work ethic, a struggling economy, and the slide of the middle class are just a few of the factors that will make it more difficult to maintain a middle-class life style. But owning a house may be the most difficult to achieve of these status symbols. Below are listed the most and least expensive housing markets for new homes in the country in 1990. The figures are based on the average cost of a new home and are drawn from a database of 291 cities encompassing all of the metropolitan areas in the country. Tops on the list are the fast-growing California counties of Ventura and Orange, where many are drawn by the promise of good weather and high employment growth.

Highest Housing Costs	Avg. Home Cost
1. Ventura County, CA	$249,498
2. Orange County, CA	$248,154
3. Nassau-Suffolk, NY	$246,800
4. San Jose, CA	$244,000
5. New London, CT	$240,180
6. San Diego, CA	$227,000
7. Los Angeles County, CA	$221,260
8. Meriden, CT	$210,000
9. Temecula, CA	$176,980
10. Hartford, CT	$175,540

Lowest Housing Costs	
1. Scotts Bluff, NE	$73,485
2. Cedar City, VT	$73,667
3. Lufkin, TX	$73,875
4. Brownsville, TX	$74,167
5. Harlingen, TX	$74,975
6. Aberdeen, SD	$75,000
6. Tyler, TX	$75,000
7. Huntington, WV	$75,400
8. Pueblo, CO	$75,900
9. Sioux City, IA	$75,960
10. Beaumont, TX	$76,460

Source: American Chamber of Commerce Researchers Association [ACCRA], Cost of Living Index, Fourth Quarter, 1990.

CITIES — LIQUOR CONSUMPTION
Brandy and Cognac

In some low-brow climes, requests for "cocktails" are received like commandments in ancient Greek and orders for aperitifs meet with outright laughter. There are, however, some unexpected corners of the geo-grid in which thinking, drinking men and women appreciate the most refined of quaffs. The following represents the top ten cities in the U.S. in annual per capita consumption of brandy and cognac per adult of legal drinking age.

City	Liters per Year
1. Milwaukee	2.268
2. Minneapolis-St. Paul	1.396
3. Washington, DC	.691
4. Baltimore	.671
5. Atlanta	.613
6. San Jose	.570
7. Chicago	.565
8. Anaheim-Santa Ana	.563
9. Oakland	.561
10. Sacramento	.561

CITIES — LIQUOR CONSUMPTION
Cordials and Liqueurs Consumption

Our Pilgrim forbears struck shore only a few hops and hearbeats from historic Boston, and that metro has endured as an island of civility ever since. A subtle sign of this Old World sophistication is the regional predilection for liquers and cordials in place of beer and hard booze. The following represents the top ten cities in the U.S. in annual per capita consumption of liqueurs and cordials per adult of legal drinking age.

City	Liters per Year
1. Boston	2.633
2. Milwaukee	1.475
3. Detroit	1.422

PLACES

		City	Liters per Year
4. Bergen-Passaic, NJ	1.374		
5. Newark, NJ	1.355	1. Rochester, NY	1.346
6. Middlesex-Somerset, NJ	1.347	2. Nassau-Suffolk, NY	1.343
7. Monmouth-Ocean, NJ	1.326	3. New York	1.333
8. Denver	1.160	4. Buffalo	1.299
9. Philadelphia	1.032	5. Washington, DC	1.270
10. Chicago	.990	6. Baltimore	1.082
		7. Ft. Lauderdale, FL	1.022
		8. Orlando	1.022
		9. Miami-Hialeah	1.014
		10. Boston	1.008

CITIES — LIQUOR CONSUMPTION

Gin Towns

Gin is the most sublime and opinionated of hard liquors. In drinks, it is obtuse, mating with few soft beverages. But when it finds a worthy partner, most notably tonic, the sensation can seldom be matched. The following represents the top ten cities in the U.S. in annual per capita consumption of gin per adult of legal drinking age.

City	Liters per Year
1. Atlanta	1.626
2. Washington, DC	1.187
3. Sacramento	1.156
4. Tampa-St. Pete.-Clearwater, FL	.962
5. Orlando	.955
6. Ft. Lauderdale, FL	.951
7. Miami-Hialeah	.950
8. Middlesex-Somerset, NJ	.901
9. Bergen-Passaic	.899
10. Newark	.895

CITIES — LIQUOR CONSUMPTION

Rum

Virtually any bar in America offers a literally dizzying array of hard and soft liquors. All have some virtues, all cater to many vices. Rum, however, holds a singular spot in the gulping galaxy. Its torrid tropical history and easy camaraderie with popular mixes make it an enduring favorite. The following represents the top ten cities in the U.S. in annual per capita consumption of rum per adult of legal drinking age.

CITIES — LIQUOR CONSUMPTION

Scotch

Scotch is a universal alcoholic favorite, but for impenetrable, possibly dark reasons, the New York metro area and New York State has become the Scotch-drinking capital of the U.S. Seven of the ten most Scotch-soaked metro's in the nation, in point of fact, fall within that region. Scotch is the preferred drink among those who dwell in the business world's stratosphere, a bond passed down through the blue blood of America's elite. New York is the home to the largest array of those members of the corporate culture, and, for better or worse, scotch helps fuel the wheeling and dealing that keeps that culture going. The following represents the top ten cities in the U.S. in annual per capita consumption of scotch per adult of legal drinking age.

City	Liters per Year
1. Rochester, NY	1.477
2. Buffalo, NY	1.464
3. New York	1.462
4. Middlesex-Somerset, NJ	1.435
5. Monmouth-Ocean	1.432
6. Nassau-Suffolk	1.430
7. Bergen-Passaic	1.419
8. Ft. Lauderdale, FL	1.290
9. Orlando	1.273
10. Miami-Hialeah	1.271

PLACES

CITIES — LIQUOR CONSUMPTION
Tequila!

All liquors carry their own mythos and mystique, but few can match the primal terror and tropical exhilaration that accompanies face to face contemplation of a chilled shot of Tequila. Other drinks carry heavy reputations for potency and volatility, but few can go tongue-to-tongue with the king of the jungle. The following list represents the top ten cities in annual per capita consumption of tequila among adults of legal drinking age.

Cities	Liters per Year
1. Denver	.471
2. Phoenix	.467
3. Dallas	.427
4. Fort Worth-Arlington	.420
5. San Antonio	.417
6. Anaheim-Santa Ana	.414
7. Oakland	.410
8. Houston	.408
9. San Francisco	.407
10. Riverside-San Bernardino	.405

CITIES — LIQUOR CONSUMPTION
Vodka

In these days of Glasnost and good tidings, vodka is more popular than ever on these shores. That potent Eastern concoction, in many ways, is the purest and cruelest of popular liquors, mixing seamlessly (and dangerously) with a bevy of beauteous beverages. The following list represents the top ten cities in the country in terms of annual per capita consumption of vodka among adults of legal drinking age.

Cities	Liters per Year
1. Orlando	2.773
2. Ft. Lauderdale, FL	2.736
3. Tampa-St. Pete.-Clearwater	2.713
4. Miami-Hialeah	2.693
5. Monmouth-Ocean, NJ	2.379
6. Middlesex-Somerset, NJ	2.368
7. Newark	2.359
8. Atlanta	2.345
9. Bergen-Passaic, NJ	2.311
10. Washington, DC	2.284

CITIES — LIQUOR CONSUMPTION
Whiskey A Go-Go's

Consuming raw, hard whiskey is one of the knottiest and most enduring male rites of passage. To many, a shot of whiskey is tantamount to punishment, and poses a daunting challenge to mind, body and mouth. To others, it is the saucy elixir of nightlife, and a link to our mannish pasts. The following list represents the top ten cities in the country in annual per capita consumption of whiskey among adults of legal drinking age.

City	Liters per Year
1. Louisville, KY	1.837
2. Washington, DC	1.507
3. Norfolk-Newport News, VA	1.493
4. Memphis	1.424
5. Nashville	1.395
6. Charlotte-Gastonia-Rock Hill	1.378
7. New Orleans	1.331
8. Denver	1.238
9. Baltimore	1.200
10. Kansas City	1.168

CITIES — LIQUOR CONSUMPTION
Biggest Boozers

No one likes to be accused of excessive drinking, and cities — in this regard — are no different than the people who populate them. Sadly, it is our nation's most socially volatile metros, D.C. and Miami, which must answer for the highest per-capita consumption of liquor in the nation. The following ten cities like their drinks hard and fast — they are the top ten towns in total annual per

Washington has the highest per capita consumption of liquor in the country.   Photo courtesy Washington DC Convention and Visitors Assoc..

capita consumption of eight distilled liquors among adults of legal drinking age.

Cities	Liters per Year
1. Washington, DC	9.017
2. Miami-Hialeah, FL	8.313
3. Tampa-St. Pete.-Clearwater	8.279
4. Atlanta	7.776
5. Sacramento	7.583
6. Denver	7.224
7. Oakland	7.186
8. San Francisco	7.133
9. San Jose	7.123
10. San Diego	7.085

CITIES — MAIL
You Never Write: Most Mail Per Person

Some people seem to have an absolute magnetism for mail—junky and otherwise—while others quasi-mystically repel it. Even the most affable and genial among us may be short on words or sour on written correspondence. Those who like to get and give mail, apparently, however, like to cluster at certain mail hubs in the civilized world. Hate a cluttered mail-box? Steer clear of the the towns on this list. Here's your zip code to zip code guide of the top postal towns in the country.

City	Pieces of Mail Per Person Per Year
1. Hartford, CT	8,383
2. Orlando, FL	7,764
3. Fort Lauderdale, FL	5,998
4. Atlanta, GA	5,554
5. Tampa, FL	5,273
6. Minneapolis, MN	4,976
7. Richmond, VA	4,473
8. Des Moines, IA	4,436
9. St. Louis, MO	4,223
10. Oakland, CA	4,197

Source: U.S. Postal Service

CITIES — MANUFACTURING
Most and Least Reliant on Manufacturing

America still talks of itself as a great industrial nation, but such talk is colored mostly by nostalgia and wishful thinking.

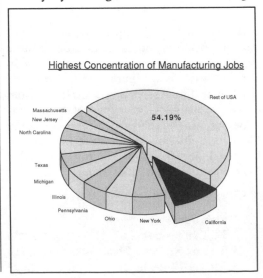

Highest Concentration of Manufacturing Jobs

Rest of USA 54.19%

Massachusetts
New Jersey
North Carolina
Texas
Michigan
Illinois
Pennsylvania
Ohio
New York
California

PLACES

Though our overall global economic and financial decline is not so bad as the many prophets of doom would have us believe, the erosion of our traditional industrial base is self-evident. A city that bases most of its earning on the profits of its manufactures today may find itself in deep fiscal peril.

The Top Ten	Mfg. Earnings (% of total)
1. Kokomo, IN	63.7
2. Elkhart-Goshen, IN	61.0
3. Anderson, IN	57.8
4. Flint, MI	56.4
5. Hickory, NC	53.3
6. Danville, VA	51.6
7. Pascagoula, MS	50.6
8. Steubenville-Weirton, OH-WV	50.0
9. Anderson, SC	49.2
10. Rochester, NY	48.2

The Bottom Ten

1. Anchorage, AK	2.1
2. Santa Fe, NM	2.6
3. Bremerton, WA	3.4
4. Las Vegas, NV	3.6
5. Naples, FL	3.9
6. Grand Forks, ND	4.2
7. Honolulu, HI	4.3
8. Jacksonville, NC	4.3
9. Washington, DC-MD-VA	4.4
10. Tallahassee, FL.	4.5

CITIES — MARIJUANA
Marijuana-Related Emergency Room Visits

The purported adverse medical effects of marijuana and related THC derivatives are the subjects of innumerable technical and lay debates. There is little doubt, however, that these drugs can cause short term loss of memory, contribute to general malaise, and promote lung disease. Opponents also rail against the casual marijuana user's supposed easy slide into harder, more debilitating illegal substances. Whatever the case, it's a fact that crimes and injuries often attend the use of pot. Below are the cities in which

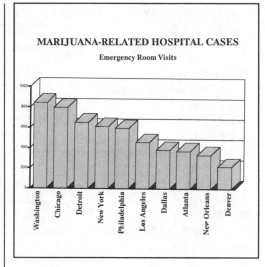

MARIJUANA-RELATED HOSPITAL CASES
Emergency Room Visits

pot was most prevalent in emergency room trauma patients. The ranking is by the number of 1989 emergency room visits in which marijuana was detected on the patient.

City	Instances
1. Washington, D.C.	843
2. Chicago	794
3. Detroit	650
4. New York	611
5. Philadelphia	595
6. Los Angeles	455
7. Dallas	381
8. Atlanta	369
9. New Orleans	333
10. Denver	218

Source: "Overview of Selected Drug Trends," NIDA Drug Abuse Warning Network.

CITIES — MARITAL STATUS
Singles Only

Sometimes the singles life swings, at cool bars, in fast cars, with easy acquaintances. Other times, the solo life is lonely, flat, boring and depressing. Like everything else in life, the decision to remain or return to singledom is a double-edged affair. We must each choose for ourselves. Below we have listed the top ten cities in the country, in terms of sheer numbers, for meeting one's prospective mate. Topping the list of soloists is the Big Apple.

City	Single-Person Households (000)
1. New York	1,118.2
2. Los Angeles-Long Beach	852.0
3. Chicago	605.2
4. Philadelphia	467.9
5. Detroit	392.4
6. Boston-Salem-Brockton-Lowell	391.7
7. Washington, D.C.	368.9
8. Houston	291.4
9. Minneapolis- St. Paul	245.1
10. Atlanta	243.9

Source: Sales and Marketing magazine, Survey of Buying Power

CITIES — MURDER
Murder Capitals, I

A car with blazing guns drives past a darkened corner crowded with youths. Bodies crumble to the ground. Blood flows into a storm sewer as life escapes from the dying victims. Yes, murder is a familiar scene in some of our nation's cities. People shoot their spouses with guns meant for self-defense. Drug deals go bad. Kids shoot each other over perceived slights — basketball jackets or maybe the expensive shoes they couldn't afford. Not surprisingly, our nation's capitol, with its tremendous economic problems, is also the country's murder capitol. Among large cities, Pittsburgh is the safest with a lowly 4.6 murders per 100,000 people. Interestingly, although New York leads the nation every year in the total number of murders it logs on its streets, it ranks only thirteenth in per capita murders.

City	Murders Per 100,000
1. Washington, D.C.	59.5
2. Detroit	57.9
3. Atlanta	48.8
4. Denver	43.4
5. New Orleans	42.4
6. Dallas	36.0
Newark	36.0
8. St. Louis	32.9
9. Baltimore	30.6
10. Oakland	30.5
11. Kansas City	29.9
12. Memphis	26.0
13. New York City	25.8

Source: U.S. Federal Bureau of Investigation, *Crime in the United States*, annual.

CITIES — MURDER
Murder Capitals, II

Every 24 minutes someone is murdered in the United States. The total murder volume increased four percent throughout the nation from 1988 to 1989, and at a similar rate from 1989 to 1990. Over the last five years of the 1980s, the number of murders increased by 13 percent, but, interestingly, the decade saw an overall decline in the number of murders of 7 percent, as the 1980 nationwide murder total was an all-time high. But 1991 is shaping up to be the most murderous year

Washington is the nation's capital in more ways than one. D.C.'s murder rate leads the nation. Photo: DC Conventiona nd Visitors Assoc.

on record, with such murder hot spots as Washington, D.C. and Chicago logging a staggering increase in the total number of murders in the first six months of the year. The following ranking lists the ten cities with populations of 10,000 and over, with the most total murders.

City	Murders (total), 1989
1. New York	1,905
2. Los Angeles	877
3. Chicago	742
4. Detroit	624
5. Philadelphia	475
6. Houston	459
7. Washington	434
8. Dallas	351
9. Baltimore	262
10. New Orleans	251

Source: "Crime in the U.S.," Uniform Crime Reports, U.S. Dept. of Justice, Federal Bureau of Investigation, 1990.

CITIES — POPULATION CHANGE
Greatest Population Change, 1980-1990

America is, as they say, a nation on the move. And where we are moving, by in large, is South and West. Americans are flocking like U-Haul–propelled lemmings to to the deserts of Arizona, Texas and California. Sun, sex, success, sincerity—whatever you seek, so shall ye find in these tan cities. The cities with the largest decrease in population are the rusted out hulks of America's once-proud industrial heartland. Cities listed have seen the greatest change in population from 1980 to 1990 among cities with a 1990 population of at least 100,000.

Fastest Growing	% Change, 1980-90
1. Mesa, AZ	89.0
2. Rancho Cucamonga, CA	83.5
3. Plano, TX	77.9
4. Irvine, CA	77.6
5. Escondido, CA	68.8
6. Oceanside, CA	67.4
7. Bakersfield, CA	65.5
8. Arlington, TX	63.5
9. Fresno, CA	62.9
10. Chula Vista, CA	61.0

Fastest Declining	% Change, 1980-90
1. Newark, NJ	-16.4
2. Detroit, MI.	-14.6
3. Pittsburgh, PA	-12.8
4. St. Louis, MO	-12.4
5. Cleveland, OH	-11.9
6. Flint, MI	-11.8
7. New Orleans, LA	-10.9
8. Warren, MI	-10.1
Chattanooga, TN	-10.1
9. Louisville, KY	-9.9
10. Macon, GA	-8.8

Source: U.S. Bureau of the Census.

CITIES — POPULATION DENSITY
Near to the Madding Crowd: The Most Densely Populated Cities in America

Do you like the rush of the crowd, body against body against body? Want to know what your neighbors' favorite albums are? What kind of fish they like to cook for dinner? What they say to each other in the midst of intimacy? In these, the densest of American cities, people live vertical, apartment-house lives. One gets to know one's neighbors habits, preferences, tendencies. This life abounds in the rush of constant contact, or alternately, the pain of loud neighbors and street noise. City living has its benefits: you can get coffee and danish any hour of day or night, but the closest thing to nature one sees are the rats digging through one's garbage. Significantly, four of the ten most densely populated cities are in the New York metropolitan area. Manhattan itself has a stagering density of 68,015 people every square mile. Number eight on the list, Inglewood, is a "suburb" of Los Angeles (as if Los Angeles itself isn't a suburb).

PLACES

City	People per Sq. Mile
1. New York City	24,387
2. Patterson, New Jersey	16,701
3. Jersey City, New Jersey	16,487
4. San Francisco	15,768
5. Chicago	13,054
6. Boston	12,242
7. Philadelphia	12,110
8. Inglewood, California	11,677
9. Miami	10,819
10. Yonkers, New York	10,000

Source: U.S. Bureau of the Census

CITIES — POPULATION DENSITY

Far From the Madding Crowd: Least Densely Populated Cities

America has always been known for its vast, wide-open spaces. Where then, do all of our 250 million inhabitants live? If you're looking to get away from it all, if you want some *space* in between you and your neighbor, check out the list below. Good fences make good neighbors, according to Robert Frost, but distance, too, antinomously, brings us closer together. The towns below offer the most of that wide-open American landscape to each inhabitant, while still preserving something of an urban environment. Figures are drawn from the U.S. Bureau of the Census numbers for population density in cities with a population of 25,000 or more.

City	People per Sq. Mile
1. Butte-Silver Bow, MO	47
2. Suffolk, VA	125
3. Anchorage, AK	136
4. Oak Ridge, TN	324
5. Chesapeake, VA	395
6. Palm Springs, CA	407
7. Cape Coral, FL	465
8. Concord, NH	511
9. Edmond, OK	581
10. Enid, OK	686

Source: U.S. Bureau of the Census.

CITIES — POVERTY
Most and Least Poverty Stricken

Poverty is commonplace in America, and its symptoms are seldom scarce in our great cities. But the true urban sad spots in this nation, the poorest of our cities, are much less known. Our images of urban poverty center around the inner sectors of our largest cities. In actuality, urban poverty is most concentrate in our small and mid-sized metropolitan areas. The following are the ten poorest and ten richest metropolitan areas in the country out of the top 275, as judged by the percentage of people living below the poverty level. The most poverty-stricken towns are those along the border with Mexico, where a large number of poor immigrants from south of the Rio Grande have settled, at least for the moment. The regions that know poverty the least are primarily in the upper midwest.

Highest Poverty	% Below Poverty Level
1. McAllen-Edinburg-Mission, TX	35.2
3. Brownsville-Harlingen, TX	31.8
4. Gainesville, FL	23.1
5. Pine Bluff, AR	22.7
6. Las Cruces, NM	22.7
7. Bryan-College Station, TX	22.3
8. El Paso, TX	21.7
9. Florence, SC	21.4
10. Tallahassee, FL.	21.1

Lowest Poverty	
1. Sheboygan, WI	4.9
2. Casper, WY	5.8
3. Appleton-Oshkosh-Neenah, WI	6.2
4. Rochester, MN	6.6
5. Cedar Rapids, IA	6.8
6. Minneapolis-St. Paul, MN	6.8
7. Reno, NV	7.0
8. York, PA	7.2
9. Manchester-Nashua, NH	7.2
10. Janesville-Beloit, WI	7.2

Source: U.S. Census Bureau.

PLACES

CITIES — RADIO
Holiest Radio Audiences

Although the trial of Jim and Tammy, and the tribulations of Jimmy Swaggart, have dealt a serious blow to American televangelism, fundamentalist Christianity remains an extremely vital national force. While ratings and revenues for televised religious programming have suffered general decline, listenership and proceeds for radio-based ecclesiastical fare are on the upswing.

Area	Religious market share (%)
1. Shreveport, La.	13.1
2. Jacksonville, Fl	9.5
3. Huntington, W. Va.	6.9
4. Lancaster, Penn.	6.6
5. Birmingham, Ala	6.4
6. Memphis, Tenn.	5.7
7. Eugene, Ore.	5.6
8. Greensboro, N.C.	5.5
9. Billings, N.D.	5.2
10. Fresno, Calif.	4.9

Source: American Radio Magazine.

CITIES — RADIATION
Most Irradiated

We are surrounded by radiation but we seldom give thought to it. The sun shines upon the earth and bathes us with light and several other forms of radiation such as ultraviolet (a tanning source) and infrared (heat). The cosmos generates a significant amount of background radiation, which also impacts on the earth. Even the earth itself generates background radiation that seeps into the environment. The twentieth century has added a new dimension to awareness of radiation; mankind has begun to control and apply it. In medicine, the use of radioactive elements has greatly improved research techniques, and we are all aware of the destructive force available from nuclear explosives and the energy potential of nuclear reactors. The management of radiation generation and disposal has become a "hot topic" of discussion and the following rating is a result of such concern. The Environmental Protection Agency has measured environmental levels of radioactivity at established testing areas and keeps a quarterly record. Focusing on items that we ingest (rather than radiations we are subjected to by being in an environment) the following rating concerns radioactive elements in drinking water and pasteurized milk. We list here the cities in which the drinking water contains up to .3 nCi of tritium per liter.

Location	Tritium level (nCi/l)
Detroit, MI	.5
Charlotte, NC	.5
Berkeley, CA	.4
Bismarck, ND	.4
Concord, NH	.4
New York City, NY	.4
Columbia, SC	.4
Hartford, CT	.3
Idaho Falls, ID	.3
Conowingo, MD	.3
Jefferson City, MO	.3
Columbia, PA	.3
Philadelphia, PA	.3
Barnwell, SC	.3
Lynchburg, VA	.3
Madison, WI	.3

CITIES — RAIN
Rain or Shine?

Whether you're an asthmatic looking for a crisp, dry climate or a swamp dweller seeking moss hanging from trees, the United States has got the climate for you. The diverse shades of precipitation are striking. From the arid, desert-like climate of the Southwest to the wet, muggy cities of the Old South and the snowy streets of Juneau, Alaska, you can choose your rainfall to the tenth of an inch. If you are a backyard gardener, you might want to choose your city by the favorite climate of your favorite plant! On the other hand, you might just wonder how wet the other Americans are. Here are the soggy totals for the rainiest American cities.

PLACES

Rainiest

City	Avg. Annual Rainfall (Inches)
1. Mobile, Alabama	64.64
2. New Orleans	59.74
3. Miami, Florida	57.75
4. San Juan, Puerto Rico	53.99
5. Juneau, Alaska	53.15
6. Jackson, Mississippi	52.82
7. Jacksonville, Florida	52.76
8. Memphis, Tennessee	51.57
9. Little Rock, Arkansas	49.20
10. Columbia, South Carolina	49.12
11. Nashville, Tennessee	48.49

Driest

The driest cities in the country are for the most part located in the booming American Southwest, and part at least of that boom can be attributed to technologies that bring water to the desert. But it is a real question how much more development and population growth these areas can support, given the limited supplies of water available to them. One can only drain a river so much for an upstream city until the towns downstream start drying out.

City	Ave. Annual Rainfall (inches)
1. Phoenix, Arizona	7.11
2. Reno, Nevada	7.49
3. El Paso, Texas	7.82
4. Albuquerque, New Mexico	8.12
5. San Diego, California	9.32
6. Boise, Idaho	11.71
7. Cheyenne, Wyoming	13.31
8. Great Falls, Montana	15.24
9. Salt Lake City, Utah	15.31
10. Bismarck, North Dakota	15.36

Source: Statistical Abstract of the United States.

CITIES — REAL ESTATE
Best Investment Real Estate Market, 1990-1994

Looking for someplace to put your money? Try West Coast real estate. In a survey of leading economists and professionals in the real estate industry, five West Coast metropolitan areas — Los Angeles, Seattle, Orange County, San Francisco and San Diego — came out on top in expected investment performance. Such optimism among real estate professionals is further indication that the economic might of the country is shifting from its traditional centers in the big Northern cities. Metros in the Northeast did not fare as well in the survey — one-fifth of all respondents expected their real estate firms to be less active in the coming years. Nearly 30% of the respondents named New York City as the most overpriced commerical real estate market in the country.

Best Real Estate Investment Market

1. Los Angeles
2. Atlanta
3. Seattle
4. Washington

The nation's capital is the leading market for office space in the country. Restrictive building codes ensure that the metro area grows out, not up. Photo: DC Convention and Visitors Assoc.

PLACES

5. Chicago
6. Orange County
7. Dallas-Ft. Worth
8. San Francisco
9. San Diego
10. Orlando
Source: Ernst & Young.

CITIES — REAL ESTATE
Leading Office Markets

The go-go eighties saw a boom in the construction of office space. Now, with more sober economic times on the horizon, the amount of new construction of office space is expected to decline. Still, it won't be bad times for everybody. The markets that inspired investors' confidence in the late 1980s continue to be the ones that are expected to perform best, according to a survey of economists and real estate professionals. It's just that those expectations should be tempered somewhat. The West coast is expected to perform particularly strongly in the office market, with Los Angeles and Seattle leading the way.

Leading Office Markets

1. Washington, D.C.
2. San Francisco
3. Los Angeles
4. Chicago
5. Seattle
6. New York
7. Atlanta
8. Dallas-Ft. Worth
9. San Diego
10. Houston
Source: Ernst & Young.

CITIES — RELOCATION
Most Popular Cities to Move To

Some reports indicate that Americans move on an average of once every two years. Where are we going? South, it seems. According to the 1990 census, the fastest growing states are still those in the Sunbelt, and the fastest declining are the northern in-

dustrial states. The attraction of Orlando is its booming tourist industry, centered around Walt Disney World. But there really is very little in the way of a city there, in traditional terms, if columnist Dave Barry is to be believed. The figures below are based on the number of households moving into these metropolitan areas minus the number of households moving out, taken from moving industry estimates.

The Most Popular Destinations

1. Orlando
2. Tampa
3. Atlanta
4. Norfolk
5. Jacksonville
6. Nashville
7. Houston
8. Seattle
9. Las Vegas
10. Phoenix

The Most Popular Departure Sites

1. New York
2. Los Angeles
3. Hartford
4. Philadelphia
5. Denver
6. Chicago
7. Miami
8. Boston
9. Providence
10. Detroit
Source: Ryder Truck Rental, Inc.

CITIES — SEGREGATION
Most Segregated, Black

We all know that segregation of minorities in the United States is a fact, but just how ingrained this segregation is has now been quantified. University of Chicago sociologists Douglas Massey and Nancy Denton have identified five dimensions of minority segregation, and, using information from the U.S. Census Bureau, have established an index that reveals the extent of segregation in 60 major American cities.

PLACES

The five dimensions of segregation that Massey and Denton reveal are: 1) Evenness, or dissimilarity, the degree to which the percentage of minority members in particular residential areas reflects the overall percentage of minorities in a metropolitan area. In highly segregated areas, neighborhoods depart greatly from the overall racial make-up of the city. 2) Exposure, the degree to which minority and majority members can be in potential contact in shared neighborhoods. 3) Clustering, the degree to which minority neighborhoods are contiguous. The most segregated metropolises are those in which the minority groups inhabit one large, contiguous area. 4) Centralization, or the extent to which minority neighborhoods are concentrated around the central business district and away from suburban areas. 5) Concentration, which is the size of the physical area which minority populations inhabit. Minority populations densely concentrated in a small geographic area means greater segregation.

Massey and Denton devised formulas for each of these five factors that assign a figure from 0 to 1.000 for each city in their study; the closer to 1.000, the worse the city is for that type of segregation (for the exact methodology, see the source). The figures are interesting in that they reveal the existence of what the researchers have termed "hypersegregation," or the excessive segregation of the community in all five identifiable categories. By adding together the indexes for the five categories of segregation, we have come up with an index of this hypersegregation (the higher the score, the more segregated the city). For instance, some cities that have a high degree of minority centralization may not be bad in terms of clustering or exposure; on the other hand, hypersegregated cities are those that are in the upper levels in all five categories.

Below are the cities in which black populations are the most and the least segregated. The top ten account for approximately one-quarter of the black population in the United States, meaning, as Massey and Denton put it, that "blacks in these cities are very unevenly distributed among tracts and live in small, densely settled, monoracial neighborhoods that are part of large agglomerations of contiguous tracts clustered tightly around the city center. Residents of such an environment would be very unlikely to come into regular contact with a member of Anglo society, except through participation in the labor force, an option that is denied to the quarter of central-city blacks who are underemployed or unemployed. Blacks without jobs would rarely meet, and would be extremely unlikely to know, an Anglo resident of the same metropolis."

The maximum score achievable is 5.000; Chicago scored .878 for evenness, .828 for exposure, .793 for clustering, .872 for centralization, and .867 for concentration, making it the American city in which black segregation is most profound. On the other hand, the least segregated cities contain only about 1.5 percent of the total black population in America, so, the researchers point out, "very few blacks experience a residential pattern that might be called 'integrated'."

Most Segregated, Black	Index
1. Chicago	4.258
2. Detroit	4.252
3. Cleveland	4.247
4. Milwaukee	4.118
5. Newark	4.041
6. Gary-Hammond-E. Chicago, IN	3.996
7. Philadelphia	3.769
8. Los-Angeles/Long Beach	3.734
9. Kansas City	3.717
10. Baltimore	3.712

Most Integrated, Black	Index
1. Anaheim-Santa Ana, CA	0.648
2. Albuquerque, NM	1.243
3. Salt Lake City-Ogden, UT	1.407
4. El Paso, TX	1.479
5. San Jose, CA	1.557

PLACES

6. Tucson, AZ	1.731
7. Riverside-San Bernardino, CA	1.804
8. Nassau-Suffolk, NY	2.240
9. Sacramento, CA	2.273
10. San Antonio, TX	2.295

Source: Douglas S. Massey and Nancy A. Denton, "Hypersegregation in U.S. Metropolitan Areas," Demography, August 1989.

CITIES — SEGREGATION
Most Segregated for Hispanics

Unlike African-Americans, Hispanics do not suffer from the widespread segregation along the five dimensions identified by Massey and Denton (see previous entry). Very little clustering, concentration, centralization, dissimilarity or isolation is evident in the 60 cities in which Hispanic and Black populations were studied. Massey and Denton conclude that only "low to moderate levels of segregation were observed for Hispanics on all dimensions. . . . Moreover, several of the largest Hispanic concentrations in the United States are not highly segregated on *any* dimension at all, including Los Angeles, San Antonio, Miami, and San Diego." If we use an overall score of about 3.400 as an indicator of hypersegregation, then it is clear that in no city do Hispanics suffer from the extreme degree of segregation that blacks do in some of the cities in the previous entry.

Most Segregated, Hispanic	Index
1. New York	3.038
2. Paterson-Clifton-Passaic, NJ	2.989
3. Chicago	2.891
4. Bakersfield, CA	2.870
5. San Antonio, TX	2.810
6. Los Angeles-Long Beach	2.795
7. Corpus Christi, TX	2.733
8. Gary-Hammond-E. Chicago, IN	2.433
9. Milwaukee	2.368
10. Philadelphia	2.367

Most Integrated, Hispanic	Index
1. Fort Lauderdale	.558

2. Salt Lake City-Ogden	.752
3. Portland, OR	.984
4. Norfolk-Virginia Beach,	1.002
5. Atlanta	1.091
6. Nashville-Davidson, TN	1.103
7. Louisville, KY	1.155
8. Cincinnati	1.254
9. Albany-Schenectady-Troy, NY	1.266
10. Pittsburgh	1.288

Source: Douglas S. Massey and Nancy A. Denton, "Hypersegregation in U.S. Metropolitan Areas," Demography, August, 1989.

CITIES
Most Segregated

By adding together the scores for Black and Hispanic segregation in the previous two entries, we have developed an overall segregation score for the cities in the study by Massey and Denton. The three largest metropolitan areas in the United States are also the three most segregated, with Chicago topping the list of the most segregated city in the country. And a simple drive through that racially beleaguered city will show how entrenched the racial divisions are: at one point you'll be driving through a neighborhood where all the faces are of one color. But cross a dividing line such as a major street, a railroad overpass or a public park, and suddenly the racial makeup is radically different. In a hypersegregated city, such boundaries are not just geographic but psychological, and politicians and social reformers in Chicago and other cities have been learning just how hard it is to erase those psychological boundaries that divide the races in the United States. For the most part, the most integrated metropolitan areas in America are those in which black populations are small to begin with, and in which Hispanic populations are either small or very well integrated into the community.

Most Segregated	Index
1. Chicago	7.149

The lure of the sun. Orlando, Florida, home of Disneyworld, is the most popular spot to relocate to, according to rental truck company figures.

2. New York	6.639
3. Los Angeles-Long Beach	6.529
4. Milwaukee	6.486
5. Cleveland	6.476
6. Gary-Hammond-E. Chicago, IN	6.429
7. Paterson-Clifton-Passaic, NJ	6.375
8. Philadelphia	6.136
9. Newark	6.098
10. Detroit	5.950

Most Integrated

1. Salt Lake City-Ogden	2.159
2. Anaheim-Santa Ana	2.573
3. San Jose	3.275
4. Nassau-Suffolk, NY	3.553
5. Albuquerque	3.564
6. Sacramento	3.582
7. Fort Lauderdale	3.690
8. Norfolk-Virginia Beach	3.725
9. Riverside-San Bernardino	3.752
10. El Paso	3.837

Source: Douglas S. Massey and Nancy A. Denton, "Hypersegregation in U.S. Metropolitan Areas," *Demography*, August, 1989.

CITIES — SIZE
Most Area

The biggest cities in America are not necessarily those that come first to mind at the mention of those words. Although Los Angeles, America's sprawling neo-Second City, is among the ten physically largest cities in the country, the remaining two of the Big Three, New York and Chicago, do not crack the list. Here, then, are the most spaced-out cities in the United States.

Top Ten	Square Miles
1. Anchorage, AK	1,732.0
2. Jacksonville, FL	759.7
3. Oklahoma City, OK	604.0
4. Houston, TX	572.7
5. Nashville-Davidson, TN	479.5
6. Los Angeles, CA	465.9

Anchorage, America's "biggest" city. Photo: Alaska Division of Tourism.

7. Phoenix, AZ	375.0
8. Indianapolis, IN	352.0
9. Dallas, TX	331.4
10. San Diego, CA	329.0

Source: U.S. Bureau of the Census.

CITIES – SMELL
Best-Smelling Populace

Pittsburghers spend the most money of anyone in the United States on bath soap and deodorant. We conjecture that the long years of grime and soot from the city's steel mills gave its residents an inferiority complex that they fight by compulsive performance of ablutions. Afterwards they lay the deodorant on, thick and heavy. On the other hand, the sweet-smelling citizens of Phoenix and Tucson spend only one-quarter the amount on bodily odor protection as their comrades in Steeltown. Below are the yearly average expenditures on deodorant for the top ten cities in the country.

City	Yearly Expenditures on Deodorant
1. Pittsburgh	$8.04
2. Grand Rapids/Kalamazoo	$7.45
3. Salt Lake City/Boise	$6.70
4. Boston/Providence	$5.73
5. Seattle/Tacoma	$5.60
6. Dallas/Ft. Worth	$5.24
7. Houston	$5.12
8. Hartford/Springfield/N. Haven	$5.12
9. Portland, ME/Concord, NH	$5.00
10. Denver	$4.93

Source: Arbitron/SAMI.

CITIES – SNOWFALL
Snowiest American Cities

Like the white stuff? Do you enjoy skiing to work? Shoveling your driveway? Pulling your groceries back from the store on your kid's sled? If snowball fights and making snow angels are your ideas of wintertime fun, take a look at our list of America's snowiest cities. These snow-covered burgs are America's winter wonderlands, places where kids tunnel like gerbils to friends houses; where principals never cancel school because of inclement weather; and where every self-respecting citizen keeps a set of chains in the trunk of his or her car. In compiling this list the U.S. National Oceanic and Atmospheric Administration counted ice pellets as well as snow.

City	Average Annual Snowfall (inches)
1. Sault St. Marie, Michigan	114.9
2. Juneau, Alaska	99.9
3. Buffalo, New York	92.3
4. Burlington, Vermont	77.9
5. Portland, Maine	71.5
6. Albany, New York	65.5
7. Concord, New Hampshire	64.3
8. Denver, Colorado	60.3
9. Great Falls, Montana	58.3
10. Salt Lake City, Utah	58.2

Source: U.S. National Oceanic and Atmospheric Administration, Comparative Climatic Data, annual.

PLACES

CITIES — SOCIAL SECURITY
Concentrations of Social Security Recipients

The aging of the American population is a widely reported phenomenon. The high rates of public pensioners in many locales are clear warnings of the difficult times ahead. These, then, are the social security capitals of the country. Not surprisingly, the nine top cities for social security recipients are in the retirement havens of Florida, while the cities with the lowest numbers of social security recipients are college towns — Iowa City, Champaign and Provo.

Most	Soc. Sec. Recipients/1,000 Pop.
1. Sarasota, FL	372.5
2. Bradenton, FL	297.4
3. Fort Myers-Cape Coral, FL	278.0
4. Daytona Beach, FL	275.9
5. West Palm Beach-Boca Raton-Delray Beach, FL	261.3
6. Ocala, FL	256.4
7. Tampa-St. Pete.-Clearwater, FL	254.3
8. Fort Pierce, FL	239.0
9. Naples, FL	223.8
10. Scranton—Wilkes-Barre, PA	218.9

Fewest	Soc. Sec. Recipients/1,000 Pop.
1. Bryan-College Station, TX	79.2
2. Houston-Galveston, TX	80.5
3. Fayetteville, NC	83.2
4. Midland, TX	83.3
5. Casper, WY	84.4
6. Odessa, TX	85.4
7. Provo-Orem, UT	88.4
8. Iowa City, IA	88.9
9. Lawton, OK	89.9
10. Champaign-Urbana, IL	91.3

Source: U.S. Bureau of the Census.

CITIES — SPEED
Overall Pace of Life

The cities of the Northeast have always prided themselves on their image of hustle and bustle — cities on the go. On the other hand, as we know, out West and down South folks are more laid back. Now there's scientific research that supports this common view. Robert Levine, Ph.D., a professor of psychology at California State University, Fresno, has studied the pace of life in a variety of large and small towns across the country. A team of researchers measured the pace of life — how fast people on the street walked, how quickly a bank teller performed a transaction, the talking-speed of postal employees, and the percentage of people wearing wrist watches — in 36 towns. Levine's research found that the rats do indeed race the fastest in the Northeast — with Boston, Buffalo and New York City leading the list, and four other Northeastern cities placing in the top ten. The slowest city in the study is the fun-and-sun capital of Los Angeles, which placed well down on the list in walking speed, next to last in talking speed (it must take a long time to decide whether

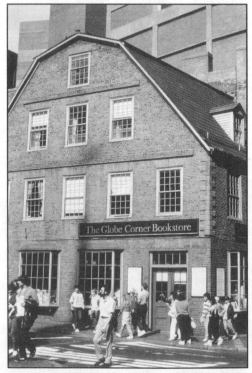

Boston is the fastest-moving city in the country.

PLACES

someone's a close enough acquaintance to call him "dude") and by far the worst in money-counting. There is a serious side to the study of how fast a city moves: Levine points out that there is a close correlation between a cities pace of life and heart disease.

Fastest

1. Boston
2. Buffalo
3. New York
4. Salt Lake City
5. Columbus
6. Worcester, MA
7. Providence, RI
8. Springfield, MA
9. Rochester, NY
10. Kansas City, MO

Slowest

1. Los Angeles
2. Sacramento
3. Shreveport
4. San Jose
5. Memphis
6. Fresno
7. East Lansing, MI
8. San Diego
9. Nashville
10. Oxnard, CA

Source: Robert Levine, "The Pace of Life," *Psychology Today*, October, 1989.

CITIES — SPEED
Fastest and Slowest Bank Tellers

Everybody hates waiting in line, but in some places the lines are longer than in others. What accounts for those long queues at the teller window in L.A.? Speed researchers timed how long it took bank clerks in 36 cities to give change for two $20 bills or to give two $20 bills for change. The results showed that tellers were slowest out West, in Los Angeles, San Francisco and San Diego, while money changed hands quickest in Chattanooga, Rochester, N.Y. and Kansas City.

Fastest Bank Tellers

1. Chattanooga, TN
2. Rochester, NY
3. Kansas City, MO
4. Paterson, NJ
5. Philadelphia, PA
6. Boston, MA
7. Buffalo, NY
8. Houston, TX
9. Providence, RI
10. Memphis, TN

Slowest Bank Tellers

1. Los Angeles, CA
2. San Francisco, CA
3. San Diego, CA
4. East Lansing, MI
5. Sacramento, CA
6. Chicago, IL
7. Oxnard, CA
8. San Jose, CA
9. Dallas, TX
10. Atlanta, GA

Source: Robert Levine, "The Pace of Life," *Psychology Today*, October, 1989.

CITIES — SPEED
Motor Mouths: Fastest Talkers

If you ever felt you've been "fast-talked" into a used-car purchase in Columbus, Ohio, now you know why. In studying the pace of life, Columbus was found to have the quickest talkers in the country. Researchers timed how long it took postal workers to to explain the difference between various classes of mail to determine how many syllables people in various cities squeeze into every second. The clerks in Columbus prattled at a rate of 3.9 syllables per second, compared to a sloth-like 2.8 for their counterparts in Los Angeles. And a Southern drawl doesn't slow down the folks in Georgia: Atlanta was found to have the second fastest-talkers in the study.

Fastest Talkers

1. Columbus, OH

2. Atlanta, GA
3. Detroit, MI
   Chicago, IL (tie)
5. Bakersfield, CA
6. Boston, MA
   Worcester, MA (tie)
8. Indianapolis, IN
9. Providence, RI
   St. Louis, MO (tie)

Slowest Talkers

1. Sacramento, CA
2. Los Angeles, CA
3. Detroit, MI
4. Shreveport, LA
5. Chattanooga, TN
6. Knoxville, TN
6. San Jose, CA
8. Louisville, KY
9. New York City
10. Canton, OH
    Rochester, NY (tie)

Source: Robert Levine, "The Pace of Life," *Psychology Today*, October, 1989.

CITIES — STRESS
Tense Towns: Cities With the Highest Stress

Las Vegas and Reno may be meccas for sin-seekers, but they also play havoc on the nerves. These towns are both a paradise and an inferno for risk-takers, where folks are made or broken on a spin of the wheel. All-night gambling, with free drinks to boot, takes its toll on residents and visitors alike, and thus in a study which ranked the relative psychological well-being of 286 cities, Reno and Las Vegas placed last. The study looked at four indicators of psychological and social pathology — alcoholism, suicide, divorce and crime. The sister cities in sin ranked one-two at the bottom of the scale of all 286 cities in the first three of these categories. Even without the divorce figures, which are skewed by the numbers of people from out of state who seek divorces in Nevada, the two cities place last in the stress index.

It's win or lose on every spin of the wheel. Reno and Las Vegas are the most stressed-out cities in the country.

Surprisingly, all of the ten most stressful cities on the list are from the West and South — Florida, California, Nevada, Texas and Arkansas; indeed, of the top 25 most stressful towns, only one — New York City, of course — is in the fast-paced Northeast. Obviously, there's more to determining a city's psychological health than simply the relative bustle of its streets and markets. Laid-back L.A., it turns out, suffers from inordinately high incidences of alcoholism, crime and suicide; only in divorce the divorce rate is it below the average. All is not well, it seems, in paradise. The easiest-going towns include a number with large universities, which attract well-educated middle- and upper-class residents.

Most Stressful

1. Reno, NV
2. Las Vegas, NV
3. Miami, FL
4. Lakeland/Winter Haven, FL
5. North Little Rock/Little Rock, AR
6. Panama City, FL

PLACES

7. Odessa, TX
8. Jacksonville, FL
9. San Francisco/Oakland, CA
10. Los Angeles/Long Beach, CA

Least Stressful

1. State College, PA
2. Grand Forks, ND
3. St. Cloud, MN
4. Rochester, MN
5. McAllen/Pharr/Edinburg, TX
6. Altoona, PA
7. Bloomington, PA
8. Provo/Orem, UT
9. Utica, NY
10. Akron, OH

Source: *Psychology Today*.

CITIES – SUBURBS
Largest Suburban Centers

Ah, suburbia, how our tired, unwashed souls long for thee! How thou hast supplanted the city of yore, with greener lawns, wider driveways, safer schools and boring malls. Cry not for Metropolis, O car commuter, or thou shalt miss the gathering of yon P.T.A. The following are the metro areas with the biggest suburban populations.

Suburban Region Population (thousands)

1. Los Angeles-Long Beach	4,571.8
2. Philadelphia	3,180.6
3. Detroit	3,136.8
4. Washington, D.C.	3,095.8
5. Nassau-Suffolk, NY	2,963.3
6. Boston-Salem	2,669.9
7. Atlanta	2,512.0
8. Riverside-San Bernadino, CA	2,318.6
9. St. Louis, MO	2,021.0
10. Anaheim-Santa Ana	1,871.2

Source: Sales and Marketing magazine, Survey of Buying Power

CITIES – TAXES
Municipal Taxes

We may hate government and taxes, but we can't do without the first, and they can't do without the second. Of course, this equation always sits a little better with John Quincy Public when he gets more or less what he pays for. Disgruntlement with government, therefore, is most justified when many greenbacks buy precious few social service goodies. In fact, as Americans are ever-increasingly inundated with such financial burdens as inflation, recession and skyrocketing taxes, there still exist some cities in which taxes remain low. Perhaps these aren't the most urbane of metropolises, but for those who wish to lower their costs of living, these cities could be of considerable value. The following ratings illustrate the ten lowest municipal taxes in the U.S., as well as the ten highest municipal taxes for comparison. A surprising number of the top tax town are in New Jersey, not considered a hot-bed of tax rebellion. The figures were drawn from a database of cities or towns with a population of 25,000 or more.

Ten Lowest   Municipal Taxes per Cap.

1. Sayreville, NJ	$28
2. Linden, NJ	$33
3. El Dorado, AR	$44
3. Florissant, MO	$44
5. Kearny, NJ	$50
6. Casper, WY	$52
7. Cheyenne, WY	$54
8. Beavercreek, OH	$56
8. Merilleville, IN	$56
9. La Puente, CA	$59
9. Fort Smith, AR	$60
10. West Memphis, AR	$61

Ten Highest   Municipal Taxes

1. Washington, DC	$2,515
2. Atlantic City, NJ	$1,894
3. New York, NY	$1,464
4. Alexandria, VA	$1,160
5. Beverly Hills, CA	$1,090
6. Newton, MA	$1,005
7. Yonkers, NY	$846
8. White Plains, NY	$837
9. Hartford, CT	$833
10. Milford, CT	$824

PLACES

Source: County and City Data Book, U.S. Department of Commerce, Bureau of the Census.

CITIES — TAXES
Property Taxes

Home ownership is an integral part of the American dream, but in the towns listed below, property taxes make that dream a nightmare for most, and unattainable for the others. Here are the cities with the highest per capita property taxes, where ownership truly costs the most.

Highest Taxes

City	Property Tax, Per Capita
1. Washington, DC	$727
2. Boston, MA	$611
3. New York, NY	$588
4. Anchorage, AK	$492
5. Richmond, VA	$489
6. Rochester, NY	$473
7. Baltimore, MD	$400
8. San Francisco, CA	$383
9. Jersey City, NJ	$371
10. Virginia Beach, VA	$312

America's anti-tax capitals are in the libertarian Western states, where land is plentiful and relatively cheap. Below are the cities where property taxes take the smallest bites from the checkbook.

Lowest Taxes

City	Property Tax, Per Capita
1. Mesa, AZ	$8
2. Columbus, OH	$24
3. Mobile, AL	$25
4. Toledo, OH	$32
5. Tucson, AZ	$34
6. Colorado Springs, CO	$42
7. Tulsa, OK	$45
8. Riverside, CA	$48
9. Akron, OH	$49
10. Aurora, CO	$52

Source: U.S. Bureau of the Census.

CITIES — TEENS
Teen Pregnancy

Teenage pregnancy is a burden on our social system. Young mothers ill-prepared for the responsibilities of parenthood make increased demands, both for themselves and their infants, on the nation's already thinly-stretched safety net. One more teen mother most often means one more underprivileged youth without a high school diploma, unemployable. This cycle of poverty repeats itself with depressing regularity in the cities below with the most teen pregnancies per 1,000 population.

Highest	Teen Pregnancies/1,000 Pop.
1. Newark, NJ	25.5
2. Baltimore, MD	23.7
3. St. Louis, MO	21.7
4. Shreveport, LA	21.3
5. Atlanta, GA	20.7
6. Detroit, MI	20.4
7. Louisville	19.6
8. Cleveland, OH	19.6
9. Fort Worth, TX	19.3
10. Cincinnati, OH	19.2

Lowest	
1. San Francisco, CA	8.1
2. Anchorage, AK	8.5
3. Arlington, TX	8.7
4. Seattle, WA	8.9
5. Virginia Beach, VA	9.3
6. San Diego, CA	9.6
7. Anaheim, CA	10.1
8. St. Paul, MN	10.6
9. Portland, OR	10.7
10. Minneapolis, MN	10.7

Source: U.S. Census Bureau.

CITIES — TELEVISION VIEWING
Biggest Vidiots

The average American family watches television forty-nine hours a week. That's longer than most people work in a week, and only a little bit shorter than the amount of

PLACES

time spent sleeping — a lot of sharing, caring time we spend with our friends the Huxtables, the Bundys and the Simpsons. Imagine the potential energy of 250 million people and 49 hours a week — more than 12 billion man/hours spent in front of the tube that might go towards finding a cure for cancer, developing a new microchip, solving the hunger problem. Video viewing has replaced talking, eating dinner, traveling, attending church and everything else as the primary means of familial interaction in America. It's how the American people solidify their bond with each other. That is, until someone steals the remote control.

City	TV Viewing, Hrs./wk.
1. Dallas/Ft. Worth	56:45
Detroit	56:45
3. Houston	55:30
4. Atlanta	54:15
5. Philadelphia	53:00
6. Boston	50:30
Chicago	50:30
Sacramento/Stockton	50:30
9. Hartford/New Haven	49:15
Los Angeles	49:15
Memphis	49:15
New Orleans	49:15
New York, Seattle-Tacoma	49:15
Washington, D.C	49:15

Source: Nielsen Media Research.

CITIES — VIDEO VIEWING
Play It Again, Pop: Most VCRs

The video cassette recorder has revolutionized our paltry couch-potato lives and spelled disaster for the networks, the neighborhood cinema, and advertisers. The preponderance of U.S. VCRs has triggered the release of an almost unimaginable volume of celluloid fare on cassette, from old movies and television programs to self-help videos and tips on hunting. The chilled-out citizens of Anchorage are the most avid VCR viewers. One can just imagine those Alaskans hunkered down with industrial-sized canisters of popcorn and a stack of videos as high as a moose's eye, prepared for those endless sub-arctic evenings.

Metro Area	% Households with VCRs
1. Anchorage	86
2. Las Vegas	84
3. Los Angeles	74
4. San Francisco	72
5. San Diego	72
6. Chicago	71
7. Reno	70
7. Sacramento	70
7. New York	70
10. Atlanta	69

Source: Nielsen Media Research.

CITIES — VIDEO VIEWING
Can't Play it Again: Highest Concentrations of Video-deprived Children and Adults

Though cable, Nintendo, VCRs and all they engender are insurmountably swell, there are still those among us who sometimes prefer to curl up with a few thousand carefully chosen written words, or indulge in the brisk art of conversation. Such nostalgic hordes may be most easily found in the following locales, where VCRs are scarcest.

City	% Households without VCRs
1. Minneapolis	62
2. St Louis	61
3. Oklahoma City	61
4. Kansas City	61
5. Jacksonville	61
6. Cincinnati	60
7. Cleveland	60
8. Albuquerque	60
9. Tulsa	59
10. San Antonio	58

Source: Nielsen Media Research

CITIES — WEALTH
The Wealthiest Cities in America

It's not surprising that the top four wealthiest cities in America are in Connecticut — George-Bush-blueblood-Groton-Yale,

PLACES

morning-commute-to-Wall-Street country. In fact, seven of the top ten cities in terms of average household income are within commuting distance of New York—though fashionably far enough away to "insulate" oneself, as Tom Wolfe says, from the great unwashed. On the other hand, Stamford, Connecticut, has become a booming city in itself for corporate headquarters, as some companies look to distance themselves somewhat from the chaos of New York. Other rich locales are found in the farmlands outside Chicago, in the D.C. metro area, and in rustic New Hampshire. Many of the poorest cities in the country are located near the border with Mexico and contain a large number of recent immigrants from south of the border. The following are the richest and poorest metro areas in the country, as measured by average household income.

Richest	Avg. Household Income
1. Stamford, CT	$91,549
2. Norwalk, CT	$83,187
3. Westport, CT	$67,225
4. Danbury, CT	$61,061
5. Nassau-Suffolk, NY	$58,464
6. Middlesex-Somerset, NJ	$57,101
7. Lake County, IL	$56,841
8. Nashua, NH	$55,979
9. Washington, DC-MD-VA	$55,355
10. Bergen-Passaic, NJ	$54,704

Poorest	
1. McAllen, TX	$21,257
2. Laredo, TX	$22,086
3. Brownsville-Harlingen, TX	$22,224
4. Jacksonville, NC	$24,791
5. Clarksville, TN	$25,431
6. Yuba City, CA	$25,817
7. Pine Bluff, AR	$25,883
8. Pueblo, CO	$25,956
9. Rapid City, SD	$26,292
10. Houma-Thibodoux, LA	$26,257

Source: U.S. Bureau of the Census.

CITIES—WHITE POPULATION
Whitebread America: Most Caucasian Metropolitan Areas

Integration is imperfect, but ongoing nonetheless. Interestingly, it is the cities with the lowest minority populations that are the most integrated, as we see in a separate rating. In these tightly held, brightly lit, ivoried citadels, black faces are few and far between, but at least what small populations there are do not suffer the debilitations of segregation found in the major cities.

Metro Area	% Black Population
1. Salt Lake City, UT	0.8
2. Anaheim-Santa Ana, CA	1.3
3. Minneapolis-St. Paul, MN	2.5
4. Portland, OR	2.9
5. Phoenix, AZ	3.2
6. San Jose, CA	3.7
7. Seattle, WA	3.8
8. Denver, CO	5.3
9. Riverside-San Bernadino, CA	5.5
10. Boston-Brockton-Lowell, MA	5.6

Source: Sales and Marketing Magazine, Survey of Buying Power

CITIES—WIND
America's Windiest Cities

Except for Honolulu, which faces Mamala Bay and the Pacific Ocean, America's windiest cities are in dusty, wind-swept Plains states, on the shores of the Great Lakes or, like Boston, ports to the rough northern Atlantic Ocean. These wind-blown metropolises may some day be surrounded by electricity-generating windmills. However, today, they gain little benefit from the tremendous energy they are subject to. Interestingly, Chicago, which is sometimes called the "Windy City," is ranked 21st out of 68 American cities surveyed by the U.S. National Oceanic and Atmospheric Administration. Legend has it that the city got

PLACES

its moniker not from its atmospheric conditions but from its wind-bag politicos.

City	Avg. Wind Speed
1. Cheyenne, Wyoming	12.9
2. Great Falls, Montana	12.8
3. Boston, Massachusetts	12.4
4. Oklahoma City, Oklahoma	12.4
5. Wichita, Kansas	12.3
6. Buffalo, New York	12.0
7. Milwaukee, Wisconsin	11.6
8. Honolulu, Hawaii	11.5
9. Duluth, Minnesota	11.2
10. Sioux Falls, South Dakota	11.1

Source: U.S. National Oceanic and Atmospheric Administration, *Comparative Climatic Data*, annual.

Hold onto your hat, cowboy! Cheyenne, Wyoming, not Chicago, is America's windiest city. Photo courtesy Wyoming Travel Commission.

CITIES, WORLD — AIR POLLUTION

Particulate Matter

Even before the destruction of Kuwait's oil fields by the retreating forces of Saddam Hussein, and the resulting blackening of the skies over the liberated country, Kuwait had the worst air in the world in terms of particulate matter in the air. One hesitates to ponder the long-term health and environmental effects from the thick clouds of black smoke billowing from burning wells. Already in the two months since the war ended, scientists had noted a severe climate change throughout Kuwait, with temperatures up to 15 degrees below normal. This drop in temperature has triggered plants to bloom in the spring instead of the fall; they subsequently die when the temperature once again rises. The environmental tragedy of Kuwait is an unprecedented one, recalling the "nuclear winter" scenarios developed to anticipate the environmental effects of a full-scale nuclear war. The list below reflects the ten worst cities for air pollution in the GEMS Monitoring Network in terms of annual average concentrations of particulate matter recorded from 1980 to 1984. More than half of the recording cities in the network registered levels above the suggested guidelines.

The Ten Worst

1. Kuwait City, Kuwait
2. Shengyang, China
3. Xian, China
4. New Delhi, India
5. Beijing, China
6. Calcutta, India
7. Tehran, Iran
8. Jakarta, Indonesia
9. Shanghai, China
10. Guangzhou, China

Source: World Health Organization.

PLACES

CITIES, WORLD — AIR POLLUTION

Sulfur Dioxide Emissions

Sulfur dioxide is one of the most prevalent atmospheric pollutants in industrialized countries. SO2 is a principal cause of environmentally destructive acid rain and also causes respiratory illness in people. The burning of fossil fuels accounts for almost 90% of man-made sulfur dioxide emissions world-wide. The lists below represent the ten worst and ten best cities for average sulfur dioxide levels in the air, for cities in the Urban Air Quality Monitoring Project of the GEMS Environmental Research Center in London. The list was determined by observing the median concentrations of sulfur dioxide in the air over the period from 1980 to 1984. Although Asian cities account for four of the ten worst cities in terms of sulfur dioxide air pollution, on a continent-wide scale, European levels are twice those of Asia and North America, due in large part to the relative density of industry on that continent. The good news is that monitors have noted a steady decline in sulfur dioxide levels in many western industrial nations since the implementation of emission controls strategies. The Soviet Union and other former Eastern block countries for the most part did not participate in the monitoring network during the period under observation, and so air-pollution levels in those areas are not yet fully known.

Ten Worst

1. Milan, Italy
2. Shengyang, China
3. Tehran, Iran
4. Seoul, S. Korea
5. Rio de Janeiro
6. Sau Paulo, Brazil
7. Xian, China
8. Paris, France
9. Beijing, China
10. Madrid, Spain

Ten Best

1. Craiova, Poland
2. Melbourne, Australia
3. Auckland, New Zealand
4. Cali, Colombia
5. Tel Aviv, Israel
6. Bucharest, Romania
7. Vancouver, Canada
8. Toronto, Canada
9. Bangkok, Thailand
10. Chicago, U.S.

Source: World Health Organization.

CITIES, WORLD — CONFLICT

Most Fought Over

You can either say it's property value or a persistent curse, but some land seems to have more than its fair share of battles fought over it. Leading the way, not too surprisingly, is the city of Jerusalem, which has had nine major wars fought within its bounds, beginning with the Romans, leading through the Crusades and up through the First World War and the Arab-Israeli conflict. These include only battles that involved the city changing hands via invaders that took over or uprisings that threw out the entrenched power. It doesn't touch on the petty skirmishes and confrontations that seem to surround that beleaguered city on a daily basis. Here, then, are the world cities that have been host the most fighting. The number for Baghdad includes its recent bombing in the Persian Gulf War.

City	Number of Wars
1. Jerusalem	9
2. Adrianople (Edilne)	7
3. Constantinople (Istanbul)	7
4. Rome	7
5. Warsaw	6
6. Pavia	5
7. Baghdad	5
8. Alexandria	4
9. Paris	4
10. Prague	4

PLACES

11. Ravenna   4
Source: *Encyclopedia of Battles*.

CITIES, WORLD –
COST OF LIVING
Most Expensive World Cities

The cost of living is something we are all concerned with, especially as it continues to rise! This index is a flexible standard when applied to the world as a whole, as can be seen in the following rating. Such a measure of the expense of staying afloat is even more important to those posted by the U.S. diplomatic service to foreign cities. The State Department estimates the cost of living in its various outposts and determines an allowance for its minions in their far-flung places of employ. The cost of living allowance is based on a yearly income between $25,000 and $47,000 U.S.; costs are shown for family and individual wage earners. Costs for housing, education, foreign taxes and insurances are excluded in these estimates. These are the most expensive places to live, measured by State Department allowances.

City	Family	Single
1. Tokyo	$54,500	$50,800
2. Geneva	$36,200	$33,200
3. Paris	$30,700	$26,200
4. The Hague	$25,600	$21,200
5. Madrid	$24,500	$22,000
6. Lisbon	$22,600	$19,000
7. Luxembourg	$22,600	$16,800
8. Manama, Bahrain	$22,300	$19,700
9. Bermuda	$22,100	$18,500
10. Mexico City	$22,000	$19,100

Source: U.S. State Department.

CITIES, WORLD –
GARBAGE
The World's Trashiest Cities

For years we have heard savants speak of the "disposable society," and today we come face to grimacing face with its legacy. Although the third world boasts some of the dirtiest cities in the world, their garbage production (a function, in the end, of disposable wealth) cannot nearly compete with the output of the microwave generation. The citizens of tinsel town generate an obscene three kilograms (almost a pound and a half) of trash a day, amounting annually to three times the average person's body weight. And this doesn't even include such cultural effluence as *Leonard, Part 6*.

City	Per Capita Daily Waste (kg)
1. Los Angeles	3.00
2. Washington, D.C.	2.10
3. Seattle	1.86
4. New York	1.82
5. Cincinnati	1.50
6. Hamburg, Germany	1.30
7. Tokyo, Japan	.93
8. Quito, Ecuador	.92
9. Tel Aviv, Israel	.89
10. Panama City	.87

Source: UN Center for Housing, Planning and Building.

CITIES, WORLD –
POPULATION
Projected Population, 2000

It's a small world, but in some ways it's getting bigger. Although zero population growth is a goal of most nations on the globe, fertility rates do not reflect this fact. Many of the capitals of Catholic Latin America are speeding toward hyper-population, while others have passed that point long ago. Below are the projected most populous cities in the year 2000. The majority of the cities listed here are third-world nations.

City	Projected Population
1. Mexico City	26,300,000
2. Sao Paulo	24,000,000
3. Tokyo	17,400,000
4. Calcutta	16,600,000

105

PLACES

5. Bombay	16,000,000
6. New York	15,500,000
7. Seoul	13,500,000
Shanghai	13,500,000
9. Rio de Janeiro	13,300,000
Delhi	13,300,000
10. Buenos Aires	13,200,000
Cairo	13,200,000

Source: International Statistical Handbook of Public Transport, International Union of Public Transport, Brussels.

CITIES, WORLD — POPULATION DENSITY
Most Densely Populated

Feel the need to reach out and touch someone? Here are the places where it's easiest. It has been said that we must come once again to love and appreciate our neighbors and re-extend the notion of community. Nonetheless, in some neighborhoods around the world, this proves to be more difficult than in others. Oftentimes, we do not have to reach out to our neighbors, because they are right there, in the way, at arms length or even closer. These are the world cities that are the most over-stuffed.

City	Persons Per Square Mile
1. Hong Kong	43,443
2. Lagos, Nigeria	39,905
3. Dhaka, Bangladesh	36,567
4. Jakarta, Indonesia	26,006
5. Bombay, India	24,288
6. Ho Chi Minh City, Vietnam	21,873
7. Ahmadabad, India	21,293
8. Shenyand, China	20,669
9. Tianjin, China	20,418
10. Chengdu, China	17,431

Source: U.S. Bureau of the Census

CITIES, WORLD — POVERTY
Slumming It

Poverty is ugly, and the cities in which that contagion have gone rampant too often are loathsome, self-perpetuating affronts to human decency. In many sectors of the third world, sixty percent or more of the urban population makes its home in squalid, underbuilt, over-populated ghettos. The renovation or abolishment of such dark human holes is a global imperative.

City	% Pop. in slums or squatting
1. Addis Ababa, Ethiopia	90
2. Yaounde, Cameroon	90
3. Douala, Cameroon	87
4. Buenaventura, Colombia	80
5. Mogadiscio, Somalia	77
6. Ibadan, Nigeria	75
7. Lome, Togo	75
8. Santo Domingo, Dom. Rep.	72
9. Casablanca, Morocco	70
10. Nairobi, Kenya	70

Source: Advertisnig Age.

CITIES, WORLD — PUBLIC TRANSIT
Busiest Public Transit Systems

Despite the disappearance of the gas lines of the seventies, we are still very much in the midst of an oil crisis. Conservation is a major item on the national agenda, and switching from individual motor transport to mass public alternatives is one of our most viable options. But as the list below reveals, Americans have a long way to go to match the public-transit consciousness of the rest of the world — only one American city, New York, is in the top ten in number of public transit travelers. Below are the busiest metro transit systems in th world, measured in millions of passengers annually.

City	Millions of Passengers per Year
1. Moscow	2,426
2. Tokyo	1,694
3. Bombay	1,407
4. Paris	1,156
5. Mexico City	1,117
6. New York City	1,006

PLACES

		County	Number of Farms
7. Buenos Aires	930		
8. Osaka	835	1. Fresno, CA	7,394
9. Leningrad	763	2. San Diego, CA	6,180
10. Calcutta	600	3. Tulare, CA	5,568

Source: International Union of Public Transport, Brussels.

County	Number of Farms
1. Fresno, CA	7,394
2. San Diego, CA	6,180
3. Tulare, CA	5,568
4. Lancaster, PA	4,991
5. Stanislaus, CA	4,611
6. Yakima, WA	4,581
7. San Joaquin, CA	4,475
8. Riverside, CA	3,907
9. Greene, TN	3,881
10. Clackamas, OR	3,489

Source: U.S. Bureau of the Census.

COUNTIES—ECONOMIES
Hottest Economies

When we contemplate a move that is still many years in the future, Americans tend typically to apply criteria more appropriate to the selection of vacation spots. When a move is actually imminent, however, we are bound to think along much more pragmatic lines. First among these, usually, is the availability of gainful employment. According to demographic and economic experts, the following counties will experience the most dramatic job growth over the next decade.

County	New Jobs, Next 10 Years
1. Orange, California	674,000
2. Los Angeles, California	652,000
3. Harris, Texas	452,000
4. Maricopa, Arizona	434,000
5. San Diego, California	420,000
6. Dallas, Texas	371,000
7. Santa Clara, California	304,000
8. Fairfax, Virginia	258,000
9. King, Washington	253,000
10. Broward, Florida	246,000

Source: NPA Data Services; *American Demographics*, January, 1991.

COUNTIES—FARMS
Most Farms

America is no one homogeneous entity—in fact, that is part of the nation's great appeal. So, it is little surprise that within this increasingly technological society, a tremendous agrarian economy still flourishes. Here are the most cultivated counties in all the land, as measured by the number of farms within county borders.

COUNTIES—FARMS
Small Farm U.S.A.

Despite the trend toward larger, more productive farms, there still exists a great number of small, family owned and family operated farms in the U.S. Small farms—defined here as those under 50 acres—are most prevalent in the land-scarce isles of Hawaii, and in Southern California, where residential areas are continuing to encroach on the farmer's traditional domain. These are the counties with the most farms under 50 acres as a percentage of all farms operating within the county.

County	Percent Small Farms
1. Honolulu, HI	93.1
2. San Diego, CA	87.4
3. Hawaii, HI	87.2
4. Los Angeles, CA	86.1
5. King, WA	83.8
6. Maui, HI	82.7
7. Dade, FL	82.5
8. San Bernardino, CA	80.5
9. Orange, CA	80.1
10. Salt Lake, UT	79.4

Source: U.S. Bureau of the Census.

COUNTIES— POPULATION DENSITY
Most Densely Populated

The values of leisure time, family and material wealth are indisputable, by a

PLACES

surprising few of us fully recognize the luxury and comfort of adequate (or even excessive) "personal space." In this age of the metropolitan megalopolis and the efficiency apartment, square footage is an increasingly rare and valuable commodity—most particularly in these over-packed counties:

County	Population per Square Mile
1. Manhattan, NY	67,181
2. Kings, NY	32,760
3. Bronx, NY	28,419
4. Queens, NY	17,645
5. San Francisco, CA	16,282
6. Philadelphia, PA	12,080
7. Hudson, NJ	12,023
8. Suffolk, MA	11,603
9. Washington, D.C.	9,938
10. Baltimore City, MD	9,410

Source: U.S. Bureau of the Census, City and County Data Book

COUNTIES—POPULATION GROWTH

Fastest Growing

Despite the natural tendency to view economic situations in stark black-and-white, the cyclical amassing and dispersion of wealth in contemporary America is characterized by the intersection of countless gray regions. The flight of capital, material and population may well wreak devastation in the area from which it departs, but often, it simultaneously brings prosperity and renewed vigor to the area to which it relocates. These are some of the counties enjoying the benefits of the American urge to pull up stakes and move on when things start going bad.

County	% Growth (1980-86)
1. Matanuska, Alaska	119.0
2. Hernando, Florida	74.8
3. Kenai Peninsula, Alaska	70.7
4. Osceola, Florida	68.7
5. Flagler, Florida	66.5
6. Gwinnett, Georgia	65.9
7. Esmeralda, Nevada	65.1
8. Uinta, Wyoming	63.5
9. Fayette, Georgia	62.9
10. Nye, Nevada	61.1

Source: U.S. Bureau of the Census, City and County Data Book

COUNTIES—REVENUES

Highest Governmental Revenue

Big government is by nature neither bad nor good. Our elected officials must justify their levels of expenditure and employment. Each situation is unique. Below are the counties with the highest revenues gathered from their citizenry and their businessmen and women. The duty of those citizens and businesspeople is to look into those revenues and establish whether their tax dollars are being spent justly. If you live in one of these counties, you might want to check out what you're getting for your money.

County	1990 Govt. Revenue ($ millions)
1. Los Angeles	$7,572.1
2. Montgomery, MD	$2,200.0
3. Fairfax, VA	$2,081.3
4. Orange, CA	$1,870.1
5. Dade, FL	$1,705.4
6. Nassau, NY	$1,620.0
7. Prince Georges, MD	$1,478.1
8. San Diego	$1,439.4
9. Suffolk, NY	$1,288.0
10. Baltimore	$1,222.9

Source: City & State Magazine.

COUNTIES—SIZE
Largest

Out of the brave, innocent explorations of Columbus and other pre-industrial seekers has grown a urban nation whose appearance would strike its simple founders dumb. The seats of political, cultural and industrial power that man has wrought in this region—

PLACES

in a mere matter of a half millennium, a drop in time's bucket in the old world — would be utterly unintelligible in the idioms of our forbears of even the last century, accustomed to the friendly ministrations of the county sheriff and judge. Here, then, are the most populous counties in the land.

County	Population
1. Los Angeles, CA	8,295,900
2. Cook, Illinois	5,297,900
3. Harris, Texas	2,798,300
4. Kings, NY	2,293,200
5. San Diego, California	2,166,800
6. Orange, California	2,164,300
7. Wayne, Michigan	1,923,300
8. Queens, NY	1,900,200
9. Maricopa, Arizona	1,833,100
10. Dallas, Texas	1,769,500

Source: U.S. Bureau of the Census.

COUNTRIES — ABORTION
Most Abortions

Over the past several years, the trend toward liberalization of abortion laws has continued — almost everywhere, that is, except for here in the U.S., where abortion rights are under attack in many states, and the executive and judicial branches of the federal government continuous move to the right has led to a number of setbacks for abortion rights activists. Forty percent of the world's population live in countries which allow abortion on request, and another 25 percent can receive abortions if the life of the mother is in danger. The trend toward liberalized abortions began in the 1950s in the countries of Eastern and Central Europe, before the development of modern contraceptive methods but after the imposition of communist rule, which tore down the social and religious obstacles to abortion. In the majority of countries of the west, half of all abortions are obtained by young, single women; in the U.S., 83 percent of all abortions are obtained by unmarried women. On the other hand, in Eastern Europe and the developing world, abortion is most common among married women with two or more children. The rate of mortality from legal abortions in developed countries is 0.6 deaths per 100,000 procedures. China, which, facing severe population growth, has instituted widespread programs to limit growth, leads the world in total number of abortions annually.

Country	Abortions, 1987
1. China	10,394,500
2. Soviet Union	6,818,000
3. United States	1,588,600
4. India	588,400
5. Turkey	531,400
6. South Korea	528,000
7. Japan	497,800
8. Romania	421,400
9. Yugoslavia	358,300
10. Italy	191,500

Source: Stanley K. Henshaw, "Induced Abortion: A World Review, 1990," Family Planning Perspectives, March/April, 1990.

COUNTRIES — ABORTION
Highest Abortion Rate

Eight of the ten countries with the highest rates of abortion are those that have either until very recently been under the cloak of communism or remain so. According to the most recent reliable data, Romania leads the world in induced abortions. In such Eastern European countries as Romania, the Soviet Union and Bulgaria, over half of all pregnancies are terminated. In the United States, the ratio is 29.7 abortions for every 100 known pregnancies. The developed country with the lowest abortion rate in which abortion is legal is the Netherlands, where 9 percent of all pregnancies end in abortion. According to Stanley Henshaw of The Alan Guttmacher Institute, the most pressing need in the reduction of unintended pregnancy and abortion in Western developed countries is improved contraceptive use among young, unmarried women. In Eastern Europe, on the other hand, the greatest concern is providing contraceptive

PLACES

services and supplies to married women, and encouraging their use. The following are the countries with the highest abortion rates, measured in induced abortions per 100 pregnancies.

Country	Abortion Rate
1. Romania	56.7
2. Soviet Union	54.9
3. Bulgaria	50.7
4. Yugoslavia	48.8
5. Cuba	45.3
6. South Korea	43.0
7. Czechoslovakia	42.2
8. Hungary	40.2
9. Singapore	32.7
10. China	31.4

Source: Stanley K. Henshaw, "Induced Abortion: A World Review, 1990," Family Planning Perspectives, March/April, 1990.

COUNTRIES – ACCIDENTS
Most Accident-Prone Peoples

Accidents will happen wherever and whenever you go. There are, however, some spots where accidents seem to happen more often than in others. Whether such clumsiness is the result of excessive relaxation, outright carelessness or the will of God, one can never surely say. Here however, are the most troublesome spots for accidental deaths.

Nation	Rate per 100,000
1. Hungary	73.6
2. France	62.4
3. Austria	51.4
4. Switzerland	50.9
5. Poland	49.9
6. Ecuador	48.8
7. Portugal	48.2
8. New Zealand	45.2
9. Greece	43.4
10. Bulgaria	40.4

Source: National Center for Health Statistics.

COUNTRIES – AGE
Oldest

Age is a fundamental criterion in establishing the legitimacy of nations and their governments. Of the more than 160 independent countries on Earth, a mere 45 existed in their current forms before the turn of the century. The Napoleonic wars resulted in the births of many new geopolitical entities, as did the cessation of hostilities in WW I. Now, however, some of those geo-political patchwork constructions are falling apart, not the least of which is the once fearsome Soviet Union, as ethnic groups gravitate toward older associations and assert their independence. The following are the oldest continuous countries in the world.

Nation	Year Founded
1. Ethiopia	B.C. 3,000
2. San Marino	c. A.D. 400
3. France	486
4. Japan	c. 500
5. United Kingdom	1066
6. Hungary	1101
7. Andorra	1278
8. Switzerland	1291
9. Monaco	1338
10. Spain	1492

COUNTRIES – AGRICULTURE
Most Fertile Land

As the bread basket to the world, it's often said that the United States is blessed with the most fertile soil in the world, but while that may be figuratively true – in that our Constitutional freedoms are the fertile soil for individual expression and growth – in terms of actual crop yield, the U.S. does not even place in the top ten, as the list below demonstrates. However, the U.S. territory of Puerto Rico does lay claim to the most productive soil in the world. That Caribbean island enjoys a cereal crop yield of on average of 8,443 kilograms per hectare (hectare is a unit of measure equal to 2.471 acres). The U.S. can afford to serve as the world's breadbasket because of its sheer size, and its crop yield is still quite good at 4,618 kg/hectare. In fact, with a crop yield on average of 3,837 kg/hectare, North and Central America enjoy an agricultural productivity 66% higher than the world average of 2,552. Europe leads the world in agricultural productivity, with an average of 4,234 kg/hectare. Asian farmers get 2,523 kg of cereal crop per hectare, followed by South America at 2,038 and Africa at a staggering 1,077 kg/hectare. These figures are based on the average crop yield measured by kilograms per hectare of cereals over a three-year period from 1984 to 1986.

The Top Ten	Kg/Hectare
1. Puerto Rico	8,443
2. Netherlands	6,934
3. Belgium	6,116
4. United Kingdom	6,081
5. Reunion Island	5,039
6. Japan	5,901
7. Switzerland	5,721
8. France	5,655
9. South Korea	5,625
10. Ireland	5,468

Source: Food and Agriculture Production Yearbook.

COUNTRIES — AGRICULTURE
Least Fertile Land

Agriculture, it is said, was invented in Africa, where man first tied a plow to the back of an ox and sowed a field. Unfortunately, in many cases this is still the way cultivation takes place in many African nations. On average, a hectare of land in Africa yields only 1,077 kilograms of cereal crops — that's a mere 42% of the world average and about one-fourth the productivity of the farmland in Europe. Primitive agricultural techniques combined with seemingly perennial drought conditions, political turmoil

and relatively low levels of agronomical education combine to hinder the efforts of African farmers and create the conditions for the famines that have plagued the continent over the past decade. Not all African countries suffer these conditions, however. For instance, the Nile floods create an incredibly fertile strip of land through Egypt, and thus the Egyptian farmer enjoys a crop yield of 4,471 kg/hectare, almost as much as a U.S. farmer, and 25 times that of a farmer in Botswana, which suffers from the least productive land in the world. The following list presents the ten countries with the lowest agriculturally productivity, as measured by average yield of cereal crops over the three-year period from 1984 to 1986; eight of the ten worst are African nations.

Country	Kg/Hectare
1. Botswana	178
2. Niger	366
3. Mauritania	431
4. Angola	461
5. Namibia	485
6. Sudan	508
7. Central African Rep.	513
8. Vanuatu	518
9. Virgin Islands	518
10. Chad	531

Source: Food and Agricultural Production Yearbook.

COUNTRIES — AGRICULTURE
Most Agricultually Mechanized

While many third-world farmers still use ox-drawn plows or even simple sticks to cultivate their land, farmers in the advanced nations have long since abandoned muscle power in favor of machine power. Along with the McCormick reaper and a few other mechanical advances, the tractor has freed the farmer from reliance on the ox, the horse, the mule and his own back to plow and sow his field. The most agriculturally mechanized country in the world is the

PLACES

United States, with more than four million tractors in use, or about one-fifth of all the farm tractors in the world. The bottom ten in this list are places that either can't or don't have to rely on home-grown agricultural production; many of them are tourist-rich island nations or oil-rich Gulf states.

Most Tractors	Number of Tractors
1. United States	4,674,333
2. U.S.S.R	2,750,000
3. Japan	1,696,067
4. Germany	1,634,975
5. Italy	1,198,215
6. China	861,068
7. Poland	806,339
8. Brazil	748,333
9. Canada	658,200
10. Spain	611,148

Fewest Tractors

1. Br. Virgin Islands	4
2. St. Helena	5
3. Djibouti	6
4. Hong Kong	7
5. Niue	10
6. American Samoa	12
7. Montserrat	14
8. Cape Verde	16
9. Kuwait	17
Kiribati (tie)	17
10. Grenada	27

Source: Food and Agriculture Organization Production Yearbook.

COUNTRIES — AGRICULTURE
Most Agriculturally Advanced

Perhaps the truest index of the level of agricultural advancement is the comparison of mechanization with the amount of arable land. Japan and Europe on average have the most advanced agricultural levels in the world, using this criterion. The top ten are led by Iceland, which suffers from a veritable tractor traffic jam with 1,754 tractors per hectare. Of the countries with a large-scale agricultural industry, Japan leads with 403 tractors per hectare. European countries average about 200 tractors per hectare; by comparison, the United States has only 25 tractors for every hectare of arable land, but still manages a very high crop yield. Many African nations have *no* tractors for their arable land.

The Top Ten	Tractors/hectare
1. Iceland	1,754
2. Japan	403
3. Switzerland	269
4. Austria	226
5. Netherlands	221
6. Germany	204
7. Ireland	196
8. Norway	174
9. New Zealand	158
10. Belgium	147

Source: Food and Agriculture Organization Production Yearbook.

COUNTRIES — AIR POLLUTION
Carbon Dioxide Emissions

In addition to being a major component in what we breathe out when we breathe, carbon dioxide is a product of the burning of fossil fuels. In earlier days, we needn't worry much about carbon dioxide emissions, since the compound is converted by plants into life-sustaining oxygen, providing a natural system to offset the increase. But the past several decades have seen an increase in carbon dioxide emissions concurrent with the destruction of the rain forests in Asia, South America and the Pacific Northwest. These rain forests are called by many scientists "the lungs of the world"; the loss of them, combined with the continued high level of carbon dioxide emissions from the industrialized nations, could seriously upset the planet's fragile ecological balance. Below are the worst perpetrators in terms of carbon dioxide emissions from fossil fuels,

PLACES

ranked by millions of tons of emissions annually.

Country	Tons Annually (million)
1. United States	1,135.3
2. U.S.S.R.	900.9
3. China	413.1
4. Germany	263.5
5. Japan	226.4
6. United Kingdom	141.0
7. Poland	111.9
8. France	110.8
9. Canada	108.2
10. India	105.1

Source: Environmental Data Report, GEMS Monitoring and Assessment Research Centre, United Nations Environment Programme, 1989.

COUNTRIES — AIR POLLUTION

Sulfur Dioxide Emissions

National levels of sulfur dioxide emissions are a measure not only of air pollution but of governmental laxity in controlling such environmental toxins. Sulfur dioxide finds its way into the air—and into our lungs—from the burning of fossil fuels. It can cause respiratory illness and is a major contributor to the creation of acid rain. Happily, western industrial nations have, at least to some extent, recognized the problem that sulfur dioxide emissions present and have implemented either voluntary or obligatory emission controls on autos and industrial sources of SO2 pollution. In the period from 1980 to 1986, annual sulfur dioxide emissions have decreased by more than half in France, from 3,392,000 tons to 1,580,000; during the same period, emissions in the U.S. were cut 20 percent, from almost 27 million tons to just over 21 million—still not a healthy level, but at least a start. Below are the ten largest national producers of sulfur dioxide in the world.

Country	Tons Annually (thousands)
1. United States	21,200
2. China	12,570
3. U.S.S.R.	11,100
4. Germany	6,626
5. Poland	4,300
6. Canada	3,940
7. United Kingdom	3,740
8. Czechoslovakia	3,050
9. Spain	2,877
10. Yugoslavia	1,800

Source: Environmental Data Report, GEMS Monitoring and Assessment Research Centre, United Nations Environment Programme, 1989.

COUNTRIES — AIR TRAVEL
Flightiest

Americans do their business on the fly—literally. Successful business ventures require a personal touch, and in this great big land of ours, the only way to keep that personal touch is by winging it. Jet-setting businessmen and women account for a large proportion of the total business that American air carriers do, and airlines love it, because businessmen most often travel on short notice, and can't take advantage of cheaper advanced-purchase tickets. On almost any daytime flight, you can see these harried suits hacking away at their lap-top computers, happily ignoring the in-flight meal. Contrarily, airlines continually have to woo pleasure travelers with bizarre discount fares that must be purchased months in advance with no opportunity to change one's ticket. But just try getting a hold of those airlines on the last day of one of their airfare wars. Is this the way they run Aeroflot? Doubtful. Even in the age of perestroika, figures for domestic travel in the Soviet Union are unavailable, although that nation has the largest—and some say shabbiest—commercial airline in the world. Before the Soviets ever hope to match the west in the global marketplace, they had better master the intricacies of the various frequent-flyer

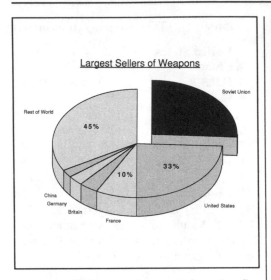

Largest Sellers of Weapons

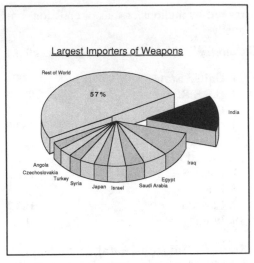

Largest Importers of Weapons

programs. Below are the ten nations that fly the most, on business and pleasure.

Country	Air Travel (million km)
1. United States	5,807
2. United Kingdom	444
3. Japan	418
4. Canada	375
5. Germany	290
6. France	288
7. Brazil	255
8. Australia	241
9. Mexico	176
10. Italy	151

Source: Environmental Data Report, United Nations Environment Programme, 1989.

COUNTRIES—ARMS EXPORTERS

The Arms Merchants: Largest Sellers of Weapons

One of the most graphic lessons of the showdown in the sands (Desert Storm), was that the wanton sales of leading-edge weapons to loose-cannon, third world megalomaniacs must be checked. The problem, of course, is that the American government has kept the economy on a war footing for a half a cen-

tury, and our defense industry relies implicitly on the ability to subsidize its over-priced wares by indiscriminate sales to nervous-Nelly autocrats. In fact, for all the chest-thumping about third-world hot spots, the top five arms exporters in the world are the nations that had, until very recently, been the main combatants in the Cold War. They find in those third-world markets a vicarious battleground for the ideological and geo-political struggle. Weapons systems got a good tryout—at a profit, no less. With the serious contraction of its once widespread empire, its loss of former client-states, and its dangerous internal turmoil, one expects that the Soviet Union will soon relinquish its top spot on the list of global arms exporters.

Nation	Share of World Market
1. Soviet Union	35.0%
2. United States	32.8%
3. France	10.3%
4. Britain	5.1%
5. Germany	4.0%
6. China	2.9%
7. Netherlands	1.4%
8. Sweden	1.1%
9. Brazil	1.1%
10. Czechoslovakia	0.9%

PLACES

Source: International Peace Research Institute.

COUNTRIES— ARMS IMPORTERS

The Arms Buyers: Largest Importers of Weapons

In 1990, Iraq accounted for one tenth of the world's open market for arms (not to mention that nation's gray and black market acquisitions). Iraq's frenzied weapons purchasing was surpassed only by third world giant India. That the Western world did not view this situation with alarm is a testament both to our statesmen's capacity for denial, and to the Machiavellian doings of the defense lobby. Is it just a coincidence that six of the top ten world importers of weapons were either direct or indirect participants in the Persian Gulf war? The sad fact is that since the official end of that conflict, Israel has signed a new arms-purchase agreement with the U.S., and China has made public its plans to sell missiles to Syria. Iraq, too, is not quite pacified in the way our leaders had hoped or, indeed, had painted it to be at the conclusion of the vaunted "100-hour" war. We await with baited breath the next thrid-world flare-up. On the other hand, the revolutionary leaders in Czechoslovakia have vowed to take their nation out of the international arms market, and the recent treaty ending the Angolan civil war should limit that African nation's arms purchases. Undoubtedly, though, some other budding nations will step in to fill the arms-sale void.

Nation	Share of World Market
1. India	14.8%
2. Iraq	10.0%
3. Egypt	6.3%
4. Saudi Arabia	4.8%
5. Israel	4.6%
6. Japan	3.7%
7. Syria	3.7%

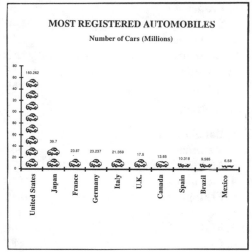

MOST REGISTERED AUTOMOBILES
Number of Cars (Millions)

United States 160.262; Japan 39.7; France 23.87; Germany 23.237; Italy 21.359; U.K. 17.5; Canada 13.65; Spain 10.318; Brazil 9.585; Mexico 6.58

8. Turkey	3.4%
9. Czechoslovakia	3.4%
10. Angola	3.1%

Source: International Peace Research Institute

COUNTRIES— AUTOMOBILES

Most and Fewest Cars Per Person

America is a car culture, make no bumpers about that. We like to rove, roar, rave and rock and roll in our bitchin' Camaros, 4x4s and Model Ts. It is little surprise, then, that we lead the world in per capita car ownership. Nor is it shocking that the look-alike nation to the North is a bumper-to-bumper second place winner. On the other hand, rush hour in such auto-deprived countries as Bangladesh, Rwanda and the Maldive Islands must be a breeze, unless you're unlucky enough to be carpooling in the same vehicle with 1,000 other of your hapless compatriots. Let's at least hope the buggy is a four-door.

The Top Ten	People per Car
1. United States	1.54
2. Canada	1.90
3. Switzerland	2.31
4. Iceland	2.32

115

5. France	2.34
6. Sweden	2.40
7. Luxembourg	2.44
8. Germany	2.63
9. Norway	2.66
10. Qatar	2.69

The Bottom Ten

1. Bangladesh	1,608
2. Rwanda	1,364
3. Maldive Islands	975
4. Vietnam	870
5. Ethiopia	819
6. Nepal	713
7. Mali	660
8. China (PRC)	582
9. Burundi	468
10. India	429

Source: United Nations.

COUNTRIES — AUTOMOBILES
Most Registered Vehicles

It is time for us to face some simple facts in America, and one of the first things that we should own up to is that we are obsessive, unyielding, sometimes wanton road hogs. With more than one hundred and sixty million vehicles on the road, our society has at last become truly treaded-out. All the frenzied exhortations to carpool, use mass transit, walk, bike, cut down on trips and conserve energy can't stem the most basic American desire to hit the road. And we are fast approaching the day when every American will be able to do so in his or her very own personal auto. Whether there will be anywhere to go by then is another matter.

Country	Number of Cars
1. United States	160,262,000
2. Japan	39,700,000
3. France	23,870,000
4. Germany	23,237,000
5. Italy	21,359,000
6. United Kingdom	17,500,000
7. Canada	13,650,000

8. Spain	10,318,000
9. Brazil	9,585,000
10. Mexico	6,580,000

Source: United Nations.

COUNTRIES — BEER
Biggest Beer Producers

As big a stink as is made about hoity-toity imported brews, America still leads the world in beer production. Though our products (barring Miller) may not be the champagnes of beer, we can still hold a candle and keg to any suds-sipping vat-meisters. Most of the U.S. production is made for domestic consumption. Below are the biggest beer producers in the world.

Country	Barrels
1. United States	195,123,375
2. Germany	102,670,000
3. Soviet Union	57,949,000
4. England	52,580,000
5. Japan	42,032,000
6. Brazil	24,713,000
7. Czechoslovakia	21,267,000
8. Mexico	20,121,000
9. Canada	19,259,000
10. France	18,821,000

Source: The Brewer's Almanac.

COUNTRIES — BEER
Biggest Suppliers of Beer to U.S.

When it comes to filling their empty beer bellies, the snootiest of American consumers turn their pointy noises up at most domestic suds. Beer, to such folk, is not a mere drinking experience. No, no. To them it is an oral travel odyssey, where exotic brews transport them to the rugged shores of the Rhine (Becks), the torrid jungles of Mexico (Corona) and the rollicking Prussian beer halls of New Jersey (Lowenbrau). We might expect our cosmopolitan brothers in other scenic world spots to be similarly subject to such imaginative brew fancy. Judging from the statistics on their imports of American beer, however, this is — sadly — not the case (or keg)...

Country	2.25-Gallon Cases
1. Netherlands	35,308,000
2. Canada	29,961,000
3. Mexico	23,265,000
4. Germany (W.)	14,296,000
5. United Kingdom	2,959,000
6. Ireland	2,948,000
7. Australia	2,133,000
8. Japan	2,077,000
9. China (PRC)	803,000
10. Denmark	789,000

Source: Jobson's Liquor Handbook.

COUNTRIES — BIRTH RATE
Highest and Lowest

Population growth is a daunting global problem, for its solution lies in the individual discretion of billions of individual souls. In this era, a birth rate of 25 per 1,000 population per annum has been identified as the upper limit of acceptable procreation. Currently, 121 of the world's 166 nations exceed this rate. The group of African nations which have the world's highest birth rates is the same basic group which has the world's highest infant mortality rate and its lowest life expectancy. These countries are growing in population but not nearly as their huge birth rates might suggest, as these nations have neither sufficient health facilities nor the basic needs of food and shelter for their rapidly procreating populations. Intensive birth control counseling and education could alleviate the problem, but the puritanical U.S. opposition to abortion and other family planning counseling means that this country's vast resources cannot be mobilized against the problems of excessive birth rates either here or in the rest of the world. Conversely, it is the nations of Europe, particularly northern Europe, which have the lowest birth rate, with a continental birth rate of 13.8 births per thousand inhabitants. They are followed by the U.S.S.R. with 18.3 births per thousand

and then Oceania, North America, Asia, South America and finally Africa which has a birth rate of 45.2 births per thousand.

The Ten Highest	Births /1,000 pop.
1. Malawi	53.1
2. Niger	50.9
3. Rwanda	50.7
4. Nigeria	50.5
Benin	50.5
6. Tanzania	50.3
7. Mali	50.1
Uganda	50.1
9. Mauritania	50.0
10. Ethiopia	49.3

The Ten Lowest	
1. Sweden	10.1
2. German Federal Republic	10.6
3. Switzerland	10.8
4. Denmark	10.9
5. Luxembourg	11.0
6. Italy	11.6
7. Netherlands	11.7
Norway	11.7
9. Hungary	12.1
10. Belgium	12.2

Source: *World Resources 1988-89*, A Report by The World Resources Institute and The International Institute for Environment and Development in collaboration with The United Nations Environment Programme, Basic Books, Inc., New York.

COUNTRIES — BIRTHS, ILLEGITIMATE
Most Bastardly

In this nation, conceiving (and bringing forth) a child out of wedlock has always carried a social stigma. In other regions of the world, however, illegitimate birth remains a rule, rather than an exception. Such relaxed behavior is prevalent even in tourist meccas like Barbados and Antigua, despite the perceived conservative sexual practices of their inhabitants. Indeed, the ten leading nations in illegitimate births are all Caribbean or Central American countries. Imagine the confusion on Father's Day.

Nation	% of illegitimate births
1. Guinea-Bissau	88.7
2. St. Kitts-Nevis-Anguilla	82.8
3. São Tome & Principe	82.4
4. Antigua	77.3
5. Montserrat	76.6
6. Barbados	73.3
7. Grenada	72.8
8. Panama	71.6
9. El Salvador	69.7
10. Dominican Republic	66.6

Source: U.N. Demographic Yearbook

COUNTRIES — CAT TRADE
The Skin Trade: Biggest Traders in Endangered Cat Skins

World total exports of cat skins in 1986 came to 192,402; this represents a substantial drop from the 462,210 exported in 1980. Whether this decline is due to the increased vigilance on the part of customs officials in enforcing bans on trade in skins of endangered species, increased consumer reluctance to purchase clothing and other products made from the skins of endangered animals, or simply a sharp decline in the overall number of animals, is unclear. What is clear is that the U.S. remains a major player in the skin trade, importing more than 17,000 skins and exporting more than 65,000. The overall figures include skins of the cat family, Felidae. A substantial number of skins measured by weight (7,872 lbs. plus 4,115 kg) or by length (1450 meters plus 7 feet) are not included in the figures below, since it is impossible to determine how many animals those weights or lengths represent.

Top Importers	Number of Skins
1. Germany	82,240
2. Canada	21,109
3. United States	17,543
4. Japan	14,321
5. Italy	9,505
6. Denmark	7,976
7. France	7,701
8. Switzerland	6,657
9. Spain	2,261
10. Greece	1,897

Top Exporters	Number of Skins
1. China	68,274
2. United States	65,419
3. Canada	24,104
4. Switzerland	7,622
5. Germany	6,908
6. Bolivia	6,624
7. Israel	4,573
8. U.S.S.R.	2,855
9. Denmark	1,048
10. South Africa	931

Source: Environmental Data Report, GEMS Monitoring and Assessment Research Centre, United Nations Environment Programme, 1989.

COUNTRIES — CHILD LABOR
Largest Concentrations of Child Laborers

The U.S. and most Western developed nations banned child labor in the early days of the labor movement. But such is not the case in many developing countries. A nation that sends a child to do an adult's work is certainly underdeveloped, in the deepest sense of that word. Yet, no matter how we decry the participation of unformed juveniles in the workforce, that participation is an indisputable reality in the vast majority of world nations. In troubled, impoverished sections of Asia, nearly a third of all workers are under the age of fifteen.

Country	Employed Children/100 pop.
1. Bhutan	42
1. Mali	42
1. Rwanda	42
4. Upper Volta	40
5. Nepal	37
Central African Republic	37

PLACES

Madagascar 37
8. Botswana 34
9. Ivory Coast 34
10. Burundi 31

Source: U.N. Committee on Children

COUNTRIES — CHOLERA

Highest Number of Cholera Cases, Africa

No, Sierra Leone is not the director of those Clint Eastwood spaghetti Westerns. Over the past decade, it has been the worst country in Africa for cholera epidemics. Incidences of cholera most often are the result of poor sanitation and corrupted drinking water. In 1986, Sierra Leone was struck by the worst cholera epidemic in Africa in a decade; more than 10,000 people were afflicted, of whom 800 died. Other serious epidemics in which more than 1,000 incidences were counted broke out in Tanzania, Senegal, Burkina Faso, Mali and Mauritania just in the three years from 1985 to 1987. Reports of a cholera epidemic in South America in 1991 have been denied by officials there, while fears of an epidemic in Iraq following the severe pounding the country's infrastructure took during the brief Persian Gulf war luckily have not yet been realized. Cholera has even been known to break out in the U.S. in recent years.

Country	Cholera Cases, 1985-87
1. Sierra Leone	10,761
2. Mauritania	3,877
3. Tanzania	3,493
4. Mali	2,364
5. Zaire	1,812
6. Senegal	1,313
7. Burkina Faso	1,258
8. Burundi	1,199
9. Cameroon	1,130
10. Kenya	1,023

Source: Epidemiology Bulletin, World Health Organization, Brazzaville, Congo, 1989.

COUNTRIES — CONDOM USE

Highest

Armor, sheath, mackee, rubber, pigskin, prophylactic — its names have changed over the years, but the same trustworthy condom has been around since English authors discussed being "sheathed" while having intercourse with London prostitutes during the late 18th century. And modern authors from Nabakov to Phillip Roth have made the "mackee" the subject of both comic and serious discourse. In view of the AIDS crisis and the protection condoms provide against disease, worldwide condom use is again on the upswing. Our data is for married couples only. Dates of information gathering vary according to country.

Country	Condom Use
1. Japan	44.6%
2. Finland	32.0%
3. Denmark	25.0%
4. Sweden	25.0%
5. Singapore	24.3%
6. Costa Rica	19.4%
7. United Kingdom	25.0%
8. Norway	16.0%
9. Trinidad and Tobago	15.0%
10. Poland	14.0%
11. Czechoslovakia	13.0%
12. Hong Kong	12.9%
13. Mauritius	10.8%

Source: *World Resources 1988-89*, A Report by The World Resources Institute and The International Institute for Environment and Development in collaboration with The United Nations Environment Programme.

COUNTRIES — CURRENCY

Easiest Place to be a Millionaire

Here's how to be a millionaire, quickly! It's surprisingly easy to do — all you have to do is leave the country and exchange your currency. Of course, you won't be a millionaire in U.S. dollars, but it's the name that counts, right? Here are the least valuable currencies

PLACES

to trade in on the world market, in terms of their value against the dollar, and how much American money one needs to earn a million in various foreign currencies.

Country	1$ =	Million
1. Peru	13100 Inti	$77
2. Mexico	2814 Pesos	$356
3. Italy	1177 Lira	$850
4. Paraguay	883 Guarani	$1,133
5. Ecuador	737 Sucre	$1,357
6. Korea	666 Won	$1,502
7. Greece	158 Drachma	$6,329
8. Azores	148 Escudo	$6,757
9. Portugal	137 Escudo	$7,299
10. Japan	137 Yen	$7,299

Source: "Best and Worst" original.

COUNTRIES — DEATH RATES
Highest and Lowest

In a statistic which should surprise no one, the desperately poor countries of Africa have the world's highest death rates. What is a surprise however, is the low figure presented by certain wealthy oil producing states and two unspectacular yet relatively peaceful players in Central America (figures from Kuwait are from before the Persian Gulf war). Interestingly, no "developed" countries are in the bottom 20 of lowest death rates. Perhaps it is the strain of modern life and the toll of meat and other fatty foods. Americans, with a score of 9.0 deaths per 1,000 inhabitants, die at a rate faster than all but four countries in our hemisphere. In the Americas, we are surpassed only by politically repressive Haiti, and desperately poor Bolivia, Peru and Uruguay.

Ten Highest	Deaths/1,000
1. Sierra Leone	27.6
2. Gambia	26.9
3. Afghanistan	23.9
4. Somalia	22.6
5. Ethiopia	22.3
6. Guinea	21.9
7. Niger	20.9
8. Mali	20.8
9. Angola	20.6
10. Central African Republic.	20.1

Ten Lowest	Deaths/1,000
1. Kuwait	3.1
2. Bahrain	4.0
3. Costa Rica	4.2
United Arab Emirates	4.2
5. Qatar	4.3
6. Fiji	5.0
7. Panama	5.2
8. Albania	5.4
Guyana	5.4
Venezuela	5.4
Korea, Dem. People's Rep.	5.4

Source: *World Resources 1988-89*, A Report by The World Resources Institute and The International Institute for Environment and Development in collaboration with The United Nations Environment Programme, Basic Books, Inc., New York.

COUNTRIES — DEFENSE CONTRACTS
Largest Foreign Holders of U.S. Defense Contracts

Despite the perversity of the revelation, the Western world is largely fueled by the sale, lease, loan, transport and use of armaments. And, while the U.S. disburses untold billions to its domestic defense industry, it also invests considerable sums in the developmental and manufacturing projects of many foreign nations and institutions. While these institutions receive nothing like the hundreds of millions bestowed upon American research universities and institutions, the sums are still significant. Below are the foreign institutions that are the top beneficiaries of the U.S. Department of Defense's largess. First among these is a closest historical political partner, the United Kingdom.

120

PLACES

Contractor	D.O.D. Contracts ($000)
1. U. K. Ministry of Defense	14,848
2. Royal Norwegian Nav. Material	11,371
3. Nat. Center/Space Studies, Fr.	2,576
4. Culman Laboratory (U.K.)	1,880
5. Soreg Nuclear Res. Ctr. (Israel)	783
6. Israeli Min. of Defense	710
7. Societe Gen. de Tapis (France)	560
8. Royal Norwegian Council	359
9. Weizman Institute (Israel)	342
10. York University (Canada)	305

Source: Dept. of Defense

COUNTRIES — DEVELOPMENT
Most Developed

We Americans like to think of ourselves as the most advanced, developed people on the planet. Well, think again. The following Human Development Index was devised by the United Nations Development Program. The index measures a country's social and economic development using a formula based on a country's degree of deprivation of life expectancy, literacy rate and real gross domestic product. The list below represents the ten countries that rank the highest on this measure of development, with Japan leading the way, followed by Western European nations, Canada and Australia. The development score for the United State is .961, still fairly high, but behind Finland, Germany, Italy, New Zealand, Belgium and Spain and on a par with Austria and Ireland. The U.S.S.R. had a development index of .920. Countries scoring in the middle of the pack, with indexes of around .500, include Honduras, Egypt and Laos.

Country	HDI
1. Japan	.996
2. Sweden	.987
3. Switzerland	.986
4. Netherlands	.984
5. Canada	.983
Norway	.983
6. Australia	.978
7. Iceland	.975
8. France	.974
9. Denmark	.971
10. United Kingdom	.970

Source: Human Development Report 1990, Oxford University Press.

COUNTRIES — DEVELOPMENT
Least Developed

In the previous entry, we listed the most developed countries in the world — those that enjoy the highest literacy, life expectancy and economic power. Here we list the other side of the coin, the true developmental backwaters of the world, where life expectancy is low, literacy is uncommon and the economies are primitive. All of the ten least developed countries, we see, are in Africa. Djibouti has the lowest rating of all countries on the Human Development Index — with a per-capita GNP of $480 and a life expectancy of just 47 years. Clearly the nations of the Third World have far to go in the most basic areas of nutrition, education, health care and economic development before they can hope to improve their lot. This would be the greatest peace dividend one could imagine — the developed nations of the world ceasing their petty squabbling over trade and ideology and lending a helping hand to the less-privileged around the world.

Country	HDI
1. Djibouti	.073
2. Guinea-Bissau	.074
3. Gambia	.094
4. Niger	.116
5. Mali	.143
6. Burkina Faso	.150
Sierra Leone	.150
7. Chad	.157
8. Guinea	.162
9. Somalia	.200
10. Mauritania	.208

PLACES

Source: Human Development Report 1990.

COUNTRIES – DRIVING
Worst Drivers

When it comes to taking the road in Europe, steer clear of the Mediterranean countries. The Portuguese, normally a quiet, easygoing people, somehow turn into raving lunatics on the roadway, accounting for the highest traffic fatality rate among all developed nations. Many blame outdated driver's education and testing programs in which Portuguese drivers can receive their licenses without ever taking a car out onto a highway. Others blame drunk driving, excessive speed, poor auto and road conditions in the newly industrialized nation, and a general sense that the road is the best place to relieve tensions. In contrast, the staid residents of northern climes – Denmark, Germany, the U.K., even the United States, suffer a fatality rate only about one-quarter that of the Portuguese and a third that of the Greeks.

Country	Deaths/million vehicles
1. Portugal	1,163
2. Greece	764
3. Spain	635
4. France	439
5. Denmark	376
6. Italy	285
7. Germany	265
8. United Kingdom	255
9. United States	248
10. Netherlands	236

Source: *New York Times*.

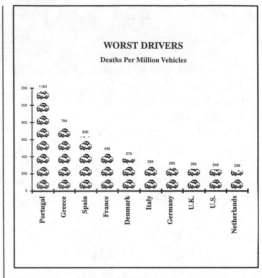

WORST DRIVERS
Deaths Per Million Vehicles

divorce rate easily leads the developed world. Only the fickle folks of the Maldive Islands and Djibouti surpass us in breaking the knot. Indeed, save for the U.S. and the Soviet Union, the top countries for divorces are all island nations.

Country	Divorces/1,000 pop.
1. Maldives	27.1
2. Djibouti	6.9
3. United States	5.3
4. Kiribati	5.0
5. Bermuda	4.5
6. FalkLand Islands	4.3
7. Puerto Rico	3.6
8. Soviet Union	3.5
9. Australia	3.2
10. Guam	3.2

Source: U.N. Demographic Yearbook

COUNTRIES – DIVORCE RATE

Most Fickle Nations

America, to its jaded citizenry, is a new Babylon. Central to this contention is the dissolution of the traditional American family unit. Indeed, these United States have witnessed an unprecedented erosion of marital stability. Today, our per capita

COUNTRIES – ECONOMIES
Most Economically Powerful

Although the United States suffers from a great variety of simultaneous ailments, it still boasts the highest gross national product on the globe. Trailing distantly are the lumbering Soviet Union and upstart Japan. The second tier of nations muster far lesser economic might, but the emergence of the

PLACES

new Europe in 1992 may well enhance that continent's already powerful influence and prestige in world economic affairs.

Country	GNP ($ millions)
1. United States	2,582,460
2. Soviet Union	1,212,030
3. Japan	1,152,910
4. West Germany	827,790
5. France	627,700
6. United Kingdom	442,820
7. Italy	368,860
8. China	283,250
9. Brazil	243,240
10. Canada	242,530

Source: U.S. Commerce Dept.

COUNTRIES—ELEPHANTS
African Elephant Populations

It's said that an elephant never forgets; but if recent trends in elephant populations continue, the elephant himself may be only a memory by the middle of the next century, at least in a wild, free-roaming state. Elephant populations in Africa have been on a steep and steady decline over the past several decades, except in places where poaching is strictly controlled. In these latter countries—Botswana, Malawi, Namibia, South Africa and Zimbabwe—elephant populations have actually shown a slight annual increase (0.7%). However, in regions where elephants are unprotected from poachers, the average decline is 8.7%. In Selous National Park in Tanzania, elephant numbers have fallen from about 110,000 to 55,000—a loss of 50%—since 1986. As usual, man is by far the main culprit. Habitat loss in some elephant areas is minimal because human settlement in those regions is sparse, but in other areas, the encroaching human populations put a great burden on the elephant. But the real threat comes from poachers who continue to kill elephants only for their ivory, although there have been strict limitations and now even bans on the international ivory trade. Experts presume that in the face of the ban, the ivory trade will

go underground and continue on a wholly illegal basis. The most successful method for preserving the elephant in the wild is increasing the degree of protection afforded the species, by setting aside special game reserves and national parks monitored and patrolled by committed game wardens. Below are the ten countries with the largest elephant populations in Africa.

Country	# of Elephants in the wild
1. Zaire	329,700
2. Tanzania	108,800
3. Gabon	74,400
4. Cameroon	73,300
5. Botswana	58,300
6. Zimbabwe	58,100
7. Angola	45,800
8. Central African Rep.	40,400
9. Sudan	37,200
10. Kenya	29,800

Source: "The African Elephant," United Nations Environmental Program, Nairobi, 1989.

COUNTRIES—ENVIRONMENT
Most Environmentally Conscious, Europe

When Louis Harris and Associates was asked to conduct a poll for the United Nations on environmental concerns throughout the world, strangely, Italy came out as having the populace the most concerned with environmental issues. We say strangely because in the EnviroSummit scorecard created by the G-7 Summit Environmental Accountability Project, which ranked the seven industrialized nations in the G-7 in terms of their environmental practices and policies, Italy ranked dead last (see elsewhere). Perhaps their is a gap in Italy between the political will of the leadership and the desires of the people, or perhaps the gap lies between people's realization of the problem and their ability to effect positive change, but in any event, on the environmental front, Italy is not practicing what is seems to preach. The following presents a ranking based on the level of environmental concern in European countries, in the percentage of people who consider protection of the environment and the struggle against pollution as an "urgent and immediate problem." The least concerned European Economic Community countries were France and Ireland, where only 56% of the population seemed overly concerned with environmental protection.

Country	Percent Concerned
1. Italy	85
2. Greece	84
3. Luxembourg	83
4. Germany	80
5. Denmark	77
6. Spain	72
7. Portugal	71
8. United Kingdom	67
9. Netherlands	62
10. Belgium	62

Source: "Public and Leadership Attitudes to the Environment in Four Continents," United Nations Environment Programme, 1989.

COUNTRIES — FISHING

Fish Stories

Around the world, the fishing is getting better. In a ten-year span from the mid-seventies to the mid-eighties, the total world fish catch increased by 29 percent to a whopping 87 million tons. The most prolific fishermen in the world are the Japanese, who rely on fish as a major protein source in their diet, much as Americans used to rely on beef. On the other hand, it's not surprising that the worst fishermen in the world come from land-locked Luxembourg, where there is no commercial fishing industry to speak of. Even the similarly land-locked Lesothans do better than Luxembourgers — the kingdom, completely surrounded by South Africa, manages to pull 14 tons of fish from

its lakes and streams yearly. But you should see the ones that get away! The following rating represents countries by the total fish catch, marine and fresh water, in the three years from 1984 to 1986.

Best Fishermen	Fish Catch, Tons
1. Japan	11,798,902
2. U.S.S.R.	10,791,883
3. China	6,901,892
4. Chile	4,958,443
5. United States	4,840,464
6. Peru	4,354,268
7. India	2,870,427
8. South Korea	2,743,216
9. Indonesia	2,370,720
10. Norway	2,161,126

Worst Fishermen	Fish Catch, Tons
1. Luxembourg	0
2. Lesotho	14
3. Swaziland	44
4. Mongolia	372
5. Bermuda	589
6. Bhutan	1,000
7. Rwanda	1,059
8. Belize	1,375
9. Lebanon	1,467
10. Afghanistan	1,500

Source: Food and Agriculture Organization Yearbook of Fishery Statistics.

COUNTRIES — FOREIGN OWNERSHIP

Most U.S. Holdings by Foreign Countries

Non-Americans own about 5% of all U.S. assets. And despite all the recent Japan-bashing concurrent with the sale of such American icons as Columbia Pictures and Rockefeller Center, it is our friends in Britain who are our biggest investors. The following rating represents the countries who own the largest chunks of the U.S., measured by total value of direct investment.

PLACES

Country	Direct Investment (billions)
1. Britain	$120.6
2. Japan	$74.7
3. Netherlands	$62.6
4. Canada	$31.4
5. Germany	$27.4
6. Switzerland	$20.1
7. France	$18.9
8. Netherlands Ant.	$10.6
9. Australia	$5.3
10. Sweden	$5.3

Source: Time.

COUNTRIES — FOREIGN TRADE

America's Biggest Trading Partners

In the 1890s, Americans flocked to buy the novel and inexpensive dolls, pottery and Christmas decorations F.W. Woolworth had brought back from Europe. Today, in the 1990s, Americans are flocking to buy the cars, television sets and shoes a myriad of producers and importers have brought from Asia, Europe, Canada and Mexico. Far from being novel, we perceive imported goods as the norm that we prefer. We see Japanese and Korean products as high-quality bargains. Germans are masters of engineering, while Italians have a flair for style. America is still the world's largest economy, but it has transferred much of its own manufacturing to Mexico and the Far East where labor is cheaper. These statistics are from a typical month in 1990 (July).

Biggest Exporters to America

Country	Billions Per Month
1. Japan	$7,474
2. Canada	$7,237
3. Germany	$2,576
4. Mexico	$2,390
5. Korea	$1,798
6. United Kingdom	$1,671
7. China (People's Republic)	$1,618
8. Italy	$1,280
9. France	$1,261
10. Hong Kong	$987

Source: Direction of Trade Statistics, International Monetary Fund, November, 1990.

Biggest Importers From America

Despite "expert" predictions, not every American has entered the service economy. Some of us still actually make things. And guess what? The rest of the world buys them. The American farmer sends his grains, fruits and vegetables to Europe and the Far East. American appliance makers have entered the European market and are struggling for dominance worldwide. The supercomputer is still an American adventure. American arms dealers sell the F-15 and hundreds of other pieces of military hardware to friends (and future foes) around the world. The world watches *The Cosby Show*, listens to Paula Abdul records, catches Madonna's videos and follows the exploits of those lovable Teenage Mutant Ninja Turtles. Overall, America is still a powerful economy. Below is the dollar amount in goods for top ten importers of American products.

Country	Billions per Month
1. Canada	$6,059
2. Japan	$4,220
3. Mexico	$2,333
4. United Kingdom	$1,813
5. Germany	$1,498
6. Korea	$1,105
7. France	$976
8. Belgium-Luxembourg	$901
9. Netherlands	$791
10. Australia	$761

Source: Direction of Trade Statistics, International Monetary Fund, November, 1990

Biggest Trading Partners

Not surprisingly, Canada with its long American border, close population and largely integrated culture, is our biggest monthly trading partner. Most others on this list are about where you'd expect them to be. Two interesting cases are China and the

125

PLACES

Soviet Union. You know that big changes have taken place when Communist China is doing more than $2 billion in monthly trade with the capitalist United States. On the other hand, despite glasnost, perestroika and a Nobel Prize, Gorbachev's Soviet Union has failed to build such a consistently large relationship with the United States. In the future our relationships with Canada Mexico and other hemispheric partners should grow as free-trade agreements gradually envelope the Americas.

Country	Billions Per Month
1. Canada	$13,296
2. Japan	$11,694
3. Mexico	$4,723
4. Germany	$4,074
5. United Kingdom	$3,484
6. Korea	$2,903
7. France	$2,237
8. China (People's Republic)	$2,004
9. Italy	$1,840
10. Singapore	$1,538

Source: "Best and Worst" original based on Direction of Trade Statistics, International Monetary Fund, November, 1990.

COUNTRIES — GOLD RESERVES
Who's Got the Gold?

Once upon a time, all paper money was redeemable for precious metals like gold and silver. In the United States, we had as many dollars as we had gold in Fort Knox. This was called "The Gold Standard." During the Nixon Administration, we went off the gold standard and let the dollar's value be determined by variables like interest rates, inflation and international perceptions of the American economy. But even though dollars are no longer redeemable for gold, don't fret — we still have a lot of gold at Fort Knox and other depositories. In fact we have almost three times as much as the next biggest holder (Germany) and more than a quarter of all gold held by the governments

of the world. Now doesn't that make you feel good, Goldfinger? The following are the ten countries with the largest gold holdings, measured in millions of fine troy ounces.

Country	Gold (Millions Oz.)
1. United States	262.01
2. Germany	95.18
3. Switzerland	83.28
4. France	81.85
5. Italy	66.67
6. Netherlands	43.94
7. Belgium	30.23
8. Japan	24.23
9. Austria	20.39
10. United Kingdom	18.97

Source: *International Financial Statistics*, International Monetary Fund, December 1990.

COUNTRIES — HAZARDOUS WASTE
Biggest Generators of Hazardous Waste (Western & Developed)

The two major economic powerhouses in the world — Japan and the United States — account for a huge proportion of the toxic waste generated by the Western industrialized nations. Unfortunately, figures for the Soviet Union and the former Eastern bloc countries have not yet been made available, but it is assumed that, having even less strict measures against the generation and disposal of hazardous wastes, their generation of toxic wastes is even greater, and Western experts expect to find in those newly freed lands many sites as bad as the Love Canal.

Country	Tons Hazardous Waste (000)
1. Japan	292,312
2. United States	240,000
3. India	35,722
4. United Kingdom	5,000
5. Germany	4,900
6. Italy	3,500
7. Canada	3,280
8. France	2,000

PLACES

9. Hungary 1,800
10. Belgium 1,500

Source: Environmental Data Report, United Nations Environment Programme, 1989.

COUNTRIES—HEALTH CARE

Highest Percentage of GNP Spent on Health Care

With the median age of the population in steady ascent, America faces an imminent health care crisis. Despite the fact that we do not provide national health insurance or nearly adequate Medicaid care, the U.S. has already committed more of its gross national product to health care than any other nation on Earth. Mustering our resources for effective treatment of any in need health care, especially in view of the coming crunch of baby-boomers turned elderly, is our most pressing national imperative.

Nation	% on Health Care
1. United States	11.1
2. Sweden	9.1
3. Canada	8.5
4. France	8.5
5. Netherlands	8.3
6. Germany	8.1
7. Switzerland	8.0
8. Italy	6.7
9. Japan	6.7
10. United Kingdom	6.2

Source: Health Affairs

COUNTRIES—IMMIGRATION TO U.S.

The Immigrants: Nations of Birth of Legal Aliens (1981-88)

Much is said of our uninvited guests from South of the Border, but we hear little about the half million or so Latin Americans granted legal admittance to our cozy confines. Nor has the great wave of Philippine immigration been much noted. The co-min-gling of old immigrants with new has catalyzed the history of America—the time is now here for a new stew from the melting pot. Whereas Europe served as the source of most of America's immigrants in this countries first two centuries, the new breed of immigrants is made up predominantly of Asians and Latin Americans. The country should be in for some very interesting changes as the demographic make-up continues to shift from European predominance to an even more globally representative ethnic mix.

Nation	# of Immigrants
1. Mexico	569,997
2. Philippines	411,366
3. South Korea	269,766
4. China	266,824
5. Vietnam	252,853
6. India	193,378
7. Dominican Republic	183,155
8. Jamaica	160,909
9. Cuba	125,619
10. Haiti	105,169

Source: U.S. Immigration and Naturalization Service.

COUNTRIES—INFANT MORTALITY

Highest and Lowest Rates

War, famine, lack of pre-natal care, lack of sanitary conditions, lack of proper obstetrical care—the reasons for infant mortality are many. Yet while larger societal problems loom as difficult to solve, young children most often die from diseases which are readily treatable in the west, such as diarrhea, whose dehydrating effects can usually be kept at bay with fluids. Except for Afghanistan, which borders on Pakistan and the Soviet Union, all the countries with the highest infant mortality rate are on the continent of Africa. While many of these countries have recently been involved in wars, others merely struggle with dismal living conditions.

127

PLACES

Highest

Country	Infant Deaths/1000 Live Births
1. Afghanistan	183
2. Sierra Leone	169
3. Mali	169
4. Gambia	164
5. Malawi	150
6. Somalia	149
7. Ethiopia	149
8. Mozambique	141
9. Burkina Faso	139
10. Angola	137

Source: *World Resources 1988-89.*

Lowest Infant Mortality

Infant mortality is a pretty good indication of a health-care system's quality and its reach to every level of society. For instance while the white minority in South Africa might get excellent health care, the same is not true for the black majority who live with substantially less access to health care. The result is 72 infant deaths per 1,000 live births. The industrialized countries listed below all have excellent health care systems, which reach to every level of society. Most of these societies are homogeneous and very well off. In the United States there are 10 infant deaths per 1,000 live births.

Country	Infant Deaths/1,000 Live Births
1. Japan	6
Finland	6
Iceland	6
Sweden	6
5. Switzerland	7
Denmark	7
Netherlands	7
Norway	7
9. France	8
Luxembourg	8
Australia	8
Canada	8

Source: *World Resources 1988-89.*

COUNTRIES — LAND OWNERSHIP
Most Oligarchical

America — and the democracies that have followed in its serpentine social path — guarantees that its citizens receive equality of opportunity. Despite these best of efforts, the distribution of wealth, power and property in these nations remains grossly disproportionate. The failure of these progressive governments to accomplish substantive property reform, makes the gross inequities of more repressive nations seem even more bleak and irreversible. It's not surprising that strife-torn Latin America predominates in this list of the countries where a small elite owns the bulk of the countries land — for the very inequalities that such landowning oligarchy symbolizes drives the underprivileged into the arms of revolutionary idealogues. The following are the most oligarchical countries in the world, measured by the percentage of land owned by the top ten percent of all landowners.

Nation	Share Owned by top 10%
1. Barbados	95.0
2. Peru	93.0
3. Colombia	80.0
4. Mauritius	80.0
5. El Salvador	78.0
6. Guatemala	76.6
7. Jamaica	74.6
8. Nicaragua	67.0
9. Dominican Republic	62.7
10. Lebanon	57.0

Source: U.S. Agency for International Development

COUNTRIES — LEPROSY
Highest Incidences of
Leprosy, Africa

Leprosy has all but been eradicated in the United States and most developed countries; and with that eradication, the disease has all but vanished from the public eye.

PLACES

The few who are still afflicted by the illness in the U.S. are cared for just as any other patients. However, leprosy, which calls to mind the darkest images of the Middle Ages, still constitutes a major public health problem in Africa, where the incidence is more than one in 1,000. The numbers, though, have been declining in the last two decades, from 1,685,526 cases in 1966 to 534,720 cases in 1988, in response to the World Health Organization's program of monitoring and treatment of cases of leprosy in Africa.

Country	Cases per 1,000 Pop.
1. Congo	5.42
2. Ivory Coast	4.24
3. Gambia	3.68
4. Mali	3.37
5. Cape Verde	2.74
6. Central African Rep.	2.71
7. Madagascar	2.56
8. Guinea Bissau	2.42
9. Burkina Faso	2.25
10. Benin	2.08

Source: Epidemiological Bulletin, World Health Organization, Brazzaville, Congo.

COUNTRIES — LIFE EXPECTANCY

Longest Life Expectancy

We citizens of the industrialized world are modern-day Methuselas. That is, we live a long time if we don't wrap ourselves around telephone poles or succumb to disease and gang warfare. With an American life expectancy of 75 years, a kid who is ten in 1992 will probably live to see the goings on in 2057. Some in Japan and Iceland are living a full sixteen years longer than the world life expectancy of 61.1 years. Unfortunately, the disparity between life expectancy in the industrialized world and life expectancy in the rest of the world indicates more about the generally awful nutritional, sanitary and economic conditions most humans live with than it does about the good living conditions in a few advanced countries.

Country	Life Expectancy
1. Japan	77.2
2. Iceland	77.1
3. Sweden	76.8
4. Switzerland	76.5
Netherlands	76.5
6. Norway	76.4
7. Canada	76.3
8. Australia	75.7
9. France	75.2
Italy	75.2
10. Israel	75.1
Denmark	75.1

Source: *World Resources 1988-89*, A Report by The World Resources Institute and The International Institute for Environment and Development in collaboration with The United Nations Environment Programme, Basic Books, Inc., New York

Shortest Life Expectancy

While we've all seen the pictures of West African starvation on television, sometimes statistics can be even more startling than pictures. Twelve of the world's 13 lowest life expectancies are in African nations. If you are 18 in Sierra Leone, your life is already half over. You would be lucky to reach the ripe old age of 42 in Ethiopia and Somalia, countries long locked in a bloody war and lately wracked by famine and draught. And in Chad, the former French colony and the scene of many an armed struggle, 45 years is all you'd have to look forward to.

Country	Life Expectancy
1. Sierra Leone	36.0
2. Gambia	37.0
3. Afghanistan	39.0
4. Ethiopia	41.9
Somalia	41.9
6. Guinea	42.2
7. Angola	44.0
Mali	44.0
9. Niger	44.5

10. Central African Republic	45.0
Chad	45.0
Guinea-Bissau	45.0

Source: *World Resources 1988-89*, A Report by The World Resources Institute and The International Institute for Environment and Development in collaboration with The United Nations Environment Programme, Basic Books, Inc., New York

COUNTRIES – LIVESTOCK
Most Asses

Judging simply from American political campaigns and network television programming, one might get the impression that the United States is home to the most asses in the world. The four-footed variety, however, are most numerous in China, where many people still rely on muscle power as the basic means of transport and cultivation. The world population of asses is 39,857,000.

Country	Number of Asses
1. China	9,942,000
2. Ethiopia	3,915,000
3. Mexico	3,183,000
4. Pakistan	2,779,000
5. Egypt	1,865,000
6. Iran	1,800,000
7. Afghanistan	1,250,000
8. Brazil	1,249,000
9. Turkey	1,211,000
10. India	1,000,000

Source: Food and Agriculture Organization Production Yearbook.

COUNTRIES – LIVESTOCK
Most Buffaloes

India is home to more than half of the world's total number of buffaloes, accounting for more than 73,000,000 of the 135,687,000 of these beasts of burden. The buffalo (not the American bison, which we call the buffalo, but what we normally call the "water buffalo") remains a major source of power to draw the plow and pull the cart in most Asian nations. The top ten countries

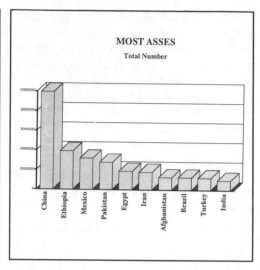

MOST ASSES
Total Number

listed here account for 93 percent of the world population of buffaloes.

Country	Number of Buffaloes
1. India	73,450,000
2. China	19,593,000
3. Pakistan	13,077,000
4. Thailand	6,284,000
5. Philippines	2,996,000
6. Indonesia	2,839,000
7. Vietnam	2,582,000
8. Egypt	2,577,000
9. Burma	2,139,000
10. Bangladesh	1,803,000

Source: Food and Agriculture Organization Production Yearbook.

COUNTRY – LIVESTOCK
Camel Jockeys

Camels are most prevalent, of course, in dry, desert regions, where their endurance and their ability to go for days or weeks without water make them the vehicle of choice for transportation and commerce. Indeed, because they have served so well as beasts of burden for several thousand years, these testy, mean-spirited animals have earned the name "ships of the desert."

Country	Number of Camels
1. Somalia	5,750,000

2. Sudan	2,783,000
3. India	1,083,000
4. Ethiopia	1.030 000
5. Pakistan	913,000
6. Mauritania	786,000
7. Kenya	665,000
8. China	541,000
9. Chad	534,000
10. Niger	414,000

Source: Food and Agriculture Organization Production Yearbook.

COUNTRIES — LIVESTOCK
Most Bovine

There's a good reason why there are so many beef cattle in India: those animals are holy, and cannot be slaughtered for food. Brazil's beef industry has boomed in recent years, but the cost has been great environmentally—in order to create more pasture land, Brazilian cattle ranchers have been systematically clear-cutting the Amazonian rain forests vital to the planet's overall ecological balance and to the continued survival of Amazonian Indians and many threatened species. Indeed, many consumers have begun to fight back, organizing boycotts of restaurants and grocery stores that sell beef from cattle raised on cleared rain forest land. The world total of beef cattle is 1,264,621,000. The world dairy total is 221,185,000.

Country	Number of Beef Cattle
1. India	197,853,000
2. Brazil	127,655,000
3. U.S.S.R.	120,500,000
4. United States	109,639,000
5. China	62,885,000
6. Argentina	53,865,000
7. Mexico	30,864,000
8. Ethiopia	26,100,000
9. France	23,171,000
10. Colombia	23,100,000

Country	Number of Dairy Cattle
1. U.S.S.R.	43,408,000
2. India	28,033,000

3. Brazil	17,135,000
4. United States	10,896,000
5. France	10,056,000
6. Poland	5,522,000
7. Germany	5,478,000
8. Mexico	5,367,000
9. Turkey	5,363,000
10. Sudan	3,500,000

Source: Food and Agriculture Organization Production Yearbook.

COUNTRIES — LIVESTOCK
Biggest Chickens

A chicken in every pot? With a worldwide population of more than 8.5 billion chickens, a politician could give every person in the world a chicken for their pot, and still have more than three billion left over. In the U.S., the situation is even more advantageous: with more than 1.1 billion chickens in the United States alone, the proverbial politician could promise a healthy four chickens in every proverbial pot.

Country	Number of Chickens (000)
1. China	1,360,000
2. United States	1,122,000
3. U.S.S.R.	1,085,000
4. Brazil	481,000
5. Indonesia	338,000
6. Japan	333,000
7. Mexico	212,000
8. France	187,000
9. India	170,000
10. Nigeria	160,000

Source: Food and Agriculture Organization Production Yearbook.

COUNTRIES — LIVESTOCK
Most Goats Gotten

Goats, like buffaloes and camels, are not the most popular livestock animals in the U.S. (although goat cheese has made great strides recently among the culinary trend-mongers). But in other parts of the world, goats serve as a vital source of milk, as well as pretty serviceable garbage disposals.

131

PLACES

Below are the top ten countries in the world for goat fanciers. The world population of goats is 486,242,000.

Country	Number of Goats
1. India	100,597,000
2. China	62,912,000
3. Pakistan	29,738,000
4. Nigeria	26,109,000
5. Ethiopia	17,263,000
6. Somalia	15,967,000
7. Turkey	14,311,000
8. Iran	13,600,000
9. Indonesia	12,118,000
10. Bangladesh	10,407,000

Source: Food and Agriculture Organization Production Yearbook.

COUNTRIES — LIVESTOCK
Horse Country

Two things played the greatest role in creating the myth of the American West: the horse and the six-shooter. A hundred years after the last badman was rounded up and four hundred years after the Spaniards first introduced it to the New World, the horse is still populous in the United States and the rest of the Americas. Admittedly, horses are no longer as vital to agriculture, transportation and law enforcement in the New World, but the legend of the cowboy still lives on in ranches across the western United States, as well as in Mexico, Brazil and the pampas of Argentina, where horse skills are more important than driver's licenses. As long as horses are still around, the legend of the cowboy will continue to thrive. Below are the top ten countries in terms of horse population; the total world population is 64,754,000.

Country	Number of Horses
1. China	10,928,000
2. United States	10,638,000
3. Mexico	6,135,000
4. U.S.S.R.	5,770,000
5. Brazil	5,481,000
6. Argentina	2,990,000

7. Colombia	1,890,000
8. Ethiopia	1,580,000
9. Poland	1,404,000
10. India	907,000

Source: Food and Agriculture Organization Production Yearbook.

COUNTRIES — LIVESTOCK
Hog Heavens

The pig has gotten a bad rap. Just because pigs like to wallow in slop and they eat like, well . . . pigs, people think hogs are foul creatures. Nothing could be further from the truth. Pigs in fact are extremely smart animals, and make wonderful pets. The tiny Vietnamese pot-bellied pig is becoming increasingly popular among lovers of exotic pets, stirring up all kinds of strife between owners of pet pigs on the one hand and condo residents and landlords on the other who still cling to the old-fashioned view of the now-noble pig. The 804,155,000 hogs around the world can truly stand proud — they have now been welcomed into the American household, alongside the dog, the cat and the gerbil. The list below represents the top ten countries in the world in pig population.

Country	Number of Pigs
1. China	321,371,000
2. U.S.S.R	78,136,000
3. United States	54,360,000
4. Brazil	32,551,000
5. West Germany	23,783,000
6. Mexico	18,874,000
7. Poland	17,740,000
8. Romania	14,481,000
9. East Germany	13,065,000
10. Netherlands	12,146,000

Source: Food and Agriculture Organization Production Yearbook.

COUNTRIES — LIVESTOCK
Sheep Land

Much as the American West was made by horsemen, the land down under was settled

PLACES

by sheepherders. Indeed, in Australia, sheep outnumber people by a factor of seven to one. Where Americans recall the rough and tumble way of life on the Chisolm Trail or in Dodge City, the ethos of the Australian Outback calls to mind the sweat and toil of the dusty sheep ranch and the shearing station. New Zealand's sheepishness is even more pronounced: there, the ovine population outnumbers humans by a whopping 17 to one. Talk about getting fleeced! The world population of sheep is a healthy 1,135,512,000.

Country	Number of Sheep
1. Australia	148,183,000
2. China	96,107,000
3. New Zealand	69,746,000
4. India	52,787,000
5. Turkey	43,166,000
6. Iran	34,333,000
7. Argentina	30,828,000
8. South Africa	30,334,000
9. Pakistan	25,045,000
10. United Kingdom	23,934,000

Source: Food and Agriculture Organization Production Yearbook.

COUNTRIES — MALE
Where the Boys Are: Most Male-Dominated Nations

With the exceptions of Israel, Ireland, Canada and Australia, every nation in the developed world has a majority of female citizens. Worldwide, however, males account for 50.12% of the human population. The high concentration of males in Asia and the Middle East is the primary demographic compensation for the female majorities of the West. Indeed, in the Islamic nations of Bahrain, the United Arab Emirates and Kuwait, men outnumber women by a whopping six to four. One explanation of this fact is the large number of male workers from Palestine, Egypt, Turkey and other nearby countries who, at least until recent events,

have flocked to the oil-rich gulf states, while leaving their spouses and families at home.

Nation	Male as % of Population
1. Bahrain	61.0
2. United Arab Emirates	60.0
3. Kuwait	59.5
4. Guam	57.2
5. Maldives	55.8
6. Pakistan	53.1
7. Jordan	53.0
8. Hong Kong	52.3
9. Solomon Islands	52.2
10. Taiwan	52.2

Source: U.N. Census of World Populations

COUNTRIES — MILITARY
Highest Military Expenditures, U.S. and Allies

War is devastating in its toll on human lives and personal serenity, but its is also the most fiscally burdensome of international calamities. Further, war is a vexing expense even in times of great political placidity. In this generation, as in the two before it, the U.S. continues to bear the brunt of this expense in its dealings with NATO and its other allies. In the coming years, however, with the relaxation of tensions between Eastern and Western Europe (indeed, with the disappearance of most of the West's

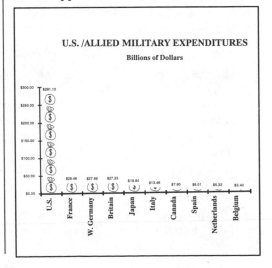

U.S./ALLIED MILITARY EXPENDITURES
Billions of Dollars

tried and true enemies), spending on the military should be less of a burden. Europe will take on a growing fiscal share of its own defense, and regional flare-ups will require a quicker, more mobile military presence, but one which, at least the American taxpayer expects, should cost less to maintain.

Country	Spending ($billions)
1. U.S.	$281.10
2. France	$28.46
3. West Germany	$27.69
4. Britain	$27.33
5. Japan	$19.84
6. Italy	$13.46
7. Canada	$7.90
8. Spain	$6.01
9. Netherlands	$5.32
10. Belgium	$3.40

Source: Department of Defense.

COUNTRIES — MURDER
Most Murderous Nations

Human nature is universal, and violence is an inevitable feature of any society. Acts of violence, however, do not occur in a vacuum. Climate certainly has an effect. The murder capitals below all lie within the tropics or in hot, arid semi-deserts — so much for paradise. Political, ideological and economic strife also serve as undeniable provocations to homicide. Herewith, then, are the established murder capitals of the modern world:

Country	Murders/100,000 pop.
1. Lesotho	140.81
2. Bahamas	22.88
3. Guyana	22.21
4. Lebanon	20.33
5. Netherlands Antilles	12.47
6. Iraq	11.94
7. Sri Lanka	11.92
8. Cyprus	11.11
9. Trinidad and Tobago	10.41
10. Jamaica	10.25

Source: Interpol International Crime Statistics

COUNTRIES — NUCLEAR POWER
Most Reactors

Since the accident at Three Mile Island and the release of the Jane Fonda vehicle *The China Syndrome*, Americans have indulged in a morbid fascination with the possibility of catastrophic meltdowns on their shores. Until the incident at Chernobyl, we had little sense of the mounting nuclear dangers beyond our borders. Now, however, we watch the world's glowing stacks with utmost anxiety. After Chernobyl, the world began to realize that nuclear power, and its potential for hazard, is a worldwide concern. Indeed, with the opening of Eastern Europe, nuclear experts are finding a plethora of ill-designed, potentially dangerous reactors built with the Soviet technology that proved less than failsafe in the Chernobyl incident. Japan, too, has recently been suffering a spate of somewhat troubling reactor difficulties. The following list represents civil nuclear power reactors; it does not count those on board nuclear-powered vessels or those for research purposes.

Country	Number of Reactors
1. United States	110
2. France	55
3. Soviet Union	46
4. Japan	39
5. UK	39
6. West Germany	24
7. Canada	18
8. Sweden	12
9. Spain	10
10. South Korea	9

Source: Intl. Atomic Energy Agency.

COUNTRIES — OIL RESERVES
Who Controls the Oil Supply

Iraq invaded Kuwait and threatened Saudi Arabia. When three of the world's top four oil suppliers engage in such shenanigans, these events, in the century of the fossil fuel, move nations. Although America does not often partake in full-fledged martial maneuvers, move we did – the motivation in this case, to many, as crudely clear as a barrel of Kuwaiti Kool Aid or Texas Tea. For all the talk of the sovereignty of the Kuwaiti people, we fought to keep the oil lines open, and to keep the life-blood of the world economy out of the hands of one ruthless despot. If Hussein had kept Kuwait and gotten his grip on the Saudi oil reserves, fully forty percent of the world's oil would have been under his control. Certainly, our excessive consumption of and reliance on petroleum is dangerous and wasteful, but until reliable alternatives can be found, access to those reserves through market channels must be preserved, or the global economic consequences are dire. Perhaps, once the euphoria of victory wears off, the dance of death in the desert will spur greater efforts to find safe, efficient, renewable energy resources – the biggest of which shines down on us every sunny day.

Nation	Barrels in Reserve (billions)
1. Saudi Arabia	255.0
2. Iraq	100.0
3. United Arab Emirates	94.5
4. Kuwait	92.9
5. Iran	58.5
6. Venezuela	58.4
7. Soviet Union	56.4
8. Mexico	56.4
9. United States	25.9
10. China	24.0

Source: Energy Information Administration

COUNTRIES – PAPER USE
Paper Tigers

You'd think that with the advent of computers in the business place, the consumption of paper in America would decline. In fact, the opposite is the case. By speeding up the work process, computers allow an ever greater generation of paper trails – everyone must have a printout, a photocopy, a spreadsheet, a "hard copy" back-up. Countless trees are felled to feed the dot-matrix and laser printers now ubiquitous in American offices. With every ream of 8" x 11" fed into the copier, another great Sequoia falls. Add to that the piles of paper generated by junk mail, paper bags, product wrapping, and, of course, newspapers, and it's no wonder America leads the world in per capita consumption of paper.

Country	Kg/yr (per cap.)
1. United States	287.0
2. Sweden	222.0
3. Canada	200.4
4. Denmark	184.1
5. Finland	180.0
6. Germany	176.3
7. Switzerland	173.7
8. Netherlands	171.0
9. Japan	169.0
10. Belgium	161.0

Source: Environmental Data Report, U.N. Environment Programme, 1989.

COUNTRIES – PARROT TRADE
Biggest Importers and Exporters of Parrots

Scientists are only now beginning to unlock the secrets of the parrot. As they do so, they are finding the birds to be remarkably intelligent – on a par, some say, with dolphins, able to recognize and label objects, colors and shapes, and, of course, speak. But even as we learn more about these fascinating creatures, their existence is threatened. Once again, destruction of their habitats in the Caribbean and South America is the main culprit. Capture and transport of the birds for sale in pet stores also threatens the many parrot species. Oddly, scientists, note, birds captured in the wild make lousy pets. Wild parrots placed in captivity often develop neurotic behavior, such as bobbing back and forth, constantly shifting from one foot to another, abnormal grooming practices like plucking out their own feathers, and aggressiveness. Furthermore, the transportation of the birds is extremely wasteful; on many airplane flights, more than half the birds being shipped die in transit. Conservationists promote the domestic breeding of parrots for sale as pets and seek a total ban on the trade in wild birds. Below we have listed the biggest culprits in the import and export of parrots.

Annual world trade in parrots amounts to more than 600,000 birds a year. The United States exported only 3,853 parrots in 1986, the same year as it imported more than 305,000 — representing a 60% increase in the number of birds imported since 1981. In comparison, Canada imported 62,956 parrots in 1981, but had dramatically cut that number to under 10,000 by 1986. Bulgaria imported only 13 parrots that same year, Greenland 6.

Top Importers	Annual Imports
1. United States	305,997
2. Germany	60,564
3. Netherlands	27,822
4. Japan	27,790
5. Belgium	20,357
6. France	18,843
7. Sweden	16,454
8. Spain	11,406
9. Canada	9,551
10. Italy	8,607

Top Exporters	Annual Exports
1. Argentina	177,992
2. Tanzania	84,228
3. Indonesia	58,832
4. Senegal	28,430
5. Uruguay	20,967
6. Peru	17,032
7. Honduras	15,816
8. India	15,445
9. Malaysia	15,012
10. Taiwan	13,840

Source: Environmental Data Report, GEMS Monitoring and Assessment Research Centre, United Nations Environment Programme, 1989.

COUNTRIES — PATENTS
Strongest Technology

Yes, the U.S. is still an economic and technological powerhouse, but, according to one measure of technology, the threat from Japan to America's cherished number one spot on the high-tech edge is even more pronounced than many thought. This index, which rates countries by the number of influential patents, shows that Japan's share of influential technology is nearly three-fourths that of the United States, and is growing rapidly. The index measures the frequency with which patents are cited in subsequent patent filings, thus gauging the importance of particular patents to the development of future technologies. A patent that is often mentioned in other patents is judged to be more important than those that go ignored. Control of significant patents puts control over the development of future technologies in the hands of its owner. The causes for concern in the American business world are many; for instance, Fuji and Hitachi have surpassed Kodak and IBM in important patents. Experts say the Japanese are moving steadily forward in most every high-tech area, not just electronics and automobiles. On the other hand, the Soviet Union is a relative midget in the patent world, with only 400 significant patents, compared to more than 100,000 in the U.S. and 76,000 in Japan.

Country	Significant Patents
1. United States	104,541
2. Japan	76,984
3. Germany	17,643
4. Great Britain	8,795
5. France	7,672
6. Netherlands	5,737
7. Switzerland	5,002
8. Canada	1,156
9. Sweden	1,124
10. Italy	1,106

PLACES

Source: *New York Times*, from CHI Research, Inc.

COUNTRIES — PRESCRIPTION DRUGS
Most Expensive Prescription Drugs

The free market has been allowed to set prices in this country for everything from tampons to brain surgery. But when it comes to basic medical care, should the workings of the market be allowed to dictate the price of health? In Europe, governments group up with large private purchasers to negotiate prices with producers, permitting a profit to the manufacturer but keeping overall prices to the consumer down to an affordable level. In the U.S., drug companies set the prices, and doctors prescribe the drugs. The consumer has little choice in what to purchase, or what to pay. In one egregious case, doctors continue to prescribe the drug TPA, which dissolves blood clots at $2,000 a dose, instead of streptokinase, which has been shown in studies to be more effective at one-tenth the cost. The average U.S. price for a Valium prescription is $9.70; in Europe and elsewhere, the same prescription is $3.60. The following list compares prescription drug prices in nine countries, with the lowest average equal to 100. In the Netherlands and Denmark, where drug prices are similar to those in the U.S., doctors are limited in the amounts they can prescribe, cutting overall drug expenditures. Only in Germany are both prices and consumption comparable to the U.S.

Country	Price Index
1. Netherlands	299
2. United States	279
3. Germany	269
4. Denmark	230
5. Britain	217
6. Italy	131
7. France	127
8. Spain	105
9. Greece	100

Source: U.S. Senate Special Committee on Aging.

COUNTRIES — POPULATION
Most Crowded

Although technological miracles like satellite telecommunications have narrowed the apparent size of the world, the growth of the planet's population (and its accompanying cities, towns and other such social encampments) continues at a brisk pace. The world's two most populated nations face enormous difficulties in the coming century, as they struggle to slow their own human growth and increase their per capita standards of living.

Country	Population
1. China	1,103,900,000
2. India	835,000,000
3. USSR	289,000,000
4. United States	248,800,000
5. Indonesia	184,600,000
6. Brazil	147,400,000
7. Japan	123,200,000
8. Nigeria	115,300,000
9. Bangladesh	114,700,000
10. Pakistan	110,400,000

Source: World Population Data Sheet, Population Reference Bureau, Inc.

COUNTRIES — POPULATION
Most Populous
(Projections for 2100)

Although the information-rich United States retains its position as one of the world's largest centers of population, the coming century should see the continued curtailment of fertility among the world's most-developed nations, in tandem with record growth among the fecund peoples of the third world. The abatement of world hunger and allied resource distribution

PLACES

questions shall continue to pose one of man's most daunting challenges, as these projected population figures for the year 2100 amply demonstrate. India will surpass China as the most populous country, with Nigeria moving into the third position, despite its great poverty. The U.S., with relatively slow population growth, will drop to seventh worldwide.

Country	Population
1. India	1,631,800,000
2. China	1,571,400,000
3. Nigeria	508,800,000
4. USSR	375,900,000
5. Indonesia	356,300,000
6. Pakistan	315,800,000
7. United States	308,700,000
8. Bangladesh	308,700,000
9. Brazil	297,100,000
10. Mexico	293,200,000

Source: World Bank, 2100.

COUNTRIES — POPULATION
Little Guys: Small Populations

In the eighties and nineties, we have reached a high-water mark in public awareness of international geography by attacking a series of previously obscure Third World wonderlands (Grenada, Panama, Iraq/Kuwait). In the future, if the U.S. government needs another little guy to pick on, it might consult the following list of the countries with the smallest populations.

Country	Population
1. Holy See/Vatican	890
2. San Marino	19,149
3. Liechtenstein	25,215
4. Monaco	27,063
5. Andorra	49,000
6. Saint Kitts-Nevis	49,000
7. Kiribati	63,833
8. Seychelles	67,000
9. Dominica	79,000
10. Antigua and Barbuda	85,000

Source: United Nations.

COUNTRIES — POPULATION DENSITY
Highest and Lowest

Population density is the kind of misleading figure it's fun to play with during cocktail parties. You can wow your friends with fascinating fictions about what it must be like to live in one of these places. But while you are fooling your friends, don't let the figures fool you. The fact is that the majority of the most densely populated countries are small nations containing large cities. And while the residents of Singapore are indeed closely packed, they are less sardine-like than the residents of Manhattan Island. Ironically, extreme crowding is a condition common to extremely destitute and extremely prosperous locales. Residents, it seems, are either too poor to get out, or too blindly anxious to get in. On the other hand, the least densely populated countries are often large countries containing large wastelands.

Highest Density	Population per sq. km
1. Singapore	46,895
2. Malta	12,281
3. Bangladesh	8,389
4. Bahrain	8,113
5. Mauritius	6,070
6. Barbados	6,023
7. Republic of Korea (South)	4,494
8. Netherlands	4,335
9. Japan	3,275
10. El Salvador	3,034

Lowest Density	
1. Mongolia	14
2. Mauritania	21
3. Australia	22
4. Botswana	23
5. Iceland	25
6. Surinam	25
7. Canada	29
8. Chad	44

PLACES

COUNTRIES— POPULATION GROWTH
Fastest and Slowest Growth

It's a wonder why some people are so worried about Germany these days. Any country that has its libido this much in check is not about to start another world war. Germany has a population growth rate of -0.11% each year. That compares favorably with Germany's vigorous birth-rate earlier in the century that helped fuel that country's tragically misguided military adventures. At today's total population of 77.3 million, German population will actually be declining by 83,000 people every year. Now if we could only give a Volkswagen to everyone in China and then feed them all wienerschnitzel, we'd have this world population thing licked for sure! Here in America our population growth rate is 0.86%, nothing to sneeze at, though some predict our population will reach 312 million before it begins to decline in the middle of the next century.

Country	Annual Growth (%)
1. Sweden	-0.11
Germany	-0.11
3. Luxembourg	-0.10
4. Denmark	-0.01
5. Austria	0.01
6. United Kingdom	0.02
7. Switzerland	0.04
8. Belgium	0.09
9. Italy	0.09
10. Norway	0.17

Source: *World Resources 1988-89.*

COUNTRIES— POPULATION GROWTH
Fastest Sheer Population Growth

Demographers tell us that the world's population will reach an incredible eight billion, two-hundred five million by the year 2025. Its going to be hard to feed, house and clothe all these people, not to mention getting them to buy Coke and wear Levis. Who knows what trouble they will cause when they find that we have more cable channels than they do? Of the chief governments involved, those in India and China have worked hard at population control, reducing their growth rates from 2.28% and 2.61% in 1965 to a present 1.72% and 1.18% respectively. But while growth rates have slowed, their sheer masses mean that even a tiny increase percentage-wise adds a yearly population increase roughly equivalent to the entire population of New York City and its suburbs. The following are the countries that add the most new citizens every year, in terms of sheer numbers.

Country	Annual Pop. Increase
1. India	13,645,000
2. China	12,859,000
3. Nigeria	3,629,000
4. Indonesia	3,020,000
5. Brazil	2,961,000
6. Bangladesh	2,819,000
7. Pakistan	2,369,000
8. United States	2,082,000
9. Mexico	2,003,000
10. Iran	1,325,000
11. Ethiopia	1,306,000
12. Philippines	1,295,000

Source: *World Resources 1988-89.*

COUNTRIES — RAILROADS
Best Rail Network

Casey Jones would be proud to know that the United States leads the world in terms of the extent of its rail network. While many in the States bemoan our lack of an extensive and convenient passenger-rail service (Amtrak notwithstanding), the sheer size of the country means that the airline industry has taken over the major part of passenger transport over long distances. However, when it absolutely, positively doesn't have to be there overnight, the railroads, along with trucking, still serve as a major means of transporting material. The following lists

PLACES

give the top ten countries in the world in terms of the total amount of railroad track and the total number of rail cars.

Country	Km track (000)
1. United States	234.6
2. U.S.S.R.	144.9
3. India	61.8
4. China	52.5
5. Germany	41.5
6. France	34.6
7. Poland	24.3
8. Canada	25.3
9. South Africa	22.4
10. Japan	19.9

County	Rolling Stock (000)
1. United States	22,932
2. China	12,266
3. India	10,713
4. Germany	8,634
5. France	7,468
6. Czechoslovakia	6,171
7. South Africa	5,553
8. United Kingdom	5,499
9. Italy	4,958
10. Japan	4,765

Source: Environmental Data Report, United Nations Environment Program, 1989(figures for the U.S.S.R. are not available).

COUNTRIES — RECYCLING
Best Recyclers

Elsewhere we saw that the United States is the largest per capita consumer of paper in the world, and decried the fate of the forests which feed that hunger for paper. But there is a way to lessen the effects of such a voracity on the world's woodlands: recycling. The United States currently recycles about 27 percent of its annual paper consumption. But, as the list below shows, that's a far cry from the leaders in the recycling arena. Tiny Hong Kong, with its limited natural resources and waste disposal opportunities, recycles fully two-thirds of all its waste paper. Clearly the U.S. has a long way

to go before overcoming the pervasive attitude of the disposable society; the first faltering steps are now being made through increased environmental awareness. The countries that recycle the least include Nigeria (2%), Malaysia (3%), Iceland (5%), and Sri Lanka (9%). The following are the leading paper recyclers in the world, in terms of paper recovery as a percentage of paper consumption.

Country	Paper Recycled (%)
1. Hong Kong	67
2. Kenya	54
3. Greece	51
4. Japan	49
5. Finland	45
Netherlands	45
Taiwan	45
Portugal	45
6. Kuwait	44
Switzerland	44
7. Panama	43
8. Mexico	41
Spain	41
9. Austria	39
10. Germany	38
Sweden	38

Source: "Materials Recycling: The Virtue of Necessity," World Watch Institute, Washington.

COUNTRIES — RELIGION
Most Christian

God is everywhere, of course, but those who believe in him are a little more spread out. As the home of the Pope and the seat of the Roman Catholic church, Vatican City is the most Christian locale on Earth. Among the nations of the West, bitterly divided Ireland is the most solidly religious.

Nation	% Christian
1. Vatican City	100.0
2. Faeroe Islands	99.9
3. Dominica	99.8
4. Niue	99.8
5. Andorra	99.6

PLACES

6. Ireland	99.5
7. Nicaragua	99.3
8. Anguilla	99.2
9. El Salvador	99.2
10. St. Christopher-Nevis	99.2

Source: U.N. Demographic Handbook

COUNTRIES — RELIGION

Least Chrisitian

Christianity pervades the Western world. It pervades its customs, its holidays and its laws. Much of the world, however, is completely immune to these traditions. Though the Moslem world is highly visible in its antipathy to Judeo-Christian faiths, Arab nations nonetheless harbor fairly significant Christian populations. It is in the ancient, mysterious lands of the East that one finds a truly pronounced dearth of Christians.

Nation	% Christian
1. China	.2
2. Comoros	.2
3. Mongolia	.2
4. Bhutan	.1
5. Maldives	.1
6. Somalia	.1
7. South Yemen	.1
8. Afghanistan	.0
9. Nepal	.0
10. Yemen Arab Republic	.0

Source: World Christian Encyclopedia.

COUNTRIES — RELIGION

Largest Jewish Population

The great waves of immigration from Europe to the United States gave to this country a rich ethnic heritage of peoples and creeds. In fact, the United States is home to more Jewish people than any other country on Earth, Israel included. Tragically, though, the small populations in Europe are more the result of genocide than immigration, as millions of European Jews perished in the Holocaust, and hundreds of thousands more fled to the fledgling state of Israel upon its founding in 1948. The healthy Jewish population in the United States guarantees our continued close ties with and commitment to Israel.

Country	Jewish Population
1. United States	5,700,000
2. Israel	3,659,000
3. U.S.S.R.	1,435,000
4. France	530,000
5. Great Britain	322,000
6. Canada	310,000
7. Argentina	220,000
8. South Africa	114,000
9. Brazil	100,000
10. Australia	85,000

Source: American Jewish Yearbook, 1990.

COUNTRY — RELIGION

Smallest Jewish Population

Looking for bagels and lox in Manila? A good kosher deli in Seoul? Forget about it. According to the American Jewish Year Book, there are only 100 Jewish people in all of the Philippines and South Korea. That's .00017 percent of the Filipino population and .00024 percent of South Koreans, lower than the percentage in such places as Egypt, Iraq and Lebanon. The following are the least-Jewish countries in the world, measured by the percentage of the population that is Jewish.

Country	Jewish Pop.	% Jewish
1. Philippines	100	.00017
2. South Korea	100	.00024
3. Egypt	200	.00039
4. Thailand	300	.00055
5. India	5,000	.00063
6. Iraq	200	.00113
7. Zaire	400	.00119
8. Dominican Republic	100	.00146
9. Kenya	400	.00167
10. Lebanon	100	.00354

Source: American Jewish Year Book, 1990.

PLACES

COUNTRIES — REPRESSION

Most Repressive Regimes

Despite our cozying up to Saudi Arabia, Syria and even Iran in the Persian Gulf crisis, these continue be some of the most repressive regimes in the world, according to Freedom House, a non-profit organization that has been monitoring the state of freedom throughout the world since 1955. Despite the new-found liberty in such formerly repressive countries as Chile and the nations of Eastern Europe, Freedom House says that nearly a third of the world's population is not free. Freedom House rates countries on a scale from 1 to 7, with 1 being the most free and 7 the least. The list below contains the countries with a rating of 7.

Iraq

Invasion of Kuwait; vast secret police apparatus; widespread human rights abuses included forced relocation, arbitrary arrest, torture and summary execution.

Iran

Public executions of opponents to the regime; thousands of political prisoners; persecution of religious and ethnic minorities.

Saudi Arabia

Continued suppression of women's rights; forcibly expelled hundreds of thousands of Yemeni workers.

Syria

Widespread secret police system; persecution of religious and ethnic minorities.

China

Harassment and jailing of Tiananmen students and other voices of democratic reform; security forces strengthened in anticipation of further protests.

North Korea

Recalled students and officials from abroad and scattered them throughout the country, hoping to dissipate ideas of democracy from outside; only nominal economic reforms under Stalinist Kim Il-Sung.

Burma

After being swamped in national elections it had called for, the military leaders refused to step down, instead arresting members of the victorious opposition.

Vietnam, Laos

Continue to affirm commitment to a one-party state.

Afghanistan

Stalemate in civil war has meant continued violence and lawlessness.

Liberia

Rival guerrilla movements and tribes engaged in bloody struggle for power after civil war that toppled Samuel K. Doe.

Somalia

Engaged in civil war to topple ruling party, which controls only the capital.

Cuba

Human rights activists jailed; in the face of communism's crumble elsewhere, Castro's grip over every aspect of Cuban society remains as strong now, or stronger, than ever.

Source: Freedom House.

COUNTRIES — R&D

Spending on R&D

The race for the economic lead in the coming decade will in large part be dictated by a country's commitment to research and development in such high-tech fields as advanced materials, semiconductors, artificial intelligence, biotechnology, digital imaging, superconductivity and high-performance computing. In these and most other cutting-edge areas, the United States is either ahead or even with Japan and Europe in terms of research and development. However, in most instances, the trend is for increased competitiveness from these two powerful foreign markets in the coming years. The great American challenge will be to strengthen the commitment to such high-tech wizardry, and to translate breakthroughs on the R&D front into useful products in the market. These are the top ten countries for spending on research and development in 1989.

Country	R&D Spending (Millions)
1. United States	$65,200
2. Japan	$26,300
3. Germany	$11,370
4. Britain	$5,723
5. France	$4,912
6. Netherlands	$3,521
7. Switzerland	$3,023
8. Sweden	$2,908
9. Italy	$2,295
10. Canada	$2,042

Source: Compustat Services, Inc.

COUNTRIES — ROAD SYSTEMS

Most Roads

In addition to industrialization and technical advancement, a major indicator of the level of country's development is its transportation system. Not surprisingly, the United States, where the car is king, enjoys the most extensive road system in the world — four times as much roadway as the Soviet Union, the largest country in the world. And we have the Cold War to thank for it. Our interstate highway system was built, at least in part, with military preparedness in mind; passenger and commercial travel wasn't the only, or even the most important, reason for the construction of our elaborate and efficient systems of interstate roadways. But even more telling of a country's development is how much of its road network is paved: for instance, Brazil has the second longest road network, but a mere eight percent of the road system in that country is paved, whereas 90% of America's roads are hard-topped, as are virtually all the roads in Western Europe. Below we have noted the ten countries with the most roadway, in kilometers, and the percentage of roadway that is paved.

Country	Km of Roadway	% paved
1. United States	6,242,200	90
2. Brazil	1,675,000	8
3. U.S.S.R.	1,549,000	n/a
4. Japan	1,098,900	65
5. Australia	853,000	50
6. Germany	539,500	99
7. United Kingdom	352,300	98
8. Poland	340,200	63
9. Spain	318,000	66
10. Italy	301,600	100

Source: World Road Statistics, International Road Federation, Geneva.

COUNTRIES — ROAD SYSTEMS

Densest Road Network

Not only is the length of a country's road system and the amount paved important, but alo key is how much of the country is actually served by usable roads. Below we have listed the countries that have the most and least dense road network, in terms of the number of kilometers of roadway per square kilometer of land. Tops on the list are Monaco, Gibraltar and Singapore — really city-states rather than countries. Beyond these anomalies, one sees that Europe and Japan have the densest road networks in the world, while African and South American countries are least served by usable roadways.

Country	Km Road/Sq. Km
1. Monaco	32.21
2. Gibraltar	8.33
3. Singapore	4.55
4. Belgium	4.20

5. Japan	2.91
6. Netherlands	2.76
7. Germany	1.98
8. Luxembourg	1.96
9. Denmark	1.63
10. France	1.46

Least Dense Road Network

Country	Km Road/Sq. Km
1. Niger	.01
Mauritania	.01
2. Botswana	.02
3. Canada	.03
Central African Rep.	.03
Egypt	.03
Ethiopia	.03
Mozambique	.03
4. Saudi Arabia	.04
Papua New Guinea	.04
5. Jordan	.06
Suriname	.06
U.S.S.R.	.06
Zaire	.06
6. Benin	.07
Senegal	.07
7. Argentina	.08
Liberia	.08
Madagascar	.08
Morocco	.08
8. Colombia	.09
9. Chile	.10
French Guiana	.10
Malawi	.10
10. Australia	.11
Cameroon	.11
Iceland	.11
Mexico	.11
Venezuela	.11

Source: World Road Statistics, International Road Federation, Geneva.

COUNTRIES — ROAD SYSTEMS

Most Crowded Roads

Gotta get somewhere fast in Monaco? The casino, perhaps, for a game of baccarat with

Rush Hour: the Grand Prix of Monte Carlo further clogs an already congested road system.

James Bond? Forget the roads. You'd be better off walking. Monaco suffers from the most congested roadways in the world, with a staggering 402 cars for every kilometer of roadway, followed distantly by Gibraltar and Hong Kong. Among larger states, the oil-rich kingdoms of Kuwait and Saudi Arabia have the most cars per kilometer, although figures for Kuwait are from before the war, and many Kuwaiti cars were destroyed by Iraqi troops, or by American planes firing on the fleeing Iraqis. Although the U.S has the most cars per capita, its roads are relatively wide open.

Country	Vehicles/Km
1. Monaco	402
2. Gibraltar	229
3. Hong Kong	216
4. Puerto Rico	148
5. Kuwait	144
6. Saudi Arabia	126

PLACES

7. Singapore	114
8. Italy	32
9. Spain	80
10. Trinidad & Tobago	63

Source: World Road Statistics, International Road Federation, Geneva.

COUNTRIES — SENIOR CITIZENS
Loneliest Senior Citizens

In some nations the elderly are venerated and catered to in their last years. The situation in this nation has been very different. In the U.S., where 30.4% of all seniors live alone, our treatment of the elderly has lately bordered on neglect. And the problem will become even worse as the baby-boom generation ages. But the U.S. is not the country where the largest percentage of senior are living alone. This neglect is widespread throughout the industrialized world. We have a moral obligation to erect and maintain nuturing, loving and affordable homes for our mothers, fathers and grandparents. Below are the countries where the largest percentage of senior citizens are living alone

Nation	% Senior Citizens Living Alone
1. Sweden	40.0
2. Norway	40.0
3. Germany	38.9
4. Denmark	38.3
5. Finland	32.9
6. France	32.6
7. Czechoslovakia	32.4
8. Belgium	31.9
9. Netherlands	31.3
10. Austria	30.9

Source: U.S. Census Bureau.

COUNTRIES — SENIOR CITIZENS
Least Lonely Seniors

Neglect of the elderly is pervasive, but hardly universal. In many traditional cultures, respect for elders is still a keynote of civilization. The United States and the rest of the West has much to learn from the veneration, love and respect that pervade Asian and so-called third-world cultures, as is demonstrated by those cultures' accepting the elderly as a member of the household.

Country	% of Seniors Living Alone
1. Fiji	2.0
2. Korea	2.2
3. Singapore	2.3
4. Philippines	3.0
5. China	3.4
6. Colombia	5.0
7. Mexico	6.4
8. Malaysia	6.4
9. Costa Rica	6.9
10. Indonesia	8.0

Source: U.S. Census Bureau.

COUNTRIES — TAXES
Highest Taxes Among Industrialized Countries

High taxes are a fact of life in industrialized countries. Someone has to pay for massive social programs, defense, education and infrastructure. Compiled from statistics published by the Tax Foundation in Washington, D.C., this list indicates the countries with the highest taxes. Americans, who pay an average of $4,944 per person each year, are far from the highest. The welfare states established in the Scandinavian countries top the list of most taxing nations. Another way of measuring taxes might be to list taxes as a percentage of gross domestic product — that is, the percentage of a country's total output that is taken by the government. The Swedes give 53.5% of their output to the government. Norway gives 49.8% and Denmark gives 50.6%. Americans give just 28.9% of their total productivity to the government.

1. Sweden	$8,385
2. Norway	$8,346
3. Denmark	$8,151

4. Switzerland	$6,707
5. Germany	$6,540
6. France	$5,802
7. Netherlands	$5,483
8. Finland	$5,499
9. Germany	$5,484
10.Austria	$5,302

Source: Tax Foundation, Washington, D.C.

COUNTRIES – TELEVISION VIEWING

World's Biggest Couch Potatoes

The more myopic among us may believe that television is a Western phenomenon, but in truth it is an absolutely global medium. While the United States finishes a respectable third in overall sets per capita, the real leaders in world video consumption, as it turns out, are the tinyish republics of Monaco and Guam. It is some comfort, perhaps, that wherever we venture on the globe we are just a few commercials from home, that in most any of the far-flung reaches of the globe – from India to Brazil to Mongolia – one can flick on the set and see the reassuring visage of Columbo or J.R. Ewing.

Country	T.V. sets per 1,000 population
1. Monaco	654
2. Guam	625
3. United States	624
4. Japan	539
5. St. Pierre & Miquelon	533
6. Virgin Islands	526
7. Bermuda	500
8. Canada	471
9. United Kingdom	404
10. Kuwait	400

Source: Book of World Rankings.

COUNTRIES – TOURISM

Where Foreign Tourists Come From

In the heady days when the dollar is booming – just after the two World Wars and in

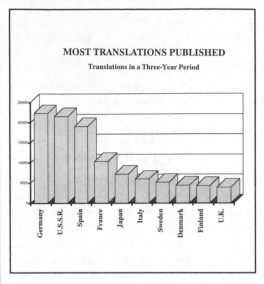

MOST TRANSLATIONS PUBLISHED
Translations in a Three-Year Period

Germany, U.S.S.R., Spain, France, Japan, Italy, Sweden, Denmark, Finland, U.K.

the mid-1980s, Americans flock to foreign shores to gawk at the treasures, both natural and man-made, of the old world. Contrarily, when the dollar is down, we welcome hordes of camera-toting tourists to our bountiful land. If you become frustrated on the streets of New York in August these days because you're hearing more German, French or Japanese than English, maybe now you'll get some idea why Parisians flood out from the City of Lights every summer to escape the invasion of their city by similar minions from abroad. And if you start to see signs posted in German on the beaches of Miami or in Japanese in Los Angeles, think of the tourist dollars flowing into this country from those wealthy lands. If they're coming to take everything we own anyway, we can at least make them pay for the pleasure while we can. These are the countries that send the most most temporary visitors, either on business or pleasure, to the United States annually.

Country	Visitors per year (000)
1. Japan	2,247
2. United Kingdom	1,397
3. West Germany	942
4. Mexico	820
5. France	473
6. Italy	271

7. Australia	265
8. Switzerland	227
9. Netherlands	176
10. Sweden	168

Source: U.S. Immigration and Naturalization Service.

COUNTRIES — TRANSLATIONS
Purloined Letters — Most Translations

Elsewhere we saw that English is by far the most translated language in the world. But who exactly is taking all that knowledge and putting it to use for themselves? Below we have noted the countries publishing the most translations in a three-year period from 1980 to 1982. By comparison, the United States ranked twelfth, with 3,795 translated works published over the three-year period. That ranks just behind Yugoslavia in the amount of information from foreign language sources published in this country.

Country	Translations Published
1. Germany	22,301
2. U.S.S.R.	21,567
3. Spain	19,108
4. France	10,379
5. Japan	7,201
6. Italy	5,960
7. Sweden	5,157
8. Denmark	4,420
9. Finland	4,355
10. United Kingdom	3,953

Source: UNESCO.

COUNTRIES — TRAVEL
Most Frequent Foreign Destinations of American Travelers

Although Americans often talk about their need to get far, far away, most often when they go away, they head for the nearest possible foreign destination. Last year, nearly thirty million of us slid across the border to Canada or Mexico, taking advantage of the last days of the debased peso or chatting with secessionists in French Quebec. In comparison, a mere 2.9 million American's journeyed to the most-popular European destination, the United Kingdom.

Destination	U.S. Visitors, 1990 (million)
1. Mexico	14.30
2. Canada	12.70
3. United Kingdom	2.90
4. France	1.90
5. Germany	1.80
6. Italy	1.20
7. Bahamas	1.10
8. Japan	.92
9. Jamaica	.75
10. Hong Kong	.69

Source: U.S. Travel and Tourism Administration

Monaco is the most urbanized country in the world. Photo: Monaco Tourist Bureau.

PLACES

COUNTRIES – URBANIZATION

Most Urbanized Nations

Progress is a two-edged sword. On the blunt edge, expansion, development and growth prolong and enhance living. On the sharp side, though, they destroy natural beauty, disrupt the in-built harmonies of human existence and foster poverty, claustrophobia and violence. In the United States, 77% of the population makes its home in urban centers; in hamlet nations like Monaco, every last man makes his stand in the houses of progress.

Country	% Urban Population
1. Monaco	100.0
2. Singapore	100.0
3. Malta	94.3
4. United Kingdom	91.0
5. Hong Kong	90.0
6. Australia	89.0
7. Israel	89.0
8. Kuwait	88.0
9. Sweden	87.0
10. West Germany	85.0

Source: U.N. Demographic Handbook

COUNTRIES – URBANIZATION

Most Rural Countries

The world's most rural countries are secluded places where Western influences seldom reach. The lives of their people are insular and completely disconnected from much of the world. Most are farmers or nomadic shephard peoples. In Bhutan, which is a tiny country at the feet of the Himalayas, barely 53,000 of the one-million inhabitants live in towns or cities. The numbers are scarcely different in any of the African nations near the top of the list. In Kampuchea (Cambodia) in South East Asia, the Khmer Rouge brutally forced many city dwellers into the countryside, systematically killing millions in the process.

Country	Percent Rural
1. Bhutan	94.7%
2. Cape Verde	94.3%
3. Burundi	92.7%
4. Rwanda	92.3%
5. Burkina Faso	91.0%
6. Nepal	91.4%
7. Oman	89.4%
8. Solomon Islands	89.4%
9. Kampuchea (Cambodia)	88.4%
10. Ethiopia	87.1%

COUNTRIES – U.S. FOREIGN AID

Biggest Recipient of U.S. Aid

When we in the U.S. make friends, we know how to treat them right. Although the domestic agenda is far from clear or resolved, humanitarian principles require that the U.S. parse billions of its hard-held dollars to ailing and developing nations across the known globe. Our biggest dependents? The war torn nations of the Gulf and the Mid-East; topping the list are two nations that, until the Camp David accords under the presidency of Jimmy Carter, had been in continual conflict since the end of the Second World War. Following those two countries by a large margin are Pakistan, with its strategic military location near the Soviet Union, India and Afghanistan, Turkey, which served as an important base for Operation Desert Storm, and the Philippines, which, until the wrath of the volcano Mt. Pinotubo was felt, served as our biggest base in the South Pacific.

Country	U.S. Aid ($000)
1. Israel	$3,000,000
2. Egypt	$2,294,687
3. Pakistan	$583,043
4. Turkey	$563,750

5. Philippines	$494,118
6. El Salvador	$382,657
7. Greece	$350,700
8. Bangladesh	$174,683
9. India	$162,802
10. Guatemala	$155,751

Source: U.S. State Department.

COUNTRIES — U.S. RESIDENTS

The Foreign Legions — U.S. Expatriates

We go abroad to escape and find or to remember and forget. When we leave, most often we do not go far or for too long. The gentle beaches of Mexico and the quirky back streets of Quebec invite us. Occasionally, we return to the motherland, taking a European summer or two. And even if we decide to stay a while, most of us still prefer to stick close to home or among our linguistic brethren in the U.K. The following are the world's countries that have opened their arms the widest to American expatriates. Students comprise a large portion of these numbers.

Country	Resident U.S. Citizens (000)
1. Mexico	396.0
2. Canada	235.1
3. U.K.	158.8
4. Philippines	156.3
5. West Germany	134.1
6. Italy	86.4
7. Australia	68.7
8. Dominican Republic	63.2
9. Israel	60.9
10. Spain	60.1

Source: U.S. Bureau of the Census

COUNTRIES — WINE

Top Wine Producers

In France, wine is a religion. Each year's crop is heralded, judged, and ultimately, consumed, with a fervor bordering on the spiritual. Gustatory Gauls can satisfy their urge for the grape in vintages ranging from the pedestrian *vin ordinaire* in a plastic jug to the rarest and most expensive bottles of Chateau Lafite. Indeed, France is the greatest wine producing nation in the world, squeezing their grapes for more than 1.6 billion gallons of wine annually, about four times the production of U.S. vineyards.

Country	Gallons of Wine (Millions)
1. France	1,607
2. Italy	1,580
3. Spain	765
4. U.S.S.R.	560
5. Argentina	537
6. United States	411
7. Germany	349
8. Romania	264
9. South Africa	255
10. Portugal	203

Most Acres Under Vintage

Country	Acres
1. Spain	3,640
2. U.S.S.R.	2,671
3. Italy	2,654
4. France	2,343
5. Turkey	1,544
6. Portugal	951
7. United States	818
8. Romania	662
9. Argentina	642
10. Yugoslavia	561

Source: Office International de la Vigne et du Vin; Chicago Wine School.

COUNTRIES — WINE

Most Productive Vineyards

Recent archaeological discoveries have suggested that man first acquired a taste for the grape at least 6,000 years ago. Ancient jars from Godin Tepe in Iran have been found with tell-tale red stains rich in tartaric acid, the residue of a now-forgotten but obviously robust Sumerian vintage. And that vintage

PLACES

had to be extra strong, because the Middle East is about the worst place in the world to cultivate wine. For instance, as the rating below shows, Syria has the least-productive vineyards in the world — vintners there must plant three acres to squeeze out one good gallon of wine. Let's hope their Sumerian forebears had better luck with the grape. The story is a little better in Turkey, Jordan and Egypt, but not much: in each of those countries, an acre of land produces less than ten gallons of wine. On the other hand, Germany enjoys the most fruitful wine-producing acreage in the world, pumping out a healthy 1,385 gallons of their sweet vintages from each acre.

Country	Gallons per Acre
1. Germany	1,385
2. South Africa	973
3. Australia	923
4. New Zealand	916
5. Canada	882
6. Argentina	836
7. France	686
8. Italy	595
9. Brazil	502
10. United States	502

Least Productive

Country	Gallons per Acre
1. Syria	.36
2. Turkey	3.9
3. Jordan	5.3
4. Egypt	8.4
5. Lebanon	40.5
6. China	58.0
7. Morocco	70.0
8. Tunisia	78
9. Algeria	79
10. U.S.S.R.	210

Source: Office International de la Vigne et du Vin; Chicago Wine School.

GOLF COURSES
Best Private and Public Courses

Since 1966, *Golf Digest* has been continually refining its criterion for selection of America's greatest golf courses. Its first list was drawn solely from the U.S. Golf Association's course ratings system, which primarily depended on distance. In subsequent ratings, more qualitative and sub-

I'm Going to Graceland. And so are 600,000 other people a year.Photo: Rogers & Cowan, Inc.

PLACES

jective factors have been taken into account: not only the toughness of the course, but its number of "classic" holes, quality of play, and aesthetic value. As the criteria state, "A great course should test the skills of a scratch player from the championship tees, challenging him to play all types of shots. It should reward well-placed shots and call on the golfer to blend power and finesse. Each hole should be memorable. There should be a feeling of enticement and a sense of satisfaction in playing the course. The design should offer a balance in both length and configuration, and the course should be properly maintained." The selection panel of 200 includes professional and amateur golfers, administrators, local officials, journalists and golf historians.

Best Private Courses

1. Cypress Point Club, Pebble Beach, CA
2. Merion Golf Club, Ardmore, PA
3. Oakland Hills Country Club, CA
4. Oakmont Country Club, Oakmont, PA
5. Olympic Club (Lake), San Francisco, CA
6. Pebble Beach Links, Pebble Beach, CA
7. Pine Valley Golf Club, Clementon, NJ
8. Seminole Golf Club, N. Palm Beach, FL
9. Southern Hills Country Club, Tulsa, OK
10. Winged Foot G.C., Mamaroneck, NY

Not a member of the country club set? You can still find great courses to play. In fact, some public and municipal courses were conceived by the same designers as the best private courses, such as Robert Trent Jones. Others courses, such as Torrey Pines, and the Edgewood Tahoe Golf Course, boast spectacular natural settings.

Best Public Courses.

1. Brown Deer Park G.C., Milwaukee, WI
2. Cog Hill G.C.#4, Lemont, IL
3. Edgewood Tahoe G.C., Stateline, NV
4. Indian Canyon G.C., Spokane, WA
5. Otter Creek G.C., Columbus, IN
6. Plumas Lake C.C., Marysville, CA
7. Tanglewood G.C., Clemmons, NC
8. Torrey Pines G.C.(South), La Jolla, CA

9. Wailua G.C., Kauai, HI
10. West Palm Beach C.C., FL

Source: *America's 100 Greatest Golf Courses—and Then Some*, William Davis, Golf Digest Publications.

HOUSES
Most Visited House-Museums

Of all the architectural wonders within the United States, isn't it fascinating that Elvis Presley's 1939 pseudo-Colonial style home attracts the most visitors—more than 600,000 a year? Architectural genius Frank Lloyd Wright did make it onto the list of the ten most popular homes in the U.S., with his stunning Falling Water in Pennsylvania.

Home/Location

1. Graceland
   Memphis, TN

2. Isabella Stewart Gardner Museum
   Boston, MA

3. Gallier House Museum
   New Orleans, LA

4. Bonnet House
   Ft. Lauderdale, FL

5. Falling Water
   Mill Run, PA

6. Victoria Mansion
   Portland, ME

7. Melrose
   Natchez, MS

8. Bayou Bend
   Houston, TX

9. Olana
   Hudson, NY

10. Gamble House
    Pasadena, CA

MOUNTAINS
Tallest

Denizens of Colorado and some the U.S.'s other mountainous climes have come to

PLACES

regard themselves as a rugged, Alpine people. The elevations on which they encamp, however, seem dwarfish beside the great peaks of the Himalayas and other Asian chains. Indeed, oxygen is so rare at the great heights of the East that even the heights of the foothills of the world's tallest peaks are literally dizzying.

Mountain/Nation	Elevation (feet)
1. Everest (Nepal)	29,108
2. K-2 (Kashmir)	29,064
3. Kanchenjunga (Nepal-Sikkim)	28,208
4. Lhotse (Nepal-Tibet)	27,890
5. Makalu (Nepal-Tibet)	27,790
6. Dhaulagiri I (Nepal)	26,810
7. Manaslu (Nepal)	26,760
8. Cho Oyu (Nepal)	26,750
9. Nanga Parbat	26,660
10. Annapurna I	26,504

MOUNTAINS

Tallest U.S Mountains

North America is unique in possessing both a vast, flat prairie regions, and the rugged mountain ranges of the West and Pacific Northwest. Although our peaks cannot compare with the great summits of Asia, they comprise an imposing continental barrier, and offer a dramatic counterpoint to our fertile lowlands. All of America's tallest peaks are in Alaska.

Mountain	Elevation (feet)
1. Mt. McKinley	20,320
2. Mt. St. Elias	18,008
3. Mt. Foraker	17,400
4. Mt. Bona	16,500
5. Mt. Blackburn	16,390
6. Mt. Sanford	16,237
7. Mt. Vancouver	15,979
8. South Buttress	15,885
9. Mt. Churchill	15,638
10. Mt. Fairweather	15,300

Source: Department of the Interior, U.S. Geological Survey

The highest peak in the U.S., Mt. McKinley.

NATIONAL PARKS
Most National Park Lands, Countries

With expanding world populations encroaching on the world's few remaining natural provinces, and industrial pollution increasingly affecting the ability of certain plants to survive, the role of national parks and protected wilderness areas is becoming

Where the Buffalo Roam: A lone bison surveys his domain in Yellowstone National Park. Photo: Wyoming Travel Commission.

PLACES

increasingly important. The national park was invented here in the United States, but since its introduction in the early part of this century, it has become a fixture on the world scene. Worldwide, parks make up a full 2.9% of national land area and cover approximately 454 million hectares, a unit which is equivalent to 1,000 square meters or 2.471 acres.

Country	Nat. Park Area (hectares)
1. United States	67,506,028
2. Australia	35,690,026
3. Canada	22,997,933
4. U.S.S.R	18,411,999
5. Indonesia	13,910,021
6. India	12,910,021
7. Chile	12,781,114
8. Brazil	11,929,634
9. Ecuador	10,619,171
10. Botswana	9,934,200

NATIONAL PARKS
Most Visited in the U.S.

Many American families who pack up their Winnebagos for a two-week vacation away from the hustle and bustle of suburbia receive a sudden, unexpected shock when they run into their first traffic jam outside a national park seemingly in the middle of nowhere. Only then do they realize that their idea of getting away from it all has led them smack into the middle of it all. In fact, last year the National Park Service counted more than 260 million visits to its facilities — or more than one visit for every American. With most people vacationing sometime during the summer, it's not surprising that America's national parks fill up quickly — perhaps there's just not enough scenery to go around. The leader on this list benefits (or suffers) from its proximity to San Francisco, the residents of which can make day trips there instead of the weekenders or summer vacationers who head off for the likes of the more remote Grand Canyon, Yellowstone and Yosemite.

Golden Gate National Recreation Area is the most visited national park in the U.S. Photo by Richard Frear, courtesy National Park Service.

Park	Visitors, 1,000s
1. Golden Gate Nat. Rec. Area	16,656
2. Blue Ridge Parkway	16,176
3. Natchez Trace Parkway	10,838
4. Lake Mead NRA	8,495
5. Great Smoky Mts. Nat. Park	8,334
6. Gateway NRA	6,748
7. Acadia National Park	5,441
8. Independence Nat. Hist. Park	5,175
9. Cape Cod National Seashore	5,020
10. Grand Canyon	3,966

Source: National Park Service.

PORTS
Largest U.S. Ports

In the era of the jet and the tractor-trailer, it is easy to forget the role that maritime freight lanes (and their principle ports) played in this nations economic and social development. Our key ports were — and

PLACES

remain—direct and visceral links to other peoples, vessels and cultures, in a fashion which airports shall never usurp. Below are the busiest ports in the United States, in terms of the annual tonnage of shipping handled.

Port	Annual Tonnage
1. New Orleans	167,917
2. New York	154,536
3. Houston	112,546
4. Valdez Harbor, Alaska	106,867
5. Baton Rouge, La	73,401
6. Corpus Christi, Texas	53,539
7. Long Beach, California	45,898
8. Tampa Harbor, Fla	44,303
9. Los Angeles	40,460
10. Norfolk Harbor, Va	39,993

Source: Department of the Army, Corps of Engineers

STATES—ABORTION
Highest and Lowest Rates

Each year in the United States, about 1.6 million abortions are performed. Since abortions became legal with the *Roe v. Wade* decision of the Supreme Court, the number of abortions grew steadily from the early 1970s until 1980; since that time, the number has remained steady. Debate has raged across the country between opponents of the practice and those who support a woman's right to choose; many states, and the federal government more recently, have attempted to limit the availability of abortions by requiring teens to notify their parents, by restricting federally funded family planning clinics from offering abortion counseling, and even by threatening doctors with jail terms for performing abortions. The number of hospitals that offer abortion services has declined over the past decade, from 1,654 in 1977 to just 1,040 in 1988, a decline of 37 percent. The large majority of abortions now are performed in clinics. Below we have listed the states with the highest abortion rate per 1,000 women of child-bearing age. Differences between states are the result of a number of factors—including the availability of abortion services, minority populations, urbanization, and individual state policies on such issues as public funding for abortions for low-income services.

Top Ten	Abortion Rate
1. D.C.	163.3
2. California	45.9
3. New York	43.3
4. Hawaii	43.0
5. Nevada	40.3
6. Delaware	35.7
7. New Jersey	35.1
8. Florida	31.5
9. Connecticut	31.2
10. Rhode Island	30.6

Bottom Ten	Abortion Rate
1. Wyoming	5.1
2. South Dakota	5.7
3. West Virginia	7.5
4. Idaho	8.2
5. Mississippi	8.4
6. Arkansas	11.6
7. Indiana	11.9
8. Utah	12.8
9. Kentucky	13.0
10. Iowa	14.6

Source: "Abortion Services in the United States," Family Planning Perspectives, May/June 1990.

STATES—ABORTION
Least Available

Lack of available abortion services can prevent women who would otherwise choose to terminate a pregnancy from doing so. For instance, in Wyoming, which has the lowest abortion rate in the country, at 5.1 abortions per 1,000 women, more than half of all Wyoming women who choose to obtain an abortion travel out of state to do so. In fact, of the ten states with the lowest abortion rate, eight of them are in the top ten in the percentage of their female residents who receive abortions out of state. It's not hard

PLACES

to figure out that for many women, especially those with low incomes, the costs, both economic and emotional, of traveling out of state for an abortion have an effect on the choices they make. The following rating presents the states in which it is hardest to get an abortion, as measured by the percentage of residents who must travel outside the state to receive abortion services.

State	% Out-of-State Abortions
1. Wyoming	51.6
2. Kentucky	29.9
3. West Virginia	27.6
4. Mississippi	27.1
5. Maryland	26.6
6. Indiana	25.9
7. Arkansas	25.8
8. South Dakota	23.3
9. Missouri	20.6
10. Idaho	19.9

Source: Stanley K. Henshaw and Jennifer Van Vort, "Abortion Services in the United States," Family Planning Perspectives, May/June, 1990.

STATES — ALCOHOL USE

Most Arrests for Alcohol-Related Offenses

Sending an authoritative, chastening message to the America's habitual drunk drivers is a national priority. Overall, the U.S. has been slowing down, sobering up and getting smart. To secure our roads for our children and ourselves will be a test of our resolve in the coming decade. The following are the states where the crackdown is most severe, measured by the number of drinking-related arrests annually.

State	Arrests, 1987
1. California	612,213
2. Texas	385,457
3. New York	179,800
4. Pennsylvania	149,268
5. Illinois	134,710
6. Florida	126,995
7. Virginia	118,079
8. Michigan	113,793
9. Ohio	108,381
10. Wisconsin	79,657

Source: U.S. Department of Health and Human Services.

STATES — ARCHITECTS

Greatest Concentrations

Although the do-it-yourself spirit of middle-America is an indisputable national resource, one of the highest marks of a society's attainment is the concentration of architects and other professional design initiates, to lay the foundation for that civilization's expansion and perpetuation. Indeed, it is no surprise that our most populous and logistically involved settlements in California and New York afford the most opportunities for certified architects.

Top Ten	Architects per 10,000
1. California	6.2
2. New York	5.1
3. Texas	4.9
4. Illinois	4.2
5. Pennsylvania	3.6
6. Ohio	3.4
7. Florida	2.9
8. Michigan	2.8
9. New Jersey	2.7
10. Massachusetts	2.5

Bottom Ten	Architects per 10,000
1. Alaska	0.06
2. Oregon	0.08
3. Nevada	0.11
4. District of Columbia	0.18
5. South Dakota	0.2
6. North Dakota	0.3
7. Delaware	0.3
8. Vermont	0.4
9. Wyoming	0.7
10. Arizona	1.1

Source: U.S. Bureau of Labor Statistics.

PLACES

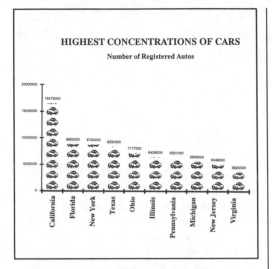

HIGHEST CONCENTRATIONS OF CARS

Number of Registered Autos

STATES — AUTOMOBILES

Highest Concentrations of Automobiles

America is a car-centered culture. Although many may bemoan this fact, none can credibly dispute it. Cars liberate us from regionalism, from tiresome, energy intensive jobs and from the company of our brothers on public transportation, but they also harness us with onerous financial burdens and vexing environmental side effects. The following are the top automotive states in the union, in terms of sheer numbers of registered automobiles.

State	Registered Cars
1. California	16,473,000
2. Florida	8,822,000
3. New York	8,764,000
4. Texas	8,330,000
5. Ohio	7,177,000
6. Illinois	6,428,000
7. Pennsylvania	6,331,000
8. Michigan	5,556,000
9. New Jersey	5.048,000
10. Virginia	3,623,000

Source: Department of Transportation, Federal Highway Administration.

STATES — AUTOMOBILES
Highest Automotive-Related Death Rates

Whatever their practical benefits, cars too often become the engines of accidental destruction in our high-speed world. Although any road comprises a potential hazard, the long, open stretches of our sparsely populated Western and Southern states have consistently proven to be our nation's most dangerous. Yes, those in the West enjoy their freedom, but that doesn't mean they're free to roam the roads with reckless abandon. The following are the states with the deadliest roadways, in number of deaths per 1,000 people per year attributed to automobiles.

State	Deaths/1,000 pop. annually
1. New Mexico	4.1
2. Mississippi	4.0
3. South Carolina	4.0
4. Arizona	3.9
5. West Virginia	3.6
6. Arkansas	3.5
7. Alabama	3.2
8. Idaho	3.3
9. Florida	3.2
10. Tennessee	3.2

Source: National Safety Council.

STATES — BANKRUPTCIES
Highest Occurrence of Business Failures

Entrepreneurship is a key component of the American character, and in sum, that trait underlies much of this nation's historical success in the world's financial arena. Inherent in the establishment of a commercial enterprise, however, is personal financial risk. Although the eighties were marked by economic recovery and growth, the high attrition rate among new businesses in the nineties is a harbinger of tougher times. These are the states where entrepreneurship has taken the biggest beating.

State	Failures/10,000 businesses
1. Colorado	248
2. Arizona	207
3. Alaska	200
4. Texas	188
5. Utah	165
6. Louisiana	156
7. Washington	141
8. California	138
9. Idaho	133
10. Nevada	132

Source: Dun and Bradstreet Corporation.

STATES — BEARS
Most Bearish States

The following figures for bear populations in the United States refer to the total numbers of bears on public, federally controlled lands, and include black, grizzly and brown bears. California, which used to count so many bears in its domain that it put the animal on its state flag, now holds less than 400 bears on its federal lands. Alaska, on the other hand, America's last great wilderness, still has a fairly healthy bear population. The bear is all but gone from the wild in East, except in specially protected areas of the Appalachians.

1. Alaska	8,700
2. Oregon	1,980
3. Colorado	1,243
4. Montana	650
5. Utah	503
6. Wyoming	433
7. California	385
8. Arizona	80
9. Eastern States	22

Source: Public Land Statistics, U.S. Dept. of the Interior.

STATES — BEER CONSUMPTION
Beer Bellies

Everyone likes a cold, frosty one now and again. But the folks in New Hampshire, it seems, get a little bit more than their fair

A grizzly at the McNeil River in Alaska, home to the largest grizzly population in the U.S. Photo by John Hyde, courtesy Alaska Dept. of Fish and Game.

share when it comes to the kegger. These New Englanders are no tee-totalers: the average New Hampshirite of legal drinking age socks away 52.4 gallons of the tasty malt beverage each year. That's more than 110 six-packs per annum, or about one every three days. At that rate, it better be less filling (we know it tastes great). In contrast, Utah, with its large, non-drinking Mormon population, guzzles at less than half that rate — fewer than 22 gallons per adult drinker per year.

Highest Beer Consumption	Gallons/Yr.
1. New Hampshire	52.4
2. Nevada	48.5
3. Wisconsin	46.7
4. Hawaii	45.0
5. Montana	43.3
6. Texas	42.2
7. New Mexico	42.0
8. Arizona	40.8

9. Alaska	40.3
10. Wyoming	40.0

Lowest Beer Consumption	Gallons/Yr.
1. Utah	21.6
2. Alabama	24.6
3. Arkansas	24.9
4. Oklahoma	25.6
5. Connecticut	26.6
6. Tennessee	26.6
7. North Carolina	26.7
8. Kentucky	27.1
9. West Virginia	27.7
10. Kansas	28.7

STATES – BIGHORN SHEEP

Largest Populations

The bighorn sheep was once prized by hunters for the impressive trophy it made. No longer. Bighorn populations are strictly protected in the last ranges they inhabit. This most impressive of American species is is found in greatest numbers in the sparsely populated areas of California, as well as in Alaska and Arizona. Smaller populations can be found in most other Western states. The list below gives state populations for bighorn sheep on federally owned land, and includes Rocky Mountain, Dall, California and Desert bighorn sheep.

State	Bighorn Sheep
1. California	3,205
2. Alaska	3,200
3. Arizona	3,095
4. Oregon	1,600
5. Colorado	1,559
6. Wyoming	1,214
7. Utah	1,065
8. Montana	1,000
9. New Mexico	80

Source: Public Land Statistics, U.S. Dept. of the Interior.

Dall rams in the Denali National Park in Alaska. California, Alaska and Arizona contain the most Bighorns in the U.S.

STATES – BLACK POPULATION
Highest Percentage African-American

Despite inequities and despair, the black populace has not abandoned the South. The highest concentrations of blacks, as a percentage of total population, still occur in the rural South. Although blacks have moved steadily toward the cities since the Second World War, much of that redistribution has been offset by differential birthrates.

State	% Black
1. Mississippi	36
2. South Carolina	31
3. Louisiana	30
4. Georgia	27
5. Alabama	26
6. Maryland	24
7. North Carolina	23
8. Virginia	19

PLACES

9. Delaware	17
10. Arkansas	17

Source: U.S. Census Bureau.

STATES — BOMBING INCIDENTS

Most Explosive States

In our violent society, shooting, stabbings, muggings and mutilations are everyday occurrences. To truly stand out, an act of mayhem must arrive with a bang. Despite the esoteric reputation of the bomb as a practical weapon of violence, the Bureau of Alcohol, Tobacco and Firearms reports thousands of bombings each year. These, then, are the most explosive states in the union, measured by annual number of bombing incidents. California may be the land of sun and surf, but it is also the state with the most incendiarists in the nation.

States	Bombing Incidents, 1987
1. California	183
2. Florida	77
3. Illinois	69
4. Texas	53
5. New York	48
6. Ohio	44
7. Michigan	37
8. Washington	32
9. Colorado	31
10. Virginia	30

Source: U.S. Bureau of Alcohol, Tobacco and Firearms

STATES — BOWLING

Most Female Bowlers

Although Americans love to watch baseball, football and basketball, when it comes time to actually participate in a sporting activity, millions turn to the oft-maligned, old, indoor standby, bowling. Although that sport has acquired a reputation as an after-work tension release for beer-toting good ole

Professional Women's Bowler Lisa Wagner sets the pace for women bowlers across the U.S. Photo courtesy the Bowler's Journal.

boys, in reality, it has achieved remarkable popularity with women. Last year, there were more than 4 million registered members of the Women's International Bowling Congress, belonging to more than 160,000 leagues nationwide. The following are the states with the most female bowlers.

States	Bowling Leagues
1. California	16,898
2. New York	12,564
3. Ohio	11,992
4. Michigan	10,734
5. Illinois	8,568
6. Wisconsin	8,418
7. Pennsylvania	7,097
8. Texas	6,950
9. Florida	6,252
10. New Jersey	4,970

Source: Women's International Bowling Congress

PLACES

STATES — CAPITAL PUNISHMENT
Most Executions

Capital punishment has always been an enormously emotional issue for politically aware Americans. On one hand, most citizens acknowledge the need to establish a strong and chilling deterrent against such heinous crimes as pre-meditated murder and kidnaping. On the other, our system is based around the presumption of innocence, the apportionment of mercy and the continuing possibility of redemption. Historically, each state, through its citizens, has grappled individually with these issues. Alaska, Hawaii, Maine, Michigan, Minnesota, North Dakota, Rhode Island and Wisconsin have never seen fit to take a life. Those states that have most frequently are listed below.

States	Executions since 1930
1. Georgia	378
2. New York	329
3. Texas	323
4. California	292
5. North Carolina	266
6. Florida	187
7. Ohio	172
8. South Carolina	164
9. Mississippi	157
10. Pennsylvania	152

Source: BJS Bulletin, Capital Punishment, 1987.

STATES — CHILD ABUSE
States of Abuse: Most Child Abuse Fatalaties

Child abuse is easy to condemn, but more difficult to curtail. In reality, not only do we disregard, neglect and traumatize our young — to a horrifying degree we have actually occasioned their demise. Here is the toll of these most atrocious of casualties, in the number of children killed through abuse, by state.

State	Child abuse fatalities, 1988
1. New York	198
2. Illinois	97
3. California	96
4. Texas	78
5. Pennsylvania	40
6. Louisiana	39
7. Missouri	28
8. Indiana	27
9. Colorado	26
10. Washington	26

Source: U.S. Dept. of Health and Human Services.

STATES — CHILDREN
Most Childish States

Miami Beach is world famous for its elderly population, just as Daytona Beach is famous for its youth-crazed Spring Breaks. Age, over the broad geography of this great nation, is a factor in all sorts of logistics and decisions. Size counts, weight counts, age counts — at their oldest, American retirement communities are indeed old, and at their youngest, college towns are exceedingly young. The state with the most school-age persons as a percent of the population is Utah, home of the friendly, fecund Mormons.

State	% of population of school age
1. Utah	26
2. Idaho	22
3. Mississippi	22
4. Wyoming	21
5. Louisiana	21

Source: U.S. Census Bureau.

STATES — CRIME
Highest Concentrations of Bank Defrauders/Embezzlers

In the past, the public has been lenient in its assessment of bunco artists, embezzlers and other white collar criminals. With the disastrous convergences of the savings and loan crisis now manifestly obvious to all, how-

PLACES

ever, the nation is taking a much dimmer and more punishing view of fiduciary pilferage. Here are the states with the highest incidences of embezzlement and bank fraud.

State	Investigations, 1987
1. California	2,277
2. Texas	1,069
3. Florida	820
4. New York	702
5. New Jersey	545
6. Georgia	544
7. Ohio	511
8. Pennsylvania	502
9. Illinois	435
10. Maryland	332

Source: F.B.I. Bank Crime Statistics

STATES — DEATH RATES
Highest Accidental Death Rates

Death is inevitable, but not on any particular occasion. Accidental death is, in principle, preventable. There are, however, regions of greater safety or graver safety. If your looking for the safest place to hide, try to avoid these scenic locales.

State	Accidental Deaths/100,000 pop.
1. New Mexico	35.1
2. South Carolina	31.7
3. Mississippi	30.9
4. Alabama	29.0
5. Montana	27.6
5. Arkansas	27.6
7. Arizona	27.2
8. Tennessee	26.7
9. West Virginia	26.5
10. Idaho	26.3

Source:U.S. National Center for Health Statistics

STATES — DEATH RATES
Highest Death Rates

One of the principle aims of any society is the prolongation of the pleasurable life-spans of its people. In contemporary America, the danger to life comes more often from accident, injury and criminal victimization than the ravages of disease. While we have solved many of the most insidious medical quandaries, it remains for us to so thoroughly address our social ills. Below are the states that suffer from the highest incidence of death per 1,000 persons annually. Washington, D.C. top spot on the list is due in no small part to its position as the murder, as well as the political, capital of the U.S.

State	Deaths /1,000 pop. annually
1. District of Columbia	13.8
2. Florida	10.7
3. Missouri	10.7
4. Pennsylvania	10.5
5. West Virginia	10.5
6. Rhode Island	10.0
7. Tennessee	10.0
8. Arkansas	9.8
9. New York	9.7
10. Nebraska	9.5

A mule deer buck at play in Wyoming. Photo courtesy Wyoming Travel Commission.

PLACES

Source: National Center for Health statistics

STATES — DEER AND ANTELOPE POPULATION

Where the Deer and the Antelope Play

"Oh give me a home where the buffalo roam, where the deer and the antelope play . . ." Well, in order to find this nirvana, you'd be best advised to head to Wyoming, where the combined deer and antelope populations on land controlled by the federal government totals nearly 370,000; in addition, Wyoming is home to the country's largest herd of buffalo, which resides in Yellowstone National Park. However, with Wyoming's struggling economy, we can't promise that you'll seldom hear a discouraging word; and for skies that are not cloudy all day, you might be better off in the desert Southwest.

State	Antelope	Deer	Total
1. Wyo.	172,852	196,938	369,790
2. Ore.	15,780	204,300	220,080
3. Colo.	12,510	199,307	211,817
4. Utah	12,550	190,000	202,550
5. Mont.	49,933	127,700	177,633
6. Calif.	6,210	101,000	107,210
7. N. Mex.	4,900	58,000	62,900
8. Ariz.	1,147	35,140	36,287

Source: Public Land Statistics, U.S. Dept. of the Interior.

STATES — DEFENSE INDUSTRY

Most Income from the Pentagon

Defense is big industry, but less so these days. With shrinking defense budgets, fewer soldiers in the field, and base closings all across the country, states must tighten their belts and come to rely less on the military Santa Claus that fueled much of the economic growth since the end of World

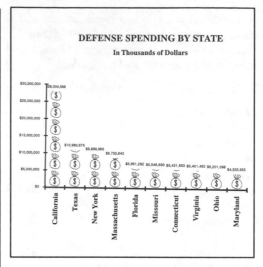

DEFENSE SPENDING BY STATE
In Thousands of Dollars

War II. California is perennially the biggest benefactor of the military-industrial complex, but with the relaxing of world tensions, it will be interesting to see if these states can turn their swords into plowshares.

Highest	DOD Dollars (000)
1. California	$28,004,588
2. Texas	$10,960,675
3. New York	$9,899,965
4. Massachusetts	$8,735,643
5. Florida	$5,661,292
6. Missouri	$5,546,590
7. Connecticut	$5,431,653
8. Virginia	$5,401,492
9. Ohio	$5,201,098
10. Maryland	$4,533,653

Lowest	
1. Montana	$62,040
2. Idaho	$62,670
3. Wyoming	$92,066
4. West Virginia	$103,441
5. Vermont	$123,646
6. South Dakota	$127,633
7. Nevada	$141,419
8. Delaware	$224,478
9. Nebraska	$225,595
10. North Dakota	$229,223

Source: *Congress and Defense.*

PLACES

STATES — DENTISTS
Highest and Lowest Concentrations

For many, the prospect of a visit to a dentist wakes dark visages of medieval dungeons and unutterable acts of torture and defilement. Nonetheless, the fast, easy availability of dental treatment is indeed a high-water mark for a community. Among our most orally conscious outposts, the data reveal, are the great Pilgrim encampments of the Eastern seaboard.

Highest	Dentists per 1,000
1. New York	7.4
2. Connecticut	7.3
3. Massachusetts	7.1
4. Oregon	6.9
5. Hawaii	6.8
6. Washington	6.8
7. New Jersey	6.6
8. Utah	6.4
9. California	6.3
10. Minnesota	6.2

Lowest	Dentists per 10,000
1. Mississippi	0.08
2. Arkansas	0.11
3. Alabama	0.18
4. South Carolina	0.2
5. Louisiana	0.3
6. West Virginia	0.3
7. New Mexico	0.4
8. Texas	0.7
9. Oklahoma	1.1

Source: Bureau of Labor Statistics.

STATES — DIVORCE
Highest Divorce Rates

In the second half of the twentieth century, we have witnessed the simultaneous erosions of the nuclear family and the environment. The once iron-clad institution of marriage has retained a fraction of its earlier stability. And in our nation, it is the clean, hot states of the West which have become the largest cauldrons for marital unrest, with Nevada and Arizona ranking first and second in divorces per capita.

State	Divorces per 1,000 population
1. Nevada	14.1
2. Arizona	7.1
3. Oklahoma	7.1
4. Arkansas	7.0
5. Alaska	6.9
5. Wyoming	6.9
7. Tennessee	6.5
8. Florida	6.3
9. Kansas	6.2
10. Idaho	6.0

Source: U.S. National Center for Health Statistics

STATES — EDUCATIONAL ATTAINMENT
Most Educated

What's the most high-brow state in the Union? The figures below list the percentage of adults in the state population with at least four years of college (this doesn't however, necessarily mean they *graduated*). Washington, D.C., is home to the highest concentration of lawyers in the United States; this, plus the large preponderance of government bureaucrats and relatively low number of blue-collar jobs in the nation's capital, helps account for its number one ranking among educated "states." Alaska is a surprising third — partially because with its high wages, even some college-educated people are willing to brave the cold climate and and the rigors of a blue collar job.

State	% pop. 4 or more years of college
1. District of Columbia	27.5
2. Colorado	23.0
3. Alaska	21.1
4. Connecticut	20.7
5. Maryland	20.4
6. Hawaii	20.3
7. Massachusetts	20.0
8. Utah	19.9
9. Virginia	19.1

PLACES

10. Washington	19.0
Vermont	19.0

Source: U.S. Bureau of the Census.

STATES — ELECTRICITY COSTS
The Biggest Charge

If one senses static in the air, it is not the result of an impending storm, but of friction. The American public is beyond weariness in its struggle against mounting utility prices. All over the nation, citizens and activists are banding together to check the excesses of the quasi-public service providers, and establish a safer, more affordable, equitable system. Here are the states in which citizens pay the most for basic electrical services, measured by the cost per million BTUs.

State	Price per Million BTU
1. Alaska	$26.38
2. New York	$25.09
3. New Jersey	$24.97
4. Connecticut	$24.55
5. New Hampshire	$24.24
6. Vermont	$23.73
7. California	$23.42
8. Rhode Island	$23.27
9. Massachusetts	$22.86
10. Hawaii	$22.52

Source: State Price and Expenditure Data System.

STATES — ELEVATION
Highest

With the "Mile High City", Denver, as its most visible, airily high symbol, Colorado is this nation's highest state. Denver, in fact, is low-lying by Colorado standards. With the other great states of the West, it provides a dramatic contrast to the adjacent plains of the Midwest.

State	Mean Elevation (Feet)
1. Colorado	6,800
2. Wyoming	6,700
3. Utah	6,100
4. New Mexico	5,700
5. Nevada	5,500
6. Idaho	5,000
7. Arizona	4,100
8. Montana	3,400
9. Hawaii	3,030
10. California	2,900

Source: Department of the Interior, U.S. Geological Survey.

Rocky Mountain High: Colorado is the highest state in the Union. Photo: Colo. Tourism Board.

STATES — ELKS
Largest Elk Population

Elks can be found all across the United States and even in such far-off U.S. possessions as Guam. The American elk population totals more than 1.5 million in 2,300 lodges around the country . . . no, wait, we're talking about real elk, not the kind with funny hats and ritualistic handshakes — *wild* elk (though if you've ever been to an Elks

PLACES

convention, you might say those guys get pretty wild, too). Below are the eight states with the largest four-legged elk populations on federally owned land. The largest single herd of elk in the U.S. can be found at the National Elk Refuge just outside of Jackson Hole, Wyoming.

State	Wild Elk
1. Colorado	47,009
2. Wyoming	28,709
3. Montana	20,000
4. Oregon	14,400
5. Utah	13,600
6. New Mexico	2,000
7. California	920
8. Arizona	20

Source: Public Land Statistics, U.S. Dept. of the Interior.

STATES—EMPLOYMENT
Employment Growth

Living in a boom town does not guarantee personal prosperity, but it certainly can be a help. And, no matter what one's personal abilities and credentials, blood does not flow freely from a stone, and jobs can not be gotten where none are given. Thus, it makes some certain sense to place oneself squarely in the path of opportunity. Try these 'stately' locales, which enjoyed the greatest job growth through the 1980s.

State	% Growth 1987-89
1. Nevada	17.1
2. Idaho	11.1
3. Washington	10.5
4. Hawaii	8.8
5. Oregon	8.7
6. Utah	8.7
7. Florida	8.4
8. Alaska	8.4
9. Maine	7.5
10. South Carolina	7.4

Source: Bureau of Labor Statistics

A herd of elk in Grand Teton National Park. Photo courtesy Wyoming Travel Commission.

PLACES

STATES — ENERGY CONSUMPTION
Biggest Energy Hogs

Despite our mounting interests in the environment and conservation, America still survives by glutting itself on irreplaceable fossil fuels. In the end, our consumption is understandable, but questionably forgivable and ultimately unworkable. The individual states, and the Federal government, must work to refine and deploy alternative fuels and more efficient products and conservation schemes.

State	Energy Expenditures Per Capita
1. Alaska	$2,840
2. Wyoming	$2,756
3. Louisiana	$2,569
4. Texas	$2,157
5. North Dakota	$2,136
6. Indiana	$1,988
7. Kansas	$1,933
8. Delaware	$1,853
9. Maine	$1,828
10. New Jersey	$1,813

Source: State Price and Expenditure Data System.

STATES — FARMING
Most Farm Acreage

Although Americans were quick in their history to build lasting and expansive settlements, the early epochs of this nation were marked by its extraordinary utilization of its land resources, and concomitant hegemony in world agriculture. Today, a relatively tiny percentage of our nation's acreage remains under cultivation, yet our productivity remains unrivaled. This development has come apace with the introduction of high-technological means to common farming (whose side-effect is the displacement of the venerable citizen-farmer).

State	Rural Acreage (Millions)
1. Texas	132
2. Montana	61
3. Kansas	48
4. Nebraska	47
5. New Mexico	45
6. South Dakota	44
7. Arizona	37
8. Wyoming	35
9. Iowa	34
10. Colorado	34

Source: USDA Crop Production.

STATES — FARMING
Greatest Farm Income

While America's fledgling hi-tech industries garner world attention, straightforward agricultural cultivation remains an unspoken but critical component of our economy. Although we traditionally associate farming with the rural expanses of the Great Plains, populous, temperate states like Washington, California and Florida are also extremely important contributors to our national agricultural output.

State	Farm Income (Millions)
1. California	$4,235
2. Texas	$2,350
3. Iowa	$2,330
4. Florida	$1,773
5. Nebraska	$1,670
6. Minnesota	$1,561
7. Wisconsin	$1,477
8. Kansas	$1,475
9. Illinois	$1,212
10. Washington	$1,196

Source: Census Bureau.

STATES — FORECLOSURES
Highest Percentage of Foreclosed Mortgages

To many, the loss of a family home is an archetypal symbol of failure and disaster. In these recessionary times, unfortunately, the relinquishing of one's home through bank foreclosure is a very real possibility. In the last calendar year, nearly one in eight new mortgages were foreclosed on. The states with the most foreclosures are also those with some of the fastest-growing populations, so as soon as a house is emptied, it is immediately reoccupied.

State	Percentage of Foreclosures
1. Arizona	12.85
2. Texas	11.57
3. Alaska	8.36
4. Wyoming	8.34
5. Colorado	7.72
6. Oklahoma	6.63
7. Arkansas	5.70
8. Louisiana	5.63
9. New Mexico	5.41
10. Mississippi	3.43

Source: U.S. Office of Economic Analysis

STATES—FOREIGN OWNERSHIP
Highest Concentrations of U.S. Employees of Foreign-Based Corporations

Everyone decries the transfer of critical U.S. commercial assets into foreign hands, but few are aware of the positive contributions many foreign companies make to our economy through the establishment of domestic subsidiaries. Though the Japanese and their Asian neighbors may take American jobs as they incrementally increase the share of the domestic durable goods markets, they return many of these jobs by establishing U.S. plants to manufacture those very goods. Below are the states in which the highest percentage of workers are in the ultimate employ of a foreign corporation.

State	1,000's of Employees
1. California	324.2
2. New York	300.1
3. Texas	207.6
4. New Jersey	169.3
5. Pennsylvania	168.5
6. Illinois	166.1
7. North Carolina	132.9

8. Ohio	132.2
9. Georgia	117.7
10. Florida	116.8

Source: U.S. Bureau of Economic Analysis.

STATES—FORESTS
Greenest States

This nation may be heading inevitably toward urban blight, but there are still plenty of forests that must be put asunder first. Georgia, the nation's woodiest state, boasts nearly twenty four million acres of forested land. Even industrial New York still maintains almost nineteen million wild acres. Here, then, are America's woodland empires.

State	Timberland (thousands of acres)
1. Georgia	23,907
2. Montana	21,190
3. Idaho	21,818
4. Alabama	21,725
5. Colorado	21,338
6. North Carolina	18,891
7. New York	18,775
8. New Mexico	18,526
9. Michigan	18,220
10. Maine	17,713

Source: U.S. Forest Service

STATES—GASOLINE COSTS
Most Expensive Gasoline

There are uncountable injustices in the world, but few things irk the consumer more than jacked-up prices at the gas pump. Although the last decade has seen a broad roll-back in retail petroleum prices, hostilities in the Persian Gulf in 1991 hyped prices sufficiently to renew consumer gas anxieties for a long time to come. Below are the states in which gasoline, the lifeline of our country, is most dear.

State	Price per Million Btu
1. Hawaii	$9.55
2. Connecticut	$8.91

3. Washington, D.C.	$8.80
4. Rhode Island	$8.40
5. Maryland	$8.18
6. Maine	$8.15
7. Alaska	$8.14
8. Delaware	$8.07
9. North Dakota	$8.05
10. Massachusetts	$7.90

Source: State Price and Expenditure Data System 1988

STATES — GIRL SCOUT POPULATION
Most Girl Scouts

Nearly 2,500,000 girls across the country are members of the Girl Scouts; another 800,000 adults are members. One in every nine girls ages 5 to 17, one in every four girls ages 6 to 8 and one in seven girls ages 9 to 11 is a Scout. Fourteen percent of girl and adult members are minorities. The following are the states with the highest populations of Girl Scouts.

State	Girl Scouts
1. California	205,859
2. New York	168,051
3. Pennsylvania	148,686
4. Illinois	146,123
5. Ohio	144,006
6. Texas	140,508
7. Michigan	110,672
8. Florida	89,987
9. New Jersey	89,196
10. Missouri	82,283

Source: Girl Scouts of the United States of America.

STATES — GOVERNMENT SPENDING
Highest Expenditures by State and Local Goverments

Everyone likes to be pampered. When that special treatment comes from usually menacing authority figures like the elective agents of Uncle Sam, it is a double treat.

Alaska leads the nation in its expenditures per capita. This is — at once — a function of the vast natural wealth and small population of that frigid state, and the high cost of providing basic services in so forbidding a climate.

State	$ Spent Per Capita (yr.)
1. Alaska	$9,956
2. Wyoming	$4,424
3. New York	$3,900
4. Minnesota	$3,281
5. California	$3,085
6. New Jersey	$3,034
7. Massachusetts	$2,993
8. Delaware	$2,990
9. Connecticut	$2,925
10. Michigan	$2,898

Source: Statistical Abstract of the United States.

STATES — GRADUATION RATES
Best and Worst Graduation Rates

Not so many years ago, a high school diploma was an invaluable possession, which separated the diligent and employable from the unkempt masses. Just decades later, the value of that degree has eroded enormously, as an undergraduate university education has become the minimum prerequisite for even relatively low-brow positions. This devaluation, however, has made the completion of a high school program all the more critical, because of the tremendous stigma and difficulties the high school dropout faces in the job market.

Highest	H.S. Graduation Rate (%)
1. Minnesota	91.4
2. Connecticut	89.8
3. North Dakota	89.7
4. Nebraska	88.1
5. Iowa	87.5
6. Montana	87.2
7. Wisconsin	86.3
8. South Dakota	81.5

Kansas	81.5
10. Wyoming	81.2

Lowest	H.S. Graduation Rate (%)
1. District of Columbia	56.8
2. Florida	62.0
3. Louisiana	62.7
4. Georgia	62.7
5. Arizona	63.0
6. Mississippi	63.3
7. New York	64.2
8. Texas	64.3
9. South Carolina	64.5
10. Nevada	65.2

Source: U.S. Department of Education, Office of Planning, Budget and Evaluation.

STATES — HEALTH CARE

Cost of Hospital Care

Medical mishaps are invariably traumatic, but for the uninsured, even the smallest health crisis represents a financial nightmare. Simply put, the cost of contemporary health care has become completely daunting and unmanageable for most, and actually out of reach for the less than well-off. The 1990s may well witness a popular referendum for the creation of some sort national health insurance collective. Below are the states in which illness hits the pocket-book the hardest.

State	Overnight charge, semi-private rm.
1. Connecticut	$396
2. California	391
4. Alaska	378
5. Delaware	350
6. Vermont	328
7. D.C.	325
8. Pennsylvania	318
9. Oregon	301
9. New York	301

Source: National Center for Health Statistics

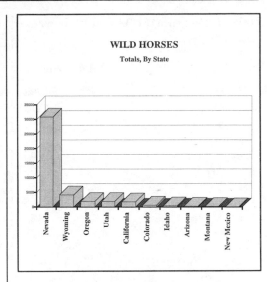

WILD HORSES
Totals, By State

STATES — HORSES

Wild Horse Populations

The Spaniards first brought horses to the New World nearly five centuries ago; before that time, they were unknown to peoples who inhabited North and South America. Eventually, though, the horse became an integral part of the lives of both the Native American population and the Europeans who sought dominion over the new-found land. Inevitably, some of those horses broke free of their domesticity and returned to the wild. The vestiges of these horses are still to be found roaming the vast open spaces of the American West, and you can own one. Like most other creatures in the wild, the 41,774 horses and burros roaming free on public land need protection to maintain a healthy ecological balance; therefore, the Bureau of Land Management maintains an adoption program for wild horses and burros, and has placed more than 96,000 animals with private individuals since the program began (and the BLM has recently instituted stricter adoption policies to prevent the commercial exploitation of adopted equines). The following list represents the states where horses truly roam free on public lands. Wild burros in the U.S. are most numerous in Arizona, where they number

PLACES

2,075, California (1,333) and Nevada (1,269).

State	Wild Horses
1. Nevada	30,798
2. Wyoming	4,115
3. Oregon	1,891
4. Utah	1,884
5. California	1,745
6. Colorado	605
7. Idaho	354
8. Arizona	225
9. Montana	128
10. Oregon	29

Source: Public Land Statistics, U.S. Dept. of the Interior.

STATES—INCOME

Highest and Lowest Per Capita Income

Per capita income varies greatly across the United States. As the table below shows, people in Connecticut enjoy more than twice the personal income of their counterparts in Mississippi. Cost of living alone cannot explain the differential. The high income levels in Connecticut and New Jersey no doubt are helped by their vicinity to the financial and legal centers in New York. The rural South and the Great Plains, on the other hand, suffer from their reliance on low-intensity economic forces such as farming.

Top	Per Cap. Personal Income
1. Connecticut	$18,521
2. New Jersey	$17,666
3. Dist. of Columbia	$17,180
4. Massachusetts	$16,720
5. Maryland	$15,652
6. New Hampshire	$15,610
7. New York	$15,506
8. Alaska	$15,324
9. California	$15,063
10. Virginia	$14,197

Lowest	Per Cap. Personal Income
1. Mississippi	$8,929
2. West Virginia	$9,426
3. Utah	$9,794
4. Arkansas	$9,814
5. Louisiana	$9,973
6. New Mexico	$10,031
7. Idaho	$10,173
8. South Dakota	$10,245
9. Kentucky	$10,299
10. North Dakota	$10,308

Source: Statistical Abstract of the United States, 1990. U.S. Bureau of Economic Analysis, *Survey of Current Business*, August issues, and unpublished data.

STATES—INFANT MORTALITY

Highest Rates

The loss of a child is the most terrible of familial tragedies. Despite advances in medicine, the possibility of miscarriage, deformity or still birth is very real in our society. Most disturbing are the disproportionately higher rates of infant mortality among disadvantaged populations. The following states suffer the highest infant mortality rates in the nation.

State	Deaths/1,000 live births
1. Mississippi	13.7
2. South Carolina	12.7
3. Georgia	12.7
4. Alabama	12.2
5. North Carolina	11.9
6. Louisiana	11.8
7. Delaware	11.7
7. Tennessee	11.7
9. Illinois	11.6
10. Maryland	11.5

Source: U.S. National Center for Health Statistics

170

PLACES

STATES—JUVENILE DELINQUENCY
Greatest Concentrations of Teen Troublemakers

Adolescence poses great discomfort and difficulty for teens, parents and society at large. Generally, these difficulties are fleeting, although they may not appear so at the time. Too often in our fragmented era, however, adolescent pranksterism proves to be a dark portent of twisted, pathological deeds in our "children's" future. Kids are turning to crime at a much earlier age and at a most alarming rate in many states of the Union. Listed below are the states where juveniles start their rap sheets earliest and in greatest numbers, measured by the number of juveniles incarcerated per 100,000 under lock-and-key.

State	Juveniles/100,0000 prisoners
1. District of Columbia	991
2. California	649
3. Nevada	631
5. Alaska	610
6. Kansas	566
7. South Dakota	557
8. Nebraska	555
9. Pennsylvania	438
10. Oregon	422

Source: U.S. Department of Justice.

STATES—LAND OWNERSHIP
Land Owned by Federal Government

Of the 2,271,343,360 acres in the United States, the federal government owns a whopping 30%, making it by far the biggest landowner in the country. More than four-fifths of the land in Alaska is under federal control, compared to less than one percent of the land in Iowa. The vast majority of federally owned land is used for national parks, forests and wilderness areas, as well as for military use. The government even makes money in some unexpected ways from its land—for instance, many of the ski resorts in Colorado are located in national forests and are leased from the government by the resort owners. Below are the states where Uncle Sam is the biggest landlord, and, contrarily, where his presence is least felt.

Top Ten	Percent Owned by U.S.
1. Alaska	81.054
2. Nevada	78.859
3. Idaho	60.632
4. Utah	60.034
5. Oregon	52.292
6. Wyoming	46.526
7. Arizona	44.518
8. California	44.468
9. New Mexico	33.107
10. Colorado	29.753

Bottom Ten	
1. Iowa	0.444
2. Rhode Island	0.670
3. Maine	0.769
4. New York	0.781
5. Nebraska	1.068
6. Ohio	1.260
7. Kansas	1.313
8. Illinois	1.383
9. Connecticut	1.444
10. Texas	1.608

Source: Public Land Statistics, U.S. Dept. of the Interior.

STATES—LEGAL SYSTEMS
Best and Worst Legal Systems

Most of us only need a lawyer to perform very basic civil functions, rather than represent us in big criminal trials. And almost everyone who has dealt with the legal system comes away frustrated to one degree or another. How well does the legal system in the U.S. serve the public? Not very, according to HALT, a legal reform group in Washington, D.C. HALT evaluated legal services in all 50 states and the District of Columbia in three areas—the availability of simplified, do-it-yourself laws, access to legal service providers, and lawyer-client relations. HALT issued points for the answers to questions in the three groups: in the first, it asked if consumer and insurance contracts were required to be written in plain English, if fill-in-the-blank statutory wills were available, if the process of registering title to land was simplified, if the small claims process was streamlined, and if a small corporation needed a lawyer for small claims court; in the second category, HALT asked if the state allowed people to hire paralegals for simple legal advice, if legal services programs for the poor are funded by interest on lawyer-held trust accounts, and if the state funds legal services for the poor; in the last category, on lawyer-client relations, HALT asked if written lawyer-client fee agreements are required, if there is exists a statewide program for lawyer-client fee arbitration, and if a client can learn a lawyer's disciplinary record.

The highest possible score on the report card was 100; the actual scores ranged from a high of 74 in California to a low of 25 in Mississippi, Nebraska and Wyoming. As HALT points out, the showing was poor overall — only two states earned a "C," and a total of only seven received what HALT called "passing" grades — scores of 60 or more. The conclusion drawn is that the American legal system, for all its talk of equal justice for all, is difficult for the average citizen to understand, does not provide equal access to legal services regardless of economic status, and seems to exist more for the benefit of the lawyer than for the legal consumer.

Worst	Score
1. Mississippi	25
Nebraska	25
Wyoming	25
2. Alabama	27
3. Louisiana	30
Pennsylvania	30
4. Arkansas	31
South Dakota	31
Tennessee	31
5. Kentucky	32
6. South Carolina	34
7. West Virginia	35
8. Iowa	36
9. New Mexico	37
10. Indiana	39

Best	Score
1. California	74
2. Washington	71
3. Minnesota	67
4. Massachusetts	63
Michigan	63
Oregon	63
5. Hawaii	61
6. Colorado	58
7. Florida	57
Maine	57
Wisconsin	57
North Carolina	57
8. New Jersey	56
Connecticut	56
9. New York	52
10. Montana	51

Source: HALT: An Organization for Legal Reform, Washington, D.C.

STATES — LIFE EXPECTANCY
Longest Average Lifespans

Although all states in our great nation are equal under constitutional doctrine, some are more equal than others. And while it is a truism that a luxurious, complete life can be carved out in any corner of the Union, it is likewise true that the average life is longer and easier to attain in some corners than others. Hawaii, constitutionally the youngest of the states, leads the nation in longevity. The remarkable durability of its population is at once a function of the nurturing climate of the islands, and of the attraction that those islands inherently hold for retirement-aged expatriates of other states and nations.

PLACES

State	Average Lifespan
1. Hawaii	78.80
2. Minnesota	76.82
3. Iowa	75.81
4. Utah	75.76
5. Nevada	75.71
6. Nebraska	75.49
7. Wisconsin	75.35
8. Kansas	75.31
9. Colorado	75.30
10. Idaho	75.19

Source: National Center for Health Statistics

STATES — LITIGATION
Best States In Which To Sue

The quality of mercy is never strained, but it often differs from place to place. The history of civil adjudication in a given state is always the best indication of the disposition of any new case. In states in which civil judges have awarded large sums to plaintiffs with similar ailments and allied complaints, judges will make similar awards to similar plaintiffs. In terms of potential profits from litigation, New York leads the land. Here are the best states in which to earn a cool million on a personal slight or a physical malady caused by someone else.

State	$1 million awards, 1962-89
1. New York	707
2. California	540
3. Florida	504
4. Texas	320
5. Illinois	216
6. Michigan	202
7. Pennsylvania	177
8. Ohio	100
9. Missouri	96
10. New Jersey	86

Source: The Lawyer's Almanac.

STATES — LOTTERY
Lotto Fools: Most Spending on Lotto

People in Massachusetts know a good investment when they see it. Their state lotto game pays off a whopping 59 cents for every dollar spent—the best payout of any state lottery. Perhaps that's why the good folks of Massachusetts spend more per capita on the lotto than any other people in America. Just think: the average Bay Stater will earn back nearly $139 of his $235 lotto outlay every year, losing just a little over 40% of what he spends. People get up in arms over any tax increase, but will gladly pay out 40 percent for the 9.4 million to 1 chance of hitting the big jackpot. Listed below are the states with the most annual spending on those elusive numerical combinations.

States	Per Capita Lotto Spending
1. Massachusetts	$235
2. D.C.	$197
3. Maryland	$185
4. Connecticut	$162
5. New Jersey	$155
6. Michigan	$132
7. Ohio	$128
8. Pennsylvania	$121
9. Illinois	$113
10. Delaware	$ 89

Source: *Gaming & Wagering Business*.

PLACES

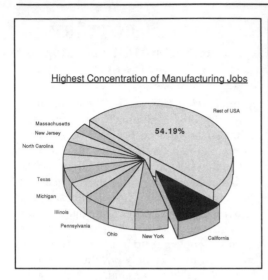

Highest Concentration of Manufacturing Jobs

Rest of USA
54.19%
Massachusetts
New Jersey
North Carolina
Texas
Michigan
Illinois
Pennsylvania
Ohio
New York
California

STATES — MANUFACTURING

Highest Concentrations of Manufacturing Jobs

The presence of industry in the modern era in a mixed blessing. Few communities can resist the lure of ready jobs for their restless populations, but fewer still can gracefully absorb the impact of environmental contamination and resource depletion. In America, unsurprisingly, the bulk of manufacturing jobs are centralized in regions of high population.

State	% of Total U.S. Mfg. Jobs
1. California	10.74
2. New York	6.90
3. Ohio	5.92
4. Pennsylvania	5.67
5. Illinois	5.38
6. Michigan	5.13
7. Texas	4.94
8. North Carolina	4.37
9. New Jersey	3.70
10. Massachusetts	3.35

Source: Census Bureau.

STATE — MARIJUANA
Softest Marijuana Laws

Most states recognize the relative harmlessness of small amounts of marijuana for personal consumption; according to Kitty Kelley, even the Reagans couldn't just say no — Kelley claims the Reagans sparked up at a dinner in while Ron was governor of California in the late 1960s (one alleged debilitating affect of marijuana is loss of memory; perhaps this one toke accounts for Reagan's lack of "total recall" concerning the Machiavellian machinations of the Iran-Contra crowd). In many regions of the country, possession of less than an ounce will get you just a fine, as long as you're not in the midst of some other illegal activity or driving. In Alaska, in fact, marijuana has been legal for personal use, although a recent referendum puts that liberty in question. On the other hand, don't get caught lighting up in Iowa or Kansas, where possession of any amount of pot, no matter how small, can lead to a jail sentence of from six months to a year and a fine of up to $2,500. The ten states below have what the editors consider to be the most lax marijuana statutes. We considered a fine to be less harsh than a jail sentence, and states that made distinctions between private or public use harsher than ones that did not.

Top Ten

1. **Alaska**
   Legal for personal use in home; personal use not in home: $0-100.

2. **Ohio**
   Possession of up to 100 grams: $0-100.

3. **Oregon**
   Possession of up to 1 oz.: $0-100; over 1 oz.: 0-10 years and $2,500.

4. **California**
   Possession of up to 1 oz.: $0-100; over 1 oz.: 0-6 months and $500.

5. **Minnesota**
   Up to 1 oz. not in vehicle: $0-100.

PLACES

6. Maine
Possession of up to 1.5 oz.: $0-200.

7. Colorado
Possession of up to 1 oz. in private: $0-100; in public: 0-15 days and $100.

8. Nebraska
Possession of up to 1 oz.: $100 and drug ed.

9. New Mexico
Possession of up to 1 oz.: 0-15 days and $100.

10. South Dakota
Possession of up to 1 oz.: 0-30 days and $100; over 1 oz. 0-1 yr. and $1000.

Source: National Organization for the Reform of Marijuana Laws.

STATES — MILITARY PERSONNEL
Highest Concentrations of Soldiery

The minions of our peacetime Army—and of its somewhat-civilianized sub-chapters, the National Guard and the Coast Guard— are scattered equitably throughout our great and broad land. In greatest numbers, they have followed the sun—to populous land rich states like California and Texas, and to sun bleached U.S. utopias like Hawaii and Florida, though most grunts rarely get the chance to sample the luxuries of their paradisiacal surroundings.

State	Military Personnel (000)
1. California	206.5
2. Texas	135.1
3. Virginia	100.0
4. North Carolina	94.8
5. Florida	75.7
6. Georgia	62.9
7. Hawaii	45.4
8. South Carolina	44.6
9. Washington	43.3
10. Colorado	42.7

Source: U.S. Bureau of the Census, Statistical Abstract of the U.S.

STATES — MINORITIES
Minority College Enrollment

Minority Americans have made substantial educational strides through the good offices of such organizations as the United Negro College Fund and through minority scholarship and assistance programs offered by federal and state governments. Whether such assistance will be permitted to continue, however, is in question, as the Bush administration challenges such assistance as discriminatory. Below are the states where minorities make up the highest percentage of college students.

State	% Minority enrollment, 1988
1. D.C.	94.6
2. Hawaii	70.9
3. California	33.0
4. Mississippi	31.1
5. New Mexico	30.7
6. New York	29.2
7. Louisiana	27.0
8. Maryland	25.1
9. Texas	25.1
10. New Jersey	20.6

Source: U.S. Dept. of Education.

STATES — MOBILE HOMES
Highest Concentrations of Mobile Homes

With skyrocketing property taxes, unworkably high mortgage rates and the dras-

Home, home on the road. Wyomingites take their houses with them when they move.

PLACES

tic costs of construction, mobile homes have become an increasingly popular alternative to conventional housing. In the rugged, open regions of the West, nearly one out of every five permanent residential structures is (in principle) mobile. But why are such residences always placed squarely in the path of tornadoes?

State	% of mobile residences
1. Wyoming	18.8
2. Montana	13.6
3. New Mexico	12.6
4. Arizona	12.1
5. Nevada	12.1
6. Alaska	10.5
7. West Virginia	10.5
8. Idaho	10.2
9. South Carolina	9.9
10. North Carolina	9.7

Source: Census Bureau

STATES — NATURAL GAS COSTS
Highest and Lowest

While our camel-loving comrades to the east control much of the world's free oil reserves, the United States boasts equally-impressive reserves of natural gas. Although transport and exploration pose major expenses in this industry, it behooves our nation to refine and develop this underexploited energy resource. In fact, natural gas prices have been falling over the past several years, to their lowest point in decades, due to the uncommonly mild winters with which the nation has been blessed for the past five years or so. The following are the states with the highest and lowest natural gas prices in the country.

Highest	Price per Million BTU
1. Hawaii	$11.52
2. Connecticut	$6.04
3. District of Columbia	$6.00
4. Rhode Island	$5.94
5. Maine	$5.64
6. New Hampshire	$5.50
7. Massachusetts	$5.46
8. New York	$5.09
9. New Jersey	$4.97
10. Maryland	$4.92

Lowest	Price Per Million BTU
1. Alaska	1.70
2. Louisiana	2.14
3. Texas	2.44
4. Oklahoma	2.80
5. Florida	2.80
6. Kansas	3.03
7. Mississippi	3.19
8. Arkansas	3.43
9. New Mexico	3.44
10. Tennessee	3.75

Source: State Price and Expenditure Data System.

STATES — PAROLEES
Thy Brothers' Keepers:
Most Citizens On Parole

As jails become more and more overcrowded, many states have no other recourse to alleviate the problem than to ease the process of parole, freeing criminals before their full sentence in order to free up prison space for new batches of convicts. This can create problems of recidivism; in addition, respect for the criminal justice system is lessened on the part of both the convict and the public in general; finally, many in the public wonder if the courts and the prison systems are taking their role seriously. Indeed, George Bush scored big points in the 1988 Presidential campaign with an ad that depicted the prison system as a revolving door. These are the states where the door spins the fastest — those with the most parolees per 100,000 members of the population.

State	Parolees per 100,000 persons
1. D.C.	789
2. Texas	570
3. Pennsylvania	423
4. Washington	310

5. New Jersey	269
6. Tennessee	257
7. Georgia	243
8. Maryland	236
9. Louisiana	230

Source: "Probation and Parole," U.S. Department of Justice.

STATES—POLLUTION
Most Toxic

According to the third annual Toxic Release Inventory conducted by the U.S. Environmental Protection Agency, the situation in the U.S. in terms of hazardous waste emissions is steadily improving. The most recent inventory notes that the amount of toxic emissions in 1989 was 1.3 billion pounds less than the 1987 release and 723 million pounds less than the figures for 1988. Environmentalists, however, dispute the figures, noting that three of the most prevalent industrial toxins—phosphoric acid, sulfuric acid and ammonium sulfate—have been withdrawn from scrutiny by the EPA; furthermore, some of the biggest polluting industries, including agriculture, mining, utilities and waste incineration, not to mention the Government's nuclear and munitions plants, are exempt from reporting. In any event, Texas and Louisiana continue to lead the nation in the amount of hazardous waste released into the environment. The following are the ten biggest state culprits in toxic waste emissions, as measured by the total amount of more than 300 types of toxic chemicals released into the air, water and land in 1989, in millions of pounds.

State	Toxic Waste (millions lbs.)
1. Texas	792.8
2. Louisiana	473.5
3. Ohio	358.7
4. Tennessee	264.3
5. Indiana	255.0
6. Illinois	248.0
7. Michigan	220.1
8. Pennsylvania	194.2

9. Florida	192.0
10. Kansas	185.1

Source: Environmental Protection Agency.

STATES—POPULATION
Largest Population and Most Seats in U.S. House

The shift in the population of the United States away from the Northeast and Midwest and toward the South and West means a shift in political power as well. Representation in the U.S. House of Representatives is determined the official census numbers, taken every ten years. The 1990 census confirms that shift of population and power. In all, a total of 19 seats in the U.S. House of Representatives will be shifted as a result of the 1990 census. Eight states will increase their representation in the 103rd Congress, which will convene in January 1993; all of those states are in the South or West. California will gain seven seats for a total of 52, Florida will gain four seats to 23, and Texas will gain three seats for a total of 30. Arizona (6), Georgia (11), North Carolina (12), Virginia (11), and Washington (9) each gain one seat. On the other hand, thirteen states will have less representation in the 103rd Congress. New York (31) will lose three seats. Illinois (20), Michigan (16), Ohio (19), and Pennsylvania (21) will each lose two seats. Iowa (5), Kansas (4), Kentucky (6), Louisiana (7), Massachusetts (10), Montana (1), New Jersey (13), and West Virginia (3) each will lose one seat.

The table below lists the official 1990 census population for the United States and the number of representatives each state will be entitled to elect to the 103rd Congress, which is scheduled to commence in January, 1993.

State	1990 Pop.	Seats
1. California	29,839,250	52
2. New York	18,044,505	31
3. Texas	17,059,805	30

PLACES

4. Florida	13,003,362	23
5. Pennsylvania	11,924,710	21
6. Illinois	11,466,682	20
7. Ohio	10,887,325	19
8. Michigan	9,328,784	16
9. New Jersey	7,748,634	13
10. North Carolina	6,657,630	12

Source: U.S. Bureau of the Census.

STATES – POPULATION GROWTH

Fastest Growing and Declining

Population growth is a symbol of where the country's populace is placing its confidence, either by procreating or by moving. In the ten years of the go-go eighties, from 1980 to 1990, Nevada, home of sun and sin, saw its population increase by more than fifty percent; in West Virginia, on the other hand, the population dropped by more than eight percent in that period, evidence of that state's flagging economic fortunes and aging population. But it remains to be seen just how much growth such places as Nevada, Arizona, California, Texas and Florida can support before their resources are tapped out. Water rights, air pollution, traffic congestion, waste disposal and destruction of the environment are the collateral costs of population growth, and the Sun Belt states that are filling up with people are also homes to some of our most pristine wilderness areas, from the Florida Everglades to the Sierras in California.

Highest	Change, 1980-90
1. Nevada	50.38%
2. Alaska	37.35%
3. Arizona	34.86%
4. Florida	32.83%
5. California	25.74%
6. New Hampshire	20.49%
7. Texas	19.38%
8. Georgia	18.56%
9. Utah	17.92%

Sun, sin and a booming economy are drawing Americans to Nevada in huge numbers.

PLACES

10. Washington	17.83%
Lowest	**Change, 1980-90**
1. West Virginia -	8.01%
2. D.C.	-4.82%
3. Iowa	-4.69%
4. Wyoming	-3.66%
5. North Dakota	-2.13%
6. Illinois	+0.11%
7. Louisiana	+0.38%
8. Michigan	+0.40%
9. Pennsylvania	+0.46%
10. Nebraska	+0.53%

Source: U.S. Census Bureau.

STATES — PRISON POPULATION

Largest Inmate Populations

The incidence of serious crime in this nation is an epic problem in itself, but the handling, supervision and rehabilitation of the perpetrators of these crimes creates a second, multi-dimensional crisis. Our courts and prisons are crowded to the bursting point. Simplistic quick fixes are not available. Resolution can only come through substantive social reform. The following are the states where the prison population is most numerous.

State	Prison population
1. California	32,607
2. Texas	31,274
3. New York	28,056
4. Florida	21,180
5. Illinois	13,951
6. Ohio	13,756
7. North Carolina	13,518
8. Michigan	11,798
9. Pennsylvania	10,785
10. Maryland	10,621

Source: Population Density in State Prisons, Dept. of Justice.

STATES — PRISON POPULATION

Most Prisoners on Death Row

Capital punishment has always presented an agonizing dilemma in our republic. In our era, the decision to take a life is vested in the governments of the individual states. In all, thousands of men await the final dispensation of their God and their governor, in the nations gallows, gas chambers and lethal-injection rooms.

State	# of prisoners
1. Florida	290
2. Texas	287
3. California	241
4. Illinois	120
5. Pennsylvania	115
6. Oklahoma	98
7. Alabama	94
8. Ohio	88
9. Arizona	84
10. North Carolina	82

Source: Sourcebook of Justice Statistics.

STATES — PRISONS

Least Secure Prison Systems

In the safe confines of a cinema or living room, dramatized prison breaks are exciting, entertaining and triumphant affairs. In reality, however, they represent the return of desperate, dangerous, corrosive elements to real communities. The overcrowding and underbudgeting of the American correctional system contributes to the alarming incidence of prison escapism. Here are the leakiest prison systems in the country, as measured by the number of escapes in a single year.

State	1987 Escapes
1. Michigan	1,488
2. California	998
3. Florida	875
4. Oregon	790
5. North Carolina	432
6. Oklahoma	391

7. Missouri	340
8. Washington	300
9. Massachusetts	284
10. Federal Bureau of Prisons	218

Source: Sourcebook of Criminal Justice Statistics.

STATES — PRISONS
Most Suicides in Local Jails

Rehabilitation is at the core of our current judicial and correctional theories. Society, as an abstract institution and collection of individualism, wishes to see criminal elements pay for their misdeeds, yet the abortive loss of life through prison suicide is an inarguably tragic and fatal end to an already misspent existence. Below are the numbers that spell out this tragedy, measured in the number of suicides among institutionalized people in a single year.

State	Suicides, 1986
1. Texas	46
2. California	32
3. Illinois	25
3. New York	25
5. Ohio	19
5. Pennsylvania	18
7. Virginia	18
8. Florida	15
9. New Jersey	14
10. Maryland	11

Source: National Study of Jail Suicides, National Center on Institutions and Alternatives.

STATES — PRISONS
Most Spacious Prison Systems

Dostoevsky said a society can be judged by the way it treats its criminals. In the bad old days, criminal conviction meant a fast, long trip to a cold, dark, cellar. Over the years, the concept of a more humane, rehabilitative correctional system has evolved. In the post-war era, however, that trend has undergone a reversal, not through any real change in the ideas of how criminals should be treated, but through the simple phenomenon of the explosion of criminality and our limited means of coping with the vast and growing numbers of the newly convicted. Prisons have become harsher, more crowded and less humane. Here, then, are the states in which inmates have the most elbow-room. Even the most spacious prison system, that of the District of Columbia, yields only 90 square feet to each inmate, which comes down to a cell less than ten by ten feet.

State	Square Footage Per Inmate
1. D.C.	90.1
2. Wyoming	89.7
3. Delaware	89.7
4. Georgia	82.5
5. New Mexico	77.5
6. Arizona	77.0
7. Arkansas	76.2
8. Colorado	76.1
9. Kentucky	71.8
10. Louisiana	71.7

Source: Population Density in State Prisoners

STATES — PSYCHIATRY
Prevalence of Psychiatric Care

Not very long ago, one had to brave major social taboos to seek psychiatric care. In this era, however, psychotherapy has become downright routine. Consider that last year in the District of Columbia there were 1,374 psychiatric office visits for every 1,000 persons in the population. That amounts to 1.374 visits per annum for every man woman and child in the capital city. Now, some might consider it reason for concern that the city of our national leaders, where the vital decisions of our day are made, leads the nation in sessions on the couch. But it's no surprise that New York appears near the top of the list. Most of the rest of the country thinks you've got to be crazy to live in New York in the first place.

PLACES

State	Psychotherapy visits/1,000 pop.
1. D.C.	1,374
2. New York	1,267
3. Connecticut	900
4. Colorado	875
5. Utah	859
6. New Hampshire	743
7. Virginia	720
8. Massachusetts	611
9. Arizona	592

Source: Mutual of Omaha Company.

STATES — PUBLIC ASSISTANCE
Highest Concentration of Citizens on Public Aid

It is a commonly held misconception that the majority of Americans receiving welfare and other public assistance are denizens of the inner city. In actuality, public aid is very much a rural phenomena, with nearly one person in five receiving some form of assistance in the troubled, agrarian South. Below are the states with the highest percentage of their populations receiving public assistance.

State	% Pop. receiving aid
1. Mississippi	18.6
2. Louisiana	16.1
3. California	8.7
4. Michigan	8.4
5. West Virginia	8.1
6. New York	7.7
7. Ohio	7.2
8. Wisconsin	7.1
9. Illinois	7.0
10. Kentucky	6.9

Source: U.S. Census Bureau.

STATES — PUBLIC SCHOOLS
Highest Expenditures per Pupil

Although the mere expenditure of dollars cannot assure an improvement in the average quality of American public education, adequate funding is a pre-requisite for the overall recovery of our teaching institutions. Wealthy, populous, highly industrialized states have traditionally lead the nation in their financial commitment to education, but in this era, smaller, progressive states have often achieved per capita parity with their wealthier neighbors. The following are the states that spend the most money on their students.

States	Ave. Expenditure per pupil
1. Alaska	$8,842
2. Wyoming	6,253
3. New York	6,224
4. New Jersey	6,177
5. Connecticut	5,552
6. D.C.	5,349
7. Massachusetts	4,856
8. Delaware	4,776
9. New Jersey	4,691
10. Maryland	4,660

Source: National Education Association, Ranking of the States, 1988.

STATES — PUBLIC SCHOOLS
Highest and Lowest Teacher Salaries

The American educational system is in a state of crisis. As a nation, we must come to grips with creeping illiteracy, overcrowding in the classroom and drugs and violence in our once-hallowed institutional halls. Although solutions in this crisis are difficult to craft, it is clear that the apportionment of more money for our chronically underpaid educators is a national priority. Below are the states that best polish the apple for their beleaguered teachers, as well as those for which the apple's skin is most dull.

Highest	Average Teacher Salary
1. Alaska	$33,500
2. D.C.	32,797
3. New York	32,000
4. Michigan	31,500

5. California	31,219
6. Rhode Island	31,079
7. Connecticut	28,902
8. Maryland	28,893
9. New Jersey	28,718
10. Massachusetts	28,410

Lowest

1. South Dakota	$18,781
2. Mississippi	19,447
3. Arkansas	19,904
4. Louisiana	20,054
5. Maine	21,257
6. North Dakota	21,284
7. West Virginia	21,446
8. Idaho	21,480
9. Vermont	21,835
10. New Hampshire	22,011

Source: U.S. Dept. of Education.

STATES—PUBLIC SCHOOLS
Student/Teacher Ratios

Student/teacher ratios—the number of students for every teacher—have been growing in recent years. The figure serves as a good measurement of the amount of individual attention each student enjoys in school. In the best state, Connecticut, there is one teacher for about every 13 students in the classroom; in Utah, the average class contains about 25 students. The national average has risen from 18.9 to 17.6 in recent years. Still, in embattled urban schools, the figures are much higher.

Best	Student /Teacher Ratio
1. Connecticut	13.3
2. Vermont	13.4
3. Massachusetts	13.9
4. Washington, D.C.	13.9
5. New Jersey	14.0
6. Wyoming	14.5
7. Maine	14.9
8. Rhode Island	15.0
9. Nebraska	15.1

10. New York	15.2

Worst	Student/Teacher Ratio
1. Utah	24.7
2. California	22.9
3. Hawaii	21.6
4. Idaho	20.7
5. Washington	20.2
6. Nevada	20.2
7. Michigan	20.1
8. Tennessee	19.6
9. Alabama	19.3
10. New Mexico	18.9

Source: U.S Dept. of Education.

STATES—PUBLIC SCHOOLS
Public School Bargains

The cost of attending four-year private college has gotten out of hand. Although we present our selves as egalitarians, Americans must realize that educational privileges, de facto, are being doled-out with elitist favoritism, as tuition and other expenses at the top private institutions soar beyond the reach of a large portion of the populace. As a saving grace, however, America has maintained its battle-worn system of public universities, the last great bargains in higher education. Below are the states in which college expenses at land-grant universities are most affordable.

State	Average Tuition and Fees, 1989-90
1. D.C.	$664
2. Texas	$959
3. Wyoming	$1,003
4. North Carolina	$1,015
5. Nevada	$1,100
6. Idaho	$1,119
7. California	$1,123
8. Alaska	$1,280
9. Hawaii	$1,293
10. Oklahoma	$1,309

Source: U.S. Dept. of Education.

PLACES

STATES — READING
Best-Read Citizenry

Nothing beats curling up with a good book in front of the fire, especially if there's nothing on TV. The peaceful folks in Iowa, it seems, are the Americans who most enjoy this past-time. Iowa leads the nation in library items checked out per capita every year. On the other hand, perhaps people elsewhere just *buy* the books, avoiding the mysterious stains and fingerprints that may accompany library items. We wonder if the rate of library fines is comparable. The following are the ten most bookish states, measured by the number of items checked out of a public library per capita each year.

State	Lib. Items Per Cap.
1. Iowa	8.37
2. Maryland	7.39
3. Kansas	7.00
4. Utah	6.84
5. Ohio	6.60
6. Washington	6.48
7. Wyoming	6.43
8. New Hampshire	6.30
9. Massachusetts	6.23
10. Minnesota	6.20

Source: American Library Directory

STATES — RELIGION
Jewish Population

European Jews, like other ethnic groups when they came to America, tended to settle first in the metropolitan areas on the East Coast, because of their proximity to Ellis Island, the ability to find work easily, and, eventually, the existence of a well-established Jewish community. New York leads the nation both in overall Jewish population and in the percent of the population that is Jewish: more than ten percent of New York's populace is Jewish. For reasons of practicality and because of real and perceived persecution, areas of the South and the Great Plains contain the fewest Jewish people, both in total numbers and in percentage. So good luck finding a latke in Idaho.

Top Ten	Jewish Population
1. New York	1,844,000
2. California	909,000
3. Florida	585,300
4. New Jersey	411,000
5. Pennsylvania	345,800
6. Massachusetts	276,000
7. Illinois	258,000
8. Maryland	209,600
9. Ohio	130,900
10. Connecticut	115,000

Bottom Ten	
1. South Dakota	350
2. Idaho	400
3. Montana	450
3. Wyoming	450
5. North Dakota	800
6. Arkansas	2,000
7. Mississippi	2,100
8. Alaska	2,400
8. West Virginia	2,400
10. Utah	3,300

Jewish Population Density

Highest	% Jewish
1. New York	10.36
2. New Jersey	5.36
3. Florida	4.87
4. Massachusetts	4.71
5. Maryland	4.62
6. District of Columbia	4.08
7. Connecticut	3.58
8. California	3.09
9. Pennsylvania	2.90
10. Illinois	2.23

Lowest	
1. Idaho	.040
2. South Dakota	.049
3. Montana	.056
4. Mississippi	.080
5. Arkansas	.084
6. Wyoming	.092
7. North Dakota	.119

PLACES

8. West Virginia	.126
9. Oklahoma	.162
10. Iowa	.226

Source: American Jewish Year Book, 1990.

STATES — RELOCATION
States Most People Leave To Go To College

When thinking about going to school, many people consider leaving the state they are in to pursue an education in an entirely different environment than they have been used to. Some people leave to explore, some people flee from oppressive local surroundings, and others simply believe that life will be better in the place they go to rather than where they come from. The state that leads the way numerically is New York; however, a comparable number of students come from other states to balance that number, so there is not too much net change. The largest net change belongs to the number two listing. It seems that the number of people who leave New Jersey far outstrip the number of new students who go there — more than 35,859 students abandon the "Garden State" annually, but only 7,147 show up to replace them! What explains New Jersey's trade deficit in college students? One reason is certainly the proximity of big name East Coast schools and the relative lack of comparable colleges in the state.

State	Number who leave for college
1. New York	38,859
2. New Jersey	35,859
3. Illinois	24,595
4. Pennsylvania	21,356
5. California	21,025
6. Massachusetts	16,885
7. Connecticut	16,141
8. Florida	15,935
9. Ohio	15,106
10. Maryland	14,687

Source: Digest of Educational Statistics

Happy to be out of New York or New Jersey? Celebrating graduation in California, home of the most out-of-state students. Photo courtesy Harvey Mudd College.

STATES — RELOCATION
States Most People Go To When Attenting School Out of State

When people go away to school and decide that an out of state school would be better or more interesting than the in-state offerings, what attracts them? It could be the prestige of the schools available (strongly suspected as the number one reason in the second through fifth listings here) or the environment the school can provide (a heavy factor in the number one rating). Whatever the reasons, a lot of people come from out of state to attend college. The following rating shows the most attractive states for prospective college students.

State	Out-of-state students
1. California	36,527
2. New York	30,262

PLACES

3. Massachusetts	28,431
4. Pennsylvania	24,917
5. Illinois	19,118
6. North Carolina	17,027
7. Florida	16,223
8. Texas	15,929
9. Arizona	15,836
10. Washington, D.C.	13,943

Source: Digest of Educational Statistics

STATES — ROAD SYSTEMS
America's Busiest Highways

Few things are more frustrating than a traffic jam on one's way to or from work. Vehicular congestion, however, is an established fact of urban life. Of our nation's public highway systems, Hawaii's modest network sees the greatest use. Following quickly behind are the urban mega-republics of New Jersey and California.

State	Miles of travel/mile of road (yr.)
1. Hawaii	1,756
2. New Jersey	1,697
3. California	1,424
4. Connecticut	1,360
5. Maryland	1,304
6. Massachusetts	1,251
7. Delaware	1,151
8. Rhode Island	1,017
9. Florida	932
10. New York	888

Source: U.S. Federal Highway Administration

STATES — ROLLER SKATING
Most Avid Roller Skaters

Although roller skating has seen the pass of two hey-days (the first in the innocent Ike Years, the second coming with the rest of the California fitness craze in the mid-1970s), it continues to enjoy tremendous popularity among hard-core fans, and may see a resurgence as prices for outdoor roller-blade skates continue to fall. The are over 40,000 registered members of the U.S. Amateur Federation of Roller Skating, participating in more than 1,100 skating clubs; the greatest concentrations are in the states listed below.

States	Roller Skating Clubs
1. California	159
2. Texas	94
3. Florida	83
4. Pennsylvania	76
5. Ohio	66
6. Michigan	62
7. Massachusetts	45
8. Illinois	39
9. Virginia	39
10. North Carolina	35

Source: U.S. Amateur Federation of Roller Skating.

STATES — SALARIES
Highest Average Salaries

Dreaming of better days? Want to go where the money is good? You'll make the most in Washington D.C., but watch out — it's also the murder capitol of the country. Alaska is good on the wallet, if you don't mind months of winter, high costs, freezing temperatures and the most rugged natural landscape this country has to offer. Those glamorous New Yorkers have money to spend and places to spend it, but the cost of living is high. Below are the best and worst paying states in the Union, in terms of the average yearly salary. Remember, these figures average the dizzyingly high profits of corporate capitalists with the minimum wages of fast food workers.

Best	Average Salary
1. Washington D.C	$30,254
2. Alaska	$28,033
3. New York	$26,347
4. Connecticut	$26,244
5. New Jersey	$25,748
6. Minnesota	$24,481
7. Michigan	$24,193
8. California	$24,124
9. Illinois	$23,606

10. Maryland	$22,500

Lowest Average Salaries

While some big corporations chase cheap labor in the Sunbelt, the states with the lowest average annual pay languish in the obscurity they have always suffered from. Six of the ten lowest paid states are in the northern plains, with huge amounts of land and few people. Mississippi, as William Faulkner depicted it, is a world unto itself.

Worst	Avg. Salary
1. South Dakota	$15,424
2. North Dakota	$16,508
3. Mississippi	$16,522
4. Montana	$16,957
5. Arizona	$17,023
6. Nebraska	$17,190
7. Idaho	$17,648
8. Iowa	$17,928
9. New Mexico	$18,259
10. Maine	$18,347

Source: U.S. Bureau of Labor Statistics.

STATES — SENIOR CITIZENS

Senior Centers: Greatest Concentrations of the Elderly

When time comes to hang up the work gear and settle down to enjoy the golden years, a good number of Americans pack up and head to Florida. There, soothed by the temperate climate and the gentle Gulf breeze, seniors can soak themselves in the sun without a pang of guilt. Indeed, Florida leads the nation in senior citizens, with nearly 18 percent of its population past retirement age. But, despite the growing popularity of the desert Southwest, many seniors choose to stay at home to luxuriate in the time they've earned. Florida is followed, not by Arizona, Nevada and California on the list of most senior states, but by such humdrum commonwealths as Pennsylvania, Iowa and Rhode Island. Here, then, are the retired states of the Union,

measured by percentage the population 65 years and older.

State	Percent Seniors
1. Florida	17.8
2. Pennsylvania	14.9
2. Iowa	14.9
4. Rhode Island	14.7
5. Arkansas	14.6
6. West Virginia	14.3
7. South Dakota	14.0
8. Missouri	13.8
8. Nebraska	13.8
8. Oregon	13.8

Source: U.S. Bureau of the Census.

STATES — SIERRA CLUB MEMBERSHIP

Highest Percentage of Sierra Club Members

The Sierra Club is one of the most prominent and powerful environmental organizations in the country, counting 640,599 members in its 56 chapters across the fifty states and in every Canadian province. But, as an organization based in San Francisco and originated primarily to preserve California's Sierra Nevadas, it's not surprising that the largest percentage of the Sierra Club's membership comes from that states. With the nation's increasing awareness of environmental issues, such organizations as

PLACES

the Sierra Club will have an increasingly important role to play in setting the national environmental agenda.

State	Total	%
1. California	210,764	32.90
2. New York	44,890	7.01
3. Illinois	23,526	3.67
4. Florida	22,922	3.58
5. Texas	22,491	3.51
6. Pennsylvania	21,569	3.37
7. New Jersey	19,224	3.00
8. Ohio	18,180	2.84
9. Washington	17,988	2.81
10. Massachusetts	16,964	2.65

Source: *Sierra*.

STATES — SIZE
Biggest

The vast, wild area of Alaska makes up fully sixteen percent of the total land mass of the United States. That's twice as much as the Texas, where the inhabitants boast that everything is bigger. America's last great frontier contains some of the most pristine — and some of the most valuable — land in the Union. In fact, one could fit 539 Rhode Islands inside Alaska. Fascinating food for thought.

Top Ten	Total Acreage
1. Alaska	365,481,600
2. Texas	168,217,600
3. California	100,206,720
4. Montana	93,271,040
5. New Mexico	77,766,400
6. Arizona	72,688,000
7. Nevada	70,264,320
8. Colorado	66,485,760
9. Wyoming	62,343,040
10. Oregon	61,598,720

Bottom Ten	Total Acreage
1. District of Columbia	39,040
2. Rhode Island	677,120
3. Delaware	1,265,920
4. Connecticut	3,135,360
5. Hawaii	4,105,600

6. New Jersey	4,813,440
7. Massachusetts	5,034,880
8. New Hampshire	5,768,960
9. Vermont	5,936,640
10. Maryland	6,319,360

Source: Public Land Statistics, U.S. Dept. of the Interior.

STATES — SODA CONSUMPTION
Most Prolific Soda Drinkers

Football and baseball get a lot of recognition as the nation's most popular pastimes, but little heed is paid to our real favorite activities, except by those who produce and sell Coke and hamburgers. To be blunt, Americans love to eat and drink. And while apple pie may or may not be the sentimental food of choice, soda is most certainly our national drink. Although wives may complain fanatically about the forest of empty Budweiser sixes and colorful street-people may hold tight to their Wild Irish Rose, it is Pepsi, Coke and Crush that keep America irrigated. In the south, Coke, not orange juice, is the breakfast drink of choice for many. In fact, Dixie is veritably awash in carbonation — the top ten states in the Union for per capita consumption of soda pop all fall south of the Mason-Dixon line. North Carolinians — every man, woman and child — gulp a gut-busting 55 gallons of the sweet bubbly each year. Below are these top ten states, ranked by per capita soda consumption.

Soda Consumption	Gallons per Capita
1. North Carolina	55.4
2. South Carolina	51.4
3. Tennessee	46.9
4. Georgia	46.2
5. Mississippi	44.3
6. Alabama	42.4
7. West Virginia	40.4
8. Virginia	40.1
9. Kentucky	39.9
10. Texas	39.7

PLACES

STATES — TAXES
Highest and Lowest Corporate Income Tax

In setting up corporate income taxes, state lawmakers must balance their need for cash with the state's need to attract and keep businesses. If taxes are too high, no businesspeople will want to set up operations. If taxes are too low, the state might go broke. For these reasons, no tax has been more tinkered with and manipulated than corporate income taxes. Some states have sliding scales, while others add "temporary" supplemental net income taxes or yearly corporate surtaxes. Below are corporate taxes regardless of supplemental taxes.

Ten Highest	Corp. Tax Rate
1. Connecticut	11.50%
2. Minnesota	9.50%
3. West Virginia	9.45%
4. California	9.30%
5. Rhode Island	9.00%
6. New Jersey	9.00%
7. New York	9.00%
8. Delaware	8.70%
9. Pennsylvania	8.50%
10. Idaho	8.00%
New Hampshire	8.00%

Lowest	Corp. Tax Rate
1. Nevada	0%
2. South Dakota	0%
3. Texas	0%
4. Washington	0%
5. Wyoming	0%
6. Michigan	2.35%
7. Arkansas	1 to 6%
8. Indiana	3.4%
9. Illinois	4.0%
10. Kansas	4.5%

Source: Tax Foundation, Washington, D.C.

STATES — TAXES
Highest and Lowest Gasoline Tax

Ever wonder why gas is so much cheaper over the state line? It's because the next state over has a lower gasoline tax and your state government has jacked the price up by pennies, nickels or even dimes per gallon. Perhaps your state government sees gas as a good means of raising revenue, or maybe the gas tax is intended as a piece of social engineering, preventing drivers from clogging over-used roads. Whatever the reason, the trend is definitely toward higher and higher gas taxes. The Federal Government recently added another five cents a gallon tax to the total, and even further taxes are on the horizon. Interestingly, three of the country's most populous states, Florida, New York and California are in the bottom five in gas taxes.

Lowest Gas Tax	Cents
1. Florida	4.0
2. New York	8.0
Alaska	8.0
4. California	9.0
Wyoming	9.0
6. New Jersey	10.5
7. Alabama	11.0
Massachusetts	11.0
Missouri	11.0
10.Colorado	12.0
Pennsylvania	12.0

Highest Gas Tax	Cents
1. Nebraska	22.3
2. Wisconsin	20.8
3. Connecticut	20.0
4. Iowa	20.0
5. Minnesota	20.0
6. North Dakota	20.0
7. Rhode Island	20.0
8. Tennessee	20.0
9. Montana	20.0
10. Utah	19.0

Source: The Tax Foundation, Washington, D.C.

STATES — TAXES
Highest and Lowest Income Taxes

Few, if any, issues get the American public more upset than state income taxes. After they pay their federal income taxes, no one wants to give more money to their state government. On the other hand, the states are the governmental entities that provide the most useful and effective services to the average citizen. The state is usually the primary funder of education. The state builds and maintains roads. The state polices highways and protects the environment, in a much more basic way than the federal government and in a more comprehensive way than small entities like cities and towns ever could. Here are the highest and lowest state income tax rates. Where states had sliding scales, we averaged the highest and lowest rates.

Highest	Income Tax Rate
1. North Dakota	8.90%
2. Massachusetts	7.50%
3. Minnesota	7.25%
4. Oregon	7.00%
5. Montana	6.50%
6. Kansas	6.20%
7. Hawaii	6.00%
Tennessee	6.00%
9. New York	5.93%
10. Wisconsin	5.92%

Lowest	Income Tax Rate
1. Florida	0%
Nevada	0%
South Dakota	0%
Texas	0%
Washington	0%
Wyoming	0%
Alaska	0%
8. Pennsylvania	2.1%
9. Illinois	2.5%
10. New Jersey	2.75%

STATES — TAXES

Highest and Lowest Sales Tax

Don't you envy the people in states where there is no sales tax? Can you imagine walking into a store where the prices listed are the prices you actually pay? It would be great! No pockets full of pennies, no worrying if you'll have enough money for the tip after you pay the tax. That's the life. On the other hand, perhaps the people of Connecticut should consider driving somewhere like New York before they buy anything too expensive. Eight percent sales tax is just too much to pay. Of course, most states with high sales tax make up for it with low income tax and most states with high income tax have low sales tax.

Highest:

1. Connecticut	8.0%
2. Washington	6.5%
3. Minnesota	6.0%
Mississippi	6.0%
New Jersey	6.0%
North Dakota	6.0%
Pennsylvania	6.0%
Rhode Island	6.0%
West Virginia	6.0%
Florida	6.0%
Texas	6.0%

Lowest:

1. Alaska	0%
Delaware	0%
Montana	0%
New Hampshire	0%
Oregon	0%
6. Colorado	3.0%
North Carolina	3.0%
Wyoming	3.0%
9. Virginia	3.5%
12 states tied for tenth.	

Source: Tax Foundation, Washington, D.C.

STATES — TAXES

Tax Freedom Day

The people at the Tax Foundation invented Tax Freedom Day to illustrate how long Americans work to pay their taxes. If, for instance, you lived in the District of Columbia, you would slave almost five months for the city and federal governments before you could keep anything you had earned. Conversely, if you lived in New Hampshire, you would work a little more than three and a half months for the common good before enriching yourself through your own labor. It's a little like summer vacation — kids in the next town over always seemed to get out of school a week or two earlier, romping on the beach or at the playground. That's how the folks in D.C. must feel about their compatriots in New Hampshire and South Dakota, for whom Tax Freedom Day comes earliest.

Earliest

1. New Hampshire	April 19th
2. South Dakota	April 19th
3. Mississippi	April 20th
4. Idaho	April 24th
5. Oregon	April 25th
6. Nebraska	April 25th
7. Arkansas	April 25th
8. Montana	April 26th
9. Iowa	April 26th
10. Indiana	April 27th

Latest

1. District of Columbia	May 23rd
2. New York	May 23rd
3. Delaware	May 18th
4. Hawaii	May 17th
5. Connecticut	May 12th
6. Maryland	May 12th
7. New Mexico	May 10th
8. Alaska	May 9th
9. New Jersey	May 9th
10. Massachusetts	May 8th

Source: Tax Foundation, Washington, D.C.

STATES — TAXES
Highest Odds of an IRS Audit

We know the folks in Utah have are a little different from the rest of the country, but does that make them so suspicious? Apparently the Internal Revenue Service thinks so. Utah taxpayers are at least three times more likely to be audited by the IRS on their federal income tax than any other citizens. In fact, they're ten times more likely

to be audited than are the honest folks of Maine, Wisconsin and Hawaii. Overall, less than one percent of all personal income tax returns were audited by the IRS in 1989. Nearly three out of four of those audited owed more money.

Highest Odds	Odds	Audits
1. Utah	1 in 21	30,842
2. Nevada	1 in 60	8,910
3. California	1 in 67	193,934
4. Georgia	1 in 73	37,602
5. Missouri	1 in 76	29,114
6. Texas	1 in 80	87,618
7. Massachusetts	1 in 85	34,407
8. Alaska	1 in 89	3,782
9. Montana	1 in 91	3,736
10. Wyoming	1 in 91	2,203

Lowest Odds	Odds	Audits
1. Maine	1 in 227	2,439
2. Wisconsin	1 in 227	9,512
3. Hawaii	1 in 222	2,323
4. North Carolina	1 in 208	14,178
5. New Jersey	1 in 204	19,576
6. Oregon	1 in 189	6,605
7. South Carolina	1 in 185	7,865
8. Virginia	1 in 175	15,927
9. Michigan	1 in 175	23,132
10. West Virginia	1 in 169	3,994

Source: *Research Recommendations*, National Inst. of Bus. Mgt.; IRS.

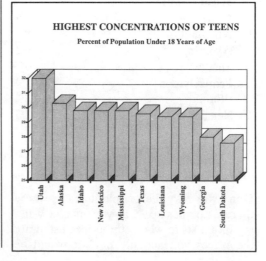

HIGHEST CONCENTRATIONS OF TEENS

Percent of Population Under 18 Years of Age

Utah, Alaska, Idaho, New Mexico, Mississippi, Texas, Louisiana, Wyoming, Georgia, South Dakota

PLACES

STATES—TEEN POPULATION
Highest Concentration of Teenagers

The phone lines are jammed, the radios are blaring and the streets are packed. All this can only mean one thing: the presence of teens. Some say that adolescence is a very difficult time; for Mom and Pop, at least, that is certainly true. On the other hand, George Bernard Shaw said youth is wasted on the young. These then, are the states that are the most wasteful.

State	% Pop. under 18 years of age
1. Utah	37.3
2. Alaska	32.0
3. Idaho	30.3
4. New Mexico	29.8
4. Mississippi	29.8
6. Texas	29.6
7. Louisiana	29.4
7. Wyoming	29.4
9. Georgia	28.0
10. South Dakota	27.6

Source: U.S. Bureau of the Census.

STATES—TOURISM
Stalking The Wild Tourist Greenback!

"I Love New York." "Illinois—You Put Me in a Happy State." "Virginia is for Lovers." "Say Yes to Michigan." Tourism is a booming business in the U.S., and states are desperate to cash in on that boom, even those states that one might not think of as tourist meccas. Florida? Yes. California? Yes. Michigan? Well . . . . States apportion money for the promotion of tourism in direct proportion to their last year's revenues from that lucrative business. The dollars spent are never astronomical, but those generated are princely indeed. Here are the states that spend the most to bring in camera-toting travelers.

Bring me your tired, your poor, your huddled masses yearning to spend free. Photo © N.Y.S. Dept. of Economic Development.

State	Tourism Promotion ($millions)
1. New York	24.3
2. Illinois	23.9
3. Texas	18.3
4. Pennsylvania	14.1
5. Michigan	11.6
6. Alaska	10.8
7. Florida	10.6
8. Virginia	9.9
8. Tennessee	9.9
10. Massachusetts	9.5

Source: U.S. Travel Data Center

STATES—TOURISM
Stalking the Wild Tourist Greenback! Part II

America is a very large country, which is fortuitous, for we are a nation of claustrophobics. As such, we like to move around, and when we do move, we like to see the new and nifty. Here are the ten states most adept in captivating that wandering imagination. Compare this list to the pre-

191

vious ranking of state spending on tourism to see which states are really getting their promotional money's worth.

State	1987 Tourist revenues (billions)
1. California	$35.8
2. Florida	$24.3
3. New York	$17.2
4. Texas	$15.7
5. Pennsylvania	$11.7
6. Illinois	$10.6
7. Michigan	$8.6
8. Nevada	$8.2
9. Ohio	$7.5
10. Virginia	$6.9

Source: U.S. Travel Data Center.

STATES — UNEMPLOYMENT
Highest Benefits

In these tough times, going on the dole is an almost universally unattractive economic option. Yet, amid the recent rain of pink slips that spell recession, few can afford to walk in total ignorance of the unemployment insurance that their chosen state provides. Here, then, are the most generous states for their out-of-work citizens.

State	Maximum Benefits ($/ week)
1. Massachusetts	$255-382
2. Rhode Island	$240-300
3. Connecticut	$234-284
4. District of Columbia	$283
5. Pennsylvania	$266-274
6. Ohio	$169-268
7. Michigan	$263
8. Minnesota	$254
9. New Jersey	$258
10. New York	$245

Source: Department of Labor, Employment and Training Administration.

STATES — UNIONIZATION
Most Unionized

The rise of organized labor in the United States has proven to be both a blessing and a curse. Protection for workers (through collective action) is an indisputable good, but the sometimes extortionist tactics of unscrupulous labor representatives often has counteracted the benefits of unionization. While heavily industrialized states like Michigan and New York are long-time union strongholds, the more-impoverished states of the South remain primarily unorganized. The following are most unionized states in the country, measured by the percentage of laborers who are organized.

State	% Workforce Unionized
1. Michigan	53.6
2. New York	48.2
3. Hawaii	41.4
4. Ohio	40.9
5. Pennsylvania	40.7
6. Indiana	37.6
7. Illinois	33.3
8. Missouri	32.4
9. Maryland	30.0
10. West Virginia	29.8

Source: Statistical Abstract of the United States

STATES — URBANIZATION
Most Urbanized Populations

Although most city dwellers occasionally entertain fantasies of idyllic escapes to pastoral wonderlands, a sizable majority of the American public makes its full-time home in or around cities. The oft-maligned New Jersey is the apotheosis of contemporary urban America, with virtually 100% of it people making their homes within 10 miles of a major population center. The most urbanized states in the union are as follows.

State	% Pop. in metro areas
1. New Jersey	100.0
2. California	95.7
3. Maryland	92.9
4. Rhode Island	92.6
4. Connecticut	92.6
6. New York	91.2
7. Florida	90.8

8. Massachusetts	90.6
9. Pennsylvania	84.8
10. Nevada	82.6

Source: U.S. Bureau of the Census

STATES — VOTERS

Most Conscientious Voters: Greatest Turnout In The 1988 Presidential Election

The newly freed minions of Eastern Europe look to the United States as their democratic ideal. But, truth be told, voters are fickle in this country. One never knows what, if anything, will move them. Sometimes they are penetrating in their analysis and their desire to grapple with central issues. At other times they vote to follow fashion, on an impulse or out of habit. Other times, they don't vote at all, ignoring or abusing the privilege for which the oppressed millions of Eastern Europe thirsted since the end of the Second World War. Here are the most conscientious Americans in terms of exercising their franchise.

State	% of registered actually voting
1. Minnesota	66.33
2. Montana	62.41
3. Maine	62.15
4. Wisconsin	61.98
5. North Dakota	61.54
6. South Dakota	61.54
7. Utah	60.02
8. Iowa	59.27
9. Oregon	58.59
10. Massachusetts	58.06

Source: Committee for the Study of the American Electorate.

STATES — WATER USE

Biggest Water Guzzlers

America is a thirsty nation. We drink to fuel our factories, we drink to spur our dusty crops, and we drink to replace the sweat that dampens our brows under the punishing sun in the South and West. Fortunately, ours is also a nation of lakes and rivers, and in many places, time, consumption and pollution have made only small inroads into our vast aquatic reserves. But in the West, water is at a premium. The Colorado River is dammed in so many places along its route to serve the Southwest that by the time it reaches its mouth in the Gulf of California, this once-mighty river is reduced to a mere trickle. And, unfortunately, the thirstiest of states is the most drought-susceptible. California has been suffering one of its most severe droughts in history, even as more and more Americans flock there. Time will tell whether the limited resources of the Golden State will be able to quench the thirst of its growing population.

State	Millions of gallons per day
1. California	49,700
2. Texas	25,300
3. Idaho	22,000
4. Florida	17,000
5. New York	15,200
6. Illinois	14,500
7. Pennsylvania	14,300
8. Colorado	13,600
9. Ohio	12,700
10. Michigan	11,400

Source: U.S. Geological Survey.

STATES — WINE

Brothers of the Grape: Biggest Wine Consumers

In the heady seventies, America acquired a taste for wine. Prior to those days, only the cultivated connoisseur could pride himself on the knowledge of various European vintages and how to serve them. But as the American wine business boomed, wine-drinking came down off its high horse and became a more egalitarian process. Dozens of new vineyards sprouted up in the 1980s to take advantage of Joe Six-Pack's newfound fondness for the grape. But the rise in consumption of wine in the U.S. has leveled off, and the playing field is littered with the broken-bottled remains of many an upstart

PLACES

vineyard. Meanwhile, Americans now revel in the consumption of the wine cooler, a sweet confection of wine and fruit juice or soft drink, more palatable to a wider range of consumer than the stodgy traditional bottle of wine. The South is the least captivated wine market in America, with a number of Southern states consuming less than a gallon of wine a year per person of drinking age, compared to nearly seven gallons in Washington, D.C. Who knows? Maybe the big wine companies will tap into that market with a drink that mixes its wine with Jim Beam. The following are the states with the highest and lowest consumption of wine per adult of legal drinking age per year.

Highest	Gallons/wine per capita (yr.)
1. D.C.	6.95
2. Nevada	4.92
3. California	4.63
4. New Hampshire	3.51
5. New Jersey	3.30
6. Washington	3.30
7. Oregon	3.23
8. Alaska	3.21
9. Rhode Island	3.21
10. Massachusetts	3.17

Sharon Pratt Dixon, mayor of Washington, D.C.

Lowest	Gallons /wine per capita (yr.)
1. Mississippi	0.63
2. Kentucky	0.74
3. Utah	0.74
4. Arkansas	0.77
5. Iowa	0.77
6. Kansas	0.78
7. West Virginia	0.78
8. Tennessee	0.87
9. Oklahoma	0.96
10. South Dakota	1.02

Source: Wine Institute of the U.S. and United States Department of Commerce.

STATES — WOMEN IN GOVERNMENT
Highest Percentage of Female Mayors

Washington, D.C. recently elected its first female mayor, Sharon Pratt Dixon, replacing the embattled Marion Barry. Across the country, more and more women are making inroads into the once all-male dominion of mayoral office. Below is a list of the top states for female mayors of cities with populations of 10,000 or more.

State	% Female Mayors
1. Colorado	28%
2. Connecticut	27%
3. Washington	25%
4. New Hampshire	25%
5. Oregon	24%
6. Michigan	22%
7. Montana	22%
8. California	21%
9. Missouri	21%

Source: National League of Cities.

TOXIC WASTE SITES
Return to the Love Canal: Worst Toxic Waste Sites In America

Despite the mounting awareness of environmental issues among the general public, relatively little progress has been made against the spread of toxic contaminants

PLACES

into our groundwaters and air. The EPA is in trouble, the toxic offenders are in trouble, the victim-communities are in trouble; everyone bemoans these facts, but monies are too scarce and the roots of the problem too widely spread. The following are the worst toxic waste sites in the country, as measured by their placement on the Superfund list. The majority of these sites are located in the Middle Atlantic states of New Jersey, New York, Pennsylvania and Delaware.

Site, Location

1. **Lipari Landfill**
   Pitman, New Jersey

2. **Tybouts Corner Landfill**
   Mantua Township, Delaware

3. **Bruin Lagoon**
   Bruin Borough, Pennsylvania

4. **Helen Kramer Landfill**
   Mantua Township, Delaware

5. **Industrial Pier**
   Woburn, Massachusetts

6. **Price Landfill**
   Pleasantville, New Jersey

7. **Pollution Abatement Services**
   Oswego, New York

8. **LaBounty Site**
   Charles City, Iowa

9. **Army Creek Landfill**
   New Castle County, Delaware

10. **CPS, Madison Industries**
    Old Bridge Township, New Jersey

Source: Environmental Protection Agency.

ZOOS
America's Best Zoos

Almost every city in the country has some kind of zoo or wild animal park. Some are small facilities with a few monkeys or lions pacing back and forth in their cages. Others are huge institutions which try to recreate an

The savannahs of Africa? No, the San Diego Wild Animal Park, top zoo in the nation. Photo by Ron Garrison, © San Diego Zoo.

animal's natural habitat in a foreign environment. To rate America's zoos, the editors of the Almanac used four statistics and three ratios. Most important was the ratio of species to budget, that is: How much money could the zoo spend on each type of animal it housed? Next came the ratio of species to acres or: How much land did animals have to roam in? The final consideration was crowding: Was the facility too crowded, was it average or were crowds sparse? The following scores are based on a formula using these factors. The ten best zoos are as follows:

Best Zoos	Score
1. San Diego Wild Animal Park	19.39
2. Washington Park (Portland)	7.04
3. Brookfield Zoo (Chicago)	5.56
4. Bronx Zoo (New York City)	4.07
5. San Diego Zoo	4.02
6. Minnesota Zoo	3.58
7. Detroit Zoo	3.41
8. San Francisco Zoo	3.15
9. Miami Metrozoo	3.10
10. National Zoo, D.C.	2.60
11. Phoenix Zoo	2.43
12. Woodland Park (Seattle)	2.26

Source: "Best and Worst" original

PLACES

Best Attendance

1. Lincoln Park Zoo, Chicago — 4.0 million
2. San Diego Zoo — 3.5 million
3. National Zoo, D.C. — 3.0 million
4. St. Louis Zoo — 2.3 million
5. Bronx Zoo — 2.3 million
6. Brookfield Zoo, Chicago — 2.0 million
7. Houston Zoo — 2.0 million
8. Milwaukee Zoo — 1.8 million
9. Los Angeles Zoo — 1.7 million
10. Cincinnati Zoo — 1.5 million

Biggest

1. San Diego Wild Animal Pk. — 1,800 acres
2. Minnesota Zoo — 488 acres
3. Miami Metrozoo — 290 acres
4. Bronx Zoo, New York City — 265 acres
5. Brookfield Zoo, Chicago — 204 acres
6. Milwaukee Zoo — 185 acres
7. National Zoo ,Washington — 163 acres
8. Cleveland Zoo — 160 acres
9. Detroit Zoo — 125 acres
   San Francisco Zoo — 125 acres
   Phoenix Zoo — 125 acres

Most Species

1. San Diego Zoo — 800
2. Cincinnati Zoo — 735
3. San Antonio Zoo — 674
4. Houston Zoo — 649
5. Bronx Zoo, New York City — 644
6. St. Louis Zoo — 619
7. Milwaukee Zoo — 605
8. Philadelphia — 560
9. Oklahoma City Zoo — 532
10. Los Angeles Zoo — 500

THINGS

ADVERTISING AGENCIES
Highest-Grossing U.S.-Based Advertising Agencies

For decades, advertising has been a volatile, unreliable sort of means from which to carve a living. As agency eats agency and dog eats dog, copywriters, creative directors and accounts jockeys move in and out as if by fricative conveyer belts. But America's unending craving to buy things means someone's got to sell those things to them, and in the tight-pursed 90s, that selling is going to get even more difficult. The discriminating consumer will be looking even harder before he leaps, even while those in the business of selling will be urging that hapless buyer ever more desperately off his precipice. Undoubtedly, in the coming times, businesses will be relying to a greater extent on the wizardry of Madison Avenue to assist the consumer in making his educated, informed purchasing decisions. Thus, for those who survive at the top of the ad world, through merger, mythos and Machiavelli, the profits are still rich. Lookee here:

Agency	1990 Revenues ($ millions)
1. Saatchi & Saatchi	$890
2. Young & Rubicam	$865
3. Backer Spielvogel Bates	$760
4. McCann-Erickson	$716
5. Ogilvy and Mather	$700
6. BBDO	$657
7. J. Walter Thompson	$626
8. Lintas	$593
9. DDB Needham	$553
10. Foote, Cone & Belding	$511

Source: Crain's Communications 1990.

AGES
The Richest Generations: Discretionary Income by Age Bracket

In these wildly woolly times, you never know who will end up with money, or how in the world they'll go about getting it. But however it comes, one can be sure that it will go just as quickly, for, as we all know, spending rises to meet income. In the large, we see that disposable cash per individual rises steadily with attainment of years, until one reaches one's fifth or sixth decade in the fast lane. By that time, one is ready for one's retirement home, or that yacht that has been tickling the fancy for years. Youngsters 15 to 24, on the other hand, have a mere $7,790 to kick around on the average year. More than an allowance perhaps, but less than a living. Below are the richest years in a person's life, as judged by the amount of discretionary money available to an individual in a household.

Age Group	Discretionary dollars
1. 55-59	$14,580
2. 45-49	$14,450
3. 60-64	$14,360
4. 50-54	$13,550
5. 65-69	$12,920
6. 35-39	$12,400
7. 30-34	$10,920
8. 25-29	$9,130
9. 15-24	$7,790

Source: U.S. Bureau of the Census.

AIDS
AIDS and the Generations

AIDS cuts across age barriers, jumps the generation gap, and stalks us all. Even fetuses are not immune—for they often pay in mortally for the ignorance and excesses of their progenitors. Two things must be learned: that age and experience provide no insulation, and that all must band together to warn of and destroy this virus. The most stricken groups are those in the age brackets from 25 to 44: three-quarter's of all known HIV infections are among people in that age span. But the elderly and the young are not immune—fully six percent of all AIDS cases are recorded to have stricken those above the age of 55. The following list gives the breakdown of the AIDS epidemic by age of the victims.

Age Group	% of known AIDS cases
1. 30-34	24%
2. 35-39	22%
3. 25-29	16%
4. 40-44	14%
5. 45-49	8%
6. 50-54	5%
7. 20-24	4%
8. 55-59	3%
9. 60-64	2%
10. 65+	1%

Source: HIV/AIDS Surveillance Report.

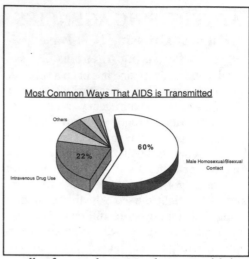

Most Common Ways That AIDS is Transmitted

AIDS
Most Common Ways That AIDS is Transmitted

It is absolutely critical that all Americans acquaint themselves with the methods by which the deadly HIV virus propagates. Each person should take this as a responsibility not only to himself, but to his family and community as well. According to most experts, AIDS can only be transmitted from one person to another through the passing of blood or semen from an infected individual to one who is uninfected. The following list reveals the most frequent means by which the HIV virus is transmitted from one person to another, as recorded among those testing positive for the virus. Sexual intercourse and the sharing of hypodermic needles are the most common means of transmission. As is evident from the list, although homosexual contacts make up the majority of transmissions, the epidemic is by no means confined to the gay community. In fact, as that community has become more educated and has begun taken more precautions to prevent transmission, the acceleration of spread of the virus has slightly quelled; unfortunately, intravenous drug users often lack education about the dangers of shared needles, and attempts among AIDS activist groups to distribute needles free to drug users has met with intense opposition.

Transmission Method	% of Total Cases
1. Male Homosexual/ Bisexual Contact	60%
2. Intravenous drug use	22
3. Male homosexual/bisexual contact combined with IV drug use	7
4. Heterosexual Contact	5
5. Other undetermined factors	4
6. Transfusion of infected blood	2
7. Hemophilia/coagulation disorders	1

Source: HIV/AIDS Surveillance Report.

AIRLINE DISASTERS
Greatest

Despite constant reassurances from the airline industry and from statisticians that commercial airline travel is the safest means of transport available, most of us still feel at least a little trepidation when stepping on board a plane. To some, the whole idea of heavier-than-air flight still seems preposterous — what could possibly get such a huge craft off the ground? Psychologists have even taken to forming therapy groups for those afflicted with a fear of flying, and several self-help books have recently been published to assist air-wary travelers in overcoming their hesitance about setting themselves aloft. However, no matter how much psychotherapy and baby-sitting, certain events give one cause for concern, like the anonymous pilots who talk about the "black-dot," or most dangerous, airports; the airline pilots who were accused of flying an early morning flight after a night of heavy drinking; news reports of the ease with which reporters pass through detection devices with weapons or drive directly out onto the tarmac through supposedly tight security; and of course, media images of wreckage and destruction on the occasion of a great air disaster. Below we have compiled the most deadly of those air tragedies. It's interesting to note that two of the ten greatest air tragedies were military shoot-downs of commercial jet-liners; another two were the result of terrorism. Six of the top ten have been deemed accidental.

Date/Description	Fatalities
1. March 27, 1977	**582**

A Pan Am 747 collides with a KLM Royal Dutch Airlines 747 on the runway in Tenerife in the Canary Islands.

2. August 12, 1985	**520**

Japan Airlines 747 crashes into a mountain in Japan.

3. March 3, 1974	**356**

Turkish Airlines DC-10 crashes near Paris.

4. June 23, 1985	**329**

Air India 747 on its way from Canada to Europe explodes in flight off the coast of Ireland; terrorist bomb is suspected.

5. August 19, 1980	**301**

Saudi Arabian L-1011 crashes during emergency landing in Riyadh.

6. July 3, 1988	**290**

Iranian A300 Airbus is mistaken for an attacking jet and shot out of the sky by the U.S.S. Vincennes in the Persian Gulf.

7. May 25, 1979	**275**

An American Airlines DC-10 plunges to earth shortly after take-off from Chicago's O'Hare Airport.

8. December 11, 1988	**270**

Pan Am Flight 103 is blown up by a terrorist bomb over Lockerbie, Scotland; all 259 on board are killed, along with 11 on the ground.

9. September 1, 1983	**269**

Korean Air Lines flight 007 is shot from the sky by a Soviet fighter plane in Soviet airspace over Sakhalin Island.

10. November 28, 1979	**257**

Air New Zealand DC-8 strikes a mountain in Antarctica on a tourist trip to the South Pole.

Source: *New York Times*.

AIRLINES
Where Has All the Baggage Gone?
Biggest Luggage Losers

How often have you been left at your hotel with nothing but the clothes on your back and the contents of your carry-on bag or purse? Below are Department of Transportation figures for the frequency of one of the most frustrating of air travel foul-ups — lost luggage. The big winner here, Southwest Airlines, benefits from the fact that it carries large number of travelers such as businessmen and others on trips of relatively short duration, thus keeping the overall number of checked bags per passenger down. Here, then, are the major airlines judged by how attentive they are to your luggage, from the worst culprits to the best performers.

Airlines	Bags lost/1,000 Passengers
1. America West	**8.61**
2. TWA	**7.52**
3. Northwest	**6.47**
4. Delta	**5.99**
5. USAir	**5.95**
6. United	**5.64**
7. Eastern	**5.52**
8. American	**4.98**
9. Pan Am	**4.54**
10. Continental	**4.44**

THINGS

11. Southwest   **2.81**
Source: U.S. Department of Transportation.

AIRLINES
Bumping: Hassle or Opportunity?

Every year, nearly half a million airline passengers are "bumped" or "bounced" (i.e. denied the right to board) from flights for which they hold tickets or reservations. Airlines normally "overbook" (that is, sell more tickets than there are seats), especially during busy seasons, in the expectation of a certain number of cancellations. In 1982, Continental Airlines, in the midst of its financial difficulties, achieved the dubious distinction of bumping a record 15.53 of every 10,000 passengers. The problems start when the number of overbooked seats exceeds the number of cancellations. But where some see problems, other see *opportunity*. In overbooking situations, airline ticketing agents often offer domestic flight vouchers for free air travel. There are some cunning travelers who know how to exploit this system to perpetually fly free. Below are the records for the major airlines in terms of the number of passengers involuntarily denied boarding. The big three — American, United and Delta — are the least bumpy airlines, in part because their wide-ranging flight schedule allows them to offer overbooked passengers quick rescheduling for a flight to their ultimate destinations. Upstart carrier America West is the most bumptious airline.

Airlines	Bumps per 10,000 Passengers
1. America West	8.71
2. Southwest	5.80
3. TWA	3.29
4. Pan Am	2.61
5. USAir	1.94
6. Continental	1.64
7. Northwest	1.00
8. Eastern	0.94
9. Delta	0.57
10. United	0.36

11. American   **0.08**
Source: Department of Transportation.

AIRLINES
Unidentified Flying Objects: The Mystery of Airline Foods

Ever since de-regulation, competition between airlines has been hot. How hot? Certainly hotter than the warmed-over salisbury steak, crusted brownie and tub of cheese spread one has come to expect of the in-flight meal. Indeed, competition is so hot that bean-counters will look anywhere for savings. One of the great legends surrounding current American Airlines honcho and hatchet-man Bob Crandall is the $40,000 he saved the airline annually by eliminating olives from the in-flight salad during his stint as Chief Financial Officer of the carrier. Yet American still remains near the top in terms of the amount it spends on food per pas-

American consistently ranks near the top in food service. Photo: Bob Takis, American Airlines.

senger. And that average, over the course of a year, adds up to over $400 million annually on victuals for American. Next on the chopping block: Bread sticks? To be fair, the bigger carriers are saddled with added food costs simply by dint of their flight schedules: International flights and longer domestic routes require more service, and extensive first-class and business-class programs mean more expensive meals. Thus Pan Am's place at the top. Stingy Southwest Airlines, on the other hand, with relatively shorter routes, can afford to cut its service to a minimum.

Airline	Food per passenger
1. Pan Am	$7.60
2. American	$6.88
3. TWA	$6.70
4. United	$6.16
5. Northwest	$5.71
6. Continental	$5.37
7. Delta	$5.18
8. Eastern	$4.44
9. Midway	$3.57
10. USAir	$3.55
11. America West	$2.74
12. Southwest	$0.12

Source: Yield Data Services.

AIRLINES
Most Popular Passenger Airlines

Commercial aviation has been a very rocky business in the last ten years or so, and the travel hysteria surrounding the Persian Gulf crisis did little to remedy this situation. At the top, competition is fierce, and price wars still flare, despite the demise of hyper-agressive bargain operators like Peoples Express. The airline to watch? Continental, as they expand their route system and go after the more-monied business frequent flier.

Airline	Passengers, 1989
1. American	80,000,000
2. Delta	77,359,000
3. United	68,200,000
4. USAir	54,919,000
5. Northwest	44,495,000
6. Continental	38,627,000
7. Southwest	34,957,000
8. Pan American	25,150,000

Source: Airline Operators Council.

AIRLINES
On-Time Performance

Gotta make a connection? Check with your travel agent. Nowadays, the Department of Transportation keeps detailed records of on-time performance for the major domestic carriers, not only overall, but for specific flights. This information is available to travel agents on their computerized booking systems. Each flight gets a score based on its past average on-time performance. Knowing this information will allow travelers to avoid chronically late flights when time is pressing. Below is a list of overall on-time performance for the major carriers, by per-

American carries the most passengers of any U.S. carrier. Photo by Bob Takis, courtesy American Airlines.

THINGS

Pan Am may be little more than history, but at least they're punctual.

centage of flights arriving within 15 minutes of their scheduled arrival time, in a typical month—in this case, September 1990 (Eastern Airlines was still operating at the time).

Airline	% of flights on time
1. Pan Am	89.2
2. Eastern	88.1
3. AmericaWest	85.6
4. American	84.6
5. United	83.8
6. Northwest	83.2
7. Continental	82.7
8. USAir	82.5
9. TWA	82.2
10. Delta	81.9
11. Southwest	81.8

Source: U.S. Dept. of Transportation.

ALBUMS
Greatest Rock Guitar Albums

The editors of *Guitar World* recently took it upon themselves to determine the greatest guitar albums in the history of rock and roll. Not an easy task, considering that "greatness" means different things to different people. Do you judge an album's greatest on the sheer technical prowess its player displays? On originality? On influence? In the end, *GW's* editors decided that the ideal rock guitar album would combine all three elements. Below is their list of the ten greatest rock guitar albums of all time.

Album/Artist/Guitar Player(s)

1. *Are You Experienced?*, **Jimi Hendrix** Experience

   Jimi Hendrix.

2. *Van Halen,* **Van Halen**
   Eddie Van Halen.

3. *Layla,* **Derek and the Dominos**
   Eric Clapton, Duane Allman.

4. *The Chess Box,* **Chuck Berry**
   Chuck Berry.

5. *Led Zeppelin IV,* **Led Zeppelin**
   Jimmy Page.

6. *Band of Gypsys,* **Jimi Hendrix**
   Jimi Hendrix.

7. *At Fillmore East,* **The Allman Brothers**
   Duane Allman, Dickey Betts.

8. *The Sun Sessions,* **Elvis Presley**
   Scotty Moore.

9. *Blow by Blow,* **Jeff Beck**
   Jeff Beck.

10. *Passion and Warfare,* **Steve Vai**
    Steve Vai.

Source: Guitar World, June 1991.

ALBUMS
Longest Winning Streak at Billboard's #1

Believe it or not, neither the Beatles nor the Rolling Stones, rock music's two most important bands, have had monster albums that have dominated the Billboard charts for long stretches of time. On the contrary, the most popular albums in history are predominantly soundtracks. What accounts for this popularity? Undoubtedly, a movie's popularity will contribute to the sale of its soundtrack album—people normally not interested in buying a pop album may be more inclined to if they liked the film. In addition, soundtracks such as *Saturday Night Fever* and *Dirty Dancing* feature a number of different artists, and may even contain music

THINGS

from different genres, such as rock, disco, jazz and oldies, thus appealing to a wider range of fans.

Record/ Year Released	Weeks at #1
1. *West Side Story* Soundtrack 1962	54
2. *Thriller* Michael Jackson, 1983	37
3. *South Pacific* Soundtrack, 1958	31
4. *Calypso* Harry Belafonte, 1956	31
5. *Rumours* Fleetwood Mac, 1977	31
6. *Saturday Night Fever* Soundtrack, 1978	24
7. *Purple Rain* Prince, 1984	24
8. *Blue Hawaii* Elvis Presley, 1961	20
9. *More of the Monkees* Soundtrack, 1967	18
10. *Dirty Dancing* Soundtrack, 1988	18

Source: Billboard.

ALCOHOL

Most Common Alcohol-Related Problems

Drinking is a problem with which we will not dispense in this country. Americans drink to be sociable, to escape, or to forget, but whatever the reason, we drink a lot. We have made one attempt at prohibition and — noting its failure — resigned ourselves to the inevitability of alcoholism, alcohol-related traffic fatalities and liver diseases. Since we can not and will not legislate away the easy availability of alcohol, we must learn to recognize the signs of its malignant incursion into previously peaceful lives. These are most common problems attributed to demon alcohol, measured by the percentage of drinkers aged 12 to 80 that report the problem.

Problem	Percent
1. Aggressive or cross while drinking	19.8
2. Unable to remember events	14.6
3. Drank too fast for maximum effect	11.9
4. Argued heatedly while drinking	11.5
5. Advised by mate to quit	11.0
6. Became inebriated while alone	9.1
7. Fears of own alcoholism	8.1
8. Can't stop drinking	7.0
9. Keep drinking after resolutions to stop	6.7
10. Advised by relative to quit	6.6

Source: U.S. Dept. of Health and Human Services, National Institute on Drug Abuse.

AMUSEMENT PARKS

Most Popular Theme and Amusement Parks

America goes to Disney, America goes to Six Flags, America goes wherever the thrills come fast and the lines come long. Big fun is big business, and the customer is always right, so long as he spends, spends, spends. So come early, come often, to these best known pleasure spots, judged by 1990 attendance

Park	Attendance (millions)
1. Walt Disney World	28.5
2. Disneyland	12.9
3. Knott's Berry Farm	5.0
4. Universal Studios Hollywood	4.6
5. Sea World of Florida	3.8
6. Sea World of California	3.3
7. Kings Island	3.2
8. Six Flags Magic Mountain	3.1
9. Cedar Point	3.1
10. Busch Gardens, Dark Continent	3.0

Source: Amusement Business Magazine.

THINGS

The Pronghorn Antelope is the fastest animal found in the U.S., second only to the cheetah. Photo courtesy Wyoming Travel Commission.

ANIMALS
Fastest

In the age of the jet and the sports car, we tend to take great speeds for granted. Just one tick of the geological clock earlier, however, man relied exclusively on the fleetness of his feet, and those of the animals he harnessed. Herewith, then, are the highest speeds ever recorded for the tortoise, the hare, and a host of God's other creatures.

The Top Ten	Top Speed (mph)
1. Cheetah	70
2. Pronghorn Antelope	61
3. Wildebeest	50
4. Lion	50
5. Thomson's Gazelle	50
6. Quarter Horse	48
7. Elk	45
8. Cape Hunting Dog	45
9. Coyote	43
10. Rabbit (domestic)	35

Slow Pokes

1. Human	27
2. Black Mamba	20

3. Six-lined Race Runner	18
4. Squirrel	12
5. Pig	11
6. Chicken	9
7. Spider	1.17
8. Giant Tortoise	0.17
9. Three-toed Sloth	0.15
10. Garden Snail	0.03

Source: Natural History Magazine.

ANIMALS
Longest Gestation Period

The human female takes roughly 270 days to bring her infant from conception to normal live birth. All in all, that is a respectable gestation period for a sizable mammal, but it cannot compare with the 645 the average mother elephant puts into the process, or the 450 days the also portly rhino puts in. Animal psychologists are yet to determine whether post-partum depression lasts a comparable time for these beasts.

Species	Gestation Period (days)
1. Elephant	645
2. Rhinoceros	450
3. Giraffe	425
4. Bactrian Camel	406
5. Zebra	365
6. Ass	365
7. Horse	330
8. Cow	284
9. Human	270
10. Moose	240

Source: The Biology Data Book

ANIMALS
Number of Animal Pelts
Per Fur Coat

Any fur larger than a simple stole is a rag tag agglomeration of the flattened skins of numerous slaughtered small animals. The average mink coat is composed of some sixty pelts—that's *sixty* animals killed for each coat. Fifteen dam-builders make one beaver coat; while sixteen threatened coyotes make a fair-sized cloak. Next time you don that

THINGS

luxurious pelt, take time to think how much blood has been spilt so you can preen in front of your fellow fur-wearers. What, indeed, is the attraction?

Fur	Pelts Per Coat
1. Mink	60
2. Sable	50
3. Muskrat	50
4. Opossum	45
5. Red Fox	42
6. Raccoon	40
7. Otter	20
8. Lynx	18
9. Coyote	16
10. Beaver	15

Source: People for the Ethical Treatment of Animals.

ARCHITECTURAL FIRMS
Tops in Billings

Appropriately enough, the architectural firm with the highest annual billings is also the designer of the world's tallest building, the Sears Tower in Chicago. Skidmore, Owings and Merrill, founded in Chicago in 1936 and now also with major offices in New York, San Francisco, Los Angeles and London, had billings of close to $200 million in 1990. SOM, as the firm is known, has dominated the field of corporate architecture for most of its existence, being repsonsible for such influential modern skyscraper structures as Lever House in New York City, the John Hancock Tower in Chicago and the Sears Tower. During the 1980s, the firm's domination was challenged by sixth-ranked Kohn Pedersen Fox Associates, who introduced the post-modern style to tall building design, and by Perkins and Will on SOM's own turf in Chicago.

The Top Ten

1. Skidmore, Owings and Merrill
2. Helmuth Obata & Kassabaum, Inc.
3. RTKL Associates, Inc.
4. The Ellerbee Becket Co.
5. The Kling-Lindquist Partnership
6. Kohn Pedersen Fox Associates
7. Perkins & Will
8. Handen Lind Meyer Inc.
9. Swanke Hayden Connell Ltd.
10. The Hillier Group

ARMIES
Fodder for the Cannon: World's Biggest Armies

Lines of marching men move in perfect unison; Migs and F-16s carry deadly weapons of destruction; tense masses of men poise on either side of disputed borders—the world's biggest armies stand on the brink at the world's hot spots. Compiled by the U.S. Arms Control and Disarmament Agency, the numbers here refer to active-duty military personnel, including paramilitary forces where those forces resemble regular units in their organization, equipment, training, or mission. Reserve forces are not included. Figures for Iraq are from prior to the invasion of Kuwait and the subsequent Operation Desert Storm; U.S. authorities have not been forthcoming with the extent of the devastation that the U.S. Armed Forces and their coalition partners wrought on the hapless Iraqi army, but estimates run to as high as 100,000 killed. Even with that depletion of manpower, the Iraqi army, as of this writing, remains a potent power in terms of sheer numbers. Moreover, with the relief of tensions between NATO and the Soviet Union, significant cuts are expected in both U.S. and Soviet forces, such as the initial 25 percent cut in American military personnel proposed by the Pentagon.

Armed Forces	Personnel
1. Soviet Union	4,400,000
2. China	3,530,000
3. United States	2,279,000
4. India	1,502,000
5. Vietnam	1,300,000
6. Iraq	900,000
7. Turkey	879,000

THINGS

8. North Korea	838,000
9. South Korea	604,000
10. Pakistan	573,000
11. France	559,000
12. Brazil	541,000

Source: U.S. Arms Control and Disarmament Agency, *World Military Expenditures and Arms Transfers*, annual.

AUTOMOBILES — ACCELERATION
Fastest

In the sorry seventies—in the face of fuel embargoes, long gasoline lines and the dreaded "moral malaise"—the death of the great American muscle car was proclaimed. But, like Mark Twain said, reports of this death were greatly exaggerated. The country's attitude has changed since those touchy-feely times. The Reagan Revolution taught us to feel good about ourselves again, and the new motto became "If you've got it, flaunt it." What better way to flaunt your lack of concern about such worries as fuel efficiency and carbon monoxide emissions than in the bigger, bolder, brasher muscle cars now coming out of Detroit? Just as the nation's passions turned to the bulked up, steroid hulks on the professional wrestling circuit, we turned back to the big boys to give us cars we can be proud of. American born and bred, the monster Chevy Corvette ZR-1 is the most muscular car on the market, blasting from 0 to 60 in a neck-snapping 4.4 seconds. From the Camaro to the Corvette to the Mustang, the America's back on top of the high-speed world, feelin' good about ourselves as we hurtle on toward the millennium, radio blastin' through the sun roof. These are the production cars with the greatest acceleration from 0 to 60.

Top Ten	Seconds, 0-60
1. Chev. Corvette ZR-1	4.4
2. GMC Cyclone	4.9
3. Chev. Corvette L98 Coupe	5.3
Mitsubishi 3000GT VR-4	5.3

The high-performance Chevy Corvette ZR-1, top production car in acceleration and braking. Photo courtesy General Motors.

4. Acura NSX	5.4
Pontiac 20th Trans Am	5.4
5. Porsche Carrera 4	5.5
6. Chev. Camaro IROC-Z	5.8
Lotus Esprit Turbo	5.8
7. Porsche 928 GT	5.9
8. Nissan 300ZX Turbo	6.0
Porsche 911 Speedster	6.0
9. Ferrari Testarossa	6.3
Mazda RX-7 Turbo II	6.3
10. Ford Mustang LX	6.4
BMW M5	6.4
Dodge Stealth R/T Turbo	6.4

Source: Motor Trend.

AUTOMOBILES — ACCELERATION
Slowest Acceleration, 0-60

Okay, okay. For some people, laying tracks isn't the most important aspect of driving. If you feel no overwhelming urge to blow the car next to you off the line when the light turns green, the autos below won't give you much problem. Then again, you probably won't get any chicks, either. The list of the cars with the slowest acceleration from 0 to 60 miles per hour contains those trendy "off-road" vehicles like the Suzuki Sidekick, the Isuzu Amigo and the Geo Tracker, as well as several versions of the newly popular minivan, such as the Toyota Previa and the Plymouth Grand Voyager. The list is

THINGS

rounded out by subcompact cars high on mileage but short on performance – the Subaru Justy and the Hyundai Excel.

Car	Acceleration (0-60), seconds
1. Suzuki Sidekick	15.8
2. Subaru Justy	14.5
3. Isuzu Amigo SX 4x4	14.2
4. Toyota Previa All-Trac	13.6
5. Daihatsu Rocky SE	13.3
6. Geo Tracker	13.2
7. Daihatsu Charade SE	13.1
8. GMC Safari AWD	12.6
Plymouth Grand Voyager LE	12.6
Pontiac Trans Sport	12.6
9. Hyundai Excel	12.5
Mitsubishi Mirage LS	12.5
10. Chev. Lumina APV	12.2

Source: Motor Trend.

AUTOMOBILES – BRAKING
Best Braking

High performance doesn't just mean quick acceleration, hot handling and a top speed above the sesquicentennial mark. Good brakes are an essential component of any performance package, if only to show Smoky that you're serious about stopping when he pulls you over. The Chevrolet Corvette ZR-1 not only has the best acceleration of any production model automobile, but it also possesses the best brake system, measured by the distance needed to bring the car from 60 miles per hour down to a dead stop – a mere 109 feet, or a little over 30 yards. That may not be stopping on a dime, but it's not far from a Susan B. Anthony dollar. Other muscle cars that appear on both the best accelerating and best braking lists include the Mitsubishi 3000GT VR-4, the Acura NSX, the Mazda RX-7 Turbo II and the Dodge Stealth R/T Turbo.

Car 60-0, Feet

1. Chev. Corvette ZR-1	109
2. Porsche 928 GT	112
3. Mazda RX-7 Turbo II	115
4. Isuzu Impulse RS	116
5. BMW 318is	117
Dodge Stealth R/T Turbo	117
Mitsubishi 3000GT VR-4	117
Nissan NX 2000	117
6. Volvo 740 Turbo Wagon	118
7. Mercedes-Benz 560SEC	119
Nissan 240SX SE	119
8. Acura NSX	120
Porsche 944 S2 Cabriolet	120
Sterling 827Si	120
9. Acura Integra GS	122
Toyota Celica All-Trac T	122
10. Merkur Scorpio	123
Subaru Legacy Sport Sedan	123

Source: Motor Trend.

AUTOMOBILES – BRANDS
World's Most Powerful Automobile Brands

The Landor ImagePower Survey/1990 polled 10,000 consumers in the three largest markets in the world – the United Sates, Japan and Western Europe – to establish the most powerful brand names in the world. Landor's ranking of "ImagePower" is the combination of consumer familiarity and esteem for particular brand names. Automobile name-plates make up 15 of the top 50 brands in the world, but, sadly, only one of those auto brands – Ford – is American, and even it rates in the top ten more for its familiarity than for its esteem. The most powerful automobile brand in the world, in terms of familiarity and esteem, is the German car maker Mercedes-Benz.

The Top Ten

1. Mercedes-Benz
2. Toyota
3. Rolls Royce
4. Honda
5. Ford
6. Volkswagen
7. Porsche
8. BMW

THINGS

9. Jaguar
10. Nissan
Source: Landor Associates.

AUTOMOBILES — COLLECTIBLE

Most Valuable Collectors' Cars

That old Chevelle SS convertible might be worth something after all. While some of these collectible cars are foreign makes that were already out of reach in 1980, many were in the grasp of the middle class and some were probably bought by teenage gear-heads with the money they made working at the local malt shop. A 1970 Plymouth Super-bird Hemi, now worth $100,000 cost, just $5,000 in 1980 and less if it wasn't in mint condition. Likewise, the mint condition 1970 Chevelle SS 454 Convertible you bought for $4,800 in 1980 is now worth upwards of $120,000. The most valuable class is the convertibles; but all cars had to be in mint condition to command their full value.

Model	Price Rise Between '80 and '90
1. Ferrari 250 GTO 1962-64	9300%
2. Mercedes 500/540K Roadster 1934-36	6600%
3. Ferrari 275 GTB 1964-66	5710%
4. Ferrari 365 GTB	4360%
Daytona Spyder 1968-73.	4360%
5. Bugatti Atlantic, 1936	2500%
Aust. Martin DB5, 1957	2500%
Chevelle SS 454 Conv., 1970	2500%
Daytona Coupe, 1968-73.	2500%
Ferrari Testa Rosa 1956-60	2500%
10. Hispano Suiza J-12 1932-35	2000%
Plymouth Superbird Hemi, '70	2000%

Source: *Chicago Tribune.*

AUTOMOBILES — CUSTOMER SATISFACTION

Car Satisfaction Index

In case you haven't heard, Acura is the highest regarded car in America. For the fourth year, in a row Honda's luxury division has won J.D. Power and Associates Customer Satisfaction Survey Product Quality and Dealer Service Survey. Aside from Acura, the Japanese and Europeans dominate the race for quality and customer satisfaction. Among Americans, only Cadillac and Buick hit the top ten. While foreigners may be leading the way to perfection, consumers can take comfort in the fact that surveys like this are forcing all car makers to improve the quality of their products.

Make	Satisfaction Index
1. Acura	154
2. Mercedes-Benz	148
3. Toyota	144
4. Cadillac	142
5. Honda	140
6. Nissan	135
7. Subaru	130
Buick	130
9. Porsche	129
10. BMW	127

Source: J.D. Power and Associates Customer Satisfaction with Product Quality and Dealer Service Survey.

AUTOMOBILES — FUEL ECONOMY

Best and Worst Mileage

In an era of unpredictable energy prices, one has difficulty deciding between frugal fuel efficiency and gas guzzling luxury. Of course, to those who can afford the Rolls-Royce Silver Shadow, whose fuel efficiency rivals that of the Abrahms tank, fuel economy is of no import to them. On the other hand, those with both economy and ecology in mind should favor the GEO Metro XFI, since high mileage cars save energy and are better for the planet in the long run. The following list, abstracted from E.P.A. statistics, shows the cars with the best and worst miles per gallon. If two versions of the same car qualified for the top ten in mileage, we listed only the one with the best fuel economy.

Best Mileage

Model	City	Hwy.
1. Geo Metro XFI	53	58
2. Honda CRX HF	49	52
(with shift indicator light)		
3. Geo Prizm	45	50
(manual transmission)		
4. Suzuki Swift	45	50
(1.0 liter engine, manual trans)		
5. GEO Metro LSI	45	50
(manual transmission)		
6. Honda CRX HF	43	49
7. Volkswagen Jetta	37	43
(1.6 liter engine)		
8. Daihatsu Charade	38	42
(1.0 liter engine, manual trans)		
9. Ford Festiva	35	42
(manual transmission)		
10. Honda Civic	33	37
(4-speed manual transmission)		
Toyota Tercel	33	37
(four speed manual transmission)		
Ford Escort FS	31	41
Suburu Justy	33	37
(manual transmission)		
Pontiac LeMans	31	40
(1.6 liter, 5-speen manual trans)		

Worst Mileage

Model	City	Hwy
1. Rolls-R. Bentley Cont.	10	13
Rolls-.R. Corniche III	10	13
Rolls-R. Bentley Eight		
/Mulsanne S	10	13
Rolls-R. Bentley Turbo R	10	13
Rolls-R. Silver Spirit II		
/Silver Shadow	10	13
Lamb. DB 132/Diablo	9	14
7. Ferrari, Testarossa	10	15
8. Ferrari, F40	12	17

BMW M5	11	20
10.Jaguar XJ-S Convertible	13	17
Mercedes-Benz 560SEL	14	17
Mercedes-Benz 560 SEC	14	17
Jaguar XJ-S Coupe	13	18
Porsche 928 S4	13	19
(five speed manual)		

Source: Environmental Protection Agency.

AUTOMOBILES — QUALITY
Initial Quality Survey

Ever buy a new car? Its funny how you've always got to take it in for something. Maybe its that whirring coming from the engine or you think "I'll just take it back to the dealer and see why its making that awful grinding sound every time I shift from first to second." You know the story. It happens to everyone. Well, almost everyone. The cars we've listed here go back to the dealer less than any other cars on the market, at least during the first 60 to 90 days. Our results come from the J.D. Power and Associates 1990 New Car Initial Quality Study and represent responses from the respected market research firm's annual survey of car owners.

Model	Problems Per 100
1. Toyota Cressida	63
2. Mercedes-Benz E-Series	71
3. Toyota Camry	72
4. Lexus LS400	74
5. Mercedes-Benz S-Class	76
6. Buick LeSabre	82
7. Nissan Maxima	89
8. Infinity Q45	91
9. Toyota Corolla	94
10. Mazda Miata	99

Source: J.D. Power and Associates.

AUTOMOBILES — QUALITY
Best Initial Quality Among Operating Units

This category speaks not to the integrity of a single model but to the overall average initial quality of an operating unit or name-plate. It averages the scores of all the different models you might see in a showroom. So while Honda had no individual cars in the top ten, the overall quality of its entire line ranks it with the industry's leaders. As you can see, the spread between number one and number ten is quite large. As a point of reference, the industry's average was 140 problems per 100 cars over the first sixty to ninety days. Lexus is a division of Toyota, Buick is part of General Motors, and Acura is a division of Honda. Again, as with auto models, the list of the ten most reliable makes contains only one American name.

Make	Problems per 100 Cars
1. Lexus	82
2. Mercedes-Benz	84
3. Toyota	89
4. Infiniti	99
5. Buick	113
6. Honda	114
7. Nissan	123
8. Acura	129
9. BMW	139
Mazda	139

Source: J.D. Powers and Associates

AUTOMOBILES – SAFETY

Head Injuries

This crash test data derives from the National Highway Traffic Safety Administration (NHTSA) New Car Assessment Program. Each year, NHTSA tests approximately 35 cars in simulated head-on 35-mph crashes with devices ("dummies") in the cars to measure the forces of impact to the head, chest, and femur (leg). The results are listed in ascending order from from lowest (injury is unlikely) impact force to highest (injury is likely) in the three areas (head, chest, legs) tested. Test data from the head are used to calculate the head injury criterion (HIC), a measure of the potential for brain injury. According to the tests, some cars might offer better protection to one area of the occupant's body than another area. The

score given here is an average of the driver's and passenger's score. Models that were structurally similar, such as the Olds Calais and the Buick Skylark, were judged the same. The car that comes out the best in terms of protection from head injury is the sporty Pontiac Fiero 2-door model. One assumes that the severe sloping of the windshield offers some ability to mitigate the force of the impact to the head. Other cars that scored well include such sporty models as the Volkswagen Jetta, the Dodge Daytona, the Ford Mustang and the Chevy Camaro. In fact, American cars make up a good percentage of the top-scoring cars in this rating; on the other hand, only two of the bottom ten in this category are Detroit products, and those models are vans.

Lowest Head Injury Score

Model/Year	Head Injury Score
1. Pontiac Fiero 2dr, '84	333
2. Volkswagen Jetta 4dr, '81	339
3. Dodge Daytona 2hb, '89	348
4. Olds Calais/Buick Skylark/ Pontiac Grand Am 4dr, '87	367
5. Ford Mustang LX 2hb, '87	390
6. Chevy Camaro/ Pontiac Firebird 2dr, '83	392
7. Ford Escort 2hb, '81	423
8. Buick Century/Chevy Celebrity/ Olds Ciera/Pont. 6000 4dr, '82	437
9. Volvo DL Wagon 4W, '85	442
10. Audi 100 Sedan 4dr, '89	447

Highest Head Injury Score

Model/Year	Head Injury Score
1. Peugeot 504 4dr, '79	3506
2. Renault Fuego 2dr, '82	3126
3. Chevy G-20 Van, '88	2558
4. Renault Sportwagon 4W, '84	2387
5. Honda Prelude 2HB, '80	2332
6. Ford Club Wagon Van, '90	2255
7. Isuzu Impulse 2HB, '84	2111
8. Renault Alliance Conv. 2dr, '85	2099
9. Peugeot 505S 4dr, '89	2087
10. Honda Civic 2HB, '80	2066

Source: National Highway Traffic Safety Administration.

AUTOMOBILES — SAFETY
Chest Injury

The following are best and worst automotible scores in the NHTSA's tests for chest injury. As in the Head Injury tests, according to the NHTSA, some cars might offer better protection to one area of the occupant's body than another area. For instance, in the top-rated model, the Buick Century, the driver's chest injury score is 36, but the passenger's score is only 21, indicating that in a collision, the driver is at a slightly greater risk than the passenger. This is understandable, since on the driver's side, the steering wheel poses an added threat absent on the passenger side of the automobile. According to the NHTSA, the chest measurement in G's (a "G" is a unit acceleration) is used as an indicator of the potential for chest injury. The following are the cars that scored the lowest and the highest in the NHTSA's chest injury tests. The total score given is an average of the passenger and the driver scores. In the ranking that we have devised from this information, ties are broken by the by lowest driver-side total, since in many driving instances there will be no passenger in the front seat. (Models that were structurally similar, such as the Buick Century, Chevy Celebrity, Olds Ciera and Pontiac 6000, were rated together). The models tested were not equipped with airbags; it is yet to be determined the extent of the effect airbags will have on the scores, but certainly it will make all cars safer.

Lowest Chest Injury Score

Model/Year	Chest Injury Score
1. Buick Century/Chevy Celebrity/ Olds Ciera/Pontiac 6000, '84 (Wagon score for same models: 30)	27
2. Buick Skylark/Olds Calais/ Pontiac Grand Am 4dr	31
3. Volvo DL Wagon, '85	32
4. Chevy Camaro/ Pontiac Firebird, '83	33
5. Volks. Jetta, '81	33
Audi 100 Sedan 4dr, '89	33
6. Honda Civic CRX 2dr, '84	34
7. Suburu XT 2dr, '86	34
8. Buick LeSabre '90	34
9. Chrysler LeBaron GTS/ Dodge Lancer 4dr '85	34
10. Ford Escort 2hb, '81	35

Highest Chest Injury Score

Model/Year	Chest Injury Score
1. Nissan 310 GX 2dr, '80	88
2. Suburu GLF 4dr, '72	83
3. Toyota Corolla 4dr, '80	81
4. Mazda 626 2dr '80	78
5. Chevy G-20 Van, '88	77
6. Mitsubishi Tredia 4dr., '84	72
7. Chrysler Lebaron 2dr, '87	72
8. Honda Civic 2dr, '79	70
9. Mitsubishi Mighty Max, '83	70
10. Renault Le Car 2HB, '80	69

Source: National Highway Traffic Safety Administration.

AUTOMOBILES — SAFETY
Leg Injuries

As with the previous two entries, this crash test data comes from the National Highway Traffic Safety Administration New Car Assessment Program, in which approximately 35 cars each year are tested in head-on 35-mph crashes with test dummies to determine the potential for injuries to drivers and front-seat passengers in the areas of the head, chest and leg. The following are the best and worst scores for models in the leg tests. Forces on the upper legs (measured in pounds) are indicative of the potential for injury to the femurs (the thigh bones). Scores above 2250 in the leg injury data collected under the NHTSA's test conditions indicate that leg injury is probable. The rankings below give the average of the driver and passenger results, with the score indicating the impact on the femur in pounds.

THINGS

The winner here is the spacious Lincoln Marquis/Ford LTD, which offers ample protection to the legs in a 35-mph crash. In fact, the average scores for even the worst-scoring model fall below the 2250 level for likely leg injury; however, a number of models scored above that level for either the driver or the passenger.

Lowest Leg Injury Score

Model/Year	Leg Injuiry Score
1. Lincoln Marquis/Ford LTD, '83	149
2. Toyota Tercel 4X4, '83	188
3. Mitsubishi Mighty Max, '83	233
4. Volkswagen Scirocco, '82	245
5. BMW 318I, '85	285
Isuzu Trooper I, '90	285
6. Isuzu I-Mark, '86	299
7. Mitsubishi Montero, '83	305
8. Jeep Cherokee, '84	310
9. Mazda GLC 4HB, '81	313
10. Isuzu Spacecab, '88	327

Highest Leg Injury Score

Model/Year	Leg Injury Score
1. Honda Civic CRX 2dr, '84	2169
2. Suzuki Sidekick, '89	2143
3. Volkswagen Vanagon, '88	1954
4. Dogde/Plymouth Colt Vista Wagon 4W, '86	1930
5. Toyota Cressida 4dr, '81	1786
6. Ford Club Wagon Van, '90	1714
7. Renault Le Car 2HB, '80	1708
8. Eagle Medallion 4dr, '89	1676
9. Chevy Cavalier 2HB, '82	1671
10. Ford Thunderbird II 2dr, '80	1610

Source: National Highway Traffic Safety Administration.

AUTOMOBILES—SAFETY
Deaths on the Road

Pure Muscle! The power and thrill of the great American muscle cars is an unmatched driving experience. Unfortunately, letting that Corvette or Camaro go flat-out on a winding country road is more than just exhilarating—it's deadly. So it isn't surprising that these two models head the list of the most deadly automobiles. They are owned predominantly by young males—the most accident prone of all drivers. Also among the top ten are a number of models with less muscle but also less size—sub-compacts like the Chevy Chevette and Sprint and the Honda Civic. It remains to be seen whether the addition of airbags will have a dramatic effect on the death rates in either muscle cars or sub-compacts.

Most Deaths

Model	Deaths/10,000 Cars
1. Chevrolet Corvette	5.2
2. Chevrolet Camaro	4.9
3. Dodge Charger/Shelby	4.5
4. Ford Mustang	4.4
5. Nissan 300ZX	4.2
6. Chevrolet Chevette 4-door	4.1
Chevrolet Sprint 2-door	4.1
8. Honda Civic CRX	3.9
9. Pontiac Firebird	3.8
10. Plymouth Turismo	3.6
Pontiac Fiero	3.6

Source: Insurance Institute for Highway Safety.

Fewest Deaths

Big cars provide a lot of protection in the event of an accident. The family wagon

The Chevy Cavalier is among the autos involved in the fewest fatalities in the nation. Photo courtesy General Motors.

THINGS

proves not only to be a great way to get the whole family around town, but to keep them out of harm's way. The owners of Cadillac de Villes, Lincoln Town Cars and other luxury autos also enjoy safety as an added by-product of their conspicuous consumption. Where safety is concerned, the old Detroit axiom that "bigger is better" is indeed true.

Model	Deaths/10,000 Cars
1. Audi 5000 4-door	1.1
Cadillac Fleetwood DeVille 4-door	1.1
Cadillac Fleetwood De Ville 2-door	1.1
Chevrolet Cavalier Station Wagon	1.1
Olds Cutlass Ciera Station Wagon	1.1
Toyota Cressida 4-door	1.1
Volkswagen Jetta 4-door	1.1
8. Lincoln Town Car	0.8
9. Ford Taurus Station Wagon	0.7
10. Volvo 740/760 4-door	0.6

Source: Insurance Institute for Highway Safety.

AUTOMOBILES — SALES
Top Selling

Looking at this list two things immediately jump out. The first is that pickups were the two biggest sellers in 1990. The second is that the Honda Accord was the biggest selling regular car in the United States. In fact American Honda which also had a big seller in the Civic came very close to passing Chrysler as the number three seller of cars in the United States. Overall, American car manufacturers continue to loose ground to Japanese owned plants operating in the United States. Among the big three, only General Motors gained market share in 1990. The Japanese product is now perceived as better than the American one. If Detroit is going to get back in the game, it has got to improve its quality image.

Model	Units Sold
1. Ford F-Series Pickup	522,034
2. Chevrolet C/K Pickup	487,508
3. Honda Accord	417,179

The Ford Taurus, top selling domestic car in the U.S. Photo courtesy Ford Division.

4. Ford Taurus	313,274
5. Chevrolet Cavalier	295,123
6. Ford Escort	288,727
7. Toyota Camry	284,595
8. Ford Ranger	280,610
9. Chevrolet Corsica/Baretta	277,176
10. Honda Civic	261,502

AUTOMOBILES — SALES
Top Domestically Made Cars

In 1990, Ford's incredible Taurus again topped the list of domestically manufactured cars. The distinctively styled and versatile automobile has been a hit since it and its sister vehicle, the Mercury Sable, were first introduced in the mid-1980s. The Chevy Cavalier, the most popular car with first-time buyers, made a strong showing in second, and the Ford Escort, long the most popular car in the world took third, with more than 288,000 units sold. Among imports, Honda's Accord and Civic and the Toyota Camry were right up there with the big boys in Detroit. Despite foreign ownership, these cars were manufactured with American labor right here in the good old U.S. of A.

Model	Units Sold
1. Ford Taurus	313,274
2. Chevrolet Cavalier	295,123
3. Ford Escort	288,727
4. Chevrolet Corsica/Beretta	277,176
5. Honda Accord	276,878
6. Chev. Lumina/Monte Carlo	218,288
7. Ford Tempo	215,290

THINGS

8. Toyota Camry	212,587
9. Pontiac Grand Am	202,149
10. Honda Civic	187,240

Source: *Automotive News*.

AUTOMOBILES—SALES
Top Ten Imported Cars

This list shows just how completely the Japanese now dominate the imported car market. Pure and simple, we love their cars. The European manufacturers (like the Americans) do not seem able to keep up, either in price or in perception of quality. Despite "Farvegnugen" (whatever that means) Volkswagen, once the dominant player in the imported car market with its ubiquitous "Beetle" model, sold a piddling total of 129,705 units in the U.S. in all of 1990. That's less than Honda sold of just one model, the Accord. With the entrance of Hyundai, the Koreans are beginning to make a mark of their own, al though the Korean cars have received few of the accolades of their neighbors to the north. The scene continues to change, but the Japanese seem firm in their grip; experts expect the Japanese to extend their hold on the American market from about 25% to about 33% by the end of the decade, despite the continued increase in the quality of American nameplates.

The Chevy Camaro isn't just for gearheads anymore. Now many cops are stocking up on the classic muscle car.

Model	Units Sold
1. Honda Accord	133,683
2. Nissan Maxima	100,067
3. Hyundai Excel	100,590
4. Toyota Corolla	92,258
5. Toyota Tercel	90,808
6. Geo Storm/Spectrum	86,257
7. Acura Integra	83,599
8. Honda Civic/CRX	80,880
9. Toyota Celica	78,521
10. Nissan Stanza	76,615

Source: *Automotive News*.

AUTOMOBILES—SPEED
Fastest Cop Cars

Watch out, bad guys: Smoky's got a new set of wheels. Crooks are getting more sophisticated, and speeders getting more daring on the highways, so America's police forces are looking to a new breed of police packages. Don't be surprised if in some locales, you spot the local officer at the wheel of a Ford Bronco, S-10 Blazer, Jeep Cherokee or other off-road vehicle, especially in small towns or out West. On the other hand, only Ford and Chevy continue to make police packages for general police work. The folks at *Motor Trend* checked out the new generation of police cars that Detroit is offering to state, county and municipal law enforcement agencies across the country, and rated them on speed, acceleration and braking. The top performing squad car currently available is the Chevrolet Camaro, a 5.7-liter V-8 coupe with four-speed automatic transmission that can rocket from zero to 100 in a mere 17 seconds. The Ford Mustang LX wasn't far behind the Camaro, either in top Speed (135.5 to the Camaro's 150) or in acceleration. These figures should make any thug think twice before contemplating a high-speed freeway chase with state troopers sporting these models

	Speed
Car	Top Speed (mph)
1. Chevrolet Camaro	150.0

2. Ford Mustang LX	135.5
3. Chevrolet Caprice	130.0
4. Ford Taurus	129.4
5. Ford Crown Victoria	121.3
6. Chevrolet Caprice Wagon	109.0

Acceleration

Car	Seconds, 0-100
1. Chevrolet Camaro	17.3
2. Ford Mustang LX	18.8
3. Chevrolet Caprice	29.2
4. Ford Taurus	29.6
5. Ford Crown Victoria	34.5
6. Chevrolet Caprice Wagon	42.2

Braking

Car	Stopping Distance from 60mph (ft.)
1. Chevrolet Camaro	144.7
2. Chverolet Caprice	145.3
3. Chevrolet Caprice Wagon	159.8
4. Ford Taurus	167.2
5. Ford Crown Victoria	167.6
6. Ford Mustang LX	185.4

Source: Motor Trend.

AUTOMOBILES—THEFT
Most Often Stolen

Can you picture someone else behind the wheel of your cherished new car, your prized possession, taking a whiff of that new-car smell, the one you shelled out so many somoles for the privilege of? Well, if you've recently plunked down some pretty pennies for the models below, you better get accustomed to that image. Or you better have a pretty good automotive security system. These are the models the car thieves prefer over all others. Tops on the list are high-performance sports-car models, but, surprisingly, thieves also love the look, the feel and the *safety* of the Yuppiemobile Volvo 740 and 760.

1990 Models

1. Nissan 300ZX
2. Ford Mustang
3. Volkswagen Jetta 4-door

The venerable Mustang is the most prized American car among auto thieves.

4. Cadillac Brougham
5. Mercury Cougar
6. Nissan Maxima
7. Honda Civic CRX
8. Volvo 740
9. Volvo 760 4-door
10. Ford Thunderbird

Source: Highway Loss Data Institute.

1989 Models

1. Hyundai Excel
2. Chevrolet Beretta/Corsica
3. Chevrolet Camaro
4. Ford Escort/EXP
5. Chevrolet Cavalier
6. Ford Mustang
7. Pontiac Firebird/Trans Am
8. Nissan Sentra
9. Ford Tempo
10. Ford Taurus

Source: NHTSA.

1988 Models

1. Chevrolet Cavalier
2. Pontiac Grand Am
3. Ford Mustang
4. Nissan Sentra
5. Chevrolet Corsica
6. Ford Escort/EXP
7. Ford Tempo
8. Toyota Camry
9. Honda Accord
10. Ford Taurus

Source: NHTSA.

THINGS

AUTOMOBILES — TIRES
Top Tires

The National Highway Traffic Safety Administration, in addition to testing cars for safety, also checks out tires. Its findings are that tire quality is getting better. The NHTSA grades safety features of tires, such as braking traction and temperature resistance, on a letter scale, with "A" being the best score. Treadwear, measure of the comparative tread life of a tire, is on a numerical basis. In 1985, only two tires received an "A" rating and a treadwear score above 200; in the most recent ratings, more than 100 tires fit this bill. The following is a list of the tires that received both an "A" rating in safety-related features and a treadwear score of at least 300.

Tire	Treadwear Score
1. Goodrich Comp H4 (exc. 13" & 15")	340
Goodrich Comp V4	340
3. Riken Classic STX-70 (14" & 15")	320
4. Riken STX-70 (13")	300
Riken Classic STX 70 (13")	300
Goodrich Comp H4 (13" & 15")	300
Goodrich 95H, 107H	300
Goodrich Euro T/A (14" & 15")	300
General XP2000 AS (P215/70R14)	300
Goodyear Eagle GA H/V (P195/60R15)	300
Sumitomo HTR-70 (14" & 15")	300
Uniroyal Rallye GTH	300
Hoosier A/S	300

Source: National Highway Traffic Safety Administration.

AUTOMOBILES — USED
Most and Least Valuable

For some, a car is mere transportation. For others, it's an investment. For the poor Yugo owner, it's a nightmare. A car can lose up to twenty percent of its original value the moment the happy buyer drives it off the lot. Below is a list of the cars with the best and worst depreciation records over five years. The winners, not surprisingly, are imported luxury cars and sports models; the loser, the hapless Yugo. The percentage given is that of the original value after five years.

Most Valuable	Value after 5 years
1. Porsche 911, Carrera, Cabriolet	79%
2. Honda CRX HF	76%
3. Mercedes-Benz 190E 2.6	73%
4. Volvo 240 DL	73&
5. Chevrolet Corvette	69%
6. Jaguar XJ6 Sovereign	69%
7. Mercedes Benz 300 SEL	69%
8. Honda Accord DX	67%
9. Toyota Corolla Deluxe	67%
10. Honda Prelude Si	65%
11. Toyota Celica GT	64%

Least Valuable	Value after 5 years
1. Yugo	25%
2. Dodge Daytona Shelby	34%
Audi 200	34%
4. Pontiac 6000 S/E	35%
Mercury Topaz LS	35%
6. Ford Escort Pony	36%
Ford Escort LX	36%
Dodge Daytona ES	36%
9. Pontiac Grand Prix	37%
Oldsmobile Cutlass Ciera Intl.	37%
Audi 80, Audi 90, Ford Tempo LX	37%

Source: Intellichoice, Inc.

BANKS — AMERICAN
Largest American Commercial Banks

One mark of a great nation is its ability to foster financial institutions whose influence extend beyond its physical borders. Although the swollen coffers of America's largest commercial banking institutions represent equal parts of prosperity and risk, it is indisputable that the agglomeration of large, central stores of wealth provides the nation with the ability to undertake sweeping projects, and to weather short-term shifts in the winds of international finance.

THINGS

While many American banks have seen tough times in the last five years, few doubt their long-term health. Below are the largest commercial banks with headquarters in the U.S., terms of total assets.

Bank	Assets (millions)
1. Citicorp	$207,666
2. Chase Manhattan Corp.	$97,455
3. BankAmerica Corp.	$94,647
4. J.P. Morgan Co.	$83,923
5. Security Pacific Corp.	$77,870
6. Chemical Banking Corp.	$67,349
7. First Interstate Bank Corp.	$66,710
8. Bankers Trust	$58,193
9. Bank of New York	$57,942
10. Wells Fargo & Co.	$47,388

Source: Dun and Bradstreet.

BATTLES
Bloodiest

The twentieth century has yielded many extraordinary advances in military technology. We can now kill more, better and faster than ever before. Of the battles that follow, only two are not from either WWI or WWII. They include one from the Korean conflict and the other from the worst retreat in history, Napoleon's march from Russia. The World Wars, which galvanized so much of humanity in the struggle to kill each other, make up the bulk of this record, including the grimmest statistic of all, the bloodiest battle. In World War I, near the town of Ypres in southwest Belgium, the massed Allies slugged it out with the massed Central powers in the bloodiest single battle of history. Over 380,000 men were killed on each side, with wounded and missing running at 600,000 for the allies and slightly less for the Central powers. The British commander Haig visited the battlefield only once, and had to be taken away in incredulity at what he was ordering his men into. Madly, in the First World War, the European powers fought not once, but time and again for the same shell-pocked, devastated, bloody ground; the Italians and the Austrians

fought a stupefying *eleven* Battles of the Isonzo in the course of three years, with no clear-cut decision on either side on that front (Caporetto, the Austrian breakthrough, came further north). The sheer horror of the battles on the Western front in the First World War should have convinced the world of war's futility, but sure enough, World War II erupted anyway. There is a certain numbness that settles on the mind upon reading these ratings, but here are the numbers anyway. Casualties include dead, wounded and missing from both sides.

Battle/War	Total Casualties
1. Ypres I World War I	1,800,000
2. Somme River I World War I	1,265,000
3. Po Valley World War II	740,000
4. Moscow World War II	700,000
5. Gallipoli World War I	500,000
6. Artois-Loos World War I	428,000
7. Berezina River War of 1812	400,000
8. Stalingrad World War II	350,000
9. 38th Parallel Korean War	320,000
10. Somme River II World War I	300,000

Source: Encyclopedia of Battles

BEER
Best-Selling Domestic Brews

As we turn the corner on a new decade, America seems to have cooled its affections for foreign quaffs, and renewed its interest in home-based hop houses. The rise of the "micro-brewery" — small, local brewers that turn out a premium product in relatively small numbers for avid fans — heralds a turn in taste back toward the good old U.S.A. The new "domesticity" is everywhere: at the ball park, in the living room, even at the yacht club. Our heads may not always be completely clear when we drink, but we do know enough to buy American. Bud still runs way ahead of the pack, with a firm grip on America's malted taste buds. Bud and its parent company, Anheuser-Busch of St. Louis, maintain a firm grip on the American beer market — A-B products account for over 40% of all the beer consumed in the United States. For a while, Bud seemed threatened by Miller Lite, with its popular jock-filled "Tastes Great, Less Filling" ads, but in 1982 Anheuser-Busch kick-started their Bud Light brand, whose success has reaffirmed A-B's dominance in American suds.

A tall, frosty Budweiser is overwhelmingly the beer of choice for American beer-drinkers. Bud sells more beer than the next four brews combined.

Beer Brand	1990 Sales (barrels, 000)
1. Budweiser	50,025
2. Miller Lite	19,700
3. Budweiser Light	10,800
4. Coors Light	10,500
5. Busch	9,100
6. Miller High Life	7,500
7. Old Milwaukee	6,950
8. Milwaukee's Best	6,700
9. Coors	5,150
10. Miller Genuine Draft	4,700

Source: Beer Marketer's Insights.

BEERS
Top Beer Imports

Imported beer has been a status symbol in the United States, but how do particular beers reach this status-symbol level among the millions of gallons of imported brew flooding into the U.S. every year? Certainly aggressive marketing, as in the case of Heineken and Beck's, is important. But even the Mexican makers of Corona were surprised by the sudden mystique their beer attained in the U.S. in the 1980s. In fact, you could drive over the border into Mexico and buy a case of Corona for what you'd pay for one bottle of the stuff in a trendy Southern California bar. But fads go as quickly as they come, and some trendy beers can go on the wane. Who knows which could be the next imported-beer Cinderella story: Thailand's Singha, Italy's Peroni, Mamba Beer from Kenya . . . ? The following are U.S. sales figures for imported beers, in millions of 2.25 gallon cases, for the year 1989.

Beer	Cases (mill)	Share
1. Heineken	31.8	26.7%
2. Corona Extra	17.3	14.5%
3. Beck's	10.1	8.5%
4. Molson Golden	9.9	8.3%
5. Moosehead	6.0	5.0%
6. Labatt's Blue	5.8	4.9%
7. Amstel Light	4.5	3.8%

8. Tecate	3.2	2.7%
9. St. Pauli Girl	3.1	2.6%
10. Foster's Lager	3.0	2.5%

Source: Jobson's Liquor Handbook.

BIRDS
Rarest

The California condor chick that recently hatched in the San Diego Zoo has a face only a mother could love; but the rest of us should feel a cause for hope that this species, of which there is only one known in the wild, can be saved through an active program of captive breeding and eventually reintroduced to the wild. However, numerous obstacles threaten the existence of this and other species, not the least of which is the continuing encroachment of man on the natural habitat of these rare creatures. Even the whooping crane, whose numbers showed steady increase since an active protection program began in the 1950s, still exists in such small numbers that a single cataclysmic event, such as a disease within the population, can wipe out the entire species in one blow. In fact, the whooping crane population, which had gradually grown from only 15 in 1941 to 198 in 1988, suffered a severe setback in 1989, when its number dropped a frightening 69% in one year, down to 136. Sadly, despite our efforts, the continued survival of these rare species is a matter more of luck than anything else.

Bird	Number, Worldwide, Wild
1. California Condor	1
2. Northern Bald Ibis	7
3. Seychelles Magpie Robin	19
4. Pink Pigeon	20
5. Cahow	35
6. Puerto Rican Parrot	35
7. Mauritius Kestrel	46
8. St. Lucia Amazon	100
9. Whooping Crane	136
10. Short-tailed Albatross	165

Source: Environmental Data Report, United Nations Environment Programme, 1989.

California Condor chick "Amalyi" with hand-puppet mother. Photo by Ron Garrision, © San Diego Zoo.

BOOKS
Most Influential

There's been a lot of debate recently about the Great Books—whether such a "canon" should remain part of the educational curriculum, or, indeed, whether one can even judge a work's "greatness." The original concept behind the Great Books series, developed by Robert M. Hutchins and Mortimer Adler, was to bring together the works that were most fundamental in forming and espousing the driving ideas of our society and our culture—from philosophy and political science to mathematics and even fiction. The debate now raging is over the "Euro-centric" nature of the traditional canon of great books—the fact that these works were overwhelmingly the creations of dead white European men, and that alternate views of the world—female, ethnic,

THINGS

modern, African, Latin American, Asian — are slighted. Be that as it may, there are quantitative methods of establishing just what the most influential works in the world are. One of these methods is citation analysis, which measures the number of times a particular work is mentioned in academic writing. An analysis performed by the editors of the Arts and Humanities Citation Index® yielded this list of the most-cited works published in the twentieth century, in a seven-year period from 1976 to 1983. The most cited work in that period was *The Structure of Scientific Revolutions*, a work by Thomas S. Kuhn that explored the ways in which scientific ideas are formulated and scientific theories developed from those ideas. Second on the list, surprisingly, is a work of fiction, James Joyce's *Ulysses*. Philosophy is well-represented in the top ten, with Ludwig Wittgenstein's *Philosophical Investigations*, as well as the works by the French thinkers Jacques Derrida, Roland Barthes and Michel Foucault and German phenomenologist Martin Heidegger. These great books, it seems, represent a wide variety of viewpoints.

Book/Author	Citations
1. *Structure of Scientific Revolutions* Thomas S. Kuhn	855
2. *Ulysses* James Joyce	710
3. *Anatomy of Criticism* Northrop Frye	699
4. *Philosophical Investigations* Ludwig Wittgenstein	668
5. *Aspects of the Theory of Syntax* Noam Chomsky	640
6. *The Order of Things* Michel Foucault	488
7. *Of Grammatology* Jacques Derrida	475
8. *S/Z* Roland Barthes	454
9. *Being and Time* Martin Heidegger	450
10. *European Literature and the Latin Middle Ages* Ernst R. Curtius	434

Source: Current Contents, April, 1987.

BOOKS
The Cost of Reading

No wonder nobody reads anymore. Judging from the average price of a hardcover book these days, it's much cheaper to head down to Blockbuster and rent a video for three dollars. And videos, being a passive entertainment, don't take nearly the amount of mental effort on the part of the viewer as reading does for the reader. Reading is even more physically challenging: try eating popcorn while holding a book with one hand and turning the pages with another. If God had meant us to read, he would have given us three hands. The most expensive books, not surprisingly, are weighty tomes in technical fields such as science, technology and medicine; lighter fare such as kids books and fiction are a bargain by comparison. The following are average per-volume prices for 1989

Hardcover

The Most Expensive	Avg. Cost, Hardcover
1. Technology	$44.26
2. Science	$43.46
3. Medicine	$39.71
4. Law	$38.12
5. General Works	$37.47
6. Education	$36.54
7. Language	$35.66
8. Art	$35.43
9. Music	$35.39
10. Sociology, Economics	$35.03

The Cheapest	Avg. Cost, Hardcover
1. Juvenile	$12.13
2. Fiction	$18.44
3. Home Economics	$21.44

4. Biography	$24.43
5. Travel	$26.53
6. Religion	$26.63
7. Poetry, Drama	$27.45
8. Literature	$30.46
9. History	$31.73
10. Philosophy, Psychology	$33.34

Trade Paperbacks

The Most Expensive	Avg. Cost
1. Science	$26.75
2. General Works	$25.87
3. Law	$23.42
4. Medicine	$21.94
5. Business	$20.92
6. Education	$18.95
7. Sociology, Economics	$18.54
8. Music	$18.25
9. Language	$17.56
10. Art	$16.92

The Cheapest

1. Juvenile	$6.61
2. Fiction	$9.78
3. Religion	$11.00
4. Poetry, Drama	$11.07
5. Biography	$11.36
6. Home Economics	$12.08
7. Technology	$13.66
8. Literature	$14.78
9. Philosophy, Psychology	$14.93
10. History	$15.18

Source: The Book-Trade Almanac, 1990-91.

BOOKS
Best-Selling Paperback Books, All-time

Everyone loves a paperback. They're lighter and easier to carry around, easier to handle on the subway or at the beach. Tucked into the back pocket, a paperback can make anyone look like a member of the *literati*. The list below represents the most popular books in this form. Several of the winners in this category, including Orwell's *1984* and *Animal Farm* and J.D. Salinger's *Catcher in the Rye* did well when they came out, but

because of their lasting message, have earned permanent spots on the reading lists of many high school English classes. Spock's *Baby and Child Care* has made its way onto the shelves of nearly 40 million new mothers in the U.S. and abroad. We didn't know there were that many pointy-eared Vulcans around.

Book/Author	Millions of Copies Sold
1. *Baby and Child Care* Dr. Benjamin Spock	39.2
2. *How to Win Friends and Influence People* Dale Carnegie	17.4
3. *The Hobbit* J.R.R. Tolkien	14.5
4. *1984* George Orwell	12.8
5. *The Exorcist* William Peter Blatty	12.4
6. *The Thorn Birds* Colleen McCullough	10.9
7. *Animal Farm* George Orwell	10.5
8. *Mythology* Edith Hamilton	10.0
9. *Catcher in the Rye* J.D. Salinger	9.7
10. *Love Story* Erich Segal	9.5

Source: Publisher's Weekly, May 26, 1989.

BOOKS
Best-Selling Children's Books, All-time

The paperback children's book market is dominated by a handful of extremely popular and successful authors—Judy Blume, S.E. Hinton, and Laura Ingalls Wilder with her *Little House* books account for six of the ten best-selling children's paperbacks of all-time. Hinton and Blume

THINGS

especially address modern problems kids face in growing up. The list of best-selling hardcover children's books, on the other hand, is dominated by classics such as *Peter Rabbit* and *Mother Goose*, and, of course, Dr. Seuss.

Paperback

Book/Author/Publisher   Sales (millions)

1. *The Outsiders*   **5.855**
   S.E. Hinton (Dell/Laurel-Leaf, 1968)

2. *Are You There, God?*
   It's Me, Margaret   **5.278**
   Judy Blume (Dell/Yearling and Laurel-Leaf, 1974)

3. *Charlotte's Web*   **4.607**
   E.B. White, illus. by Garth Williams (Harper Trophy, 1973)

4. *Tales of a Fourth-Grade Nothing* **4.582**
   Judy Blume (Dell/Yearling, 1976)

5. *Little House on the Prairie*   **3.803**
   Laura Ingalls Wilder, illus. by Garth Williams (Harper Trophy, 1971)

6. *The Little Prince*   **3.667**
   Antoine de Saint-Exupery (HBJ, 1968)

7. *Little House in the Big Woods*   **3.495**
   Laura Ingalls Wilder, illus. by Garth Williams (Harper Trophy, 1971)

8. *That Was Then, This Is Now*   **3.351**
   S.E. *Hinton (Dell/Laurel-Leaf, 1972)*

9. *Where the Red Fern Grows*   **3.347**
   Wilson Rawls (Bantam, 1974)

10. *Superfudge*   **3.243**
    Judy Blume (Dell/Yearling, 1981)

Hardcover

The figures in these lists cover sales from the date of original publication throught the end of 1988. The lists are based on actual sales as reported by publishers; they reflect domestic sales only.

Book/Author/Publisher   Sales (millions)

1. *The Tale of Peter Rabbit*   **9.000**
   Beatrix Potter (Frederick Warne, 1902)

2. *Pat the Bunny*   **4.857**
   Dorothy Kunhardt (Golden Books, 1940)

3. *The Littlest Angel*   **4.665**

S.E. Hinton, author of "The Outsiders."

Judy Blume, top children's author.

Charles Tazewell (Children's Press, 1946)

4. *The Cat in the Hat*   **3.693**
Dr. Seuss (Random House, 1957)

5. *Green Eggs and Ham*   **3.683**
Dr. Seuss (Random House, 1960)

6. *The Children's Bible*   **3.654**
Golden Books, 1965

7. *The Real Mother Goose*   **3.600**
Illus. by Blanche F. Wright (Rand McNally, 1916)

8. *Richard Scarry's*
Best Word Book Ever   **3.303**
Richard Scarry (Golden Books, 1963)

9. *One Fish, Two Fish,*
Red Fish, Blue Fish   **2.970**
Dr. Seuss (Random House, 1960)

10. *Hop on Pop*   **2.953**
Dr. Seuss (Random House, 1963)
Source: *Publishers Weekly.*

BOOKS
Most Popular Book Subjects

Despite its defeats in other intellectual, political and commercial arenas, the United States remains the world's most prolific publisher and consumer of printed materials. Although, as a nation, we demonstrate an enormous interest in the sometimes insubstantial field of fiction, our foremost demand is for practical tomes on sociology and economics. But curiously, in making up a list of Book Subjects, *Publishers Weekly* feels it necessary to differentiate between "Fiction" and "Literature." Where exactly is the line drawn? If the two were combined, then fictive literature would lead the list.

Topic	Published titles per year
1. Sociology/Economics	7,119
2. Fiction	5,144
3. Juvenile	4,212
4. Medicine	3,376
5. Science	3,118

Peter Rabbit is the top-selling hard-cover children's book of all time.

6. Religion	2,306
7. Technology	2,756
8. Biography	1,994
9. Literature	1,982
10. Philosophy/Psychology	1,656

Source: Publishers Weekly.

BOXING
Biggest Heavyweight Upsets

By the time heavyweight champion Mike Tyson signed on to fight the relative unknown Buster Douglas in Tokyo on February 10, 1990, the sporting media was treating Tyson bouts the same way in which the news media had been treating space shuttle flights before January, 1986. Just as shuttle flights had become routine, almost boring affairs, not even worth covering live by the networks, Tyson's title fights had become predictable early-round knockouts,

THINGS

hardly meriting a few paragraphs in the morning sports pages. Like the flight of the *Challenger*, with its teacher-in-space theme, Tyson's bout with Douglas needed some gimmick to attract any interest at all, this being the Tokyo locale. The Vegas oddsmakers had given Douglas only a 45-to-1 chance to wrest the title from "Iron Mike" Tyson, known for his vicious punches and his violent character, both in and out of the ring. But when the smoke cleared from that ring in Tokyo, Tyson had tumbled from boxing's firmament with a stunning, *Challenger*-like plunge in the 10th round, and folks had to stand up and take notice. The shine was off the Tyson myth, and a new folk hero had emerged in the rotund Douglas. Although Douglas turned out to be a one-punch wonder — after bulking up to a full-figured 246 pounds, he was easily dispatched by Evander Holyfield in his first title defense — the unlikely hero from Ohio had scored the biggest upset in boxing history. Here are other top upsets, with their pre-fight odds:

Winner/Loser	Odds Against
1. Buster Douglas/Mike Tyson	45-1
2. Muhammad Ali/G. Foreman	10-1
3. James Braddock/Max Baer	10-1
4. Cassius Clay/Sonny Liston	7-1
5. Leon Spinks/Muhammad Ali	6-1
6. Jersey Joe Walcott/E. Charles	6-1
7. Ingemar Johansson/F. Patterson	4-1
8. James Corbett/John L. Sullivan	4-1
9. George Foreman/Joe Frazier	3-1
10. Gene Tunney/Jack Dempsey	11-5

Source: *National Sports Review*.

BRANDS
Most Familiar Worldwide

Nothing could be more American than a burger and a Coke, but nowadays, nothing could be more international, too. Global brands have insinuated themselves into the daily lives of almost every person on the planet. Coca-Cola is available in virtually every country in the world, and according to the Landor ImagePower Survey/1990 of familiarity and esteem, the Real Thing is the most recognizable brand name in the world. Coke's global acceptance is due in no small part to American foreign policy — G.I.'s stationed overseas during and after World War II brought their taste for Coke to countries from Iceland to the South Pacific. Indeed, American brands take up six of the top ten global brands in terms of share of the world's mind. The Golden Arches places second in this category, but, interestingly, ranks much lower on the esteem scale, scoring only 85th. They may line up for Big Macs in Red Square and on the Champs Elysées, but foreigners don't really *like* those familiar patties.

The Top Ten

1. Coca-Cola
2. McDonald's
3. Pepsi-Cola
4. Sony
5. Kodak
6. Toyota
7. Nestlé
8. Disney
9. Honda
10. Ford

Source: Landor Associates.

BRANDS
Most Esteemed Worldwide

There's an interesting disparity between the rankings for familiarity and esteem in the Landor ImagePower Survey/1990. In the category of familiarity, American brands placed one, two and three. But none of those three most familiar brands are the top three esteemed brands, and only one — Coca-Cola — is in the top ten in the list of most esteemed brands. On the contrary, Japanese mega-corporation Sony owns the most well-regarded name-plate in the world. To be fair, though, some of the less recognized American brands are extremely highly regarded — for instance, Duracell is only 86th in the world in terms of familiarity, but those who know the brand certainly hold it in high esteem—seventh in the world, in fact. Here, then, are the most esteemed brands in the world.

The Top Ten

1. Sony
2. Mercedes-Benz
3. Rolls Royce
4. IBM
5. Disney
6. Coca-Cola
7. Duracell
8. Levi's
9. Kodak
10. Panasonic

Source: Landor Associates.

BRANDS

Most Powerful

The Landor ImagePower Survey/1990 polled 10,000 consumers in the world's three major markets—the United States, Japan and Western Europe, to determine the most powerful brand names in the world. Although megabrands continue to spread their influence across national borders, the survey showed that of the 6,000 brand names tested, just two—Coca-Cola and Sony—ranked in the top 40 across all three markets, and only another six ranked in the top 100 in all three markets: Disney, Nestlé, Toyota, McDonald's, Panasonic and Kleenex. The Landor survey identified the existence of an emerging class of global consumers—an under-40 market of avid media consumers willing to gobble up product regardless of where a brand's corporate headquarters are located. Think about it. Despite all the intense pleas to "Buy American," even the most xenophobic American consumer lusts after an Acura Legend and a Sony television. The following are the most powerful brand names in the world, as judged by the Landor ImagePower Survey/1990. "ImagePower" is a combination of familiarity and esteem.

The Top Ten

1. Coca-Cola
2. Sony
3. Mercedes-Benz
4. Kodak
5. Disney
6. Nestlé
7. Toyota
8. McDonald's
9. IBM
10. Pepsi-Cola

Source: Landor Associates.

BRANDS

Most Powerful Brand Names in America

Staying power is the name of the game for the ten most powerful brand names in America in the Landor ImagePower Survey/1990. All of the brands in the top ten have been around for at least thirty years. In fact, the youngest company in the group is McDonald's. When Andy Warhol painted his soup cans, he captured something uniquely American, and the survey shows that. Campbell's is the number two brand in the United States, but doesn't even rank in the top 50 worldwide. Another uniquely American phenomenon, the survey indicates, is the desire to tinker away at the workbenches on the weekend: tool-maker Black & Decker is the seventh most powerful brand name in the United States, yet it does not rank in the top 50 worldwide. Neither does NBC or Hershey's.

The Top Ten

1. Coca-Cola
2. Campbell's
3. Disney
4. Pepsi-Cola
5. Kodak
6. NBC
7. Black & Decker
8. Kellogg's
9. McDonald's
10. Hershey's

THINGS

Source: Landor Associates.

BRANDS
Most Powerful Brands in the Soviet Union

Good capitalists across the world are drooling at the prospects of the opening of free markets in the former Communist world, without the complicated bureaucratic red tape of which Lenin's heirs were so fond. Still, some brands have found a way, whether by greasing palms or through incredible patience, to penetrate perhaps the most rigid large centralized market still existing— the Soviet Union. Sony is the most powerful brand in Russia, followed by sportswear maker Adidas and American automaker Ford. The latter's prominence in the minds of the Soviet consumer may be due to the memories of the thousands of the lend-lease Ford trucks that rolled off of American ships and onto Soviet soil during the Second World War. The following are the most powerful brand monikers in the Soviet Union.

The Top Ten

1. Sony
2. Adidas
3. Ford
4. Toyota
5. Mercedes-Benz
6. Fanta
7. Pepsi-Cola
8. Volvo
9. Fiat
10. Panasonic

Source: Landor Associates.

Broadway has been drawing them in for decades. Photo © N.Y.S. Dept. of Economic Development.

BROADWAY
Longest Running Play

Broadway is no longer what it once was, in the asphalt (concrete) or in the abstract. The grand street, today, hosts more runaways that debutantes and Ditch Debonnaires, and the theaters are dominated by re-tread versions of foreign imports such as *Phantom of the Opera* and *Les Miserables*. High prices also keep many from the Great White Way. But all these rational facts aside, Broadway is still very much Broadway, and the indefinable, sometimes smutty spark has not dimmed. *Chorus Line* recently shut down its hugely successful run of 6, 137 shows. Below are the most successful Broadway shows in history, measured by the length of their runs.

Play	Run	Shows
1. *A Chorus Line*	1975-90	6,137
2. *Oh, Calcutta*	1976-89	5,959
3. *42nd Street*	1980-89	3,486
4. *Grease*	1972-80	3,388
5. *Cats*	1982-	3,437
6. *Fiddler on the Roof*	1964-72	3,242
7. *Life with Father*	1939-47	3,224
8. *Tobacco Road*	1933-41	3,182
9. *Hello, Dolly!*	1964-71	2,844
10. *My Fair Lady*	1956-62	2,717

Note: As of Dec. 31, 1990.

THINGS

BUILDINGS
America's Tallest Buildings

One tick back on the geological timescale, the American skyline was defined by trees, mountain tops and eagles' nests. Today, much of our land lies in the shadows of the great steel and concrete shelters we have erected. Of our tallest structures, the top two are of recent vintage; but the venerable Empire State building still holds its own.

Building	Height (ft.)
1. Sears Tower (Chicago)	1,454
2. World Trade Center (NYC)	1,377
3. Empire State (NYC)	1,250
4. Standard Oil (Chicago)	1,136
5. John Hancock Center (Chicago)	1,127
6. Chrysler (NYC)	1,046
7. Texas (Houston)	1,002
8. Allied Bank (Houston)	985
9. American International (NYC)	952
10. Citicorp Center (NYC)	915

The Sears Tower, world's tallest building. Photo courtesy of Sears; photographer: Bob Shimer/Hedrich Blessing.

CANCER
Most Prevalent, Worldwide

The following list represent the most common types of cancer found throughout the world. The list represents malignant neoplasms only (benign cancers are not included) and refers to the total number of incidences of each type reported in a given year (1980) regardless of the outcome. Thus, the figures refer to the total number of cases, not the number of fatalities, in the entire population. For women, the most prevalent cancers are of the breast, cervix, colon, corpus uterus, lung and ovary. Men suffer most from cancers of the lung, stomach, colon, mouth, prostate, esophagus and liver. Breast cancer is not unknown in men; several hundred American males are stricken by this cancer each year.

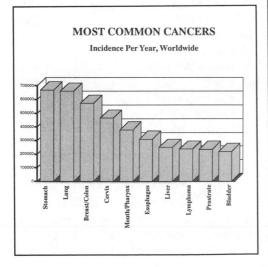

MOST COMMON CANCERS
Incidence Per Year, Worldwide

Type	Incidence, Worldwide
1. Stomach	669,400
2. Lung	660,500
3. Breast	572,100
Colon/Rectum	572,100
4. Cervix	465,600
5. Mouth/Pharynx	378,500
6. Esophagus	310,400

THINGS

7. Liver	251,200
8. Lymphoma	237,900
9. Prostrate	235,800
10. Bladder	219,400

Source: Environmental Data Report, United Nations Environment Programme, 1989.

COMIC STRIPS
Longest Continuously Running Comics in America

The comic strip of late has become more respectable, thanks in part to the Pulitzer Prize for editorial cartooning won by *Bloom County*. But as the comics become more politically active, will they lose their staying power? After all, comics have always been relegated to the back pages of the paper, as a respite from the storm and stress of the daily news and editorial pages. How else to explain the endurance of such alliterative favorites as Katzenjammer Kids, Moon Mullins and Winnie Winkle? The following is a list of the longest-running comics in American newspapers.

Comic	Year Started
1. Katzenjammer Kids	1897
2. Bringing Up Father	1913
3. Ripley's Believe It Or Not	1918
4. Barney Google & Snuffy Smith	1919
5. Gasoline Alley	1919
6. Winnie Winkle	1920
7. Moon Mullins	1923
8. Annie (Little Orphan Annie)	1924
9. Tarzan	1929
10. They'll Do It Every Time	1929

Katzenjammer Kids. Reprinted w/special permission of King Features Syndicate, Inc.

CEREALS
Most Popular Breakfast Cereals

Although cereal commercials dot the Saturday morning schedule, the breakfast in a bowl is hardly just kid stuff. In this nutritionally enlightened age, scads of health conscious, heart-healthy, high-fiber Hanks and Hannas are working cereal into their morning regimens. Soaring sales and cut throat competition have been the results, with cereals making claims and counterclaims about fiber content, recommended daily allowances, cholesterol levels, fat content and the number of bowls you'd have to eat to equal the vitamin content in each other's product. One thing is for certain, though: the next closest cereal brand, Kellogg's Corn Flakes, would have to *sell* almost twice as many bowls as it does now to match the total sales performance of the leading cereal brand, that breakfast of champions, Cheerios. The following are the top ten cereal brands, in 1990 sales.

Cereal	1990 Sales ($ Millions)
1. Cheerios	$670
2. Corn Flakes	$380
3. Frosted Flakes	$360
4. Total	$255
5. Rice Krispies	$234
6. Raisin Bran	$207
7. Chex	$200
8. Cap'n Crunch	$186
9. Shredded Wheat	$179
10. Fruit Loops	$158

Source: Superbrands 1990.

CHOCOLATES
Most Popular Chocolates

When the urge for chocolate hits, most of us will munch any sweet cocoa-derived substance that crosses our culinary path. Given the leisure and luxury of selection, however, America docs have decided favorites. Despite the growing popularity of elite, foreign chocolate makers like Tobler, Lindt, and Cadbury, the U.S. market is still dominated by these five blue-collar favorites. At the top of the list is that most sanitary of coated chocolate treats, the M&M, the product of the super-secret Mars Corporation. For between meal satisfaction, Snickers finishes a delicious second.

Candy	Total Sales ($ millions)
1. M&M's	$1,000
2. Snickers	$750
3. Reese's Peanut Butter Cup	$425
4. Milky Way Bar	$263
5. Hershey's Kisses	$249

Source: Superbrands 1990.

CIGARETTES
Most Popular Cigarette Brands

The American tobacco industry is running scared. After years of constant warnings about the dangers of cigarette smoke from the nation's most respected health experts, the American public is finally getting the message, and cigarette smoking is on the decline. Smokers are outcasts, relegated to dark, dreary corners of restaurants, airports, offices and other public spaces. In the wake of this phenomenon, the tobacco companies have taken on new strategies, one of which is diversification. Powerhouse tobacco giant Philip Morris expanded into another vice-exploitation field by buying up the Miller Beer company as well as Kraft, and the merger R.J. Reynolds and Nabisco was one of the largest and most highly contested buyouts in American business history. Other strategies include expanding into less health-regulated foreign markets such as Asia, producing lighter and lower tar-and-nicotine smokes, and targeting specific, more susceptible U.S. markets—such was the idea behind the now-infamous "Uptown" cigarette campaign, marketed at the country's urban black population. But

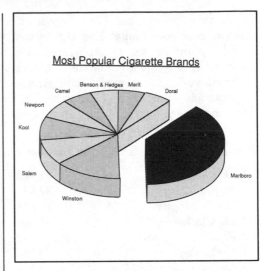

Most Popular Cigarette Brands

despite setbacks, cigarettes still do a "healthy" business, with total sales of stalwart Marlboro at nearly $10 billion annually. For the most part, the brands that cross the counter most are owned by Philip Morris or R.J. Reynolds.

Brand	1990 Retail Sales (billions)
1. Marlboro	$9.8
2. Winston	$3.4
3. Salem	$2.4
4. Kool	$2.2
5. Newport	$1.8
6. Camel	$1.5
7. Benson & Hedges	$1.5
8. Merit	$1.4
8. Doral	$1.4

Source: Superbrands 1990.

CLOTHING
Best-Selling Apparel Manufacturers

Americans like fancy pants, but nothing beats the venerable blue jean, with its slow fade, long life and comfort. Indeed, the blue jean has so pervaded our culture that they've even broken the formal dress code of many normally stodgy American restaurants and business offices. In many companies, the low-tech, jeans-and-sneakers look has replaced the suit and tie as the fashionable

THINGS

businessman's statement. Let's hear it for comfort over conformity! The U.S. is the world's point of denim-departure, with Levi's alone netting more than three billion dollars in worldwide sales of its various lines of jeans and casual slacks last year. The following are the top ten American apparel manufacturers, measured by 1990 sales.

Brand	1990 Sales (millions)
1. Levi's, Dockers	$3,628
2. Hanes, L'Eggs	$2,873
3. Lee, Wrangler	$2,533
4. Liz Claiborne	$1,400
5. Fruit of the Loom	$857
7. Leslie Fay	$786
8. Melrose, Smart Shirts	$753
9. Bass Shoes, Van Heusen	$733
10. Russell Athletic, Cross Creek	$688

Source: Superbrands 1990.

COFFEE
Best-Selling Coffee Brands

Americans are strung out on java. But the medical community is unsure just what this addiction means in terms of the nation's health. Just as some research team publishes a paper decrying the harmful effects of caffeine, another group somewhere else purports to show its beneficial medicinal qualities. In the face of such conflicting opinion, we go chugging mass quantities of the dark brew, from double-decaf capuccino in trendy urban cafes to the stalwart regular coffee served up at truckstops across the land. The leading U.S. brand, Folgers, vended more than $1 billion in caffeine-crusted java in the previous year alone. The following are the top ten coffee brands in America, measured by 1990 supermarket sales. These figures do not take into account the massive quantities of joe sucked down at local coffee counters.

Coffee	1990 Supermarket Sales (millions)
1. Folgers	$1,130
2. Maxwell House	995.3
3. Hills Bros.	238.1
4. Taster's Choice	198.4
5. Sanka	149.2
6. Nescafe	110.0
7. MJB	109.4
8. Chock Full O'Nuts	91.8
9. Yuban	73.6
10. Chase and Sanborn	69.4

Source: Superbrands 1990.

COLLEGES – ANIMAL RESEARCH
Most Frequent Institutional Users of Laboratory Animals

The animal rights movement has become surprisingly and alarmingly radicalized. Although it is easy to perceive that animal life has been indiscriminantly sacrificed in academia and industry in the past, the extremist conclusion that there is never a justification for such a sacrifice is highly debatable. Moderates in this debate recognize the validity of animal use for legitimate medical and scientific purposes. The key now is to find suitable alternatives to animal research in as many cases as possible, without seriously hindering advances in scientific and medical knowledge. The following institutions are the most prolific users of animals in laboratory research.

Inst.	Reported Experiments on Animals
1. Univ. of California	76,698
2. Univ. of Texas	33,323
3. Wilmington Med. Center	30,604
4. Univ. of Southern California	25,116
5. Univ. of Wisconsin	23,477
6. Univ. of Illinois	19,111

Source: Investor Responsibility Research Center.

COLLEGES – BIG TEN
Ph.D. Production in Big Ten Schools

The schools of the Big Ten offer a diverse curriculum that caters to the needs of their very large student bodies. Still, these schools, most of which are public and state-sponsored, produce a fair number of eventual Ph.D.'s from among their undergraduates, especially in sheer numbers. The numbers are not as great in terms of the percentage of the undergraduate student body that eventually earns Ph.D's, but that is understandable, given the public mandate of these schools, and their somewhat more open admissions policies. Given these considerations, we present here the Ph.D. institutional productivity of the Big Ten schools, ranked from first to last by the number of baccalaureate earners who go on to get a doctoral degree. None of the Big Ten schools sends more than 1% of its undergraduates on to a doctoral degree in the humanities; in fact, only one-tenth of one percent of all Purdue baccalaureates eventually are conferred a Ph.D. in a humanities discipline.

School	% Eventually Earning Ph.D.
1. Michigan	5.7
2. Illinois	5.2
3. Wisconsin	5.3
4. Northwestern	4.7
5. Purdue	4.6
6. Minnesota	3.8
7. Iowa	3.7
8. Ohio State	3.6
9. Indiana	3.2
10. Michigan State	3.1

Source: "An Analysis of Leading Undergraduate Sources of Ph.D's, Adjusted for Institutional Size," Great Lakes Colleges Association.

COLLEGES—
CONTRIBUTIONS
The Rich Get Richer:
Most Generous Alumni

Alumni and other individuals are responsible for nearly half of all voluntary support—contributions—for American colleges and universities—a total of about $4.3 billion in 1989. Other entities involved in such support include corporations, foundations and religious organizations. Most colleges in recent years have realized the great financial resources represented by alumni and have intensified fund-raising efforts to tap that resource. These efforts resulted in a 75 percent increase in voluntary support from alumni to higher education over the past five years. The following are the institutions that reap the biggest windfall from those tax-deductible contributions, measured by total 1989 voluntary support.

University	Voluntary Support
1. Stanford Univ.	$188,635,513
2. Harvard Univ.	$185,353,003
3. Cornell Univ.	$157,072,064
4. Yale Univ.	$122,755,800
5. Univ. of Pennsylvania	$121,945,814
6. Columbia Univ.	$110,422,711
7. Univ. of Southern Cal.	$102,628,589
8. Univ. of Wisc.-Madison	$102,232,856
9. Duke Univ.	$102,016,708
10. Univ. of Minnesota	$100,170,258

Source: Council for Aid to Education.

COLLEGES—
CONTRIBUTIONS
More Blessed To Give: Biggest
Individual Contributions

Once upon a time in antiquity, the doting, the church and the loving aristocracy provided almost sole financial support for the arts and education. Although we live in a benign, equitable, quasi-democratic civilization, with widescale government support of institutions both public and private, this reliance on the beneficence of individuals to support higher education is still largely the case. Higher education still relies to a remarkable degree on the generosity and publicity-hunger of a very few monied individuals, and the roll-call of contributions reads like a list of the most successful Americans—Hewlett, Packard, Annenberg, Mellon. The following are the most generous donations to universities in the past year.

University/Donor	Behest
1. **Emory University** Robert W. Woodruff	$105 million
2. **Stanford University** David Packard	$70 million
3. **University of Miami** James L. Knight	$56 million
4. **CalTech** Arnold and Mabel Beckman	$50 million
5. **Cornell University** Anonymous	$50 million
6. **Stanford University** William R. Hewlett	$50 million
7. **United Negro College Fund** Walter Annenberg	$50 million
8. **University of Richmond** E. Clairborne Robins	$50 million
9. **Yale University** Paul Mellon	$47 million
10. **University of Texas** Harold C. Simmons (Southwestern Medical Center)	$41 million

Source: *Chronicle of Higher Education.*

COLLEGES — COSTS
Most Expensive Colleges

American higher education has reached a dangerous pass. Tuition and fees at private colleges have climbed into the high monopoly-money stratosphere, while government loans, grants and subsidies have fallen to discouragingly low levels. The "education" president, George Bush, has done little to address the financial aid shortfall which confronts this country. If the problem is not taken under rapid advisement, many of our most promising students will miss the opportunity to maintain competitiveness with their foreign counterparts. "You get what you pay for," so the expression goes, but at the following prices you better be getting a whole bunch. The most expensive schools offer name recognition, a great network of alumni to help find employment after graduation, the best professors, courses, etc. Not to mention the fact that the educational environment is superior: diverse student body, plenty of activities, excellent facilities and other opportunities to learn. But are those the prices that the market itself establishes? The courts recently found the Ivy League schools guilty of fixing their prices so that no school within the group set tuitions prices that varied widely with any other. The schools argued that this practice made the prospective student's choice one based on the school itself, and not on cost; the courts decided that lack of competition made the tuition prices artificially high. Measured by 1989-90 tuition costs alone (skipping over room and board, which tacks on at least $5,000 more dollars per school year), here are the most expensive schools you can attend.

College	1989-90 Tuition
1. **Bennington College, VT**	**$16,495**
2. **Bates College, ME**	**$16,322**
3. **Dartmouth College, N.H.**	**$15,372**
4. **Hampshire College**	**$15,070**
5. **Brown University, RI**	**$14,920**
6. **Georgetown University, DC**	**$14,690**
7. **Bard College, NY**	**$14,630**
8. **Middlebury College, NH**	**$14,610**
Wesleyan, CT	**$14,610**
9. **Harvard University, MA**	**$14,560**
10. **Swarthmore College, PA**	**$14,530**

Source: National Center for Educational Statistics, Barron's Profiles of American Colleges.

COLLEGES — DEFENSE CONTRACTS
D.O.D. Contracts: Hawk Universities

Kurt Vonnegut once said, in response to Allen Ginsburg's poem "Howl," that if you want to find the best minds of our generation, you should look not to the streets of New York, but to the physics and chemistry departments of our universities. Certainly the U.S. Defense Department knows this. The Pentagon spends tens of billions of dollars each year in research and development of weapons systems, and a lot of that money goes to universities. Science departments at major research universities are involved in research on everything from the Star Wars missile defense program to high-tech nutrition to feed the Army of the next century. The leader in defense department grants is the Massachusetts Institute of Technology. The following ranking lists non-profit institutions receiving the most money from Defense Department contracts in the fiscal year 1989.

Institution	D.O.D. Grants, 1989
1. Mass. Inst. of Tech.	$410,578,000
2. Johns Hopkins Univ.	$327,647,000
3. IIT Research Institute	$78,151,000
4. Univ. of California	$56,507,000
5. Pennsylvania State Univ.	$53,950,000
6. Carnegie Mellon Univ.	$49,023,000
7. Univ. of Texas	$33,362,000
8. Stanford Univ.	$32,192,000
9. Ga. Tech Research Corp.	$31,945,000
10. Utah State Univ.	$31,705,000

Non-University Non-Profit Institution

1. Mitre Corporation	$384,216,000
2. Aerospace Corporation	$301,430,000
3. Charles S. Draper Lab.	$54,986,000
4. RAND Corporation	$50,953,000
5. SRI International	$45,624,000

Source: U.S. Department of Defense.

COLLEGES – DEGREES AWARDED

Most Bachelor's Degrees Awarded

Which schools account for the most degrees awarded to a single class? Naturally, the larger numbers come from the largest schools, but after attrition and people who don't make the four-year trek, the graduating class is always less than what it started out to be. Graduation is still the goal of most, and the people who do make it can feel justifiably proud. The following schools have awarded the most bachelor's degrees to a given class in a single year.

School	Bachelor's Degrees Awarded
1. Pennsylvania State U.	7,415
2. Ohio State U.	6,853
3. Univ. Texas, Austin	6,751
4. Michigan State U.	6,488
5. Texas A & M	6,064
6. U. Wisconsin, Madison	6,000
7. U. Illinois, Urbana-Cham.	5,938
8. U. Maryland	5,570
9. U. Minnesota, Minn./St.Paul	5,525
10. U. Alabama	5,276

Source: Digest of Educational Statistics.

COLLEGES – DEGREES AWARDED

Most Master's Degrees Awarded

Unlike undergraduate study, Master's level study and above attracts candidates to different institutions. Prestige is a factor, as indicated by the results of this ranking — most of the master's degrees come from "name" schools, private institutions rather than public. Location is also important – a large number of Master's degrees are earned by those who are currently in the workforce or returning to school after some time spent working; these students tend to gravitate toward schools in large metropolitan areas, such as New York, Los Angeles and Boston. The two schools at the top of the list, therefore, are both located in New York City, the center of the American financial and corporate community. Columbia University leads the way followed immediately by New York University. The leading bestowers of Master's degrees are as follows:

THINGS

Columbia business school graduates waving their meal tickets. Photo Joe Pineiro, courtesy Columbia University.

School	Master's Degrees Awarded
1. Columbia University, N.Y.	3,803
2. New York University, N.Y.	3,700
3. University of Southern Cal.	2,955
4. University of Michigan	2,582
5. Harvard/Radcliffe University	2,513
6. Boston University, MA	2,082
7. Ohio State University	2,042
8. University of Illinois	2,004
9. University of Wisconsin	1,983
10. University of Minnesota	1,951

Source: Digest of Educational Statistics

COLLEGES – DEGREES AWARDED
Most Ph.D.s Awarded

Where do academicians come from? Specifically, Ph.D. recipients? It seems that those interested in pursuing the doctoral degree want one of two extremes as far as educational environment. On the first, fourth and tenth of the list, the relaxing, comfortable climate of warm California and Texas seem to provide fertile grounds for nurturing scholarly work. The others on the top of the list find the darker, colder, and perhaps more introspective environments of the northeast or upper-midwest. With this in mind, the most Ph.D.s come from the following institutions:

Institution	Ph.D.s Awarded
1. Univ. of California, Berkeley	727
2. Univ. of Wisconsin, Madison	667
3. Univ. of Illinois	616
4. Univ. of Texas, Austin	612
5. Columbia Univ.	593
6. Univ. of Michigan	589
7. Ohio State Univ.	570
8. Univ. of Minnesota	508
9. Michigan State Univ.	464
10. UCLA	448

Source: Digest of Educational Statistics

The University of California at Berkeley produces more Ph.D.s each year than any other school in the country.

THINGS

COLLEGES—
ENDOWMENTS
Largest

Who's got the deepest pockets among American colleges and universities? As non-profit entities, universities pay no taxes on their properties or their endowments. They are, thus, some of the richest and most powerful organizations in the country. Three of the top four richest schools—Harvard, Princeton and Yale—are old-money Ivy League institutions. However, they've recently been joined by the *nouveau riche* of the academic world, the University of Texas, which has benefitted from Texas oil money to raid other schools' faculties for top professors and build a first-rate research university. Here, then, are the best-endowed schools in the country, in terms of their market value as of June, 1990.

School	Market Value
1. Harvard	$4,478,976,000
2. Univ. of Texas	$3,021,474,000
3. Princeton Univ.	$2,483,829,000
4. Yale Univ.	$2,336,495,000
5. Stanford Univ.	$1,775,000,000
6. Columbia Univ.	$1,460,356,000
7. Texas A&M	$1,304,536,000
8. Washington Univ.	$1,294,209,000
9. Mass. Inst. of Tech.	$1,256,165,000
10. Univ. of Chicago	$973,697,000

Source: *Chronicle of Higher Education.*

COLLEGES—
ENDOWMENTS
Best Endowed Students

Perhaps more important than total endowment, from the student's perspective at least, is the ratio of endowment to number of students. The winner in this category is the small Academy of the New Church, with a whopping $444,495 per student. In the public university arena, the Virginia Military Institute—which has counted amongst its

faculty Stonewall Jackson—enjoys the highest endowment-per-student ratio.

Private Institution	End./Stud.
1. Academy of the New Church	$444,495
2. Princeton Univ.	$398,369
3. Cal. Inst. of Tech.	$274,485
4. Harvard Univ.	$264,075
5. Rice Univ.	$242,583
6. Agnes Scott College	$235,293
7. Swarthmore College	$228,912
8. Grinnell College	$227,456
9. Yale Univ.	$221,721
10. Pomona College	$195,848

Public Institutions

1. Virginia Military Inst. Found.	$65,785
2. Ore. Health Sciences Univ Fnd.	$34,411
3. Texas A&M System	$26,091
4. Univ. of Virginia	$25,446
5. Univ. of Texas System	$24,469
6. Univ. of Delaware	$19,549
7. Georgia Inst. of Technology	$13,123
8. Univ. of Cincinnati	$12,102
9. College of William & Mary	$10,487
10. Univ. of Michigan	$9,573

Source: *Chronicle of Higher Education.*

COLLEGES—FIELDS OF
STUDY
Most Popular Undergraduate
Degrees

A few decades ago, the American higher education system saw a renaissance of Liberal Arts study. In these pragmatic, economically-troubled times, though, it is not surprising that these sublime but financially unrewarding pursuits have once again declined in popularity. With spiraling tuition costs, today's average student is asking for an education which will bring immediate, tangible results. But are we trading long-term cultural, political and, yes, economic health for immediate gain? Is anybody worried that three times as many undergraduates want to study business management than look to go into engineer-

THINGS

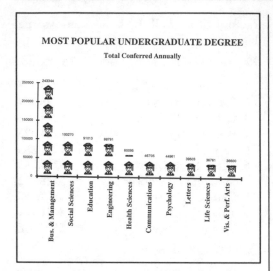

MOST POPULAR UNDERGRADUATE DEGREE
Total Conferred Annually

ing? Or that this country grants twice as many bachelor's degrees in the visual and performing arts as it does in the physical sciences? As the list below demonstrates, we've become much better at managing, advertising and selling products than we are at actually developing and building them, much better at dancing and acting than at discovering and inventing.

Field	Bachelor's Awarded Annually
1. Business and Management	243,344
2. Social Sciences	100,270
3. Education	91,013
4. Engineering	88,791
5. Allied Health & Health Sciences	60,095
6. Communications	46,705
7. Psychology	44,961
8. Letters	39,503
9. Life Sciences	36,761
10. Visual and Performing Arts	36,600

Source: U.S. Department of Education.

COLLEGES—FIELDS OF STUDY
Most Popular Master's Degree Subjects

Going on to pursue an advanced degree is an interesting decision. Masters study is more intense and focused than under-graduate study, and the numbers receiving Masters degrees are considerably less than the plethora of undergraduate awards. The choice to pursue such an advanced degree is dictated by the needs of the profession you are going into, and whether such a degree is either required or imperative for credibility in the profession. The top two subject areas fit these requirements respectively. The number one subject, education, requires a Master's in order to attain rank in the teaching profession. In the number two subject, business and management, the M.B.A. has become the standard that many businesses require for today's marketplace. What follows are the most popular Masters Degree subjects rated by number bestowed annually.

Field	Master's Awarded Annually
1. Education	75,501
2. Business & Management	67,496
3. Engineering	22,081
4. Health Sciences	18,426
5. Public Affairs	17,032
6. Social Sciences	10,393
7. Visual & Performing Arts	8,506
8. Psychology	8,204
9. Computer & Info. Science	8,491
10. Letters	6,123

Source: Digest of Educational Statistics.

COLLEGES—FIELDS OF STUDY
Most Popular Ph.D. Degree Subjects

The Ph.D. is the highest level of educational achievement. It is also the most difficult to actually attain because of the length of time in school required—the wait for many doctoral students can last more than ten years! As can be expected, the most Ph.D.s are to be found in the field of education, because it is the logical extension of the field itself. The numbers of Ph.D.s awarded is quite small—the total of all of these top ten do not add up to the 10th-ranked baccalaureate subject area. In a wry comment on wisdom through increasing education, the Ph.D. in business and management is ranked 10th, dropping from the 1 and 2 spots it occupies for the B.A. and M.B.A. The following are the top ten areas of study in which doctorate degrees are awarded annually.

Field	Ph.D.s Awarded Annually
1. Education	6,909
2. Engineering	3,809
3. Physical Sciences	3,672
4. Life Sciences	3,423
5. Psychology	3,123
6. Social Sciences	2,916
7. Theology	1,236
8. Health Sciences	1,213
9. Letters	1,181
10. Business & Management	1,098

Source: Digest of Educational Statistics

COLLEGES — FIELDS OF STUDY
Strangest Majors

If you want to major in Swahili, where do you look for a program of study? Surprisingly, according to Lovejoy's College Guide, there are more than 10 institutions that offer Swahili as a major. If you really want a "different" established major program of study (many institutions offer the option of creating your own major, but that does not enter into this rating), the following colleges are worth a look. The following rating is determined by the number of majors that are offered at 4 or fewer or institutions (any exclusive major is listed with *). This rating does not include the engineering sub-disciplines, which are legion and of which Rensselaer and M.I.T. have many. The school is listed first, with the interesting major and the number of instituions offering that major in parentheses.

Institution/Rare Major

1. Rensselaer Polytech. Inst., NY
   Strategic Studies *

Nuclear Metallurgy (2)
   Quantum Mechanics (3)
   Radio Biology (3)
   Radio Isotope Technl. (3)
   Endocrinology (4)
   Medical Physicist (4)
2. Massachusetts Inst. Tech., MA
   Bio-Mechanics (2)
   Cryogenics (2)
   Holographics (2)
   Nuclear Metallurgy (2)
   Quantum Mechanics (3)
3. Hampshire College, MA
   Brazilian *
   Finnish (2)
   Conflict-War Studies (2)
4. Stetson Univ., FL
   Orthoptics (2)
   Ornithology (3)
   Endocrinology (4)
   Icthyology (4)
5. Univ. California, Davis, CA
   Enology (Winemaking) (2)
   Pomology (4)
   Endocrinology (4)
6. Univ. of Rhode Island, RI
   Commercial Fishing *
   Aquaculture (4)
7. Rochester Inst. Tech., NY
   Glass Science (3)
   Gunsmithing (4)
8. SUNY Col. of Envirn. & Forestry
   Ornithology (3)
   Icthyology (4)
9. Univ. of New Haven, CT
   Arson Investigation (4)
   BioMed. Computing (4)
10. Nicholls State Univ., LA
   Sugar Cane Technology *
10. Univ. of Alaska, AK
   Northern Studies *
10. Maine Maritime Academy, ME
   Craft/Boat Design *
10. Slippery Rock Univ., PA
   Cruise Marketing *
10. High Point College, N.C.
   Fur Design/Marketing *

(*) = exclusive major, (#) = Number of institutions that also have programs in that subject.

THINGS

Source: Lovejoy's Guide, 19th ed.

COLLEGES— FRATERNITIES
Largest

Although it may be some years since you personally attended a kegger, polesit or other frat-house fiesta, be advised that the Greek system is still going strong, coast to coast. Although pledge volume slacked off in the hippy heydays of the sixties, the conservative climates of the Reagan and Bush presidencies have ushered in a new era of frat-brotherly love. In addition to housing, meals and companionship while in school, fraternities offer a wide network of contacts when time comes to trade in the toga for a suit and tie. Here, then, are the largest Greek organizations in the country.

Fraternal Org.	1990 membership
1. Sigma Alpha Epsilon	214,502
2. Sigma Chi	200,300
3. Lambda Chi Alpha	191,560
4. Phi Delta Theta	176,728
5. Tau Kappa Epsilon	176,072
6. Kappa Sigma	174,387
7. Sigma Phi Epsilon	171,025
8. Sigma Nu	170,000
9. Alpha Tau Omega	152,619
10. Phi Kappa Alpha	152,477

Source: National Interfraternity Conference, Inc.

COLLEGES— HUMANITIES
Top Undergraduate Colleges, Humanities

Using the criteria that examines how many undergraduates of a school go on to earn the Ph.D. in specific fields, we have compiled a list of the top colleges for development of eventual humanities Ph.D's. The schools below are ranked by the percentage of their college graduates that eventually earn a Ph.D. in a humanities discipline. It is the smaller liberal arts colleges, led by the three Pennsylvania schools Bryn Mawr, Haver-

ford and Swarthmore, that top the list here. Also making the top ten is St. John's of Maryland, which, with its counterpart in Santa Fe, New Mexico, is unique in offering the "Great Books" curriculum in which students study the seminal texts of Western civilization as opposed to elective courses in particular fields. Notably absent here are the Ivy League schools (the highest scoring of which in this category is Princeton at 3.2%, and the lowest scoring Cornell and Penn at just 1.0%) and the larger, more diverse public institutions.

School	% Humanities Ph.D.s
1. Bryn Mawr	5.7
2. Haverford	5.4
3. Swarthmore	5.2
4. Oberlin	5.1
5. St. John's (MD)	4.9
6. Amherst	4.5
7. Reed	4.0
8. Peabody Institute	3.9
Radcliffe (tie)	3.9
9. Juilliard	3.6
Wesleyan (CT) (tie)	3.6
10. Barnard	3.5
Carleton (MN)	3.5

Source: "An Analysis of Leading Undergraduate Sources of Ph.D's, Adjusted for Institutional Size," Great Lakes Colleges Association.

COLLEGES— IVY LEAGUE
Ivy League Ph.D. Production

What's the brainiest of the Ivy League schools? The list below provides a comparison, based on the percentage of undergraduate degree earners who eventually earn a doctoral degree. Tops on the scholarly list is Princeton, where 11.7% of the baccalaureates eventually earn a Ph.D. somewhere. Still, that represents a marked change from the tradition in which the Ivy League schools blazed the trail in American scholarship. Princeton, the top Ivy school in this category, ranks only 21st on the overall list of the top fifty institutions for producing

THINGS

Nearly twelve percent of all Princeton undergraduates eventually earn a Ph.D.

the scientists, humanities scholars, life scientists and social scientists that do the all-important research keeping the U.S. on the cutting edge in scientific and scholarly fields, as well as training the next generation of the intellectual elite. We leave it to another ranking to see if the Ivys fare any better in producing America's business and political leaders.

School	% Eventually Earning Ph.D.
1. Princeton	11.7
2. Harvard	9.0
3. Cornell	8.8
4. Yale	8.4
5. Brown	8.3
6. Dartmouth	7.8
7. Columbia	6.7
8. Dartmouth	4.7

Source: "An Analysis of Leading Undergraduate Sources of Ph.D's, Adjusted for Institutional Size," Great Lakes Colleges Association.

COLLEGES — LIFE SCIENCES
Top Undergraduate Colleges, Life Sciences

Life sciences mainly include biological research fields and pre-med courses. The list below represents the top ten colleges in the country ranked by the percentage of earners of Bachelor's degrees going on to earn a Ph.D. in a life sciences discipline. As the rankings show, the University of California system scores strongly in this particular field of study — with its branches in San Diego and Irvine capturing the top two spots, while the Riverside campus tied for eighth and the Santa Cruz campus placed tenth. The ubiquitous Harvey Mudd also turns up in the seventh spot, joining its number one ranking in the empirical sciences. In fact, with Cal Tech at fifth and Pomona in the ninth spot,

The University of California at San Diego is the top undergraduate producer of life science Ph.D.s.

one might say that the national center for study of the life sciences has entrenched itself in the sunny climes of California. This ranking also brings to light some other very good schools that are not household names—Earlham and Wabash in Indiana and New College of the University of South Florida—but produce a relatively large portion of life science Ph.D.s.

College	% Life Science Ph.D.'s
1. UC-San Diego	5.2
2. UC-Irvine	4.6
3. Philadelphia C. of Pharmacy	4.3
4. Reed	4.0
5. California Institute of Technology	3.8
Delaware Valley C. of Science & Agriculture (tie)	3.8
6. Swarthmore	3.1
7. Harvey Mudd	2.9
Wabash (IN) (tie)	2.9
8. UC-Riverside	2.6
Haverford (tie)	2.6
New College/U. of So. Florida	2.6
9. Pomona	2.4
Earlham (IN) (tie)	2.4
10. UC-Santa Cruz	2.3

Source: "An Analysis of Leading Undergraduate Sources of Ph.D's, Adjusted for Institutional Size," Great Lakes Colleges Association.

COLLEGES—MERIT SCHOLARS
Where the Brains Are

The National Merit Scholarship Corporation provides scholarships to the best and brightest students in the country, based on college board scores. The figures below reveal that Harvard has the most merit scholars in the freshman class; also that it has a very high *percentage* of National Merit Scholars in its entering class, compared with larger schools such as the University of Texas at Austin. The following is a list of the colleges with the most freshman National Merit Scholars enrolled in 1989.

College	Freshmen Merit Scholars
1. Harvard and Radcliffe Colleges	314
2. Univ. of Texas at Austin	217
3. Stanford Univ.	203
4. Rice Univ.	198
5. Yale Univ.	169
6. Princeton Univ.	141
7. Carleton College	123
8. Massachusetts Inst. of Tech.	113
9. Univ. of Chicago	111
10. Georgia Institute of Technology	109
Texas A&M University	109

Source: National Merit Scholarship Corporataion.

COLLEGES—PH.D. PRODUCTIVITY
Total Ph.D.s Earned by Undergraduates

A good way of determining a school's educational quality is to look at the number of Ph.D.'s that it produces from its undergraduate population. There have been several studies done on this subject in the past decade, and the figures have been made available by the National Research Council. The list below represents the top ten universities in terms of the number of baccalaureate graduates who went on to earn a Ph.D. (not necessarily from the same school as the undergraduate degree, it should be noted). The numbers refer to those receiving Bachelor's degrees in the period from 1946 to 1976 who earned Ph.D.'s between 1951 and 1980. Not surprisingly, the list is dominated by larger universities—such as Berkeley, the City University of New York, and various Big Ten schools, which grant thousands of Bachelor's degrees every year.

School	Ph.D.s Earned by U.G.s
1. UC-Berkeley	8,801
2. CUNY	6,893
3. U. of Illinois	6,761
4. U. of Michigan	6,569
5. U. of Wisconsin, Madison	6,049
6. UCLA	5,717

7. Harvard	5,554
8. Mass. Institute of Technology	5,438
9. Cornell	5,329
10. U. of Minnesota	5,321

Source: "An Analysis of Leading Undergraduate Sources of Ph.D's, Adjusted for Institutional Size," Great Lakes Colleges Association.

COLLEGES — PH.D. PRODUCTIVITY

Brain Power: Most Academically Productive Undergraduate Institutions

In the previous entry, we saw the schools that produced the most Ph.D.'s, in terms of sheer numbers, from its baccalaureates. But a truer gauge of the "institutional productivity" of colleges and universities is the *percentage* of its graduates that go on to earn Ph.D's, for this figure corrects for institutional size. The numbers below give the true brainiest schools for undergraduates. The grand winner is Harvey Mudd College in Southern California, a member of the Claremont Colleges in California that is little known by the public but highly selective and extremely prestigious in technical, scientific and engineering fields. More than forty percent of Harvey Mudd's graduates go on to earn doctorate degrees. Two other technical schools — MIT and Cal Tech — also scored highly, but the big surprises on the list are the smaller liberal arts colleges, such as Reed, Swarthmore, Haverford and Oberlin, which may be less well-known than the Ivy League schools but produce many more scholars and scientists, as a percentage of their enrollment, than their more famous counterparts.

School	Percent Eventual Ph.D.s
1. Harvey Mudd (CA)	40.7
2. California Inst. of Technology	40.0
3. Reed (OR)	25.3
4. Mass. Institute of Technology	20.9

Swarthmore (PA) (tie)	20.9
5. Haverford (PA)	18.8
6. Oberlin (OH)	17.8
7. New College / U. of So. Florida	16.1
8. Univ. of Chicago	15.6
9. Univ. of. Calif.-San Diego	14.1
10. Amherst (MA)	14.7
Carleton (MN)	14.7
Cooper Union (NY)	14.7
Pomona (CA)	14.7

Source: "An Analysis of Leading Undergraduate Sources of Ph.D's, Adjusted for Institutional Size," Great Lakes Colleges Association.

COLLEGES — R&D

Top Research and Development Universities

Below we have listed the top ten universities in the United States in terms of expenditures

Tiny Harvey Mudd College in California produces the most Ph.D.s, as a percentage of baccalaureates, of any U.S. school. More than 40% of all Mudd undergraduates eventually earn the doctorate. Photo courtesy Harvey Mudd College.

on research and development. Johns Hopkins is the leader in medical research among American universities. The rating does not include spending on arts, education, humanities, law or physical education and is expressed in terms of annual expenditures on scientific and engineering research and development.

University	R&D Spending
1. Johns Hopkins Univ.	$557,016,000
2. Stanford Univ.	$277,504,000
3. Cornell Univ.	$271,659,000
4. Univ. of Wisc.-Madison	$271,418,000
5. MIT	$270,584,000
6. Univ. of Minnesota	$252,027,000
7. Univ. of Michigan	$250,169,000
8. Texas A&M Univ.	$231,161,000
9. UCLA	$209,338,000
10. UC-San Diego	$200,472,000

Source: Chronicle of Higher Education.

COLLEGES -- SAT SCORES

Highest SAT Score

The Scholastic Aptitude Test of one of the several standardized tests that can have an impact on your chances of admission to college. It is nice to note that it is not the only factor, which is fortunate for someone who fares poorly on standardized tests. The SAT tests verbal and mathematical ability, the highest test score is 800 in each category. In the "Most Highly Competitive" group of colleges profiled in Barron's, the highest median SAT scores are listed for nearly every school (some of the top colleges, such as Yale and Harvard, merely state "SAT required" and do not list a score). Of the schools that give median SAT scores, here are the top ten.

School	Verbal	Math
1. Calif. Inst. of Tech.	650	750
2. Harvey Mudd Coll .	630	740
3. Mass. Inst. of Tech.	622	735
4. Williams College	654	682
5. Dartmouth College	630	700
6. Swarthmore College	650	680
7. Webb Inst. of Nav. Arch.	610	710
8. Pomona College	630	690
9. Amherst College	637	675
10. Wesleyan Univ.	630	680

Note: If the combined scores are equal, the single higher score sets the rating level.

COLLEGES -- SCIENCE

Slide Rule Centers: Top Undergraduate Science Schools

As with overall Ph.D. productivity, Harvey Mudd College leads the list of institutional productivity in the empirical sciences. More than one-third of Mudd's undergraduates go on to earn a doctoral degree in an empirical or "hard" scientific field. Not surprisingly, the two best-known science schools in the country—Cal Tech and MIT—round out the top three. Check the list below if you are a contemplating a career in science and trying to pick a college. These schools are the places where America's scientific future lies, and hence its ability to compete in the world marketplace of ideas in the coming century. Here are the top ten schools in the percent of undergraduates who eventually earn Ph.Ds in an empirical science discipline.

School	% U.G.s Earning Science Ph.D.
1. Harvey Mudd	34.4
2. California Inst. of Technology	33.7
3. Mass. Institute of Technology	17.1
4. Cooper Union	12.5
5. Webb Institute (NY)	11.0
6. Reed	8.7
7. Rensselaer Polytechnic Institute	7.3
Rice (tie)	7.3
8. Polytechnic Institute of New York	7.2
9. Carnegie-Mellon	6.0
10. Univ. of Calif.-San Diego	5.6

Source: "An Analysis of Leading Undergraduate Sources of Ph.D's, Adjusted for Institutional Size," Great Lakes Colleges Association.

THINGS

COLLEGES — SELECTIVITY
The Other Reason to Dread April 15: The Most Selective Schools in the Country

The Ides of April aren't feared merely by those who owe big bucks in taxes to to Uncle Sam. April 15 is the traditional date that prospective college students get the news whether they've been admitted to the school of their choice. The hardest universities to get into are, understandably, in the most highly competitive category of Barron's Profiles of American Colleges. Ivy league schools and the military academies top the list as the most selective of the crop. Considering the instant name recognition, the network of contacts established and the strength of the educational experience, it is no wonder that so many apply to these places, thereby forcing a rather brutal selection process to narrow the field. The leader among this group handles around 15,000 applications of which only 1,800 can be accepted, and only 1,400 actually join the freshman class.

Institution	% Accepted
1. U.S. Military / Naval Academy	11.3
2. Harvard University	17.5
3. Princeton University	18.3
4. Yale University	18.7
5. Stanford University	18.7
6. Cooper Union, NY	19.6
7. Georgetown University	21.1
8. Amherst College	22.1
9. Brown University	22.9
10. Bowdoin College	23.9

Source: Barron's Profiles of American Colleges, 17th ed.

COLLEGES — SOCIAL SCIENCES
Top Undergraduate Colleges, Social Sciences

Social science disciplines include sociology, anthropology, psychology, political science and other fields studying the action and interaction of the individual and social groups. The schools in which the largest percentage of undergraduates go on to receive a doctoral degree in a social science field appears below. Reed College of Oregon tops the list, with 7.3 percent of the students who received a Bachelor's degree there between 1946 and 1976 eventually earning a Ph.D in the social sciences between 1951 and 1980.

School	% Soc. Science Ph.D.s
1. Reed	7.3
2. Swarthmore	6.1
3. New College /U. of So. Florida	5.6
4. New School for Soc. Res. (NY)	5.5
5. Brandeis	5.0
6. Oberlin	4.9
7. Univ. of Chicago	4.4
8. Antioch (OH)	4.1
9. Haverford	3.9
Eckerd (FL) (tie)	3.9
10. Radcliffe	3.3
Wesleyan (CT) (tie)	

Source: "An Analysis of Leading Undergraduate Sources of Ph.D's, Adjusted for Institutional Size," Great Lakes Colleges Association.

COLLEGES — STUDENT BODY
Largest Enrollment — Campus

Would you like to be little fish in a big pond? At the Universities of Minnesota and Texas, Ohio State University and other huge campuses, students need not fear falling asleep in a lecture — there's very little chance the professor will notice among the hundreds of bodies in the lecture hall. Of course, many of the largest classes are freshman lectures, and the teacher/student ratio decreases as students sort out their majors and take more courses specific to their field of study. So don't be too daunted by these huge campus numbers.

THINGS

University/Campus	Total Enrollment
1. Univ. of Minn. – Twin Cities	61,556
2. Ohio St. Univ. Main Campus	53,661
3. Univ. of Texas - Austin	50,106
4. Michigan State Univ.	44,480
5. Miami-Dade Comm. College	43,880
6. Arizona State Univ.	43,426
7. Univ. of Wisc.- Madison	43,364
8. Univ. of Michigan-Ann Arbor	39,123
9. Univ. of Arizona	38,337
10. Penn St. Univ. Main Campus	37,269

Source: U.S. Department of Education.

COLLEGES – STUDENT BODY
Largest Undergraduate Enrollment

Choosing a college to go to is one of the complex decisions a high-schooler makes. Should you pick a tough college? A religious school? A college you can most likely be accepted at? And the questions continue: What will the teachers be like? The students? etc. The following rating ranks the colleges by undergraduate population. If you wish to become one of the faceless masses in an undergraduate population or if you just like crowds, these are the places to go. As you may surmise, state schools are the largest, with immense undergraduate populations. For schools within a state system, figures given are for the main branches.

School	UG Population
1. Univ. of Texas, Austin	38,118
2. Ohio State Univ.	33,722
3. Univ. of Toronto	31,782
4. Michigan State Univ.	31,407
5. Texas A & M Univ.	30,580
6. Pennsylvania State Univ.	29,133
7. Purdue Univ.	26,994
8. Indiana Univ.	26,347
9. Univ. of Illinois	24,973
10. UCLA	24,284

Source: Barron's Profiles of American Colleges, 17th edition 1990

COLLEGES – STUDENT BODY
Most Foreign Students

Around the world, the value of an education at an American institution is taken for granted. Students from around the world come to the U.S. to learn expertise in science, mathematics, medicine, management and a wide range of other fields, and take that knowledge back to their own countries for public and private gain. The American school that welcomes the most foreign students is Miami-Dade, the largest community college in the country, and one of the finest. One of the reasons for the large foreign enrollment is that, as a community college, the school has less strict admission standards, so foreign students don't need to master the intricacies of placement tests and admissions policies. Here are the schools at which you're most likely to meet (or even room with) a foreign student. Figures for large schools are for the main campuses.

School	Foreign Student Population
1. Miami-Dade Comm. College	5,080
2. Univ. of Southern California	3,486
3. Univ. of Texas	3,385
4. Boston Univ.	2,940
5. Univ. of Wisconsin	2,919
6. UCLA	2,859
7. Ohio State Univ.	2,790
8. Columbia Univ.	2,673
9. Univ. of Pennsylvania	2,654
10. Univ. of Illinois	2,569

Source: Institute of International Education.

COLLEGES – STUDENT BODY
Highest Percentage of Foreigners

If you like to meet people from different places without leaving the country, one way to go about doing so is to attend a school where many foreign nationals are enrolled. Many of the colleges that have high enroll-

244

ments of foreign student populations are for the most part, small schools. The leading school, Armstrong College, has a total enrollment of 100 undergraduate and 100 graduate students, but within that group over 30 countries are represented. Another interesting note is that foreign students have the most representation in specialty schools (like the three music schools in the list) rather than general institutions. What follows are the heaviest concentrations of foreign students in U.S. colleges.

School	% Foreign
1. Armstrong College, CA	55%
2. American Armenian College, CA	44%
3. Hamilton College, N.Y.	43%
4. Brigham Young University, HI	40%
Mannes College of Music, N.Y.	40%
6. Maharishi Intl. College, IA	39%
7. Hellenic College, MA	36%
8. Manhattan School of Music, N.Y.	31%
9. U.S. International University, CA	30%
Academy of the New Church, PA	30%
Curtis Institute of Music, PA	30%

Source: Barron's Profiles of American Colleges, 17th ed.

COLLEGES — STUDENT LOANS

Deadbeats: Who's the Credit Manager in Oklahoma?

It's said America has become a nation of borrowers. Indeed, many people are so over-extended on their credit that they must seek psychological as well as financial counseling. Where did we learn this nasty tendency? Perhaps at college, especially if we went to school in Oklahoma. An astounding five of the ten public universities whose students are the biggest deadbeats are in that state. Undoubtedly, this number has something to do with the economy of the state, which has been hit hard in recent years by the oil industry slump. Seems that when it comes to paying back student loans, Oklahomans would rather do it later than "Sooner." The

following list represents schools with the highest percentage of defaults on student loans made by the Guaranteed Student Loan Program. A default occurs when a borrower is 180 days past due with a payment.

Public Institutions	% Defaulters
1. Rose State College, Okla.	69.9%
2. Langston U., Okla.	53.6%
3. Alabama State U.	52.9%
4. Central State U., Okla.	49.2%
5. Northeastern Oklahoma State	49.1%
6. U. of Science and Arts, Okla.	49.1%
7. Cheyney U., Pa.	45.8%
8. Texas Southern U.	44.0%
9. Southern U. & A&M College, La.	42.8%
10. Sinte Gleska College, S.D.	41.7%

Private Institutions	
1. Tarkio College, Mo.	78.7%
2. Flaming Rainbow U., Okla.	72.7%
3. Sojourner-Douglass College	68.3%
4. Arkansas Baptist College	60.0%
5. Lane College, Tenn.	58.3%
6. St. Augustine's College, S.C.	55.1%
7. Voorhees College, S.C.	57.3%
8. Knoxville College, Tenn.	53.9%
9. Wilberforce U., Ohio	53.8%
10. Hawaii Pacific College	53.7%

Source: U.S. Dept. of Education.

COLLEGE ATHLETICS

Athlete Graduation Rates, Div. I-A

The relation of higher education to sports has always been a strange one. Every day, it seems, the papers are filled with tales of athletes receiving payoffs from coaches or boosters, illegal recruiting tactics, one team trying to snatch up a talented high school player through promises and payoffs, college athletes corrupting their bodies through steroid use, in an ever more desperate attempt to impress the pro scouts. The rewards our society grants a successful professional athlete are many, and the trade in college athletes with potential is a vast underground economy for coaches, scouts, assistants and alumni. What seems to be lost is the mission of the university to provide their athletes with an education, as well as a possible career in professional sports.

The *Chronicle of Higher Education* recently surveyed all of the NCAA's Division I schools to establish whether colleges were fulfilling their duties to assure that the student-athlete was just that—a student first and an athlete second. Of the 295 current Division I schools, 262 responded to the survey, which sought to track the percentage of freshmen entering in the fall of 1985 who graduated by August, 1989, for the student body as a whole, as well as all athletes recruited for that year. Overall, the survey found, athletes at Division I schools graduate at a *higher* rate than the student body as a whole. A little more than 56 percent of all athletes recruited for the fall of 1984 (that includes athletes in all sports, both male and female) graduated by August 1989, compared to about 48 percent for the general student body. However, a closer look at the figures reveals a more disturbing side of collegiate sports. The NCAA breaks Division I schools into three sections, I-A, I-AA and I-AAA, the latter two the less-costly, less-visible intercollegiate competition. Division I is where the big football and basketball schools play, and the news is much bleaker in those arenas. Division I-A schools graduate football players at a 42.5 percent rate, and basketball players at just 31.9 percent, a significant drop from the overall graduation rate of 50.3 percent for all students and 51.1 percent for athletes.

We give here first the Division I-A schools with the worst and the best graduation rates for athletes entering in the fall of 1984 receiving degrees by August, 1989. Of the 104 Division I schools surveyed, 92 responded with graduation rates for their athletes. The schools not responding were Brigham Young, Penn State, San Diego State, San Jose State, Temple, Tulane, Air Force Academy, Univ. of Arizona, Univ. of Miami, Univ. of Pittsburgh, Univ. of Utah, Utah State.

The big schools with the worst graduation rates for athletes are primarily public institutions located in the South and West. The schools with the best athlete graduation rates are academically well-regarded, and some are private—Duke, Notre Dame, Boston College, etc. And although Northwestern won't be winning any Big Ten titles in the major sports any time soon, Duke and Notre Dame are powerhouses with recent national titles in basketball and football. The following are the schools with the lowest and the highest graduation rate of student athletes.

Lowest	Athl. Grad. Rate
1. Univ. of Houston	18.1
2. U. of S.W. Louisiana	19.5
3. U. of Nevada-Las Vegas	21.1
4. U. of Texas, El Paso	22.5
5. Cal-State Fullerton	23.9
6. Louisiana State	24.1
7. Texas A&M	24.7
8. Univ. of New Mexico	25.3
9. Univ. of Oklahoma	27.1
10. Oklahoma State	27.5

Highest	Athl. Grad. Rate
1. Duke	95.9
2. Univ. of Notre Dame	92.8
3. Boston College	89.4
4. Univ. of Virginia	86.0
5. Northwestern	84.7
6. Stanford	84.1
7. U.S. Naval Acad.	80.3
8. Ball State	80.2
9. Rutgers	73.9
10. Vanderbilt	71.7

Source: *Chronicle of Higher Education*.

COLLEGE ATHLETICS
Football Graduation Rates, Div. I-A

As we noted in the previous entry, graduation rates in Division I sports were significantly lower for players in the marquee sports of football and basketball than they were for athletes as a whole and for the overall student body. In this rating, we look specifically at football programs. The reason for this is that football programs recruit a larger number of students than baskctball programs – several dozen at the big football schools compared to just a handful in most basketball programs – and thus gives a statistically larger pool to work with. Indeed, at 29 Division I-A schools, none of the recruited basketball players that enrolled in fall, 1984 graduated by August, 1989; at seven schools, all the recruited bas-ketball players graduated in this period, but with just one or two players at each school, these numbers are not very telling of perfor-mance of individual programs. The follow-ing are the ten lowest and ten highest graduation rates for football programs in Division I-A. The list of lowest rates in-cludes some big football guns and perennial bowl contenders, including Texas A&M, Auburn and Tennessee. But proving that succcss on and off the grid-iron are not mutually exclusive, the list of best gradua-tion rates includes some very successful football programs, most notably Notre Dame.

Worst	Football Grad. Rate
1. Texas A&M	6.7
2. Cal-State Fullerton	8.3
3. Univ. of Maryland	11.1
4. Auburn	14.8
5. Texas Tech	15.4
6. Southern Methodist*	16.0
7. Univ. of Tennessee	16.7
8. Univ. of Texas, El Paso	16.7
9. U. of Nevada-Las Vegas	17.4
10. Univ. of Louisville	18.8

Best	Foot. Graduation Rates
1. Duke	92.3
2. U.S. Naval Acad.	85.2
3. Boston College	85.0
4. Rutgers	84.2
5. Northwestern	81.5
6. Univ. of Virginia	81.5
7. Univ. of Notre Dame	81.3
8. Univ. of Hawaii	77.8
9. Stanford	71.4
10. Univ. North Carolina	71.4

* Many football players at SMU transferred after the NCAA suspended the school's program in 1987.

Source: *Chronicle of Higher Education.*

COLLEGE ATHLETICS
Football Graduation Compared with Overall Graduation

In the previous two entries, we looked at sheer percentages of athletes and football players enrolled in Division I-A schools in the fall of 1984 who received their degree by August of 1989. But this is perhaps not the fairest of assessments of college programs. At many of the schools in the survey, athletic graduation simply reflected the overall graduation trend of the school. The Univer-sity of Houston, we saw, had the lowest rate of graduation for athletes at 18.1 percent – but the overall graduation rate for all stu-dents was a mere 19.5 percent, an insignificant difference (indeed, football players graduated at a higher rate than the student body at Houston, 20.0 percent, and women athletes graduated at almost twice the rate of students in general there). Ath-letes at Notre Dame graduate at almost ex-actly the same rate as their non-athletic counterparts – 92.8 percent to 92.7 percent. So it's debatable whether the programs at such schools are to either be blamed or lauded; athletics there seems to have little influence on the graduation rate either way. At other schools with large urban and com-muter populations, administrators have questioned thc validity of the five-year graduation period in the survey, claiming that the average student at these schools takes up to six and a half years to receive a degree.

THINGS

With such questions in mind, we extrapolated from the numbers a new rating, comparing graduation rates in the marquee sport of football with graduation rates of the student body as a whole. The rating simply subtracts the football graduation rate from the overall graduation rate by August, 1989 of all students in enrolled in fall, 1984. The resulting figures can be used to determine the schools at which football programs most help and most hinder athletes in their pursuit of a college degree. Below are the schools where the difference in graduation rates between football players and the general student body is most pronounced, either in favor of the football program or to its detriment. The first list gives the schools with the best football graduation performance compared to the overall body, and the second yields the schools with the worst football graduation performance. For instance, at the best school, Colorado State, football players graduate at a rate 19.7 percent *higher* than the overall student body. Seventy percent of the 20 recruited players that enrolled at that school in 1984 graduated school by 1989, compared with an overall rate of just over 50 percent. On the other hand, in the case of the worst culprit, Texas A&M, just 6.7 percent of the players entering in 1984 graduated by 1989, a difference of more than 50 percentage points from the overall graduation student rate of 58.9 percent. The list below is from schools in Division I-A. For schools that did not respond to the survey, see the first entry.

Schools Where Football Grad. Rate is Above Overall Student Body

School	Difference (%)
1. Colorado State	19.7
2. Washington State	18.7
3. Rutgers	16.5
4. Marshall	15.5
5. Western Michigan	14.2
6. Louisiana Tech	11.3
7. Univ. of Akron	10.6
8. Univ. of New Mexico	10.4
9. Memphis State	9.1
10. Univ. of Wisconsin	6.9

Schools Where Football Grad. Rate is Below Overall Student Body

School	Difference (%)
1. Texas A&M	52.2
2. Southern Methodist*	51.3
3. Virginia Tech	47.7
4. Auburn	41.4
5. Univ. of Maryland	39.1
6. Wake Forest	38.7
7. Iowa State	28.0
8. Univ. of Tennessee	26.1
9. Purdue	26.0
10. Ohio State	25.5

* Many football players at SMU transferred after the NCAA suspended the school's program in 1987.

Most Stable Programs: Schools Where Football Grad. Rate Most Closely Reflects Overall Student Body

Finally, this rating lists the schools at which the graduation rates for football players most closely compares to the overall graduation rates of the student body. At the schools below, the difference between those rates is less than 2 percent. At Duke, the rate is exactly the same.

School	Difference (%)
1. Indiana	1.6
U. of S.W. Louisiana	1.6
2. Eastern Michigan	1.4
3. Univ. of Nebraska	0.8
Univ. of North Carolina	0.8
4. Boston College	0.1
5. Duke	0.0
6. Univ. of Houston	-0.5
7. Baylor	-0.7
8. Univ. of Iowa	-1.3

THINGS

Univ. of the Pacific	-1.3

Source: *Chronicle of Higher Education*.

COLLEGE ATHLETICS

Best Graduation Rates, Division I Overall

The previous ratings listed the schools in Division I-A, those that compete at the highest level in the major sports. The list below reflects the best and worst graduation rates of all the 262 schools in Division I — including I-A, I-AA and I-AAA — that responded to the *Chronicle of Higher Education* survey. We have listed here the schools with athletic graduation rates above 90 percent, and those below 20 percent. The list of the top schools is notable for its Ivy League members, which sponsor large intercollegiate sports programs and graduate high proportions of their athletes — truly earning them the names of *student* athletes. The top school, Gonzaga, recruited only 12 student athletes in 1984 and graduated them all by August, 1989.

Best	Athl. Grad. Rate (%)
1. Gonzaga	100.0
2. Princeton	97.4
3. Harvard	96.4
4. Holy Cross	96.0
5. Dartmouth	95.9
Duke	95.9
7. Yale	93.7
8. Duquesne	92.2
9. Drexel	91.9
10. Univ. of Hartford	90.9
11. Georgetown	90.6
12. Colgate	90.4
13. Siena College	90.1

Worst Athl. Grad. Rate (%)	
1. Texas Southern U.	9.4
2. U. of Texas, Pan American	10.0
3. Lamar U.	10.5
4. Cal. State-Northridge	10.7
5. Southern U.	12.1
6. No. Carolina A&T	12.5
7. Arkansas State	13.2
8. McNeese State	15.3
9. Northeastern Illinois	15.6
10. San Diego State U.	15.8
11. U. of Texas, Arlington	16.7
12. U. of Tennessee, Chattanooga	16.9
13. U. of North Texas	17.9
14. U. of Houston	18.1
15. Northwestern State U. (La.)	19.3

Source: *Chronicle of Higher Education*.

COLLEGE ATHLETICS

Graduation Rates, by Leagues

Colleges and universities join together in leagues to compete against each other in friendly collegiate rivalry, and to share in the wealth such rivalry generates, through ticket sales and television contracts. The first three lists here represent graduation rates for athletes, football players, and basketball players, in the top eight Division I leagues or conferences. The conferences are ranked in descending order of graduation rates for athletes. The final rating gives the extent to which football players graduate above or below the average student. Negative numbers indicate that football players graduated at a *higher* rate than the average student. The difference between football players and the regular student body is most pronounced in the Southwest Conference, where football players graduate at a rate 16.8 percent below their fellow students. Contrarily, in the Western Conference, football players actually graduate at a rate 9.1 percent higher than the overall student body.

All Athletes

League	Grad. Rate (%)
1. Atlantic Coast	66.2
2. Independents	59.0
3. Big Ten	58.0
4. Mid-American Ath. Conf.	54.4
5. Pac 10	52.9
6. Western Ath. Conf.	43.1
7. Big 8	42.3

THINGS

8. Southwest Ath. Conf.   40.6
9. Big West   39.4
10. Southeastern (SEC)   36.4

Football Players

League	Grad. Rate (%)
1. ACC	55.4
2. Independents	51.7
3. Big Ten	50.1
4. Pac 10	46.6
5. Western Ath. Conf.	43.1
6. Mid-American	42.9
7. Big 8	39.4
8. Southwest	32.5
9. SEC	32.2
10. Big West	23.8

Men's Basketball Players

League	Grad. Rate (%)
1. Big Ten	43.9
2. Pac 10	40.6
3. Mid-American	40.0
4. Big 8	34.8
5. Independents	33.3
6. ACC	32.0
7. Southwest	23.5
8. Big West	18.9
9. Western	17.6
10. SEC	14.0

Football Players Compared to Average Student

League	Difference
1. Western	-9.1
2. Independents	-0.3
3. Pac 10	3.5
4. Mid-American	3.7
5. Big 8	6.6
6. Big Ten	9.1
7. ACC	10.2
8. SEC	13.2
9. Big West	14.5
10. Southwest	16.8

Source: *Chronicle of Higher Education*.

COMPUTERS
Most Popular Personal Computers

In the seventies and early eighties, Silicon Valley and its sub-cultural Southwestern soulmates (Texas Instruments, et alia) tried to foist generation after generation of anemic, under-powered proto-micro-computers on an overly enthusiastic, premature public. As a result, for quite awhile, buyers were soured to the coming of the digital revolution to their own homes. With the advent of the affordable Apple II and the usable IBM PC all that changed quickly. Amid the aftermath, IBM has met the initial challenge from Apple, and as of this writing, the two companies were negotiating a collaborative agreement. IBM still controls the American business market for PC's, while Apple's Macintosh line comprises the computers of choice for many in the home.

The Top Ten

1. IBM PS/2-55sx
2. IBM PS/2-50z
3. IBM PS/2-70
4. IBM PS/2-30 286
5. Compaq Deskpro 386
6. IBM PS/2-30
7. Apple Macintosh SE
8. Zenith 2248
9. Apple Macintosh-II CX
10. Apple Macintosh II

Source: Computer Intelligence, ADAPSO Market Trends, 1990.

COMPUTERS – SOFTWARE
Best-Selling PC Programs

In the computer world, hardware niches and knock-offs abound, but the real creativity is definitely a software affair. The computer age has introduced many new terms to the American lexicon, but none so ubiquitous in the mainstream than "Word Processing"; the leading word-processing program is Wordperfect, with a staggering 23 percent of all software sales. In the good old days, one would just read, write and speak words; now they are "processed," like canned ham or cheese spread. What would Shakespeare say? Or Wittgenstein, for that matter? Spreadsheet programs like Lotus 1-2-3 and Excel also are now necessary tools in the daily game of American business. Numbers used to be laboriously added, subtracted, and entered into tightly-scored ledgers; now they are crunched, in higher and higher speeds, while we sit back and sip our coffee. In any event, here are America's unsung best-sellers, the software giants through which the eponymous information of the Information Age continues to flow. Happy hacking!

Software	% Market Share
1. WordPerfect	23
2. Lotus 1-2-3	21
3. Microsoft Word	8
4. Microsoft Excel	4
5. SPC (Harvard Graphics)	3
6. Borland Quattro-Pro	3
7. IBM-DisplayWrite	3
8. Ashton-Tate multiMate	2
9. Ashton-Tate dBase IV	2
10. Ashton-Tate dBase III/III +	2

Source: Computer Intelligence, Intelligence Report.

CONSUMER SPENDING
Largest Consumer Expenses

No matter what size paycheck you pull down, at one time or another, you have asked yourself "Where does the money go?" Well, wonder no further. In point of fact, the largest and most common consumer expenditures are depressingly clear. After taking care of food, clothing, shelter and transportation, the average Joe is lucky if he can still find two spare nickels to rub together for a six pack or cup of coffee. The following are the largest consumer expenses, measured by the percentage of the household budget devoted to each expense. The figures reflect some important facets of our society. For

instance, back in the early part of the century, Americans spent about forty percent of their money on shelter. That figure has been cut about in half in the subsequent decade, but we have found something to spend the savings on—transportation. Expenditures on vehicles make up roughly one quarter of the total household budget for the average family—from gasoline to repair bills to car installments. Yes, in America, the car is king, and every king requires his due.

Item	% Total Consumption
1. Vehicle Expenses	24.7
2. Shelter	20.2
3. Food and Alcohol	19.4
4. Utilities, Fuels, Public Services	8.2
5. Entertainment and Reading	5.8
6. Apparel and Services	5.2
7. Miscellaneous	4.1
8. Health Care	4.0
9. Household Furnishings	3.9
10. Household Operations	1.4

Source: U.S. Monthly Labor Review, 1990

CONTRACEPTIVES
Most Popular

Sterilization is a drastic step in contraception. Non-reversible, it means the end of the ability to procreate for those who go through with it. Yet voluntary contraceptive sterilization is the most widespread method of birth control among all those Americans who practice contraception. Of the nearly 40 percent of couples who choose this method of birth control, 70 percent opt for female sterilization and 30 percent for vasectomies. This figure can be attributed in some part to the aging of the female population (in the period from 1982 to 1988, the number of women aged 15 to 24 dropped by 1.5 million and the number aged 25 to 44, those more likely to opt for non-reversible birth control methods, rose by nearly 5.4 million). The decline of IUD use also contributes to the higher number of women relying on sterilization. Use of the pill, which had declined in the late 1970s for health con-

THINGS

cerns, has also become more popular, due to its high rate of effectiveness and convenience. Condom use has increased rapidly among teenagers and single women, but the pill remains the method of choice for the younger set.

Method	% Contraceptive Use
1. Sterilization	39.2%
2. Pill	30.5%
3. Condom	14.6%
4. Diaphragm	5.7%
5. Abstinence	2.3%
6. Withdrawal	2.2%
7. Other	2.1%
8. IUD	2.0%
9. Foam	1.1%

Source: "Contraceptive Practices in the United States, 1982-1988," Family Planning Perspectives, September/October 1990.

CORPORATIONS — ADVERTISING
Top-Spending Advertisers

No matter how much we may hate interruptions in our soap operas, sit-coms or football games, and no matter how much page turning we must do through pages of newspaper ads to find the continuation of the front-page story, most of the advertising on TV and in print actually turns a good profit in terms of increased sales. The corny stuff, the hard-sells, the Bruce Weber ads where we never even see the product: almost all are breadwinners. Despite the advent of the "zapper"—the ability to change channels instantaneously, or to fast-forward through the commercials on previously recorded programs, researchers find that relatively few viewers actually take advantage of such technology to the degree that would begin to make advertisers stand back and rethink their strategies. Indeed, with ever-new hucksters coining ever new catch-phrases to feed the pop-culture appetite for ephemera—"Bo knows . . . ," "Less filling, tastes great," "You got the right one,

baby"—and the (literally) incredible popularity of the new program-length advertisements, or "infomercials"—the American consumer is guaranteed no respite from these tried-and-true sales pitches for the foreseeable future. So, year after year, the big boys will be pouring their big bucks into the coffers of Madison Avenue. The following are the ten highest-spending advertisers on the American business scene. Philip Morris is the tobacco company that has recently expanded into buyouts of Miller Beer and Kraft foods; Procter & Gamble produces home and personal care products; Grand Met is the company that owns Burger King.

Comp.	1990 Ad Expenditures ($ Millions)
1. Philip Morris	$2,072
2. Proctor & Gamble	$1,779
3. Sears, Roebuck & Co	$1,432
4. General Motors Corp.	$1,364
5. Grand Metropolitan PLC	$823
6. Pepsico Inc.	$786
7. McDonald's Corp.	$774
8. Eastman Kodak Co.	$719
9. RJR Nabisco	$704
10. Kellogg Co.	$612

Source: Advertising Age.

CORPORATIONS — ANIMAL RESEARCH
Most Frequent Corporate Users of Laboratory Animals

American industry has done much to reduce its dependence on laboratory animals for testing purposes, but many still continue to rely on animals for research and development of products. While some use of animals is practically unavoidable in critical fields such as drug testing, a closer examination of the practice, and of available alternatives to animal testing, is high on the agenda of animal rights activists nationwide. The following are the companies that annually rely the most on experimentation on animals.

THINGS

Corp.	Experiments on Animals
1. American Cyanamid	55,460
2. Rorer Group	39,984
3. Bayer	39,983
4. American Home Products	38,033
5. ICI Americas	34,065
6. Smith Kline Beckman	33,011
7. Merck	28,499
8. Johnson & Johnson	22,541
9. Schering-Plough	20,162

Source: Investor Responsibility Research Center, Washington, D.C.

CORPORATIONS— BLACK-OWNED

Largest Black-Owned Businesses

Equal opportunity is a stated goal and policy in the business world, and prejudice has been noticed, if not remedied, in our age. But beyond the general economic malaise, black enterprise has still not achieved the economic vigor that a truly equitable social climate would create. The achievement and vision of the most-successful black-owned companies are hardly at issue; what must be adressed is the inability of enough others to emulate their successes. The following are the largest companies in the U.S. with African-Americans at the helm.

Corporation	1990 Sales (000)
1. TLC Beatrice International	$1,514,000
2. Johnson Publishing Co.	$241,327
3. Philadelphia Coca-Cola	$240,000
4. H.J. Russell & Co.	$132,876
5. The Gordy Co.	$100,000
6. Soft Sheen Products Inc.	$87,200
7. Trans Jones Inc.	$78,555
8. The Bing Group	$73,883
9. The Maxima Corp.	$58,383
10. Dick Griffey Productions	$50,162

Source: The Earl G. Graves Publishing Co., Inc.

CORPORATIONS— DEFENSE CONTRACTORS

Largest U.S. Defense Contractors

In the era of the $500 screwdriver and the 1,000% cost over-runs, an unshakable air of scrutiny surrounds the nations largest arms purveyors (many of whom are also enmeshed in the production of hair dryers, toasters and other laudable consumer goods). With the remarkable potency and efficiency demonstrated by U.S. so-called "smart weapons" in the Gulf War, however, the public has begun to reassess and forgive the capitalistic excesses of these industrial superpowers. These are the companies that make the missiles, tanks, guns and planes which so proved themselves in the sands and skies of Kuwait and Iraq.

Company	D.O.D. Contract Awards (000)
1. McDonnell-Douglas	$8,002,741
2. General Dynamics	$6,522,124
3. General Electric	$5,700,635
4. Tenneco Incorporated	$5,057,922
5. Raytheon	$4,055,346
6. Martin Marietta	$3,715,106
7. General Motors	$3,550,180
8. Lockheed	$3,508,055
9. Boeing	$3,017,839

Source: Department of Defense.

CORPORATIONS— EUROPEAN

Old World Industry: Largest European Industrial Corporations

Industry, contrary to local belief, is not an American invention. Though America put the capital "C" in Conglomerate, big business is much the same the world over! With the European cooperative economic community developing at an amazing pace, the following corporations may soon come to play much more immediate roles in our consumerist lives. Around Europe, the catchword is "cooperation," and the new megalith that will be created in 1992 will

THINGS

bring even greater challenges for American and other businesses worldwide.

Company/Business	Country
1. **Royal Dutch Shell** Oil	UK/Netherlands
2. **British Petroleum** Oil	UK
3. **IRI** State Holding	Italy
4. **Daimler-Benz AG** Engines and Vehicles	Germany
5. **Volkswagen AG** Vehicles	Germany
6. **Deutsche Bundespost** Postal and Telecommunications	Germany
7. **Siemens AG** Oil, Chemicals	Germany
8. **Unilever NV** Food Products	UK/Netherlands
9. **Philips Lamps** Holding	Netherlands
10. **ENI** Oil, Construction	Italy

Source: Superbrands 1990.

CORPORATIONS — EXPORTERS
Largest U.S. Exporters

America buys a lot more than it sells with its allies, but by any fair measure, it sells a great deal indeed. Last year, Boeing vended more than $11 billion worth of its flying wares to foreign companies and nations. General Motors did more than ten big bills (read billion) in business, and even once-crippled Caterpillar moved more than three billion in heavy duty agro-merchandise. Clearly, around the world, for marquee items such as aircraft, computers, chemicals, high technology and, yes, even automobiles, "Made in the U.S.A." still sells.

Corporation	1990 Exports (millions)
1. **Boeing**	$11,021
2. **General Motors**	$10,185
3. **Ford Motor**	$8,602
4. **General Electric**	$7,268
5. **IBM**	$5,476
6. **Du Pont**	$4,844
7. **Chrysler**	$4,649
8. **United Technologies**	$3,307
9. **Caterpillar**	$3,291
10. **McDonnell-Douglas**	$2,896

Source: The Bear Truth Investment Newsletter.

CORPORATIONS — FOREIGN REVENUES
U.S. Firms With the Biggest Foreign Revenues

For those of you who are concerned about foreign money buying up U.S. industrial assets, the following numbers should assuage your fears. Revenues from foreign operations of American-based mulinational corporations are increasing and should continue to do so, especially when the new Europe is formed in 1992. The continent will have over 325 million consumers, almsot 80 million more than the U.S. has, and American companies are mobilizing quickly to take advantage of the simplification of doing business across the European continent. Tough talk about trade barriers, though, may be an obstacle to completely free trade with the new European monolith. Asia and the Pacific Rim have also proven somewhat tougher nuts to crack than American businessmen had hoped. The American oil giant Exxon earns a whopping three- quarters of its revenue from sales outside the U.S.; General Motors, on the other hand, the largest industrial enterprise in the world, relies to a much larger degree on domestic sales—only about one-quarter of GM's total income derives from foreign sources. GM's inability to penetrate lucrative foreign markets plays a role in its continued hard times. Sales figures are in billions of dollars.

Comp.	For. Sales	Tot. Sales	% For.
1. Exxon	$63.4	$86.6	73.2
2. IBM	$36.9	$62.7	58.9
3. GM	$33.7	$126.9	26.6
4. Mobil	$33.0	$50.9	64.7
5. Ford	$31.9	$96.1	33.2
6. Citicorp	$19.8	$37.9	52.3
7. Du Pont	$14.1	$35.5	39.8
8. Texaco	$13.7	$32.4	42.3
9. ITT	$10.9	$25.2	43.3
10. Dow	$9.5	$17.6	54.1

CORPORATIONS — HIGH TECHNOLOGY
Fastest Growing High-Tech Companies

The Industrial Belt has turned into the Rust Belt, and with this corrosion of the industrial power of the country, Americans with baited breath look toward the hallowed halls of high-techdom to lift the country back into competition in the world marketplace. But here, such high-tech disasters as the Hubble Space Telescope and continued troubles at NASA have created a crisis of confidence in America's ability to contend with the high-flying Japanese and fast-charging Europeans in the high-tech arena. Such concerns, experts say, are premature. U.S. companies can and do excel in high-technology research and development. Although we are losing some ground to our friends in Japan and Europe, the U.S. is still the undisputed champ of high-tech. The challenge for the coming decades is to maintain that position; improving schools to create a better work force, and accelerating the time from conception to full production of high-tech hardware are two of the most pressing priorities in the years to come. These are the companies with the highest employment growth among those with more than 100 employees that receive at least 75% of their revenue from high technology. Sales figures are for 1989; growth refers to employment increases.

Corp.	Sales	Growth
1. Appex Waltham, Mass.	$13M	325%
2. Prairietek Longmont, Colo.	$3M	150%
3. Sybase Emeryville, Calif.	$57M	127%
4. Compuadd Austin, Tex.	$400M	100%
5. Asyst Tech. Milpitas, Calif.	$10M	93%
6. Bachman Info. Syst. Burlington, Mass.	$7M	93%
7. Farallon Computing Emeryville, Calif.	$35M	90%
8. Aion Palo Alto, Calif.	$15M	85%
9. Early Cloud Newport, R.I.	$10M	85%
10. Radius	$82M	77%

Source: Corporate Technology Information Services, 1990 Corporate Technology Directory and Database.

CORPORATIONS — INDUSTRIAL
Largest American Industrial Enterprises

No single event or resource catapulted America to its current hegemony in world affairs, but it is obvious that our nation's industrial might was fundamental in our emergence from colonial obscurity. The colossi of American business grow and recede in staggered response to the movement of the world and the economic health of the nation, but in the end, few players have entered or left the high stakes industrial game since the resolution of the first World

THINGS

War. The biggest disappearing act has occurred among meat-packing companies, such as Swift and Armour, who used to hold several of the top ten spots as late as the 1950s, before yielding to the oil, automotive, and conglomerate monoliths that dominate the American buiness scene today.

Company	1990 Sales (millions)
1. General Motors	$126,017
2. Exxon	$105,885
3. Ford	$98,274
4. IBM	$69,018
5. Mobil	$58,770
6. General Electric	$58,414
7. Philip Morris	$44,323
8. Texaco	$41,235
9. Du Pont	$39,839
10. Chevron	$39,262

Source: Fortune 500/ Service 500

CORPORATIONS – MARKET VALUE
Most Valuable

The market value of a company is the product of the share price of its stock multiplied by the number of outstanding shares. There the list of the top ten most valuable companies is a veritable stable of the warhorses of American business, led by Big Blue, IBM, on the strength of its dominance in computer markets. Philip Morris, the one-time tobacco conglomerate, has gone on a large-scale diversification program in recent years, looking to counter the effects of decline in cigarette smoking. They now own Miller Beer, Kraft and General Foods. The real performer here is Merck, the pharmaceutical company that is tops on most experts' lists of best-managed corporations. Its market value places it fifth on the list of industrial corporations, although Merck ranks only 63rd in terms of overall sales.

Company	Market Value (Millions)
1. IBM	$74,995
2. Exxon	$68,941
3. Philip Morris	$62,157
4. General Electric	$58,140
5. Merck	$40,875
6. Bristol-Myers-Squibb	$40,332
7. Coca-Cola	$34,915
8. Procter & Gamble	$30,170
9. Johnson & Johnson	$29,895
10. Amoco	$26,770

Source: Fortune.

CORPORATIONS – PRIVATE
Largest Private U.S. Companies

The American dream is fueled in large part by the stock market – its ups and downs are followed assiduously by rapt investors both big and small, watching the fortunes of their stocks wax and wane with every flutter of the economy or of world politics. But some business people prefer not to place the fortunes of their enterprises at risk in this arena. The stories of the largest privately held companies – those which do not trade their stocks on the open market – run the gamut, from the buyout of RJR Nabisco that inspired the best-selling book *Barbarians at the Gates,* to the cryptic Mars company, whose owners keep a tight lid on the family business. These then, are the most lucrative companies in the pantheon of private ownership.

Company	Revenues (Millions)
1. Cargill Intl. Marketer of Agricultural and Bulk Commodities	$43,000
2. Koch Industries Petroleum, Natural Gas, Chemicals	$16,000
3. RJR Nabisco Food Products, Tobacco	$14,000
4. Safeway Stores Supermarkets	$13,612
5. Continental Grain Commodity Trading and Processing	$13,500
6. United Parcel Service	$11,000

Package Delivery

7. Mars   **$8,541**
Candy Manufacturing, Pet Food, Rice

8. Southland   **$7,990**
Convenience Stores

9. R.H. Macy   **$7,000**
Department Stores

10. Supermarkets General   **$5,962**
Grocery Stores, Home Improvement Centers

Source: *Forbes*.

CORPORATIONS — RESEARCH AND DEVELOPMENT
Most Spent on R&D

Research and Development. That is the catch phrase when discussing a company's, and indeed a nation's, commitment to the future. America leads the world in spending on research and development — to a tune of more than $65 billion dollars in 1989. The world's largest industrial corporation, General Motors, also spends the most money on R&D of any corporation in the world — more than $5 billion in 1989 alone on its automotive and other enterprises. Other big guns in the American R&D world include auto maker Ford, computer and electronics companies like IBM, Digital, Hewlett-Packard and General Electric, the communications and chemical giants AT&T and Du Pont, the photographic products company Kodak, and United Technologies. Still, overall, the trend in R&D spending in the U.S. is cause for concern. Although spending in this area from 1988 to 1989 rose 5.6% when adjusted for inflation, that's a decline from the 6.6 percent gain in 1988. Unfortunately, as the American business climate has cooled in the late eighties, so to has investors' and executives' excitement in probing new technologies at the expense of profit. And ac-

cording to *Business Week*, the $65 billion spent by the top American companies on R&D is nearly matched by the $63 billion spent by foreign companies. These are the top ten R&D spenders in the U.S., in terms of sheer dollar outlays.

Company	R&D Spending
1. General Motors	$5,247,000
2. IBM	$5,201,000
3. Ford	$3,167,000
4. AT&T	$2,652,000
5. Digital Equipment	$1,525,000
6. Du Pont	$1,387,000
7. General Electric	$1,334,000
8. Hewlett-Packard	$1,269,000
9. Eastman Kodak	$1,253,000
10. United Technologies	$957,000

Source: *Business Week*, from Compustat Services, Inc.

CORPORATIONS — RESEARCH AND DEVELOPMENT
Spending on R&D As a Percent of Sales

The commitment to research and development should not be measured solely, or even primarily, by sheer dollar amounts thrown in that direction. Indeed, a better measure of a company's efforts in the R&D arena is the percentage of sales it pours into development of new products and ideas. For instance, although as we saw in the previous entry, General Motors leads the pack in R&D spending, its $5 billion spent on R&D in 1989 was only 4.2 percent of its sales. The real leaders in U.S. research and development are biotechnology companies such as Chiron, Genetics Institute, Centocor and Genentech, which pump from nearly 40 percent to more than 100% of sales into R&D. The following measure of R&D commitment takes R&D spending as a percentage of sales for 1989; the top ten American companies on this account are listed below.

THINGS

Company	R&D/Sales
1. Chiron	108.9%
2. Genetics Institute	92.6%
3. Centocor	63.0%
4. Daisy System	40.7%
5. Aiza	39.6%
6. Genentech	38.0%
7. Amgen	29.5%
8. Continuum	29.1%
9. Phoenix Technologies	28.2%
10. LTX	26.7%

Source: *Business Week*, from Compustat Services, Inc.

CORPORATIONS – RESEARCH AND DEVELOPMENT
Top European R&D Spenders

Europe is coming together in more ways than one. The big drive to unify its markets by 1992 will create an economic behemoth America and Japan cannot take lightly. In addition, the new political structure of Eastern Europe has opened up additional resources, from scientific research down to raw materials and manpower, for the continental powerhouse. Yes, the old world suddenly has gotten an injection of youth serum. In France, the government has stated a commitment to raise R&D spending to 3 percent of GNP; in Scandinavia, companies are teaming up with others from foreign countries to perform joint research and development; Europe is home to seven of the top ten chemical companies and six of the top ten pharmaceutical makers; and, of course, such German powerhouses as Siemens and Daimler Benz epitomize the economic might of the newly united country. All over Europe, a new confidence in the business climate is sparking renewed interest high-tech research and newfangled products, the better to compete with the established leaders, the U.S. and Japan. The following are the European companies with the biggest spending on research and development.

The Top Ten	R&D Spending (Millions)
1. Siemens, Ger.	$3.684
2. Daimler Benz, Ger.	$2.927
3. Philips, Neth.	$2.154
4. CGE, Fr.	$1.806
5. Bayer, Ger.	$1.404
6. Hochst, Ger.	$1.379
7. ABB, Switz.	$1.361
8. Fiat, Italy	$1.240
9. Ciba-Geigy, Switz.	$1.232
10. Volkswagen, Ger.	$1.198

Source: Compustat, Business Week, Innovation 1990.

CORPORATIONS – RESEARCH AND DEVELOPMENT
Top Japanese High-Tech Spenders

We all wonder at the wizardry of Japanese designs in such fields as electronics, automobiles and photographic instruments; now, the country that has proven itself internationally in these markets is turning to more serious stuff. Japan's Ministry of International Trade and Industry, unlike any agency of the U.S. government, has the power to dictate economic policy to individual Japanese corporations. The result is a coherent strategy for the Japanese economy, channeling its formidable energies into such traditionally American fields as supercomputers and semiconductors. The commitment to R&D spending is apparent in some of the big, long-term projects that MITI has been sponsoring: unmanned space experimentation, parallel processing computers, advanced material processing and machining and non-linear photonics. Given such leadership from MITI, Japanese companies are at the forefront of developing products and technologies that will lead the world into the 21st century. These are the top ten Japanese companies for R&D

THINGS

spending; this money isn't just going to televisions, stereos and VCRs.

The Top Ten	R&D (billions, 1989)
1. Hitachi	$2.19
2. Matsushita	$2.14
3. Toyota	$1.90
4. NEC	$1.78
5. Fujitsu	$1.74
6. NTT	$1.52
7. Toshiba	$1.46
8. Nissan	$1.36
9. Honda	$1.13
10. Sony	$1.01

Source: *Business Week*, from Ministry of Informational Trade & Industry, Japan.

CORPORATIONS — TRANSPORTATION

Largest American Transportation Companies

A nation that cannot move is doomed to obscurity and regionalism. In the twentieth century, America has cultivated an obsession with cars and all that comes with them (traffic jams, four-car pileups, rampant pollution, etc.). One of our great hidden strengths, however, is the multiplicity of transport opportunities available. With the emergence of new premium-service transportation and shipping companies like Federal Express, America remains at the vanguard of world transport powers.

Company	1989 Operating Revenues
1. United Parcel Service	$302.8
2. UAL	$155.0
3. AMR	$83.7
4. CSX	$75.3
5. Texas Air	$63.3
6. Delta Airlines	$38.7
7. Union Pacific	$32.3
8. US Air Group	$27.7
9. NWA	$26.3
10. Santa Fe Southern Pacific	$23.0

Source: Superbrands, 1990.

The ubiquitous UPS truck, symbol of the country's largest transportation and shipping company.

CRIMES
Most Frequent

There is, it is said, nothing new under the sun, and that adage applies particularly to criminal misdeeds. One may invent many things, but very few of us, it seems, have dreamt up new vices. Thus, it is not surprising that the most commonly perpetrated crimes are those which involve a direct monetary motive, i.e., larceny and burglary. We've left off the list minor transgressions, such as speeding and pulling the tags off of pillows and mattresses.

Offense	Rate of Incidence
1. Larceny-Theft	Every 4 seconds
2. Burglary	Every 10 seconds
3. Motor Vehicle Theft	Every 20 seconds
4. Aggravated Assault	Every 33 seconds
5. Robbery	Every 55 seconds
6. Forcible Rape	Every 6 Minutes
7. Murder	Every 24 Minutes

THINGS

Source: F.B.I. Uniform Crime Reports.

CRIMES
Costliest Criminal Acts

The true cost of crime is often difficult to assess. Beside the obvious loss of property, money or life, there is always an unquantifiable emotional cost to any serious criminal misdeed. As we move into another era of recession and deprivation, we can expect that the magnitude and frequency of money-motivated criminal acts will increase. We can only hope that the cost of these misdeeds does not extend further to human health and happiness. The resurgence of the concept of "victims' rights" may do something to redress some of the loss, both economic and psychological, involved in the perpetration of crimes. We all know that crime doesn't pay, but here are the highest-paying crimes, in any case.

Crime	Average Associated Loss
1. Bank Robbery	$3,013
2. General Residential Burglary	$1,107
3. Nighttime Residential Burglary	$1,085
4. Robbery of Commercial Prop.	$1,017
5. Office Burglary	$914
6. Robbery in Residence	$796
7. Miscellaneous Robbery	$668
8. Theft from Buildings	$665
9. Miscellaneous Larceny/Theft	$591
10. Theft from Motor Vehicles	$434

Source: F.B.I.

CRIMES
Most Popular Crimes

Although the property-related crimes of theft and larceny are still the most common felonious offenses, criminal acts involving substance abuse (and its resultant diminished states) are becoming increasingly common. D.U.I., drug possession, drunkeness and disorderly conduct are all among the nation's ten most frequent violations.

Offense	1988 arrests
1. Larceny/Theft	1,151,150
2. Driving under the Influence	1,279,121
3. Drug Abuse Violations	844,300
4. Assault (non-aggravated)	683,182
5. Drunkenness	599,295
6. Disorderly Conduct	569,475
7. Burglary	329,812
8. Aggravated Assault	302,311
9. Fraud	260,376
10. Vandalism	224,275

Source: F.B.I. Uniform Crime Reports

CRIMES
Most Popular
White-Collar Crimes

In the wake of Watergate, America has become a nation obsessed — some even say infatuated — with white collar criminals. The clever machinations of the three-piece set seldom fail to titillate and provoke. The Boeskys and the Milkens of this world are at the once admired and despised for the sheer size of the dollar amounts involved in their crimes. The results of such ambivalence, more often than not, are spells in some of the more luxurious of federal facilities. Among the white collar offenses tried in our federal courts, acts of common fraud are most frequent. Forgery and embezzlement, too, are perennial favorites, collectively resulting in almost 4,000 convictions each year. These, then, are the most popular white-collar crimes in the country.

Federal Offense	Convictions/yr.
1. Fraud (General)	2,800
2. Forgery	2,014
3. Embezzlement	1,753
4. Wire Fraud	1,428
5. Tax Fraud	1,204
6. Lending and Credit Fraud	540
7. Counterfeiting	503
8. Regulatory Offenses	491

Source: U.S. Bureau of Justice Statistics.

THINGS

CRIMES
Prison Sentences

The physical failure of our correctional system to hold and "treat" many of those convicted of serious, even violent, offenses is a national shame and dilemma. Too often, prisons are only holding pens for revolving-door criminals who reach the streets years before their full sentence has run its course. In this era of pragmatically necessitated leniency (through parole, dismissal, probation and work-release), judge and jury are forced to hand down almost comically severe, lengthy terms, in order to ensure that a truly desperate offender is not cursorily rotated back into the community. America's will to punish the hardened criminal is increasing, but the concomitant funds for newer, bigger prisons and workers to service those institutions are not forthcoming. The following are representative prison sentences for various crimes. Surprisingly high on the list are drunk-driving offenses, reflecting society's growing intolerance of this practice, which takes numerous lives, both young and old, each year. Even when getting behind the wheel, one should remember, "If you can't do the time, don't do the crime."

Offense	Average sentence (Months)
1. Forcible rape of victim, victim dies of injuries	416.5
2. Robbery at gun-point, struggling victim shot dead	365.2
3. Used gun, knife, fists to injure then kill victim	349.5
4. Forcibly raped victim and forced her to perform oral sex	202.1
5. Drove car while drunk, resulting in second-party death	141.2
6. Sold cocaine for resale	126.3
7. Robbed and wounded victim at gun-point	123.4
8. Intentionally set fire to building, $500,000 + in damage	99.9
9. Used gun, knife, pipe to injure victim, victim later recovered	92.7
10. Threatened victim with weapon, then robbed victim	68.0

Source: National Survey of Punishment for Criminal Offenses, National Conference on Punishment

DEATH
Most Common Causes

The most dangerous place in town, the pedants tell us, is one's own bathtub. If danger is measured by the number of mortal occurrences, however, hospitals must certainly be the centers of peril. As late as 1960, most people died at home; in these days of over-institutionalization, eighty percent of all deaths occur in a medical facility or nursing home. The message, unenforceable though it may be, remains, DON'T GET SICK. Diet and exercise can seriously lessen the chances of succumbing to heart disease, the number one killer in the U.S. Malignant neoplasms—cancer—are the number two killer, and life-style changes can also mitigate the threats from this scourge.

Cause	Deaths/100,000 pop.
1. Disease of the heart	312.4
2. Malignant neoplasms	195.9
3. Cerebrovascular disease	61.6
4. Accidents and adverse effects	39.0
5. Chronic pulmonary disease	32.2
6. Influenza	28.4
7. Diabetes	15.8
8. Suicide	12.7
9. Chronic liver disease/cirrhosis	10.8
10. Atherosclerosis	9.2

Source: National Center for Health Statistics

DEATH
Leading Causes of Accidental Death

When it comes to untimely deaths, cars are the worst offenders. Loaded with highly flammable gasoline, these one-ton masses of metal hurtle down strips of asphalt and end up grotesque, twisted products of tremendous collisions, their drivers mere memories. By contrast, flying is 38.8 times safer than driving. Compiled by the U.S. Center for Health Statistics, this rating shows that some of our most routine activities, driving, walking, swimming and going to the doctor are the most dangerous. Falling, and not being able to get up, is second on the list to traffic fatalities. Here are the grim statistics on the most prevalent deadly accidents.

Accident	Deaths per 100,000
1. Traffic Accidents	19.4
2. Accidental Falls	4.7
3. Drowning	2.0
3. Fires and Flames	2.0
5. Poisoning by Drugs and Medicine	1.7
6. Inhalation and Ingestion of Objects	1.5
7. Complications due to Medical Procedures	1.3
8. Guns	.6
9. Boating	.5
10. Airplane	.5

Source: National Center for Health Statistics, *Vital Statistics of the United States,*.

DICKENS NOVELS

Greatest

If you don't know what the word "Dickensian" means, check out this rating. According to our ranking of novelists, Charles Dickens is the fourth greatest novelist of all time. He was also one of the most prolific writers of his generation. So, if you haven't yet enjoyed the pleasures of a Dickens novel, here are the most important ones, rated by the amount of scholarly research that has been done on each one in a ten-year period from 1980 to 1990, as indicated in the MLA International database.

Novel	Score
1. Bleak House	140
2. Great Expectations	83
3. David Copperfield	81
4. Our Mutual Friend	48
5. Oliver Twist	43
6. Little Dorritt	42
7. A Tale of Two Cities	41
8. The Pickwick Papers	38
9. Hard Times	36
10. The Mystery of Edwin Drood	34

Source: "Best and Worst" original.

DOGS
They (Should) Only Kill Their Masters: Dog Breeds Reponsible for Most Fatal Attacks

Pit Bulls have gotten a lot of bad press, so it's no surprise to see them on this list, but the appearance of the sturdy, supportive German Shepherd and the lovable, fiery-eyed Malamute, in the same chronicle of shame will sadden fans of those breeds. The good ole St. Bernard, ever genial and compassionate on stage and screen, drops several notches in esteem as well, as he is revealed as one of nature's most consummate maneaters. To be fair to man's best friends, though, more often than not the owners of the offending mutts are to blame for negligence in the upbringing, treatment and care of their animals. Deadly dogs are not born — they are created by their owners. The following list gives the dog breeds

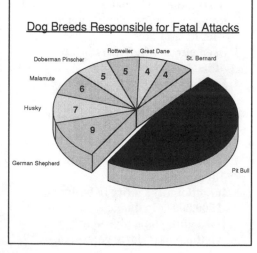

Dog Breeds Responsible for Fatal Attacks

responsible for the highest number of fatal attacks over a ten-year period from 1979 to 1989.

Breed	Known Fatal Attacks
1. Pit Bull	37
2. German Shepherd	9
3. Husky	7
4. Malamute	6
5. Doberman Pinscher	5
6. Rottweiler	5
7. Great Dane	4
8. St. Bernard	4

Source: Journal of the American Medical Association

DOGS
Most Popular Pure-Breed Dogs

Mutts are cute, cuddlesome and lovable, but pure breeds are where it's at for today's credibility-conscious canine customer. In recent years, the affable Cocker Spaniel, at number one, has been a particular favorite, while the oft-underfoot poodle has held its furry-own in the number three spot. The following are the most popular pure-breed dogs, as measured by the number of dogs registered with the American Kennel Club.

Breed	Number Registered
1. Cocker Spaniels	111,636
2. Labrador Retrievers	91,107
3. Poodles	78,600
4. Golden Retrievers	64,269
5. German Shepherds	58,422
6. Rottweilers	51,291
7. Chow Chows	50,150
8. Dachshunds	44,305
9. Beagles	43,314
10. Miniatures	42,175

Source: American Kennel Club.

DRUGS—LEGAL
Most Popular Over-the-Counter Drugs

Americans, its seems, are very prone to headaches. Perhaps it is the anxiety of our lives, or the unacceptably high noise levels in our cities. Whatever the cause, however, we want relief, and we find it, most often, at the counter of the local mart, pharmacy or convenience store. Pain-relief medications are big business, and number one at the cash register is Tylenol, which made an astonishingly quick comeback into the nation's medicine chest after the product-tampering incident of a few years back. Americans plunked down more than half a billion dollars for Tylenol, a Johnson & Johnson brand of the pain-reliever acetomeniphen. Advil, another pain medication, finished a distant second with 1990 wholesale sales of $235 million. Added evidence of our stressed-out society can be found in the non-pain relief medications on the list: Metamucil for constipation, Maalox for indigestion, Nyquil for sleeplessness.

Product	1990 Wholesale Sales (millions)
1. Tylenol	$585
2. Advil	$235
3. Anacin	$150
4. Metamucil	$125
5. Bayer	$120
6. Halls	$120
7. Robitussin	$110
8. Maalox	$110
9. Nyquil	$105
10. Excedrin	$105

Source: Superbrands 1990

DRUGS—RECREATIONAL
Most Popular Among High School Seniors

Although the eighties were marked by the re-emergence of traditional (even conservative) values among our youth, abuse of legal and illegal recreational drugs remains a problem of monumental proportions. Nearly nine out of ten American high school seniors reported significant use of alcohol within a span of two months, and nearly one in two had consumed marijuana or hashish in that same period. The following are the

THINGS

drugs of preference for "high" schoolers, in the percentage of seniors who have admitted consuming particular substances within the two months prior to the survey. Figures are from a poll taken in 1988.

Substance	Percent
1. Alcohol	87.0
2. Marijuana/Hashish	47.6
3. Stimulants	16.3
4. Sedatives	10.8
4. Tranquilizers	10.8
6. Barbiturates	9.3
7. Hallucinogens	8.8
8. Cocaine	7.2
9. Opiates (non-heroin)	6.4
10. L.S.D.	5.5

Source: "Drug Use, Smoking and Drinking by America's High School Students," U.S. Dept. of Health and Human Services.

ENCYCLOPEDIAS
Wordiest Encyclopedias

The heyday of the door-to-door encyclopedia salesman is well-past, but the days of hard sell in that field are not. Each publication offers a dizzying array of premiums, alternative configurations and nebulous claims. On the theory that the best value is the biggest book, here are the word counts for the fattest of the shelf hogs. Tops on the list is the Encyclopedia Britannica, with an amazing 44 million words spread among its three dozen volumes.

Encyclopedia	Word Length (millions)
1. New Encyc. Britannica	44
2. Encyc. Americana	31
3. Collier's Encyc.	21
4. New Standard Encyc.	10
5. World Book Encyc.	9
Academic American Encyc.	9
Everyman's Encyc.	9
Funk and Wagnall's New Encyc.	9
Merit Students Encyclopedia	9
Compton's Encyc.	9

Source: Kister's Concise Guide to Best Encyclopedias.

ENDANGERED SPECIES
Most Spending On

The bald eagle is the symbol of our country. Unfortunately, it is endangered in many places in the United States and threatened in most others (the only stable, healthy population is in Alaska). In recent years, with the passing of the Endangered Species Act, the government has taken an active role in the preservation of this and other species threatened with extinction. In addition to the U.S. Fish and Wildlife Service, such agencies as the Bureau of Land Management, Bureau of Reclamation, Bureau of Indian Affairs, the Department of Agriculture, the Forest Service, the Tennessee Valley Authority, the National Oceanic and Atmospheric Administration, the National Marine Fisheries Service the U.S. Army Corps of Engineers, and the Federal Aviation Administration have instituted programs or studies intended to promote the preservation of endangered species. The following list rates endangered or threatened species by the amount spent on their protection and recovery by state and federal agencies; the list does not include $13,300,000 spent on setting aside 16,200 acres specifically for endangered species.

Species	Annual Expenditures
1. Bald Eagle	$3,108,580
2. Grizzly & Brown Bear	$2,924,310
3. Red-Cockaded Woodpecker	$2,792,030
4. American Peregrine Falcon	$2,744,170
5. Gray Wolf	$2,205,320
6. Whooping Crane	$1,417,460
7. Southern Sea Otter	$1,300,000
8. West Indian Manatee	$1,249,450
9. Tumamoc Globe-berry	$1,167,300
10. Black-footed Ferret	$1,051,110

Source: U.S. Fish and Wildlife Service.

THINGS

ENDANGERED SPECIES

Rarest American Mammals

For all its status as the land of plenty, America has earned its wealth in large part by the exploitation of its vast natural resources. Unfortunately, this exploitation has led to what the military might call "collateral damage" — the wholesale destruction of the environment, including a large number of uniquely American species. The grizzly, once the proud master of the American West, now exists only in small numbers in the lower 48 states — estimated from 800 to 1,200 — in protected refuges such as Yellowstone. The following list represents the rarest mammals in the United States, with their estimated populations (numbers are from the World Wildlife Federation, where known). The Florida Panther is endangered by the continued desecration and destruction of its habitat in the Florida Everglades. The Key Deer, also a Florida native, exists only on one small island in the Florida Keys; each year, islanders keep a running count of the number of rare Key Deer killed by motorists traveling to and from Key West along much-used U.S. Route 1. Species for which populations are unknown include the red wolf, the Eastern cougar, which is believed extinct despite a number of recent reported sightings, the feline Jaguarundi, a few of which are thought to cross the border from Mexico on occasion, and the Vaquita, or harbor porpoise. Remember, once these animals are gone, they're gone for good.

Species	Est. Pop.
1. Florida Panther	30-50
2. Vancouver Island Marmot	100
3. Sanborn's Long-nosed Bat	135
4. Mount Graham Red Squirrel	215
5. Right Whale	240-600
6. Key Deer	300
7. Wood Bison	320
8. Morro Bay Kangaroo Rat	340
9. Sonoran Pronghorn	400-550
10. Ozark Big-eared Bat	750

ENVIRONMENTAL ORGANIZATIONS

Biggest Environmental Organizations

No question about it, America has gone green. From the massive celebrations of Earth Day to the mass effort to save the California redwoods, people are standing up for old Mother Earth. Leading the way are America's environmental organizations. Some of these organizations lobby the government for increased protection for wildlife or specific habitats, others work to inform the public and confront polluting businesses, while still others are actively involved in saving or restoring threatened lands. Recent polls show that just about every American considers him or herself an environmentalist. These are the groups on the forefront of serving that large constituency. So what are you doing to save the environment?

Organization	Members
1. National Wildlife Fed.	5,600,000
2. Greenpeace	1,400,000
3. Sierra Club	553,246
4. National Audubon Society	516,220
5. The Wilderness Society	330,000
6. Enviro. Defense Fund	125,000
7. Nat. Resources Def. Council	125,000
8. National Parks and Conservation Association	100,000
9. Defenders of Wildlife	80,000
10. Friends of the Earth	50,000
11. Izaak Walton League	50,000
12. Environmental Action	20,000
13. League of Conservation Voters	15,000

Source: *Congressional Quarterly*: Current American Government Fall 1990 Guide.

FAST FOOD CHAINS

Top Burger Joints

American chopped beef transcends socio-economic structures; it crosses ethnic borders and traverses geographic boundaries.

THINGS

More than pizza, chopped suey or apple pie, the hamburger binds this great country together. Iowa farm boys chomp on a burgers while driving in their pickups. Sophisticated New Yorkers lunch over burgers. Hollywood movie executives eat burgers with avocados. The magazine *Restaurant & Institutions* has rated some of America's most popular hamburger chains. Their satisfaction index is based on consumer surveys, with very satisfied responses receiving a grade of three, satisfied responses a grade of two and unsatisfied responses a grade of one. Ties were broken by the number of responses. McDonald's was not included in the survey.

Chain	Satisfaction Index
1. Wendy's	2.34
2. Whataburger	2.32
3. Burger King	2.26
4. Hardee's	2.25
5. Carl's Jr	2.25
6. Sonic Drive-Ins	2.25

Source: *Restaurants & Institutions*.

FAST FOOD CHAINS
Top Chicken Joints

Buk buk buk baaaaaak! Americans luv fried chicken. We take it on picnics and bring it to ball games. We eat it at family gatherings and meetings. As the Colonel says, "It's finger lickin' good." Interestingly, the chains with the highest satisfaction index are two smaller, regional outfits. Topping the list is the Atlanta-based Chick-Fil-A with 309 units. The number two place for chicken, Grandy's, has 206 units and is based in Lewisville, Texas. The latter, which has "grannies" serving as hostesses, gets especially high marks for customer service. The big three, Kentucky Fried Chicken, Popeye's Famous Fried Chicken and Church's came in third, fourth and sixth respectively. (The Almanac editors' top choice, Harold's Chicken Shack, is a chain limited to Chicago but highly recommended for those visiting the Windy City). Ratings are based on a customer-satisfaction poll which grades satisfaction from one to three. So next time you get a taste for chicken, you know where to go. Say, are you going to eat that drumstick?

Chain	Score
1. Chick-Fil-A	2.44
2. Grandy's	2.42
3. Kentucky Fried Chicken	2.33
4. Popeyes Famous Fried Chicken	2.27
5. Bojangles'	2.25
6. Church's	2.12

Source: *Restaurants & Institutions*.

FAST FOODS
Healthiest

The typical fast-food meal of which Americans are so fond—burgers, fries, a soft drink—ranks extremely low in overall nutritional value, primarily because of the fat, cholesterol and salt content. Of course, the convenience of such meals, not their nutritional value, is what makes them popular. But even if you're on the run, there are some healthy alternatives to the burgers-and-soda staple. Most fast-food joints now offer salads, and even McDonald's now is testing out pizza. The rankings of nutritional value here are based on the nutripoint system developed by Dr. Roy Vartebedian and Kathy Matthews. For a complete description of their methodology, see the source.

The Top Ten	Nutripoints
1. Wendy's Chef Salad	6.0
2. McDonald's Salad Oriental	5.0
3. Wendy's Hot Stuffed Potato	4.5
4. Roy Rogers Hot-topped Potato	4.0
5. Pizza Hut Supreme Pizza	3.5
6. P.H. Cheese Thin 'n' Crispy	3.0
7. Pizza Hut Pepperoni Pan	3.0
8. Pizza Hut Cheese Pan	2.5
9. Various Pizza Hut Pizzas	2.0

Source: *Nutripoints: The Breakthrough Point System for Optimum Nutrition,* Roy E. Vartabedian & Kathy Matthews, Harper & Row, 1990.

THINGS

FAST FOODS
Fat in Fast Food Breakfasts

Fast food is not the unmixed bag of chemicals and bio-toxins that some suspect. Nor, however, is it the on-balance best nutritional alternative open to most of us. One of the biggest culprits in the American diet is fat, which, in fast foods, is almost everywhere. The thorns in the nutritional forest are many; tread softly over these morning munchables.

Breakfast	Gram of Fat per Serving
1. Burger King Croisan'wich w/sausage	41
2. McDonald's Biscuit w/Sausage and Egg	35
3. Hardee's Sausage and Egg Biscuit	35
4. Burger King French Toast Sticks	29
5. Roy Rogers Crescent w/Sausage	29
6. Jack in the Box Pancake Platter	22
7. McDonald's Egg McMuffin	12
8. Roy Rogers Apple Danish	12
9. McDonald's Hot Cakes w/butter and syrup	9
10. McDonald's English Muffin w/butter	5

Source: Mayo Clinic Nutrition Letter

FEDERAL SPENDING
Where The Money Goes

As has been the case since Lyndon Johnson's Great Society program of the mid-1960s, the Federal Government spends most of its money on social security, national defense and medical assistance. Because of the ballooning national debt, interest continues to grow as a percentage of total spending. All other programs are comparatively minor in terms of spending. For example the government spends just 0.8% of total revenue on the administration of justice. Income security includes social security, Federal employee retirement benefits, unemployment compensation, housing assistance, food-stamps and other nutritional assistance. Health includes Medicare and Medicaid. The following are

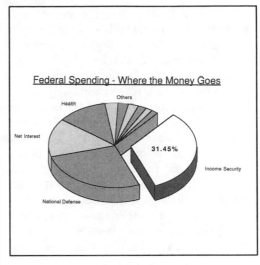

Federal Spending - Where the Money Goes

the biggest slices of the federal government pie. Are you getting your piece?

Program	Share of Fed. Budget (%)
1. Income Security	31.45
2. National Defense	25.40
3. Net Interest	14.11
4. Health	11.63
5. Education, Training, Employment, Social Services	3.10
6. Veterans' Benefits and Services	2.41
7. Transportation	2.39
8. Agriculture	1.78
9. Commerce and Housing Credit	1.71
10. Natural Resources/ Environment	1.40%

Source: Tax Foundation, Washington, D.C.

FOOD
Most and Least Nutritious

The nation's increased health-consciousness means more people are checking the nutritional value of the foods they eat. Food companies have begun advertising their fiber content, cholesterol levels, and other important nutritional information. But until recently, no one had ranked the *overall* nutritional value of various foods. In *Nutripoints*, Dr. Roy E. Vartebedian and Kathy Matthews do just that. The Nutripoints food ratings assign a point for a comparable, standard portion of each of

THINGS

over 3,000 foods. Positive points are awarded for Essentials — complex carbohydrates, protein, dietary fiber (weighted twice), vitamins, and minerals. Negative points are assigned for Excessives: total fat, saturated fat, calories, sodium, sugar, caffeine, cholesterol and alcohol, the latter two weighted three times negatively. (For the exact formula, see the source). The most nutritious foods overall are leafy green vegetables and fortified breakfast cereals. Seafood rated higher than meats and poultry. Junk foods, it turns out, are just that: most snack foods earned negative nutripoints. So dig into your turnip greens, but for heaven's sake, stay away from those sweetbreads!

The Ten Healthiest	Nutripoints
1. Turnip Greens	79.0
2. Raw Chopped Spinach	75.0
3. Bok Choy	72.5
4. Whole Wheat Total Cereal	64.5
5. Cooked Mustard Greens	62.0
6. Total Corn Flakes Cereal	57.5
7. Cooked Beet Greens	56.5
8. Product 19 Cereal	56.0
9. Parsley, Fresh	54.5
10. Raw Broccoli	53.0

The Ten Least Healthy

1. Sweetbreads	-52.0
2. Scrambled Eggs	-13.5
3. Caviar	-11.5
4. Little Debbie Snack Cake	-8.5
5. Gatorade	-8.0
6. Lipton Iced Tea	-7.5
7. Salted Butter	-7.5
8. Coconut Oil	-7.0
9. Heavy Cream	-7.0
10. Soft Drink, w/caffeine	-7.0

Source: *Nutripoints*, Dr. Roy E. Vartebedian and Kathy Matthews.

FOOD
Biggest Food Crops
Like Michael Jordan says, better get your Wheaties. Wheat is the most popular food crop in the world, followed closely by rice and corn, the big three of food production. Some of the crops on the list of top ten food crops may be unfamiliar to American palates — cassava, or manioc, for instance, a large, starchy root grown mainly in South America and a cooking staple extremely common on tropical tables. Manioc is also used to make tapioca. And most *Norte Americanos* see sweet potatoes only around Thanksgiving time. Here we list the top ten staples of the world diet, in millions of tons harvested annually worldwide.

Crop	Millions of tons Annually
1. Wheat	445
2. Rice	400
3. Corn	392
4. Pototoes	226
5. Barley	162
6. Cassava	122
7. Sweet Potato	107
8. Soy Bean	83
9. Grapes	65
10. Sorghum	58

Source: United Nations Environmental Programme.

FOOD
Most Popular
Hard to believe, but the list of what Americans eat looks pretty healthy, at least at first glance. Meat consumption is finally going down, and if it wasn't for wheat flour (used to make bread) spuds would rule. Fresh and canned vegetables and non-citrus fruits all made healthy showings. A closer look, however, would reveal that combined corn sweetener and refined sugars would top the list with 132 pounds per person per year. That might be encouraging for dentists, but it's bad news for the general health of the country. Foods that didn't make this list included chicken (44.6 pounds per year), citrus fruits (26.5 pounds per year) and pork (44.7 pounds per year).

THINGS

Food Per Capita Consumption (lbs./yr.)	
1. Wheat Flour	127.5
2. Potatoes	124.8
3. Whole Milk	105.1
4. Low Fat Milk	101.6
5. Fresh Vegetables	100.3
6. Canned Vegetables	82.8
7. Non-Citrus Fruits	70.4
8. Corn Sweeteners	70.1
9. Beef	68.2
10. Refined Cane and Beet Sugar	62.4

Source: Research Service, U.S. Department of Agriculture.

FOOD
Highest in Fiber

Long before advertising firms began capitalizing on a renewed interest in what was once called roughage, men recognized the contributions of fruit, vegetables and grains for promoting healthy digestion. Hence, the salad. Nutritionists have only recently begun to study the effects of this "non-nutritive substance," and the results are preliminary. However, studies indicate that a fiber-rich diet may help to ameliorate complaints ranging from constipation, hemorrhoids and irritable bowel syndrome to colon cancer, gallstones and diabetes. On the other hand, some high-fiber diets (like those found among villagers in Uganda) have been found coincident with zinc deficiency, sigmoid volvulus and esophageal cancer. It is estimated that the average American consumes no more than twenty grams of fiber per day; for a strict vegetarian, that number approaches sixty. At this time, there is no daily recommended allowance, but the National Cancer Insitute has suggested twenty-five to thirty-five grams daily. The figures cited below have been adjusted to reflect a single serving.

Food	Fiber, Grams/Serving
1. Pumpkin/Squash Seeds	25.5
2. Elderberries (Raw)	25.2
3. Walnuts (Black, Dried)	20.2
4. Peanuts (Oil-roasted)	19.2
5. Chia Seeds (Dried)	18.0
6. Chirimoya	15.3
7. Winged Bean Tuber (Raw)	14.8
8. Kellogg's All-Bran, Extra Fiber	13.0
9. Winged Beans (Raw)	12.5
10. Arrowhead Mills Bran Cereal	12.2

Source: *Food Values: Fiber,* Harper & Row.

FOOD
Highest in Potassium

The Food and Drug Administration has not set a recommended daily allowance for potassium, although it is recognized as an essential part of a diet. Dr. Roy Vartebedian and Kathy Mathews, in their book *Nutripoints*, have used guidelines from the National Research Council to establish a level of about 5,600 milligrams of potassium daily in a healthy diet. One of the best places to get that nutrient is the potato, which has about twice as much dietary potassium as the banana, a common source of potassium. Below we have listed the amount of potassium, in milligrams, for the top ten foods in this category. Amounts are based on a normal serving.

Food	Potassium (mg/serving)
1. Potato	844
2. Cantaloupe	825
3. Prune Juice	706
4. Avocado	602
5. Watermelon	559
6. Raisins	545
7. Dates	541
8. Tomato Juice	536
9. Apricots	482
10. Orange Juice	473

Source: Human Nutritional Information Service, U.S. Dept. of Agriculture.

FOOTBALL GAMES
Biggest Championship Blowouts

Championship games are intended to match up the best of teams from each league to battle it out for the right to call themselves

THINGS

champions. But on occasion, the match is less than even. For whatever reason – one team's vast superiority over any other, injuries to key players, a player heating up at the right moment, an entire team cooling off at the wrong time – certain professional football championships have turned into routs. The most spectacular of these pitted the Chicago Bears against the Washington Redskins in the 1940 NFL Championship game; by the end of that match-up, officials were worried that they would run out of footballs if Chicago kept scoring and kicking extra points into the stands. Final score: Chicago 73, Washington 0. Chicago's Monsters of the Midway have been on the winning end of two other championship blow-outs, the most recent being the 1986 Super Bowl against the New England Patriots. But all hasn't been roses for the Bears; in 1956, the New York Giants crushed them by 47 points. The most astounding recent rout was suffered by the hapless Denver Broncos at the hands of Joe Montana's San Francisco 49ers in the 1990 Super Bowl, by a score of of 55-10. Just two years earlier, the Broncos had been blown out in the January classic by the Washington Redskins, 42-10. Below are the most one-sided NFL Championship and Super Bowl games.

Winner/Loser Year	Score	Margin
1. Chicago/Wash., '40	73-0	73
2. Cleveland/Detroit, '54	56-10	46
3. S.F./Denver, 1990	55-10	45
4. Detroit/Cleve., '56	59-14	45
5. N.Y./Chicago, '56	47-7	40
6. Green Bay/N.Y. '61	37-0	37
7. Chicago/New Eng. '86	46-10	36
8. Wash./Denver, '88	42-10	32
9. L.A./Wash., '84	38-9	29
10. Chicago/N.Y., '41	37-9	38

FOUNDATIONS
Most Charitable

Non-profit organizations employ more civilians than the federal government and the fifty states *combined*. Associations and religious groups make up a large part of that number, but it also includes charitable, grantmaking foundations – over 25,000, in fact. The largest of these foundations concern themselves with wide-ranging regional, national and international issues – education, the environment, the arts, etc. These, then, are the biggest points of light in the American firmament, measured by their total outlay of grant payments in 1989.

Foundation	Grant Payments (millions)
1. Ford Foundation	$217.6
2. Pew Charitable Trusts	$137.1
3. W.K. Kellogg Foundation	$106.9
4. Robert Wood Johnson Found.	$98.6
5. MacArthur Foundation	$95.3
6. Lilly Endowment	$92.5
7. Andrew T. Mellon Foundation	$75.5
8. Rockefeller Foundation	$65.7
9. Kresge Foundation	$57.5
10. Weinberg Foundation	$53.7

Source: Chronicle of Higher Education.

FRUIT
Most Caloric

Fruit is a decidedly refreshing alternative to the all-too-usual bevy of junk food pseudo-sweets, but the over-anxious fruit eater must be cautioned. If you think you can munch nature's sweet bounty with utter impunity, your waistline will quickly suffer. Here are the fruits with the highest calorie content – eat them with caution and in moderation.

Fruit	Serving Size	Calories
1. Figs	5	238
2. Raisins	1/2 cup	218
3. Watermelon	slice	155
4. Mango	1 average	135
5. Apple	1 large	125
6. D'Anjou Pear	1	120
7. Prunes	5 large	115
8. Dates	5	115
9. Banana	1	105
10. Cantaloupe	half	95

THINGS

Source: Human Nutrition Information Service.

GARBAGE
Most Recycled Garbage

America has come along way in its consciousness of the perishibility of our environs, and of the needs to conserve and recycle. Still, this consciousness must be raised several notches further, if the perpetuation of our rather comfortable lives is to remain a likely proposition. Recycling is one of the many ways in which we can relieve the burden of our massive consumption of material goods on the resources available to us. The following are the goods that lend themselves most to such treatment, simultaneously lessening the demand on waste disposal and providing an alternate, cheaper source for these raw materials.

Waste Item	% Recycled, 1988
1. Non-Ferrous Metals	65.1
2. Aluminum	31.7
3. Paper and Paperboard	25.6
4. Non-classified solids	21.7
5. Glass	12.0
6. Ferrous Metals	5.8
7. Rubber and Leather	2.3
8. Yard Wastes	1.6
9. Plastics	1.1
10. Textiles	0.6

Source: Characterization of Municipal Solid Waste, E.P.A.

GOVERNMENT
Largest Federal Departments and Agencies

One hears a great deal about the excesses and inffieciencies of big government, but few of us have any concrete idea exactly how gargantuan our state apparatus actually is. Consider that the Defense Department alone employs more than a million red-white-and-blue souls. Consider also, that the Postal Service, for all the flak it fields, employs nearly as many workers (816,948) for about 1/80th of the arms budget.

Dept.	Empl.	$ (bill.)
1. Defense	1,033,730	$328.0
2. Postal Service	816,948	$4.1
3. Veteran Affairs	248,174	$29.9
4. Treasury	158,655	$248.5
5. Health & Hum. Svc.	123,959	$519.0
6. Agriculture	122,594	$55.1
7. Justice	83,932	$8.6
8. Interior	77,681	$6.2
9. Commerce	69,920	$3.6
10. Transportation	67,364	$30.2

Source: U.S. Office of Management and Budget

GOVERNMENT JOBS
Highest-Paying Government Jobs

You can't get rich in government, the conventional wisdom goes. However, you can maintain a fairly toney standard of living. Although the President and his cohort make a small fraction of what they might in less-pressured positions in the greener fields of private commerce, service and industry (or, for Vice President Dan Quayle, on the professional golf tour, a position for which he has trained hard during his time in Washington), theirs are hardly starvation wages. Besides, if things get too bad, they can always vote or lobby themselves a raise.

Position	Annual Salary
1. President	$200,000
2. Vice President	$160,600
3. Chief Justice	$160,600
4. Associate Justice	$153,600
5. Cabinet Secretary	$138,900
6. Assistant Secretary	$125,100
7. U.S. Representative	$125,100
8. U.S. District Court Judge	$125,100
9. Deputy Asst. Secy.	$115,300
10. Bureau Chief	$108,300

Source: Federal Information Center.

THINGS

HIGH SCHOOLS
Academic Champs

In the Olympics, the decathlon tests athletes in a variety of physical endeavors, from running and jumping to throwing—a test of endurance over two days. The National Academic Decathlon similarly pits American public high schools against one another, but also against an impartial scoring system. In the most recent contest, the winner was J.J. Pearce High School from Richardson, Texas, with a top score of 48,946 points, but also showing up in the top ten are two inner-city schools from beleaguered school systems: Whitney Young Magnet High School from Chicago (the city that Secretary of Education William Bennett said had the worst public school system in the country), and the University School of Milwaukee. Whitney Young is the pearl in Chicago's experimental "magnet school" program, in which talented students from all over the city are concentrated in a small number of elite, achievement-oriented schools. Clearly something about the idea is working— motivated inner-city youths achieving their potential in a public-school environment, just the way it's supposed to work.

School/Location	Score
1. J.J. Pearce High School Richardson, Tex.	48,946
2. Laguna Hills High School Laguna, Calif.	47,246
3. Whitney Young Magnet H.S. Chicago, Ill.	47,231
4. Mountain View High School Mesa, Ariz.	47,145
5. Northern Valley High School Old Tappan, N.J.	44,275
6. Framingham North H.S. Framingham, Mass.	42,519
7. Wheeler High School Providence, R.I.	42,364
8. Univ. School of Milwaukee Milwaukee, Wisc.	42,341
9. Indian Springs High School Helena, Ala.	41,388
10. Ames High School Ames, Iowa.	41,367

Source: National Academic Decathlon.

HIGHWAYS
Interstate Highways in Worst Condition

Want a sure-fire business success? Start a shock-absorber store in Missouri. The poor folks of the Show-me state suffer from the most pot-holed, bumpy interstate highways in the country. According to the Federal Highway Administration, some 43% of the more than 1,100 miles of Missouri interstate highways are in need of repair. The reason Hawaii enjoys such pristine roads, besides its climate, is the simple fact that, being an island chain, there are no interstate highways in Hawaii. The following states have the worst interstate highway systems, measured by the percentage of interstate highways in need of repair, according to the Federal Highway Administration

State	Percent	Miles
1. Missouri	43%	509
2. Alaska	42%	456
3. North Dakota	36%	204
4. Oregon	35%	257
5. Nevada	33%	179
6. Tennessee	32%	336
7. Oklahoma	29%	268
8. Rhode Island	29%	20
9. Arizona	28%	319
10. Mississippi	28%	188

Interstate Highways in Best Condition

State	Percent	Miles
1. South Dakota	0%	0
2. Hawaii	0%	0

THINGS

3. Delaware	0%	0
4. Alabama	0.1%	1
5. Wyoming	0.2%	2
6. North Carolina	1%	9
7. Nebraska	1%	5
8. Washington	1%	10
9. Utah	1%	12
10. New Mexico	1%	12

Source: Federal Highway Administration.

HIGHWAYS
Busiest

The flow of traffic in and out of urban areas presents significant challenges for city planners, especially since the exodus to the suburbs during the 1950s and '60s. As America's love affair with the automobile continued to thrive and our highway system was forced to cope with ever increasing usage, our culture developed a new malady: traffic-induced stress headaches. The mostly likely places to acquire such an affliction are in the following locations. The busiest roadway in the country is the George Washington Bridge, which spans the Hudson River and connects Manhattan with Northern New Jersey along well-travelled Interstate 95.

Route/City	Avg. daily two-way traffic
1. I-95	249,300
George Washington Bridge, New York City	
2. I-90/94	248,000
Dan Ryan/Kennedy Expressway, Chicago	
3. I-10	243,000
Santa Monica/San Bernardino Freeway, Los Angeles	
4. I-5	224,000
Seattle, WA	
5. Oakland Bay Bridge	223,000
San Francisco	
6. I-35	217,700
Dallas	
7. I-10	187,600

New Orleans	
8. I-610	169,000
Houston	
9. I-95	169,000
Miami	
10. I-5	161,000
San Diego	

Source: Federal Highway Administration.

HORSES
Highest Earning, 1990

Everybody likes to bet on the ponies, but the only people who really win in the long run are the owners and trainers of the winners; not only do their horses bring in millions in winnings during their racing career, but after those careers are over, the owners can receive equally large sums in the lucrative stud fees. Winning horses can command tens of thousands of dollars for a successful coupling. Nice life for the horse. Bettors, on the other hand, more often than not, lose whatever it is the next day that they might have won in the previous outing. These are the highest-earning thoroughbreds for the 1990 year.

Horse	Winnings
1. Unbridled	$3,718,149
2. Izvestia	$2,486,667
3. Criminal Type	$2,270,290
4. Summer Squall	$1,222,356
5. Flying Continental	$1,096,700
6. Ruhlmann	$1,095,800
7. Rhythm	$958,972
8. Home At Last	$941,065
9. Steinlen	$900,140
10. Go for Wand	$824,948

HOTELS
Largest Hotel Chains

Establishing a national or international hotel chain is a hugely capital-intensive undertaking, so it is not surprising that this recessionary era has seen the birth of very few. The hotel game is dominated by a handful of traditional players, whose individual images have changed little in modern times. The biggest noise in travel accommodations, in the last few years, has been made by stripped-down, economy chains like Motel 6, which promise clean, basic rooms at a fraction of most competitors' luxurious prices; and, at the other end of the scale, the rise of the "all-suite" hotel, which plays on the upscale traveler's desire for more space. These are the largest chains in hotel-happy America.

Chain	Rooms
1. Holiday Inn	262,002
2. Best Western	162,887
3. Days Inn	138,611
4. Sheraton	96,456
5. Hilton	96,304
6. Ramada	86,427
7. Marriott	85,199
8. Motel 6	63,341
9. Comfort Inn	62,865
10. Howard Johnson	55,684

Source: American Hotel/Motel Assoc.

HOTELS
Most Lucrative Hotel Chains, Worldwide

Home is where you hang your hat, and most often, travelers have made themselves at home at tried-and-tested, low-frills chains like Holiday Inn, Marriott or Ramada. In fact, the top hotel chains worldwide all are American-born. Well-heeled fellows and fillies worldwide prefer to park it at the upscale Hilton over other luxury locations. And folks have come in quantity to the Quality Inn.

Chain	1990 Sales ($ billions)
1. Holiday Inns	5.4
2. Sheraton Hotels	4.4
3. Best Western International	3.7
4. Marriott Corp.	3.5
5. Hyatt Hotels	2.3
6. Hilton International	1.8

7. Ramada	1.7
8. Days Inn	1.7
9. Hilton Hotels	1.5
10. Quality Inn	1.5

Source: Superbrands 1990.

INDUSTRIES—DRUG TESTING
Most Likely to Demand an Employee Drug Test

The eighties may go down in history as the decade in which U.S. industry and government decided to take an avid interest in urology. The right to privacy has been on the wane through much of the post-war epoch, and now, with the employer's right to examine an employee's urine, it has perhaps hit its all-time low. The list below rates industries by the percentage of establishments or companies within the industry that have institutionalized drug-testing programs. The most pervasive testers are those in mining, transportation and public utilities, in which the safety of employees and customers most immediately relies on the ability of employees to function with a clear head.

Industry	Percent
1. Mining	21.6%
2. Comm. and Public Utilities	17.6
3. Transportation	14.9
4. Durable Goods Manufacturing	9.9
5. Non-durable Goods Mfg.	9.1
6. Wholesale Trade	5.3
7. Finance, Industry, Real Estate	3.2
8. Construction	2.3
9. Services	1.4
10. Retail Trade	0.7

Source: Bureau of Labor Statistics, Survey of Employer Anti-Drug Programs, 1989

INDUSTRIES—GROWTH
Best and Worst 1990

Take a look at the ten fastest growing industries in the country over the last year and you'll get a snapshot of the American economy as the 1990s begin. Engineering, computers, the environment and service-related industries such as personal care are on the rapid rise, while traditional relics of the industrial age – stccl, rubber, trucking – decline. The biggest drop in growth is occurring among the once strong auto parts and equipmetn industry. Also apparent in the figures is the sad and perhaps dangerous situation of the American banking system. The figures below are for the composite market value of companies in various industries and the percent change in that value from 1989 to 1990.

Fastest Growing	Billions of $	% Grow
1. Engineering Services	8.9	53
2. Computer Software	32.9	48
3. Pollution Control	28.1	46
4. Petroleum Services	31.7	41
5. Personal Care	43.8	37
6. Electrical Products	30.2	32
7. Textiles	2.0	31
8. Misc. Services	5.4	31
9. Gas & Transmission	30.9	30
10. General Mfg.	42.2	29

Fastest Declining

1. Auto Parts & Equipment	6.9	-23
2. Hotel & Motel	8.8	-11
3. Banks – East	51.4	-9
4. Instruments	9.4	-6
5. Publishing	54.7	-6
6. Other Leisure	24.5	-5
7. Tire & Rubber	4.2	-3
8. Steel	7.2	-3
9. Computers	122.8	-3
10. Trucking & Shipping	6.7	-3

Source: Business Week.

INDUSTRIES – PROFITABILITY

Most Profitable, Last Ten Years

Health-care costs have continued to soar over the past decade – bad news for patients and for companies in terms of health care insurance. And even this jump in costs is not all good news for the health-care industry, for despite its profitability, the industry is undergoing radical changes in the delivery of services, forcing less financially sound hospitals out of business. Beyond health care, the biggest moneymakers are entertainment, servicc and retail industries. The figures below are for average annual return on equity for companies in each industry over the last ten years.

Industry	10-Year Avg.	1989
1. Health	18.7	18.4
2. Food, Drink, Tobacco	18.4	17.8
3. Entertainment & Info.	17.3	15.2
4. Business Svcs.	16.7	16.6
5. Retailing	16.7	14.4
6. Aerospace & Defense	15.7	13.4
7. Cons. Non-Durables	15.2	17.1
8. Chemicals	15.0	17.4
9. Insurance	14.4	12.0
10. Financial	14.3	13.9

Source: Forbes.

INDUSTRIES – RESEARCH AND DEVELOPMENT

Best For R&D Spending as Percentage of Sales

The big boom in the health care industry has fueled a healthy climate for research and development in that area. Spending by health care companies as a whole on R&D in 1989 was a "healthy" 8.6 percent of overall sales. Medical, biotechnology and drug companies comprise some of the biggest spenders, in terms of percentage of sales, on R&D. Computer hardware and software makers, as well as office equipment companies, also score well in this regard. However, research and development as a percentage of sales is not always a telling indicator of a company's or an industry's R&D performance. In such industries as aerospace, R&D has always been crucial for continued economic health – the "skunk

THINGS

works" of the various aircraft manufacturers, in which researchers and engineers designed and developed the great airplanes of yesterday and today, are legendary. But the aerospace industry, despite pumping 4.1 percent of sales overall into R&D, only increased its spending in this area by 2 percent; that's an actual decline when adjusted for inflation, and an indicator of the downward spiral facing the industry with the readjusting of U.S. defense policy. On the other hand, in some industries, most notably banking, research and development is not so vital to economic performance, and spending on R&D is accordingly smaller.

The Top Ten	R&D/Sales (%)
1. Health Care	8.6
2. Office Equipment	8.1
3. Electrical and Electronics	5.4
4. Leisure Time Products	4.9
5. Telecommunications	4.7
6. Aerospace	4.1
7. Chemicals	3.8
8. Automotive	3.4
9. Manufacturing	2.7
10. Conglomerates	2.3

The Bottom Ten	
1. Non-Bank Financial	0.7
2. Food	0.7
3. Fuel	0.8
4. Containers & Packaging	0.9
5. Paper & Forest Products	1.0
6. Publishing & Broadcasting	1.0
7. Service Industries	1.1
8. Metals & Mining	1.1
9. Consumer Products	1.4
10. Housing	1.9

Source: *Business Week*, from Compustat Services, Inc.

INDUSTRIES — SAFETY
Highest Occupational Injury and Illness Rates

A certain degree of risk is inherent in all human enterprises. Some tasks, however, are far more perilous than others. As it turns out, the most dangerous jobs in America do not belong to the cops, firemen, bullfighters or football stars. Surprisingly, it is America's frontline, heavy-industrial factory workers who are the true Rambos of occupational safety and health, measured in therms of the rate of occupational injury and illnesses logged per 100 employees.

Industry	Rate /100 employees
1. Ship Building and Repairing	40.1
2. Meat Packing	38.4
3. Metal Sanitary Ware	31.9
4. Prefabricated Wood Buildings	31.5
5. Mobie Homes	28.9
6. Primary Aluminum	28.6
7. Leather Tanning and Finishing	26.5
8. Canned and Cured Seafood	26.4
8. Special Product Sawmills	26.4
10. Primary Lead	25.7

Source: U.S. Bureau of Labor Statistics, Occupational Injuries and Illnesses by Industry

INDUSTRIES — SIZE
Largest U.S. Industries

Americans are flocking to the Service by the thousands. Not the U.S. Armed Services, mind you, but the civilian regiments of that same corps. Our workers — the front line commercial shock troops — are moving out of the deep trenches of industry and advancing into the service ranks. Manufacturing is old hat. In the coming days, says kind uncle Sam, we must aim to please.

Industry	Employees (thousands)
1. Health Services	8,122
2. Eating and Drinking Places	6,503
3. Business Services	5,898
4. Durable Goods	3,759
5. Transportation	3,665
6. Food Stores	3,379
7. Finance	3,363
8. Non-durable goods	2,595
9. General Merchandise stores	2,435
10. Insurance	2,165

Source: U.S. Department of Labor.

THINGS

INDUSTRIES—
UNEMPLOYMENT
Highest Unemployment

The high unemployment in the agriculture and construction industries is evidence of the susceptibility of those industries to economic downswings and dramatic climactic changes. A particularly dry growing season can be the straw that breaks the back of the small farmer, already extremely extended financially, forcing him into bankruptcy. In the construction industry, a slow housing market, bad weather, and the seasonal and project-oriented nature of the work make for high unemployment. Civil service, on the other hand, is the most secure field.

Industry	Unemployment
1. Agriculture	10.6
2. Construction	10.6
3. Mining	7.9
4. Wholesale and Retail Trade	6.2
5. Manufacturing (Nondurable)	5.7
6. Manufacturing (Durable)	5.0
7. Services	4.9
8. Transportation and Public Util.	3.9
9. Finance, Insurance, Real Est.	3.0
10. Government	2.8

Source: Handbook of Labor Statistics, August 1989.

INFLATION
Most Inflated Consumer Items

In the early eighties, the U.S. began to feel like a corner of the encroaching third world, with inflation gone runaway, and crises mounting in our schools and on our streets. The interceding years have brought some relief from the double-digit inflation of those sorry times, but the slippage of the dollar in certain areas is still impossible to ignore. For a nation that claims to be committed to equal educational opportunity for all, educational services and equipment are the expenses that have seen the most inflation from 1982 to 1989. It's good to see, at least, that the market works the way it should—as demand goes up, so do prices. The following measure of inflation takes 1982 prices as a base of 100. School supplies, the list shows, have risen almost 70 percent in that span of time; the price of medical services has also jumped by more than 60 percent, despite a continued decline in the nation's overall health care coverage.

Item	CPI Index Score
1. School Books/Supplies	169.8
2. Personal and Educ. Services	168.1
3. Medical Care Commodities	163.3
4. Medical Care Services	161.5
5. Professional Medical Services	155.8
6. Public Transportation	141.5
7. Renters' Costs	145.3
8. Homeowner's Costs	144.4
9. Entertainment Services	142.6
10. Shelter	139.5

Source: Bureau of Labor Statistics.

INFLATION
Least Inflated Consumer Items

Ah value! While it may seem that nothing is cheap, in these ultra-pricey times, certain things, at least, have remained less-outrageous than others. First among these is fuel. In the last two decades, we geared ourselves to the mentalities of embargo, shortage and price escalation. But for the brief Gulf War, the nineties look to be an era of relatively steady fuel cost. Compared to 1982 prices, the cost of fuel for our engines of commerce has actually fallen by between five and fifteen percent.

Item	CPI Index Score
1. Fuel Oil	84.9
2. Motor Fuel	94.6
3. Other Private Transp. Costs	101.8
4. House Furnishings	106.3
5. Fuel and Utilities	112.1
6. Gas and Electricity	112.4
7. Household Operation Costs	113.1
8. Private Transportation	116.4
9. Maintenance and Repair Costs	117.0

THINGS

10. Used Cars   117.6

Source: Bureau of Labor Statistics.

INVESTMENTS
Best-Performing
Investment Newsletter

Selecting an investment newsletter is a tricky business. Investment strategies proposed by a newsletter to take advantage of particular market conditions may be most unsuitable in other situations. The most telling example? The portfolio for this year's champ, the *Granville Market Letter*, has actually *lost* 86% over the last five years, even taking into account its remarkable 1989 gain. On the other hand, although the *Zweig Forecast* underperformed the S&P 500 in 1989, it is one of only two (the *Value Line Investment Survey* is the other) to outperform the market over the last 10 years. As with investments in general, so with investment newsletters, the best advice may be to diversify. The figures below compare with the S&P 500's gain of 31.6%.

The Top Ten, 1989	% Change
1. Granville Market Letter	+367.9%
2. Medical Tech. Stock Letter	+78.8%
3. OTC Insight	+62.7%
4. On Markets	+57.2%
5. Wall Street Generalist	+46.4%
6. The Oberweis Report	+41.8%
7. The Chartist	+37.9%
8. MPT Review	+37.7%
9. Value Line OTC	+37.1%
10. Timer Digest	+37.0%

The Top Ten, Last Ten Years	
1. Zweig Forecast	+484.6%
2. Value Line Inv. Survey	+438.6%
3. Prudent Speculator	+423.3%
4. The Chartist	+346.0%
5. Growth Stock Outlook	+337.2%
(Standard & Poor 500)	+361.4%

Source: *The Hulbert Financial Digest.*

JOBS
Best and Worst

What is the best job in America? Perhaps the question has no valid answer; more likely it has many. For most people, the very best job is the one they most enjoy doing. A painter for whom art is both a love and a means of making a living may believe that not only is his or her job the *best* one possible, but also the *only* one possible. Certain professionals, such as the clergy, do not feel a need to choose a vocation, believing themselves called to their occupations. But for those of us who must pick careers without the aid of divine guidance, it would be blessing enough to find a sensible, consistent system for ranking the thousands of possibilities.

The *Jobs Rated Almanac* analyzed more than 90 job-related factors that contribute to the quality of 250 careers in six primary areas: income, stress, physical demands, work environment, outlook and security. The overall ranking of best and worst jobs is

The thrill and excitement of actuarial work makes it the top job in the country. Photo courtesy Society of Actuaries.

based on the sum of the rankings in those six areas. The best job overall was found to be actuary — the person who calculates risks for insurance companies. Actuaries work in extremely comfortable surroundings, are well paid, have few physical demands, relatively low stress and extremely good security and job outlook. Compare that to themigrant farmworker toils for long hours in the field, is poorly compensated and enjoys very little job security.

Ten Best	Score
1. Actuary	73
2. Computer Programmer	185
3. Computer Systems Analyst	187
4. Mathematician	208
5. Statistician	221
6. Hospital Administrator	223
7. Industrial Engineer	228
8. Physicist	254
9. Astrologer	257
10. Paralegal	264

Ten Worst	Score
1. Migrant Farmworker	1416
2. Fisherman	1351
3. Construction Worker	1344
4. Roofer	1339
5. Seaman	1337
6. Dairy Farmer	1278
7. Roustabout	1270
8. Lumberjack	1267
9. Cowboy	1262
10. NFL Football Player	1230

Source: Jobs Rated Almanac.

JOBS — ARTS
Best Jobs in the Arts

Everyone, at some time or other, feels the artistic inclination inside of him or her. Few of us get beyond finger-painting or singing in the shower, but the lucky ones find lucrative careers in fields in which their artistic impulses are both satisfied and satisfying. From the *Jobs Rated Almanac* ranking of 250 jobs from best to worst, we have extrapolated ten careers in the arts, and ranked

them from one to ten according to their overall ranking among the 250. The best artistic career, it turns out, is that of motion picture editor, which came in at number 12 overall. Not bad, but not quite the position that anyone can pick up — film editors require a good deal of intensive technical training, and picking up a steady job often depends on the network of contacts one must develop in the film and television world. Still, editors are much better off than those who choose to fulfill themselves through the dance. In this age of cutbacks in art funding, few dancers and choreographers can get by, let alone hope for commercial success.

Job	Overall Rank
1. Motion Picture Editor	12
2. Museum Curator	60
3. Set Designer	113
4. Fine Artist	131
5. Symphony Conductor	134
6. Singer	203
7. Musician	208
8. Actor	220
9. Choreographer	225
10. Dancer	240

Source: Jobs Rated Almanac.

JOBS — CLAUSTROPHOBIA
Most Claustrophobic

Someone who suffers from claustrophobia should not pursue a career as an astronaut. In training and on space flights, astronauts are confined to extremely cramped quarters for long periods of time. Of course, astronauts undergo rigorous testing to ensure that they can cope with the mental stress from such environments, so any Don Knotts-type reluctant astronauts are presumably weeded out. A stressful, tense or competitive atmosphere, such as you'll find in a hospital operating room, on a theatrical stage, or in a courtroom, also contributes to a poor work environment. Confined spaces, heavy responsibility, and tight schedules detract from one's ability to "blow off steam" when pressure mounts. The following are the jobs claustrophobics should avoid the most; rankings are taken from the work environment scores for indoor jobs in the *Jobs Rated Almanac*.

Ten Worst

1. Astronaut
2. Surgeon
3. Dancer
4. Fashion Model
5. Psychiatrist
6. Dr. of Osteopathy
7. Photojournalist
   Actor
8. Wholesale Sales Rep.
   Auto Salesperson
9. Basketball Player
10. Attorney

Source: Jobs Rated Almanac.

JOBS — COMPETITION
Most Competitive

The following jobs have been judged to be the most competitive — in terms of entry into the field, advancement in the field, and facing win/lose situation on the job — by the editors of the *Jobs Rated Almanac*. Although none of these jobs made the list of the top careers, according to that same source, the glamour, high pay and excitement of acting, professional sports, modeling, and advertising draw many more people to these professions than can be adequately supported. Since no hard figures are available on the degree of competitiveness, occupations are listed alphabetically.

Ten Most Competitive

1. Actor
2. Advertising Account Executive
3. Architect
4. Baseball Player, Major League
5. Basketball Player, NBA
6. Fashion Model
7. Football Player, NFL
8. Jockey
9. Mayor

10. Photojournalist
Source: Jobs Rated Almanac.

JOBS — ENVIRONMENT
Best and Worst Job Environment

Since most of us spend as much or, indeed, more time at our jobs than we do in the bosom of our hearth and home, what it's like on the job has crucial impact on the quality of our lives. Choosing a job means more than just choosing a way to make a buck; it means choosing where and how you want to spend a large chunk of your time. Indeed, in one of the quality-of-life improvements that the computer and other high-tech advances is making in everyday life, a growing number of workers are now being freed of the need to report to the office every day. Through the miracle of the modem, a personal computer anywhere in the world can link up to the office's computer, freeing many a worker to stay at home, saving on commuting time, opening up more flexible work hours, allowing more time with family. Indeed, many "tele-commuters" say they are just more productive at home, away from the interruptions and tensions of the office. Informality is another growing trend in the work place. Taking the lead of the high-tech companies sprouting up in California's Silicon Valley, many companies are freeing employees from strict dress codes, creating a campus-like work environment, offering flexible schedules of their own, and offering recreational facilities. The idea is to enhance performance by loosening the reigns of conformity.

The *Jobs Rated Almanac* has ranked jobs according to their work environment, taking into account physical factors such as indoors vs. outdoors, physical demands on the job (crawling, stooping, etc.), work conditions (toxic fumes, noise, and other bothersome or dangerous facets of work), stamina and confinement; as well as emotional factors including competitiveness, life-threatening situations and public contact. Now, not all

THINGS

bookkeepers work in the same environment — one may work in a gas station while the other enjoys plush offices. But, in general, the likelihood of enjoying a pleasant work environment is largely occupation-specific. And to the extent to which it is so, these are the jobs with the best and worst working environments, measured by their overall environment score.

Ten Best	Score
1. Mathematician	1.12
2. Actuary	2.24
Statistician	2.24
3. Computer Systems Analyst	2.27
Historian	2.27
4. Hospital Administrator	2.33
5. Medical Records Technician	3.10
6. Meteorologist	3.37
7. Astrologer	4.00
8. Typist/Word Processor	4.02
9. Bookkeeper	4.09
10. Computer Programmer	4.42
Industrial Designer	4.42

Ten Worst	Score
1. Firefighter	80.04
2. Race Car Driver	63.05
3. NFL Football Player	60.04
4. Astronaut	54.58
5. Jockey	50.88
6. Police Officer	46.95
7. Lumberjack	45.44
8. Surgeon	44.96
9. State Police Officer	43.33
10. Roustabout	43.28

Source: Jobs Rated Almanac.

JOBS — GROWTH
Best and Worst

Planning a career? Here are some sure bets and some caveats. According to estimates compiled by the U.S. Bureau of Labor Statistics, many jobs in the service sector, especially medical services will open up during the 90s. Computer positions, of course, will increase, as will financial service jobs. Even travel agents and jailers will get in on the boom. While not making the top of the list, such career groups as physicians, social workers, financial managers, cooks, lawyers, nurses and teachers all also expected to show healthy gains in employment. On the other hand, you'd better stay away from electronic assembly, unskilled factory work, farming and stenography. The figures below are U.S. Bureau of Labor Statistics numbers for the fastest growing and fastest declining jobs, measured by anticipated percentage of growth in the number of positions in each field in the 1990s.

Fastest Growing	Percent Increase
1. Medical Assistants	+70%
2. Home Health Aides	+68%
3. Radiologic Technologists	+66%
4. Medical Secretaries	+58%
5. Financial Services Salespeople.	+55%
6. Travel Agents	+54%
7. Computer Systems Analysts	+52%
8. Computer Programmers	+48%
9. Human Services Workers	+45%
10. Correction Officers and Jailers	+41%

Fastest Declining	Percent Decrease
1. Precision Elec./Elec. Assemblers	-44%
2. Farmers	-23%
Stenographers	-23%
4. Telephone/ Cable TV installers	-21%
5. Sewing machine operators	-14%
Mixing Machine operators	-14%
7. Textile machine operators	-13%
Machine feeders and offbearers	-13%
9. Hand Packers and Packagers	-12%

Source: U.S. Bureau of Labor Statistics.

JOBS — MEDIA
Best Jobs in Media

The media — television, radio, publishing — gets more than its share of knocks in our society. Whenever someone's fortunes — a politician, an athlete, an actor or actress — take a dip, who do they blame first? The media. Yet this self-same entity is the one in which our heroes are created, our fantasies are fulfilled, and our great ideas are disseminated. Perhaps nowhere else and at no other time was this polarity of opinion about the media so egregious as in the Reagan era. The radical right at the same time vilified the press for its supposed left-wing leanings while at the same time heralding the accomplishments of the "Great Communicator," who so masterfully manipulated the print and broadcast media to sway the American public towards the desired ends. The media: we love it, we hate it, but we can't live without it. Here are the best careers in this beleaguered but bedazzling field, measured by overall rankings in the *Jobs Rated Almanac* compilation of 250 careers.

Job	Overall Score
1. Print Editor	17
2. Broadcast Newswriter	22
3. Broadcast Technician	33
4. Advertising Account Executive	75
5. Newscaster	95
6. Disk Jockey	110
7. Commercial Artist	115
8. Reporter	126
9. Book Author	137
10. Photographer	141

Source: Jobs Rated Almanac.

JOBS — MURDER
Most Homicides on the Job

Ever wonder why cabbies seem so worked up all the time? Perhaps it's because they face the greatest danger of being murdered on the job of any worker in the employment force, according to a study by the National Institute for Occupational Health and Safety. As with most other occupations high on the murder list, taxi-driver murders usually occur in the midst of an armed robbery. The reason cabbies are so prone? An isolated, mobile crime spot, a solitary captive victim normally looking the other way, easy access to cash, and 24-hour availability. The latter also plays a big role in the making convenience store clerks the second most numerous homicide victims on the job. In-

deed, of the 310 men on death row in Florida, fully ten percent are there for a convenience store homicide. Some cities, such as Gainesville, Florida, now require convenience stores to keep at least two employees on the job during night-time hours, to discourage potential robberies. Legislators and convenience store employees are also calling for bullet-proof glass and even for armed guards on duty.

Jobs	Homicides /100,000 workers
1. Taxi Driver	3.45
2. Convenience Store Clerk	2.22
3. Trucker	1.62
4. Gas Station Attendant	1.30
5. Retail Sales Clerk	0.89
6. Restaurant/Bar Worker	0.72

Source: National Institute for Occupational Health and Safety.

JOBS — OFFICES
Cushiest Offices

The office can be a prison for some, but a palace for others. Highly compensated lawyers enjoy the best overall office environments — indeed, the greatest sign of success for a lawyer in many a firm is the coveted corner office. Senior partners at big law firms lounge in spacious surroundings with superb views, serviced by fully stocked bars, cable television hook-ups, and even showers for those late-night legal sessions. Your noble representatives in Congress also enjoy some office amenities to make up for the slave wages they bicker about so frequently. In general, the higher one goes on the corporate-governmental ladder, the more comfortable one becomes.

Top Ten Cushiest Offices

1. Attorney
2. Senator/Congressman
3. Bank Officer
4. Advertising Account Executive
5. Public Relations Specialist
6. Insurance Agent
7. Stockbroker

THINGS

8. Architect
9. Engineer
10. Reporter
Source: Jobs Rated Almanac.

JOBS—OUTLOOK
Best and Worst Outlooks for Those with a College Education

A lot of people scrimp and save to go to college. Anyone who may be in doubt about whether it is worth the struggle would be wise to review the list that follows. The top 25 jobs for college men and women have some for the best outlooks among *all* jobs. In fact, the lowest scores among those with the 25 outlooks for the college educated all come from the top third of the 250 jobs ranked in the *Jobs Rated Almanac* job-outlook ratings. Even jobs that made the "worst" list don't have such bad futures. Except for the unlucky historian, most of the worst score are within the top half of the outlook scale.

Ten Best

1. Commissioned Officer
2. Hospital Administrator
3. Actuary
4. Civil Engineer
5. Physicist
6. Print Editor
7. Motion Picture Editor
8. Physician's Assistant
9. Stockbroker
10. Registered Nurse

Ten Worst

1. Historian
2. Public Relations Specialist
3. Personnel Recruiter
4. Market Research Analyst
5. Economist
6. Teacher
7. Parole Officer
8. Dietitian
9. Archaeologist
10. Social Worker

Source: Jobs Rated Almanac.

JOBS—OUTLOOK
Best and Worst Outlook for Jobs Requiring No Education

In many occupations requiring no formal education, professional advancement depends to a large extent on a person's job performance, the building up of a clientele, and a reputation for quality service. Most of the top ten jobs in this category are oriented toward sales, personal service, art or sports fields, in which performance and reputation are key. The losers in job outlook for non-degreed workers are predominantly construction jobs, which are traditionally unstable, because construction is seasonal and hiring levels are closely tied to fluctuations in the economy. Framing and fishing are also highly unstable fields. Computerization will cloud the job outlook for cashiers. Rankings are based on outlook scores from the *Jobs Rated Almanac*.

Ten Best

1. Auto Salesperson
2. Carpet/Tile Installer
3. Shoe Repairer
4. Sports Instructor
5. Barber
6. Fine Artist
7. Photographer
8. Vending Machine Repairer
9. Jockey
10. Cosmetologist

Ten Worst

1. Migrant Farmworker
2. Construction Worker
3. Forklift Operator
4. Plumber
5. Roofer
6. Truck Driver
7. Bricklayer
8. Cashier
9. Butcher
10. Fisherman

THINGS

Source: Jobs Rated Almanac.

JOBS — PAY
Highest Paying

Although most would admit that making a living is the primary reason why they work, for a large portion of people, income is, in fact, *not* the single deciding factor in choosing *this* career over *that* one, or even this employer over any other. Much more goes into a career or job decision than simply concerns about pay — location is a factor, as is job satisfaction, opportunity for advancement, even glamour. Success for some may be owning a BMW, a sailboat or a vacation home, but for others it may be the reward of passing on cherished ideals through teaching, or it may be the abstract rewards of public service, or again the intellectual challenge of an academic career at the expense of a more lucrative private-sector position. But no one will ever scoff at a big paycheck. The key is to find the right match between one's inner desires and motivations and the purely material need to put bread on the table. The following are the highest paying jobs with employment of more than 50,000 people nationwide, measured by workers' median weekly salary. Lawyers, the list shows, earn the most money of any occupation as a group. Indeed, starting salaries for lawyers fresh out of law school now reach up into the $80,000-dollar range in New York City. If you can see yourself getting by in a pin-striped suit in some big Wall Street law firm, more power to ya. On the other hand, in a country in which day care is one of the primary concerns of the working household, it is reprehensible that child-care workers are some of the lowest-paid people on the totem pole. Until a fair, efficient and safe day-care policy can be worked out, either by businesses or by government, working parents and their children, and ultimately the country itself, will continue to suffer.

Top Ten	Weekly Salary
1. Lawyers	$990
2. Airline Pilots/Navigators	$807
Chemical Engineers	$807
3. Electrical and Electronics Eng.	$803
4. Aerospace Engineers	$801
5. Physicians	$792
6. Mechanical Engineers	$766
7. Marketing, Adv. & PR Managers	$753
8. Pharmacists	$748
9. Civil Engineers	$735
10. Educational Administrators	$712

Bottom Ten	Weekly Salary
1. Private Child Care Workers	$127
2. Food Counter Worker	$167
3. Child Care Worker, Non-Private	$183
4. Private Cleaners and Servants	$185
5. Kitchen Workers	$191
6. Food Preparation Workers	$195
7. Waiter's Assistants	$199
8. Cashiers	$202
9. Waiters and Waitresses	$203
10. Textile Sewing Machine Op.	$205

Source: Occupational Outlook Quarterly, Fall 1990.

JOBS — PAY
Best Paying With Less Than 4 Years of College

Who says you've got to go to college to make it in this world? There are a number of good positions for those with less than four years of college that still offer substantial potential for income (here we are talking about fields that employ a large number of workers, not limited professions such as movie star, professional actor or news anchor, that are high-paying but may not require a college degree). Unionization certainly helps when it comes to blue-collar salaries, and some of the highest-paying field where a college degree is not essential are supervisory positions in heavily unionized fields such as transportation and manufacturing. Other blue-collar jobs that command high pay are those that also require specialized training or expertise, such as telephone repair and tool-and-die making. So just because you

THINGS

don't have a degree, don't fret. There are still a number of good opportunities available. These are the top paying careers in which more than 50,000 workers are employed, measured by the percent of workers earning more than $600 per week.

Job	% Earning $600+ per week
1. Rail Transportation Occupations	58
2. Police and Firefighting Supervisors	55
3. Computer Syst. Analysts /Scientists	52
4. Tool and Die Makers	51
5. Telephone Installers and Repairers	47
6. Mechanics and Repair Sup.	46
7. Data Processing Equip. Repairers	44
8. Computer Programmers	38
Electrical Equip. Repairers	38
9. Plant and Systems Operators	37
10. Firefighters	36
Production Supervisors	36
Construction Supervisors	36

Source: Occupational Outlook Quarterly, Fall 1990.

JOBS—PAY
Best-Paying Professional Careers

The top seven professional occupations ranked by income are all in the field of health care. this reflects a willingness in the market to compensate health care professionals for the pressures they are saddled with and the responsibilities that we entrust to them, namely, our well-being. However, registered nurses are near the the bottom on the pay scale for professionals—earning a mere $26,073 annually—helping to explain the serious shortage of qualified nurses that plagues the health care industry. The sacrifices in time and money for proper training and licensing, not to mention the long hours once that license is earned, do not pay off for registered nursed the way they do for most other health care professionals. Surprisingly, lawyers rank only in the middle of the pack in professional income, although the law is considered a very lucrative field.

Top Ten	Avg. Salary
1. Surgeon	$164,724
2. Psychiatrist	$93,916
3. Dr. of Osteopathy	$87,200
4. Chiropractor	$72,267
5. Dentist	$65,400
Orthodontist	$65,400
6. Veterinarian	$50,140
7. Aerospace Engineer	$44,680
Civil Engineer	$44,680
8. Attorney	$43,474
9. Industrial Engineer	$43,450
Mechanical Engineer	$43,450
Electrical Engineer	$43,450
10. Psychologist	$43,382

Source: Jobs Rated Almanac.

JOBS—PAY
Best-Paying Outdoor Jobs

When people consider outdoor occupations, what usually comes to mind a a worker toiling under the hot sun on a construction or road crew, and getting little financial reward. Well, it ain't necessarily so. Few may think of professional baseball players, who enjoy some of the most glamorous and highest paying of all jobs, while scampering about on the field of dreams under the summer afternoon sun or on lazy mid-summer evenings. for those with more earthbound talents, lucrative outdoor occupations include professional and research positions in such areas as geology, oceanography and surveying. Those who love the outdoors or are looking to escape an oppressive office environment need not resign themselves to low pay or overly strenuous work.

Top Ten	Avg. Ann. Income
1. Major League Baseball Player	$424,896
2. NFL Football Player	$209,090
3. Major League Umpire	$52,560
4. Geologist	$41,420
5. Oceanographer	$38,695
Zoologist	$38,695
6. Line Installer	$31,174
7. Surveyor	$30,210

8. Electrician	$29,474
9. Conservationist	$28,196
10. Jockey	$27,490

Source: Jobs Rated Almanac.

JOBS—PERKS
Gold-Plated Washroom Keys: Jobs With the Most Added Incentives

Perks are those extra privileges that employers offer to their workers to supplement income. Some workers' perks add up to little more than a free cup of coffee in the morning, a chance to browse through the company's subscription to various magazines, and a few stolen pencils or paper clips. In most cases, though, employers have realized that offering perks is a convenient method of attracting desirable new employees and the lest expensive way of meeting employee demands for additional income. Perks such as use of company cars, membership in frequent flyer VIP clubs, even the cherished key to the executive washroom, add, if not to the wallet, at least to the employee's sense of belonging, easing the stressful work day. The editors of the *Jobs Rated Almanac* measured jobs by their share of the seven most common work perquisites — expense account allowances, housing and meal subsidies, use of company cars and planes, access to private secretaries and assistants, use of private offices, employee-sponsored membership in social or athletic clubs, and business-related travel opportunities. The rankings show a correlation between job stress and perks offered — half of the top ten jobs for office goodies also landed in the top 50 most stressful occupations. Seems that perks may make these stressful jobs just that much more bearable.

Top Ten	Perk Score
1. Attorney	72.0
2. Hotel Manager	67.5
3. Clergyman	63.7
4. Basketball Coach	63.3

5. Senator/Congressman	63.0
6. Engineer	62.6
7. Bank Officer	53.5
8. Stockbroker	51.3
9. Photojournalist	48.7
10. Astronaut	46.7

Source: Jobs Rated Almanac.

JOBS—PHYSICAL DEMANDS
Most and Least Physically Demanding

Some jobs allow you to coast; others make you sweat. Every job requires some sort of transference of energy—either physical or mental—toward a desired end. This rating measures jobs in the first category. But physical demands are not simply those requiring great strength. Child care workers must have stamina to make it through a day of screaming, running kids; other jobs, such as mail delivery or surveying, although not in themselves demanding of physical strength, tax the body through exposure to weather; even sedentary jobs like violinist or piano player requires strength and suppleness of hand. So the rating of the most and least physically demanding job presented here and derived from the *Jobs Rated Almanac*, takes into account a variety of factors to measure the physical energy a job entails — the hazards faced on the job, the need for stamina, and the weather and environmental conditions faced, in addition to the amount of lifting, pulling, pushing, standing, walking, stooping, kneeling, crawling, climbing, walking, running and crouching a worker performs on the job. The most physically demanding job according to this system is that of the firefighter, who faces life-threatening hazards in extremely uncomfortable conditions while performing numerous physically strenuous tasks. Many firefighter are also on call at all hours of the day or night, further taxing the body's systems. The least demanding job is that of astrologer. Little physical energy is required in order to plot the position of the planets and evaluate what they portend.

Ten Most Demanding	Score
1. Firefighter	50.55
2. Farmer	43.45
3. Roustabout	38.34
4. Lumberjack	37.68
5. Ironworker	37.63
6. NFL Football Player	36.03
Cowboy	36.03
7. Migrant Farmworker	35.03
8. Dairy Farmer	34.23
9. Garbage Collector	34.21
10. Sheet Metal Worker	33.84

Ten Least Demanding	
1. Astrologer	3.00
2. Broadcast Newswriter	3.32
Newscaster	3.32
3. Statistician	3.36
Hotel Manager	3.36
Actuary	3.36
Mathematician	3.36
4. Economist	3.41
Market Research Analyst	3.41
5. Accountant	3.46
6. Advertisting Account Executive	3.61
7. Bank Officer	3.66
8. Federal Judge	3.78
9. social Woker	4.23
10. Senator/Congressman	4.37

Source: Jobs Rated Almanac.

JOBS – PHYSICAL DEMANDS

Most Physically Demanding Jobs Requiring a College Education

Many college graduates expect cushy office jobs upon graduation, and understandably, since the majority of the least physically demanding jobs are professional or academic positions, many of which involve heavy work with pure or applied mathematics and statistics (though, interestingly, computer-related occupations are not in the top ten – so much for the so-called "computer nerd"). Other college graduates, however, prefer the rugged outdoors as their offices. Research and hands-on positions in the life and earth sciences, which entail a good deal of field work, make up half of the ten most physically demanding jobs for which a college degree is required. Health care and engineering positions round out the top ten. Rankings are based on physical-demands scores in the *Jobs Rated Almanac*.

Most Demanding	Score
1. Conservationist	16.84
2. Zoologist	15.29
3. Agricultural Scientist	14.60
4. Physical Therapist	13.69
5. Geologist	13.47
6. Electrical Engineer	11.39
7. Oceanographer	11.23
8. Registered Nurse	11.21
9. Optometrist	11.01
10. Mechanical Engineer	10.44

Source: Jobs Rated Almanac.

JOBS – PUBLIC SERVICE

Best Public Service Jobs

Feel the call of public service? Want to work for your fellow man? Check out the list below. Derived from the *Jobs Rated Almanac* ranking of 250 jobs in terms of overall quality, these are the best jobs that minister to the needs of the populace. Surprisingly few of the top-rated public service jobs in the list are standard governmental positions, and even those – federal judge, parole officer, tax examiner – require specialized knowledge, training, certification or expertise. The common public sector jobs most sought-after – mail carrier, clerk, secretary – although replete with good benefits and retirement packages, offer little in the way of income advancement or perks and are highly competitive; even the job security so cherished by public-sector employees is threatened as governmental agencies from the federal level on down to the smallest municipality face severe budget limitations in the coming years. Some of the best public-service jobs, strangely, are those in the military and the clergy—strange bed-fellows, indeed.

Job	Overall Score
1. Urban/Regional Planner	27
2. Federal Judge	42
3. Postal Inspector	55
4. Parole Officer	57
5. Tax Examiner/Collector	61
6. Commissioned Officer	71
7. Protestant Minister	72
8. Warrant Officer	78
9. Rabbi	87
10. Social Worker	90

Source: Jobs Rated Almanac.

JOBS—QUOTAS AND DEADLINES
Crack that Whip: Most Quotas and Deadlines on the Job

Quotas and deadlines are inescapable facets of the working life. Each occupation has its own set of performance requirements and time constraints. Even the philosopher must put aside his dialogues and meditations long enough to teach a few classes and publish the occasional academic paper. Fortunately, most people enjoy a moderate degree of structure in their work lives. Quotas and deadlines proves them with direction and motivation. In some occupations, however, time and performance pressures may become so intense that they provoke stress and anxiety. The following are the occupations judged by the editors of the *Jobs Rated Almanac* to suffer the strictest and most numerous quotas and deadlines on the job. Absent from the list, interestingly, are print and broadcast media occupations, for while deadline pressure can be intense in these fields, they are nothing compared to as-sembly-line work.

Ten Worst

1. Automotive Assembler
2. Bookbinder
3. Stockbroker
4. Machinist
5. Migrant Farmworker
6. Precision Assembler
7. Stevedore
8. Fisherman
9. Photographic Process Worker
10. Dressmaker

Source: Jobs Rated Almanac.

JOBS—SAFETY
Most Dangerous Occupation

Work, for most in history, has been an extremely hazardous way to pass the days. Democracy, enlightenment and technology have lowered the risk to today's workers rather considerably, but carelessness and uncontrollable mishaps still take their considerable tolls each working day. The rating below of the most dangerous industrial undertakings is compiled by taking the sum of the number of injuries per thousand workers and the number of lost work days per 100 workers. Water transportation is, according to this system, the most hazardous field of work, followed by mining, trucking and various manufacturing fields. No white-collar jobs were in the top ten.

Industry	Injuries + Lost Days
1. Water Transport	381
2. Coal Mining	361
3. Trucking/Warehousing	338
4. Primary Metal Mfg.	333
5. Lumber and Wood Mfg.	311
6. Fabricated Metal	311
7. Food Processing	305
8. Stone/Clay/Glass Mfg.	290
9. Special Trade Construction	288
10. Heavy Construction	282

Source: U.S. Bureau of Labor Statistics

JOBS—SAFETY
Most Common Causes of Deaths on the Job

For those stuck in a hum-drum office job, the 9-to-5 regimen may be a deadly bore. But

THINGS

for many, work is just plain deadly. These are the most common causes of deaths on the job, ranked by the percentage of all worker deaths attributed to each cause. As the list indicates, automobile accidents account for the highest percentage of deaths among the work force—more than one-quarter of all employee fatalities are auto-related. The second-leading on-the-job killer is heart attacks, dropping from its top ranking in overall causes of death. Those who work outdoors, with heavy machinery and with dangerous equipment are at a much greater risk of dying on the job than the average office drone.

Cause	% of All Worker Deaths
1. Highway Vehicles	27%
2. Heart Attacks	11%
3. Industrial Vehicles or Equipment	11%
Falls	11%
4. Electrocutions	10%
5. Assaults	4%
Struck by Objects	4%
Caught Under or Between Objects	4%
Explosions	4%
6. Aircraft Crashes	3%
Gas Inhalation	3%
7. Plant Machinery Operations	2%
8. Fires	1%

Source: U.S. Dept. of Labor.

JOBS—SECURITY
Most and Least Secure

In uncertain economic times (and what times aren't, these days), job security takes on added importance. A steady paycheck, freedom from the fear of unemployment, firing, or work-related illness or injury, and the knowledge that other jobs are available in one's occupation, even if that requires relocation, all help in creating peace of mind. What, exactly, is job security? For some, it's the freedom to choose your job location. For others, it's the ability to stand up to a pushy or obnoxious boss, knowing you're indispensable to the company. For all, security means financial stability and

emotional tranquillity. But security in some regard often requires sacrifice in another. The *Jobs Rated Almanac* measured jobs on a variety of factors, including outlook, unionization and job classification, which can strengthen security, and threats to life and other physical hazards, competitiveness and high unemployment rates, which hamper security. On this system, even zero unemployment is no guarantee of security—the military, for instance, is all-volunteer, and one can only be dismissed on discipli-nary grounds; but soldiers face life-threatening situations, and thus military jobs do not top the list. But even negative job growth does not necessarily hamper job security—although philosophers, anthropologists and other academics may see a decline in the overall number of jobs in their fields in the coming years, tenured college professors enjoy relative immunity from layoffs and dismissals. So once you're in, you're in for life. The following are the most and least secure jobs in the work force.

Most Secure	Score
1. Hospital Administrator	197.30
2. Civil Engineer	192.90
3. Industrial Engineer	183.50
4. Bank Officer	182.15
5. Technical/Copy Writer	181.00
6. Geologist	179.90
7. Statistician	179.80
8. Paralegal	179.25
9. Broadcast Technician	178.75
10. Biologist	178.20

Least Secure	Score
1. Migrant Farmworker	15.35
2. Roofer	28.70
3. Construction Laborer	32.55
4. Drywall Applicator/Finisher	46.30
5. Const. Machinery Operator	47.60
6. NFL Football Player	48.00
7. Bricklayer	49.80
8. Insulation Worker	50.80
9. Forklift Operator	53.80
10. Carpenter	58.85

THINGS

Source: Jobs Rated Almanac.

JOBS — STRESS

Most and Least Stressful Occupations

"Job-related stress" became a buzz-word in the 1980s. Declining economic fortunes abroad and hard times at home have increased the pressures on the American worker to produce more in less time. The pace of economic life has quickened, work tools have become more complicated and harder to use, competition more threatening to security, financial deals bigger. All of this threatens the psychological well-being of the worker. Yet, despite the fact that the increased pace of the office takes its toll on office workers, very few of them face the possibility of death because of their performance. No more stressful situation can arise of the job than the responsibility for the safety of oneself or others. This, then, is the most telling criterion in judging a job's stressfulness. The following ratings of job stress are from the *Jobs Rated Almanac*, which assigned overall scores to 250 jobs based on 22 weighted factors involved in contributing to job stress. Factors most heavily weighted included lives being at risk, physical demands, competitiveness, deadlines, environmental conditions, and public scrutiny or contact. Firefighters and most others in the top ten scored near the top for each of the most heavily weighted categories — those involving physical, as opposed to psychological, well-being. So the next time you feel stressed out staring at a computer screen all day, just be thankful you're not leaping out of the window of a flaming building with a baby in your hands.

Ten Most Stressful	Score
1. Firefighter	115.15
2. Indy Race Car Driver	110.61
3. Astronaut	103.71
4. Surgeon	103.55
5. NFL Football Player	101.53
6. Police Officer	99.91
7. Dr. of Osteopathy	94.01
8. State Police Officer	92.69
9. Air Traffic Controller	88.68
10. Mayor	84.21

Ten Least Stressful	Score
1. Musical Instrument Repairer	4.69
2. Industrial Machine Repairer	10.56
3. Medical Records Technician	14.45
4. Pharmacist	14.79
5. Medical Assistant	16.81
6. Typist/Word Processor	20.08
7. Librarian	20.33
8. Janitor	20.40
9. Bookkeeper	20.44
10. Forklift Operator	20.45

Source: Jobs Rated Almanac.

JOBS — STRESS

Low Stress, High Pay

Is your job relaxing and cushy, or do you feel you're underpaid for the pressure you endure at work? To some people, the the pleasure and satisfaction they receive from work transcends such factors as stress and income. Book authors and newscasters might actually thrive on the pressure of their jobs, or may hope for the fame and fortune that comes to a lucky few in these fields. On the other hand, if you like money but hate stress, the list below gives the highest paying occupations with little pressure, and the careers to avoid for all but the most dedicated, those for whom neither high stress or low income are important. Farmers and fishermen, for instance, might prefer the traditional family business to other, more lucrative and less stressful livelihoods. Winners in this category tend to be academic research occupations, in which holders of advanced degrees dominate the work force, or jobs which involve tasks few have the precise technical know-how to perform. Ratings are derived from figures in the *Jobs Rated Almanac*.

THINGS

Best

1. Actuary
2. Piano Tuner
3. Petroleum Engineer
4. Lithographer/Photoengraver
5. Historian
6. Chemist
7. Physiologist
8. Biologist

Worst

1. Fisherman
2. Book Author
3. Cowboy
4. Taxi Driver
5. Seaman
6. Dairy Farmer
7. Newscaster

Source: Jobs Rated Almanac.

JOBS — TRAVEL
See the World: Occupations With the Most Free Travel Opportunities

Most of us cherish the occasional chance to take off on a trip, even if only on business. But ask the true frequent business flyer what he thinks of his twice-weekly jaunts to Milwaukee, Huntsville or Topeka, and one gets a truer perspective on the supposed glamour of business travel—stomach-churning taxi rides through rush-hour traffic to make a flight, only to face long delays at unfamiliar airports, waking up in a strange bed every other morning, eating unfamiliar food, seeing little of one's family until the weekend, only to have the cycle repeat itself on Monday morning. Yes, America's business is more and more done on the fly these days, but for the frequent flyer, the lure of travel wears thin after a while. On the other hand, some jobs are implicitly flight-oriented—i.e. flight attendant and pilot—so if you don't like the jet-set life, better consider another field. These are the careers with the most travel opportunities annually.

Top Ten	Trips per Year
1. Flight Attendant	240
2. Pilot	192
3. Senator/Congressman	100
4. Baseball Player	80
5. Wholesale Sales Representative	60
6. Nuclear Plant Decon. Technician	50
7. NBA Basketball Player	41
8. Astronaut	34
9. Baseball Umpire	30
10. NCAA Basketball Coach	25

Source: Jobs Rated Almanac.

JOBS — TRAVEL
Going in Style: The Well-Heeled Travelers

Businesses are beginning to cut back on the travel extravagances they previously allowed their employees. Most businesses are looking very closely at the bottom line to see if those first-class seats and stays in luxury hotels are really necessary. Expect business travel to be sharply down-graded in the coming years. Gone will be the four-star hotels and restaurants, the Cadillac limousines, the nightly entertainment expenses. In the mean time, some still travel in style. The following ranking lists the members of the work force who travel in style—in terms of the best meals, accommodations, airline class, expense accounts, and automotive travel. These are the travel dinosaurs of the business world, who will be slimming down as American business becomes leaner and meaner in the 1990s.

Job	Travel Score
1. Bank Officer	69.5
2. Stockbroker	56.0
3. Attorney	51.0
4. NBA Basketball Player	50.0
5. Clergyman	42.0
6. NFL Football Player	40.0
7. Photojournalist	39.0
8. Travel Agent	38.2
9. Hotel Manager	37.5
10. Insurance Agent	36.0

THINGS

Source: Jobs Rated Almanac.

JOBS — TURNOVER
Occupations with the
Most Turnover

Turnover in occupations is most prevalent at the lower levels of the job ladder. Service-oriented positions such as child-care worker, cashier, bartender and waiter offer quick-cash opportunities for young workers, college students, people in-between jobs, and itinerants. The positions are relatively low-paying, but require little in the way of experience or training. Few aspire to these occupations as career goals, except perhaps waiters and bartenders in the more prestigious restaurants. High turnover, however, does mean that a sort of private-sector safety net is available for those who find themselves temporarily put out of higher-level work. Whether that safety net will grow or shrink in the coming years is hard to say.

Job	Turnover Score
1. Construction Worker	37.4
2. Child-Care Worker	35.9
3. Waiter/Waitress	32.5
4. Bartender	32.2
5. Cashier	30.4
6. Retail Salesperson	28.9
7. Receptionist	28.5
8. Roofer	25.6
9. Maid	23.3
Janitor	23.3
10. Typist/Word Processor	23.2

Source: Jobs Rated Almanac.

JOBS — WORK WEEK
Occupations with the Longest and
Shortest Work Weeks

People used to talk about "banker's hours" in reference to those who had short work weeks. But perhaps the phrase should be recast as "baseball players' hours." According to research performed by the editors of the *Jobs-Rated Almanac*, baseball players and umpires, as well as basketball players, enjoy the shortest work weeks of any workers in their survey of 250 jobs, clocking in just 30 hours a week. Bank officers, on the other hand, worked an average of 48.8 hours, and bank tellers 40.2 hours. Firefighters log the most hours on the job, a with a lengthy week of 56.2 hours.

Longest	Work Week (hrs.)
1. Firefighter	56.2
2. Dr. of Osteopathic Medicine	54.5
Psychiatrist	54.5
Physician's Assistant	54.5
Surgeon	54.5
3. Farmer	52.7
Dairy Farmer	52.7
4. Protestant Minister	52.2
Rabbi	52.2
Catholic Priest	52.2
5. Zoologist	51.0
6. Undertaker	50.8
7. Federal Judge	50.5
Attorney	50.5
8. Roustabout	49.5
9. Tool-and-Die Maker	49.4
10. Pharmacist	49.3

Shortest	Work Week (hrs.)
1. Baseball Player	30.0
Baseball Umpire	30.0
Basketball Player	30.0
2. Waiter/Waitress	36.2
Dishwasher	36.2
3. Cashier	37.2
4. Maid	37.9
Child-Care Worker	37.9
Bartender	37.9
5. Receptionist	39.1
Ticket/Travel Agent	39.1
6. Cook	39.2
7. Medical Assistant	39.6
Dental Hygienist	39.6
8. Nurse's Aid	39.7
9. House Painter	39.8
Retail Salesperson	39.8
10. Telephone Operator	40.0
Military Personnel	40.0
Astrologer	40.0

THINGS

Practical Nurse   40.0
Source: Jobs Rated Almanac.

JUICES
Most Popular Juice Brands

The second coming of the health craze has done wonders for sales of juice. After decades of naive trust in dentally detrimental tonics like Coca Cola and Kool Aid, Americans are turning back to simpler, healthier alternatives. Topping the list of juice giants are those venerable purveyors of the orange elixir, Tropicana and Minute Maid. Get juiced, America! It's good for you!

Juice	1990 Sales ($ millions)
1. Tropicana	$1,113
2. Minute Maid	$1,024
3. Ocean Spray	$730
4. Hi-C	$335
5. Dole	$300
6. Welch's	$291
7. Citrus Hill	$270
8. Five Alive	$190
9. Veryfine	$187
10. Hawaiian Punch	$180

Source: Superbrands 1990.

JURY AWARDS
Biggest, 1990

There is a movement under way in this country, headed up in large part by large corporations and insurance companies, called Tort Reform. The movement is meant to limit the amount of damages a defendant is liable for and the discretion of juries in setting that amount in a civil or personal injury lawsuit. According to Lawyers Alert, a magazine of the legal profession, there were more than 600 jury awards over $1,000,000 in 1990. Who pays? Those same corporations and insurance companies, mainly. The movement has made strides in the past several years, influencing some state legislatures to pass laws capping monetary awards, but the following list of the top ten jury awards in civil or P.I. suits, compiled by Lawyers Alert, shows that the tort reform movement is failing. Has the court system become nothing more than another lotto game, where any injury offers the chance at mega-bucks, or are these awards merely the jury's way of righting a wrong inflicted upon an innocent victim by an faceless, uncaring and unrepentent corporate society? Unless one wants to argue for the elimination of the jury system in such cases, it seems the monetary awards in personal injury and other civil cases will only continue to rise.

Case/Description	Award
1. Asthma Drug	**$77 Million**

Awarded to the family of a three-month old boy whom doctors in Chicago overdosed with the drug theophylline, then with its antidote, eventually causing brain damamge.

2. Insurance Fraud	**$55 Million**

Agents of an insurance company defrauded a widow out of her husband's death benefit.

3. Police Brutality	**$51 Million**

Five New York City cops ambushed, beat and jailed a white civil rights worker on false charges in what the judge called "a horror story that one cannot imagine having taken place in the United States" (he hadn't yet seen the Los Angeles beating videotape).

4. Drunk Driving	**$50 Million**

A beneficiary of a multi-million dollar trust fund with a record of police trouble broadsides a teenager's car with his pick-up truck while drunk, killing the teen.

5. Auto Accident	**$45 Million**

A woman left in a brain-injured comatose state by a truck which swerved into her lane won this settlement in absentia.

6. Swimming Pool Injury	**$44 Million**

A seven-year-old boy suffers brain damage when he falls into his neighbor's pool; the babysitter, a friend's mother, is held responsible.

7. Food Preservative $43 Million
A chemical company is held liable in the deaths of two shrimp fishermen who die after breathing fumes from a chemical that preserves the color of their catch; the chemical company had not put adequate warnings on the product.

8. Nursing Home $39 Million
A nursing home is held responsible when an 84-year-old patient strangles herself while trying to get out of her bed restraints; the family had never consented to the restraint.

9. Benzene $34 Million
A benzene supplier is forced to pay $34 million after a Coast Guard instructor dies from leukemia contracted from repeated exposure to benzene; once again, the company had not properly warned of the danger of its product.

10. Libel $34 Million
A newspaper is charged with libel after assigning a reporter who had been arrested for wiretapping to a story about his own prosecutor. The reporter seeks vengeance in the story; the newspaper faces the largest libel suit ever brought against an American news organization.

Source: Lawyers Alert.

JUVENILE DELINQUENCY
Most Common Acts
In adulthood, we often review our childhoods and middle years through rather darkly tinted glasses. Horseplay, mischief — even petty criminaltiy — are tokens of those liminal times of life. The security and decency of our society depends on the eventual recognition and repentance of these then-minor missteps. These are the most common acts of juvenile delinquency, measured by the percentage of the total

adolescent population that has at one time or another participated in the act.

Act	Percentage Participating
1. Didn't Return Change	18
2. Drank Liquor as Minor	15
3. Stole From Employer	9
3. Carried Hidden Weapon	9
5. Evaded Payment	5
6. Used Checks Illegally	2
6. Fraud	2
6. Paid Someone for Sex	2
9. Stole From Family	1
9. Pressured for Sex	1

Source: National Youth Survey Project.

LAKES
Largest Man-Made Lakes
One of the great technological accomplishments of the industrial age has been the ability to establish and maintain reliable stocks of water in naturally arid regions. The use of man-made resevoirs is at the center of contemporary irrigation doctrine. Additional, though, man has constructed great lakes for more sublime, hedonistic purposes, creating an endless succession of ready-made resort towns and summer photo-opportunities.

Lake	Thousands of Acre-feet
1. Owen Falls, Uganda	166,000
2. Kariba, Zimbabwe	147,218
3. Bratsk, U.S.S.R.	137,220
4. High Aswan, Egypt,	120,000
5. Akosombo, Ghana	115,000
6. Daniel Johnson, Canada	110,256
7. Guri, Venezuela	59,42
8. Krasnoyarsk, U.S.S.R.	57,006
9. Bennett W.A.C., Canada	55,452
10. Zeya, U.S.S.R.	51,075

Source: Department of the Interior

LAKES
Largest Natural Lakes
Amid its other extraordinary geological distinctions, it is often forgotten that North

THINGS

America embodies the world's most magnificent concentration of inland seas. Of the planet's ten principal natural lakes, North America is home to three. Such is our great aquatic heritage.

Lake	Area (sq. miles)
1. Caspian Sea, USSR-Iran	152,239
2. Superior, U.S.-Canada	31,820
3. Victoria, Tanzania-Uganda	26,828
4. Aral, USSR	25,659
5. Huron, U.S-Canada	23,010
6. Michigan, U.S.	22,400
7. Tanganyika, Tanzania-Zaire	12,700
8. Baikal, U.S.S.R.	12,162
9. Great Bear, Canada	12,000
10. Nyasa, Tanzania-Mozambique	11,600

Source: Department of the Interior

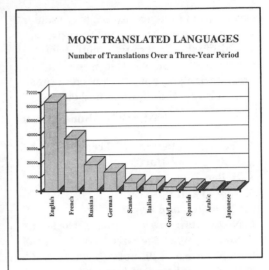

MOST TRANSLATED LANGUAGES
Number of Translations Over a Three-Year Period

LANGUAGES
Most Translated

Judging from the preponderance of translations from English into other language, it seems apparent that the most important written work in the world is being done in English these days. Either that, or we are seriously overlooking the important contributions to science, literature, and scholarship being created around the world. The following is a list of the ten most translated languages in the world, measured by the number of books translated from the source language into at least one other language over a three-year period from 1980 to 1982.

Language	Translations
1. English	63,069
2. French	37,154
3. Russian	18,607
4. German	13,288
5. Scandanavian Langs.	5,590
6. Italian	4,237
7. Greek or Latin	2,566
8. Spanish	2,185
9. Arabic	697
10. Japanese	548

Source: UNESCO.

LAW FIRMS
Fastest Growing Law Firms

Some of us are made slightly nervous by great demonstrations of prosperity by our accountants and barristers. What, we might wonder, is the source of their new-found wealth. Or, even more particularly, whom? When the corporate firms grow, however, we can be conforted by the fact that if they are stealing, they are stealing from big business— a comfort to some.

Firm	% Growth since 1987
1. Keck, Mahin & Cate	113.1
2. Thompson, Hine and Flory	97.7
3. Morrison and Foerster	95.9
4. Womble Carlyle Sandridge & Rice	89.8
5. Graham and James	84.2
6. Hopkins and Sutter	80.7
7. Haynes and Boone	80.4
8. Milbank, Tweed, Hadley, McCloy	72.9
9. Kelley Drye & Warren	70.6
10. Oppenheimer Wolf & Donnelly	66.9

Source: The Lawyer's Almanac

LAW FIRMS
Lawyers With Heart?

Pro bono, legal work provided free of charge to worthy causes, is an inbuilt facet of modern corporate and firm law. Staff lawyers, from first-year associates to senior partners, are expected to put forward a substantial number of hours in public service each year. For many, this is not only a humanitarian act, but also a needed break from their repetitious, pressured chores.

Firm	AMLAW Pro Bono Rating
1. Wilmer, Cutler and Pickering	80
2. Holland and Hart	79
3. Heller, Ehrman, White & McAuliffe	74
4. Arnold and Porter	70
5. Covington and Burling	69
6. Nixon, Hargraves, Devans & Doyle	68
7. Morrison and Foerster	68
8. Debevoise and Plimpton	66
9. Davis, Graham and Stubbs	66
10. Cahill, Gordon and Reindel	53

Source: American Lawyer.

LIBRARIES
Top University Research Libraries, U.S.

This rating is based on an index developed by the Association of Research Libraries to measure the relative size of university libraries. The factors in creating the index include the number of volumes held, number of volumes added during the previous fiscal year, number of current serials, total expenditures, and size of staff. It does not measure a library's services, the quality of its collections, or its success in meeting the needs of users.

Library	No. of Volumes
1. Harvard Univ.	11,781,270
2. Univ. of Calif.-Berkeley	7,366,672
3. UCLA	5,976,588
4. Stanford Univ.	5,753,147
5. Yale Univ.	8,718,619
6. Univ. of Illinois-Champaign	7,561,615
7. Columbia Univ.	5,894,135
8. Univ. of Texas	6,066,136
9. Univ. of Michigan	6,237,521
10. Cornell Univ.	5,144,830

Source: Chronicle of Higher Education, from Association of Research Libraries.

LIQUORS
Best-Selling Liqour Brands

Although many of us cannot stand the straight tastes of the hard liquors which we consume, most often we are quite specific and insistent about the brands which we order. Drinking 'premium' liquors like Stolichnaya or Absolut vodka may do little for our taste buds, but, apparently, it does much for the respect that we are accorded by other, more-bargain conscious drinkers.

Brand	1990 Retail Sales ($ millions)
1. Bacardi	$739
2. Smirnoff	626
3. Jack Daniels	474
4. Seagram's 7	416
5. Absolut	354
6. Jim Beam	334
7. Dewar's	315
8. Seagram's Gin	307
9. Canadian Mist	306
10. Seagram's VO	302

Source: Superbrands 1990.

LITIGATION
Injuries and Insults Most Likely To Result in Million-Dollar Civil Verdicts

Certain injuries elicit more sympathy from judges and juries than others. Death is always a big favorite in the sob story category, followed closely by brain damage, amputation and paraplegia. All this, however, should not be taken to imply that it would work to one's profit to contract these injuries. After all, you could always lose your court case.

Injury	Verdicts Returned from 1962-89
1. Death	968
2. Brain Damage	718
3. Amputation	331
4. Paraplegia	275

5. Quadraplegia	257
6. Emotional Distress	222
7. Leg	201
8. Multiple Injuries	148
9. Burns	144
10. Disc	92

Source: The Lawyer's Almanac

LIVESTOCK
Most Numerous Livestock Animals

Doctors tell us chicken is a heart-healthy food, low in fat and high in protein. The world has taken notice — chickens are the most numerous livestock animals worldwide. The great benefit of chickens is that they are a source for two food products, meat and eggs. Let's hope that livestock don't take the hint from Orwell's *Animal Farm* and get any ideas about taking over — we'd be outnumbered by more than two to one by chickens, sheep, cattle pigs and goats. The following are the most numerous livestock animals in the world; for top countries in each category, see "Countries — Livestock."

Animal	Number, Worldwide
1. Chickens	8,583,000,000
2. Sheep	1,135,512,000
3. Beef Cattle	1,264,621,000
4. Pigs	804,155,000
5. Goats	486,242,000
6. Dairy Cattle	221,185,000
7. Buffaloes	135,687,000
8. Horses	64,754,000
9. Asses	39,857,000
10. Camels	17,317,000

Source: Food and Agriculture Production Yearbook.

MAGAZINES — AD REVENUE
Who Earns the Most Ad Revenue

Occasionally, one is moved to dish out a high denomination greenback for twelve months dalliance with one of the glossier of serial substances. Even at $3 a copy and up, however, odds are that your favorite upscale magazine is a bargain. Subscription fees often counterbalance only a fraction of the actual price of producing a slick fashion rag or design mag. The real bucks? Advertising. Ad revenue is the make-or-break factor for most periodicals. Upscale readership can often offset relatively low readership — magazines targeting specific readership groups are the current trend, and glossies that target the well-to-do merely have to show advertisers the figures for their readers to have them flocking to the ad pages. But, despite continued refinement of the target audiences, the magazines with the highest ad revenue continue to be those with the widest appeal among the population in general — the weekly news magazine *Time*, *Sports Illustrated*, *People* and *TV Guide*.

Publication	1990 Ad Revenues
1. Time	$373,385,017
2. Sports Illustrated	$336,671,529
3. People Weekly	$325,201,199
4. TV Guide	$322,985,623
5. Business Week	$260,575,042
6. Newsweek	$255,918,694
7. Fortune	$187,284,536
8. Forbes	$157,696,940
9. U.S. News	$152,843,252
10. Better Homes & Gardens	$152,433,109

Source: Publishers Information Bureau.

MAGAZINES — CIRCULATION
Top Ten Consumer Magazines by Circulation

The magazine with the widest circulation in the country, *Modern Maturity*, is an organ of the largest association in the country, the American Association of Retired Persons. Armed with this mouthpiece, AARP has in recent years become a strong political lobbying force for the rights of the elderly and against cuts in benefits. Women, the list below shows, are the stronger magazine readers—the fifth through tenth most popular magazines in the country are specifically targeted at women.

Magazine	Circulation
1. Modern Maturity	21,430,990
2. Reader's Digest	16,343,599
3. TV Guide	15,867,750
4. National Geographic	10,890,660
5. Better Homes and Gardens	8,005,311
6. Family Circle	5,461,786
7. Good Housekeeping	5,152,245
8. McCall's	5,088,686
9. Ladies' Home Journal	5,038,297
10. Woman's Day	4,705,288

Source: Advertising Age, Feb. 22, 1990.

MAGAZINES — READERSHIP

Top Periodicals by Readers' Median Household Income

Reading is a highly egalitarian undertaking, but many of our most distinguished periodicals find their ways almost exclusively into privileged, monied hands. High-brow demographics usually mean greater advertising revenue, with advertisers paying to reach a better-heeled clientele, so it is unlikely that these capitalist tools will change their toney tunes anytime soon. Below are the ten magazines with the wealthiest readership, as measured by their readers' median household income. You don't need to make $50,000 a year to read the New York Times Magazine, but, on the other hand, merely reading such a tome won't guarantee a comfortable living.

Periodical	Readers' Income
1. New York Times Magazine	$50,395
2. Inc.	$49,281
3. Wall Street Journal	$48,983
4. Barron's	$48,083
5. Forbes	$46,962
6. The New Yorker	$46,555
7. Financial World	$44,917

Modern Maturity, the most widely circulated periodical in the country.

8. Ski	$44,128
9. Tennis	$43,832
10. Business Week	$43,083

Source: Simmons Market Research Bureau.

MALLS

Largest Shopping Malls in the U.S.

The American mall is a world unto itself, with its own restaurants, its own banks, its own police force, its own class structure and its own rebellious teen population. Southern California is the mall capital of the country—in fact, one might say that the entire L.A. basin is one big outdoor mall, connected by freeways instead of corridors. Indeed, Torrance, California is a mall-rat's paradise, the home of by far the largest shopping mall in the country, the Del Amo Fashion Center, with nearly 370 stores. And if Southern Californians can't find a parking space in that shopping mecca, they can take a quick drive up the freeway to nearby

THINGS

Lakewood Center Mall, although at 235 it has only about two-thirds the number of places to let the cash and credit fly. America is often called the land of opportunity, and the super-mall is where that opportunity is most egregiously displayed—from store to shining store. These, then, are the largest legacies of the free market. If you can't find it here, it ain't made.

Mall/Location	# of Stores
1. **Del Amo Fashion Center** Torrance, CA	367
2. **Randall Park Mall** North Randall, OH	250
3. **Woodfield Mall** Schaumburg, IL	240
4. **Woodbridge Center** Woodbridge, NJ	240
5. **Lakewood Center Mall** Lakewood, CA	235
6. **Gallery at Market East** Philadelphia, PA	225
7. **Fairlane Town Center** Dearborn, MI	225
8. **Sharpstown Center** Houston, TX	225
9. **King of Prussia Plaza** King of Prussia, PA	217
10. **Century III Mall** West Mifflin, PA	200
Green Acres Shopping Center Valley Stream, NY	200
Lakeside Sterling Heights, MI	200
Valley View Center Dallas, TX	200

MARINE MAMMALS
Rarest

Once whales, seals, dolphins and other marine mammals roamed the seas freely, threatened only by natural predators and natural disaster. Sadly, the period of massive exploitation of marine mammals for oil, fur, and as collateral casualties of the fishing industry has depleted populations of many species to the point of extinction. Where once more than 100,000 humpback whales dwelt in the waters of the Atlantic and Pacific, now a mere 10,000 survive. The numbers for certain seals and sea lions are even more depressing: from an original total of several million in the mid-19th century, the population of Juan Fernandez Fur Seal has dwindled to less than 1,000. Efforts to preserve marine mammals have met with varied success: a ban on commercial whaling has curtailed the exploitation of those marine mammals, but not halted it out-right—the Japanese still take hundreds of whales for "scientific research." Bans on tuna harvested by methods that entrap and kill hundreds of dolphins in a single net may yet help preserve those wise denizens of the deep. For the West Indian manatee, found in the waters of Florida, the greatest danger is not from fishermen but from pleasure boaters, who continue to destroy the gentle manatee through reckless boating procedures. The following are populations for some of the rarest marine mammals still in existence. Figures are estimates from various environmental sources.

Marine Mammal	Est. Population
1. **Caribbean Monk Seal**	near extinction
2. **Juan Fernandez Fur Seal**	750
3. **West Indian Manatee**	,000
4. **Guadalupe Fur Seal**	1,600
5. **New Zealand Fur Seal**	2,000
6. **Hooker's Sea Lion**	4,000
Right Whale	4,000
7. **Bowhead Whale**	7,200
8. **Fraser's Dolphin**	7,800
9. **Amazon Manatee**	8,000
10. **Humpback Whale**	10,000

Source: Environmental Data Report, United Nations Environment Programme, 1989.

THINGS

MEDIA
Top-Grossing Media Corporations

Communications has been the great growth field of the twentieth century. Beyond the telly and telephone, our lives have been moved toward a marginal fast-forward by a dozen innovations and accelerations in this realm. Big corporations with links to air and radio media, and even some lesser players, are getting in on the action. The television world was stunned in the mid-eighties when the relatively lightweight Capital Cities bought up the American Broadcasting Company. Shortly thereafter, big corporate gun General Electric snapped up RCA and, with it, NBC. CBS's TV empire has thus far remained aloof from the merger-mania, but it has sold off many of its other assets, most notably its record division to the Japanese company Sony. Other dominant corporate forces hereabouts include the parent of *USA Today*, Gannett.

Corporation	1990 Revenues ($ Millions)
1. Capital Cities/ABC	$4,767
2. Time Warner	$4,575
3. Gannett Co.	$3,518
4. General Electric	$3,392
5. CBS, Inc.	$2,960
6. Advance Publications	$2,882
7. Times Mirror Corp.	$2,807
8. TCI	$2,353
9. Knight-Ridder	$2,262
10. Tribune Co.	$2,095

Source: Advertising Age.

MERGERS AND ACQUISITIONS
Biggest

The eighties was the decade of the deal, a time when investors bought and sold businesses like commodities. Some deals were friendly and mutually beneficial. Others were hostile, even war-like, with cash as the primary weapon. Corporate raiders like T. Boone Pickens captured America's fancy while wreaking havoc in boardrooms across the country. No one had ever seen anything like it before. Wall Street whiz kids like Michael Milken invented the junk bond to finance these transactions; he and others then went to jail for manipulating the market and trading on inside information. Some of the mergers were meant to solidify or strengthen a company's position within a market. Such was the mad, mean-spirited scramble in the oil industry, with Chevron buying out Gulf, Texaco snapping up Getty, and British Petroleum purchasing Standard Oil; even outside companies were getting into the action, with U.S. Steel taking on Marathon Oil and Du Pont picking up Conoco. Other companies sought to expand into related industries; thus Time merged with Warner Communications to create a giant media entity with its fingers in many communications pies. The pace of mergers and acquisitions has slowed somewhat in the past few years, but it seems unlikely that we will ever get back to the innocent, less freewheeling atmosphere of the peaceful 1960s. These, then, are the biggest mergers and acquisitions to date.

Company/Acquirer/Year	Price
1. RJR Nabisco Kohlberg Kravis Roberts, 1988	$24.9 bil
2. Warner Communications Time 1989	$13.9 bil
3. Gulf Oil Chevron 1984	$13.3 bil
4. Kraft Philip Morris, 1988	$11.5 bil
5. Squibb Bristol Myers, 1989	$11.5 bil
6. Getty Oil Texaco, 1984	$10.1 bil
7. Conoco Du Pont, 1981	$8.0 bil
8. Standard Oil British Petroleum, 1987	$7.9 bil
9. Federated Department Stores	$7.4 bil

THINGS

Campeau, 1988

10. Marathon Oil   **$6.5 bil**
    U.S. Steel, 1981

MIXED DRINKS
Most Popular Mixed Drinks

No doubt about it: Americans are drinking less. But when it comes to drinking in the bar, they are trading up and experimenting with a wide variety of different spiritous mixed drinks, premium wines by the glass, beers, non-alcohol beers and "virgin cocktails" (sans alcohol). Price seems no longer a factor. More than 250 barpeople responded to a Beverage Network survey, asking them to name the most popular standard mixed drinks and the hottest specialty drinks. The responses show that tonics and martinis continue to dominate the standard drinks picture. The popularity of the martini is most prevalent in upscale nightclubs, country clubs and white-table restaurants. Overall, the call for mixed drinks made with white spirits — vodka, gin, rum and tequila — is strong, accounting for 71% of the standard mixed drinks ordered at the bar.

Drink

1. Tonic (Gin or Vodka)
2. Martini
3. Screwdriver
4. Bloody Mary
5. Rum & Cola
6. Margarita
7. Bourbon and Cola
8. Scotch & Soda
9. 7 & 7
10. Bourbon and Water
11. Manhattan
12. Whiskey Sour
13. Daiquiri

Source: Beverage Network Publication, division of The Beverage Media Group, Ltd., November, 1990.

MOVIES — ACCLAIM
Top Movies, 1980-1990

The top movies were rated according to three factors: (1) Academy awards (including best picture, best director, actor or actress); (2) box office and video rental grosses; and (3) critical response. In the first category, 25 points each were awarded for best picture, best director and best actor/actress, and 10 points for best supporting actor/actress. In category two, high box office gross was awarded 25 points, high video rental 10 points. In category three, each movie critic's vote counted for seven points, with six critics' assessments being used. *E.T. The Extra-Terrestrial* is the all-time top money making movie, with *Batman* running a close second. However, *Rain Man* made it to the top of list because not only was it a box office and video rental smash, but it also received 1988 Academy Awards for Best Director and Best Actor categories, along with numerous kudos from the critics.

Movie	Total Score
1. Rain Man	121
2. Tootsie	77
3. The Last Emperor	71
4. Raging Bull	67
5. Hannah and Her Sisters	62
6. Indiana Jones and the Last Crusade	42
7. Batman	35
7. Lethal Weapon 2	35
10. E.T. The Extra-Terrestrial	32

Source: "Best and Worst" original.

MOVIES — ACCLAIM
Most Acclaimed, 1990

Premiere magazine reviewed the reviews of the 99 major film releases of 1990 to find the best films and the biggest dogs of the year. *Premiere* evaluated each review for each film gave the film a rating, from 4 stars to -2. We added together those score to compile the list of the best and worst films of 1990. Below are the compiled scores from those 99 films.

THINGS

The highest possible score was 76; the lowest possible -38. The top-rated film of 1990, according to this method, was the Martin Scorcese film *Goodfellas*, a view of the underworld both bloody and comic; although nominated for an Academy Award as best picture, it lost out to *Dances With Wolves*, which placed only fourth on our list. The biggest dogs of the year were such star vehicles as Bill Cosby's ill-received flop *Ghost Dad*, the Mel Gibson-Goldie Hawn stinker *Bird on a Wire*, and *Revenge*, which proved that even Kevin Costner can make a bomb on occasion, despite his deft touch with *Wolves*. Here, then, are the best and worst of the class of 1990.

Most Acclaimed	Total Score
1. Goodfellas	69
2. Reversal of Fortune	64
3. The Grifters	55
4. Dances With Wolves	50
5. Monsieur Hire	49
6. The Freshman	48
7. Longtime Companion	46
8. Men Don't Leave	46
9. Mr. & Mrs. Bridge	45
10. The Russia House	44

Least Acclaimed

1. Ghost Dad	-30
2. Bird on a Wire	-28
3. Revenge	-27
4. The Bonfire of the Vanities	-25
5. The Adventures of Ford Fairlane	-24
5. Another 48 Hours	-24
7. Robocop 2	-21
8. Stella	-19
9. Days of Thunder	-10
Rocky V	-10

Source: *Premiere*.

MOVIES — COST
Most Expensive Ever Made

There are many things that contribute to a film's going over budget — long production delays, problems with shooting on locations, stars' salaries that jump through the roof with each new sequel, and, perhaps most noticeably, the ego of the director. The classic case of the over-budget movie was Michael Cimino's *Heaven's Gate*. After winning critical acclaim, including the Best Picture and Best Director Oscars for *The Deer Hunter*, Cimino's studio, United Artists, gave him free reign to achieve his artistic vision. The resulting $40 million mega-flop led to the dissolution of the once-proud UA studios, which had been founded by Charlie Chaplain and Mary Pickford in the days of the silent movies. A mere ten years after the *Heaven's Gate* fiasco, Cimino's $40 million seems like a mere drop in the bucket when such flops as *Days of Thunder, Tango and Cash, Ishtar* and *Santa Claus*(?!), which previously would have broken most studios, simply get passed over in silence. In Hollywood more than most places, money doesn't buy quality, not to mention success. The preponderance of dogs and pointless sequels on the list of most expensive movies proves that point, as does such recent, low-budget successes as *Metropolitan* and *The Terminator*. Speaking of the latter, as we go to press, the sequel *Terminator II* is rumored to be perhaps the most expensive film ever made, at a cost estimated at anywhere between $85 and $110 million.

Movie	Production Cost
1. Die Hard 2	$70 Mill.
Who Framed Roger Rabbit?	$70 Mill.
2. Total Recall	$65 Mill.
The Godfather, Part III	$65 Mill.
3. Rambo III	$58 Mill.
4. Days of Thunder	$55 Mill.
Tango and Cash	$55 Mill.
Ishtar	$55 Mill.
Superman	$55 Mill.
5. Superman II	$54 Mill.
6. The Adventures of Baron Munchausen	$52 Mill.
7. Annie	$51.5 Mill.
8. The Cotton Club	$51 Mill.
Hudson Hawk	$51 Mill.

THINGS

9. Another 48 Hours	$50 Mill.
Batman	$50 Mill.
Coming to America	$50 Mill.
Santa Claus	$50 Mill.
10. Dick Tracy	$46 Mill.

Source: *New York Times*.

MOVIES — GROSS
All-time Top Grossing Films

Although a host of halogen-hot stars and directors overtly fuel the glow in and around Tinseltown, two names dominate any discussion of celluloid super-success: Steven Spielberg and George Lucas. These genial gents are responsible for six of the most profitable films of all time. The incredible worldwide popularity of Lucas's Star Wars trilogy and Spielberg's lovable *E.T.* demonstrate most clearly the fact that the movies are a place we go to escape from reality, rather than confront it. In fact, of the ten top-grossing films of all time, listed below, eight of them deal with fantasies — replete with superheroes, aliens, and the supernatural. Another concerns a oversized, murderous shark. Only *Beverly Hills Cop* can be in any way called realistic. Watch and learn, la-la land.

Title	Receipts (millions)
1. E.T.	$367.70
2. Star Wars	$322.7
3. Return of the Jedi	$263.7
4. Batman	$251.2
5. Jaws	$245.0
6. Raiders of the Lost Ark	$242.4
7. Beverly Hills Cop	$234.8
8. Empire Strikes Back	$223.2
9. Ghostbusters	$221.1
10. Ghost	$211.1

Source: Baseline II Inc.

MOVIES — LENGTH
When's Intermission? Longest Films Ever Released

Some movies are long; others simply seem to be. The following list details the top ten longest movies ever made for commercial release. The appropriately named *The Cure for Insomnia*, shown only once, consisted entirely of footage of a person asleep. The Hollywood productions below, *Cleopatra* and *Heaven's Gate*, cost exorbitant amounts of money and were commercial and critical flops, the latter even resulting in the eventual financial ruin of its studio, United Artists. On the other hand, *Berlin Alexanderplatz*, the German director Werner Fassbinder's adaptation of Alfred Döblin's novel of Weimar Germany, *Little Dorritt*, a two-part adaptation of the Dickens novel, and *Shoah*, a documentary about the Holocaust, met with extreme critical and some financial success, despite their lengths. The following are the the longest movies ever made and commercially released.

Movie	Length
1. The Cure for Insomnia	85 hours
2. Mondo Teeth	50 hrs.
3. Berlin Alexanderplatz	15 hrs. 21 m
4. Shoah	9 hrs. 21 m
5. Empire	8 hrs.
6. Little Dorritt	5 hrs. 57 m
7. Les Miserables	5 hrs. 5 m
8. Greatest Story Ever Told	4 hrs. 20 m
9. Cleopatra	4 hrs. 3 m
10. Heaven's Gate	4 hrs.
11. Gone With the Wind	3 hrs. 42 m

Source: *The Guiness Book of Movie Facts*.

MOVIE STUDIOS
The Biggest Box: The Movie Biggies By Market Share

In these disparate days, the economics of risk and reward have dictated that Hollywood commit its redoubtable resources to a relatively few films per year. These few products, in turn, are concentrated in even fewer, well-accessorized hands. Herewith, the nations largest distributors, producers and refiners of prime celluloid. With the encroachment of cable television, video and

THINGS

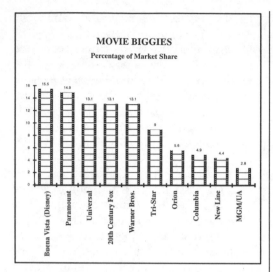

MOVIE BIGGIES

Percentage of Market Share

other media into Hollywood's once unique entertainment domain, many of the studios are either diversifying or themselves being bought up by foreign interests.

Studio/Distributor	% Share
1. Buena Vista (Disney)	15.5
2. Paramount	14.9
3. Universal	13.1
4. 20th Century Fox	13.1
5. Warner Bros.	13.1
6. Tri-Star	9.0
7. Orion	5.6
8. Columbia Pictures	4.9
9. New Line Cinemas	4.4
10. MGM/UA	2.8

Source: Baseline II, Inc.

MOVIE STUDIOS — INDEPENDENT

On My Own: America's Largest Independent Film Companies

In the Golden days of Hollywood, Louis Mayer, Lew Wasserstein and a few other founding ramrods ruled Hollywood from the comfort of their own casting couches. In that corner of the Wild West, the small-world flavor still lingers, but a few scrappy independents have muscled in on the green fields of the majors. Here's your guide to the players.

Studio	1990 Gross Receipts (Millions)
1. New Line Cinema	$170.0
2. Miramax Films	$27.0
3. Samuel Goldwyn Co.	$20.0
4. Cinecon Entertainment	$7.0
5. Concorde Pictures	$5.3
6. Corsair Films	$5.0
7. Helmdale Film Corporation	$4.5
8. Avenue Pictures	$3.3
9. Taurus Entertainment	$3.0
10. Skouras Pictures	$1.8

Source: Baseline II, Inc.

MURDER

Most Popular Methods

We live in violent times. But, in point of fact, everyone who has ever lived has done so in violent times. Although the methods of waging personal war vary somewhat from town to town and time to time, the fundamental motives remain the same. To expunge the violence of society will require an elevation of psychological and moral consciousness, the first of which, perhaps, is breaking the National Rifle Association's hold on Congress and passing a nationwide gun-control law — seeing as guns are the weapon of choice for murderers.

Technique	Victims, 1988
1. Gunshots	11,084
2. Cutting/Stabbing	3,496
3. Blunt Object	1,143
4. Strangulation	1,546
5. Arson	258
6. Other	742

Source: F.B.I. Uniform Crime Reports

MURDER

Most Likely To Kill

It is an unfortunate fact of human existence that there is no truly safe quarter from personal violence. One never knows from what direction an attack may come, although hopefully it will not come at all. The most likely souls to do us mortal harm, the F.B.I. says, are acquaintances, but not friends. The facts also reveal that are chances of getting it from a friend or wife are almost one in 20. So choose your acquaintances carefully, and make friends with them quickly. Sadly, roughly one victim in thirty goes at the hands of his or her own child.

Relationship To Victim	% all Homicides
1. Acquaintance	29.1
2. Unknown Relationship	23.1
3. Stranger	13.1
4. Friend	4.7
5. Wife	4.1
6. Girlfriend	2.6
7. Husband	2.4
8. Other Family	2.3
9. Son	1.6
10. Daughter	1.4

Source: F.B.I. Uniform Crime Reports

NAVIES
Strongest

Naval power is the most significant factor in any issue concerning world conflicts. When the British Navy deterred the Spanish Armada in 1588, forcing them to lose more than 50% of their force, they claimed dominance as the first world naval power, then proceeded to become the first "real" world power. In this regard, we present the following rating. Naval forces are controlled by men and not machines, so the first point totals are determined by men. For every 1,000 naval personnel, 1 point is attributed. For every 1,000 Marines (special training accounted for) 2 points are attributed. Machines being vital, as well as being extraordinarily destructive, the following values have been attributed: strategic submarines (carrying nuclear warheads) 3 points each; attack submarines, 2 points each; aircraft carriers (being the most

potentially destructive and versatile platforms) 5 points each; all other battle ships, including destroyers, frigates, missile carrying ships, etc., 1 point each, and all other support ships (troop carriers, supply ships, etc.) one-quarter point each. According to this system, the most powerful navy in the world is that of the U.S.S.R. But the Soviet Navy faces severe limitations, despite its size and destructive power. These include the lack of suitable warm-water ports within the Soviet Union that have easy access to the open sea, and their weakness in aircraft carriers, the true measure of naval power since the Second World War. The U.S. fields more than a dozen carrier battle groups, of which the Soviets have none (although they do sport several smaller carriers). The world's top navies are listed below.

Country	Score
1. U.S.S.R.	2414
2. U.S.A.	1753
3. China	1576
4. U.K.	338
5. Taiwan	314
6. Turkey	270
7. France	255
8. Spain	188
9. Norway	182
10. India	177

Source: "Best and Worst" original.

NEWSPAPERS — CIRCULATION
Top Ten Daily Newspapers in Circulation

The newspaper industry is fighting a bitter war with television for the hearts and minds of the American people. The result has been the "televisionization" of the American newspaper, as witnessed by the popularity of the USA Today format: color pictures, elaborate graphics, easy-to-read charts, bold headlines, and, most of all, short stories so that the attention spans of readers are not

THINGS

taxed. Still, the most popular daily in the U.S. remains the staid *Wall Street Journal*, which doesn't even use black-and-white pictures, much less color. The paper still employs those strange pointillist drawings in place of photography in their pages.

Paper	Daily Circulation
1. Wall Street Journal	1,835,713
2. USA Today	1,325,507
3. New York Daily News	1,194,237
4. Los Angeles Times	1,107,623
5. New York Times	1,068,217
6. Washington Post	772,749
7. Chicago Tribune	720,155
8. Long Island Newsday	700,174
9. Detroit News	690,422
10. Detroit Free Press	626,434

Source: World Almanac.

NEWSPAPERS — CIRCULATION
Sunday Newspaper Circulation

Curling up with a nice, bulky Sunday paper is a weekend tradition which shows little sign of strain — everyone wants to read the comics, check out the latest batting averages, scope the classifieds for job listings, and dream of those unattainable paradises profiled in the Travel section. And the lingerie ads in the Sunday Magazine are always worth a glance. The New York Times still maintains a very respectable circulation, but surprisingly, the Big Apple paper has been topped by a rag from a much more modest market — the newly merged Detroit News/Free Press.

Newspaper	Sunday Circulation
1. Detroit News/Free Press	1,563.6
2. New York Times	1,506.2
3. New York Sunday News	1,448.8
4. Los Angeles Times	1,400.6
5. Chicago Tribune	1,123.7
6. Washington Post	1.133.4
7. Philadelphia Inquirer	992.1
8. Boston Globe	784.6

9. San Francisco Chronicle	710.8
10. Long Island Newsday	704.1

Source: Newspaper Advertising Bureau, Inc.

NEWSPAPERS — READERSHIP
Most Readers per Copy

What's black and white and read over and over? Answer: Your daily newspaper. Despite their inherent affordability, newspapers are frequently re-cycled before they ever hit the scrap heap. Ad reps often pitch their product's "pass-around" rate, in addition to circulation, as a hidden measure of the number of readers a paper reaches. In lobbies and in waiting rooms; on trains and on planes; through the office and through the house, second-hand copies go round and round. These are the papers that reach the most readers per copy.

Paper	Readers per Copy
1. San Francisco Examiner	4.42
2. Reading Eagle	3.77
3. New York Daily News	3.56
4. Charleston Gazette	3.54
5. Daily News of Los Angeles	3.48
6. Chicago Sun-Times	3.42
7. Providence Journal	3.41
8. San Bernardino Sun	3.34
9. New York Times	3.33
10. Milwaukee Sentinel	3.26

Source: Scarborough's Newspaper Audience Ratings Study.

NOVELS — AMERICAN
Greatest American Novels, All-time

Every writer dreams of creating the Great American Novel. But it's already been done. The top two novels on our list of greatest American books of all-time are the undisputed masterpieces of American fiction — at least they are now. Mark Twain's *Huck Finn* has had to fight being banned from school libraries for whatever reason as

THINGS

recently as ten years ago. Melville's work went unrecognized upon its publication — its greatness only gradually became recognized. We rated novels in the same way as writers — by the total number of citations in the MLA International Bibliography of literary and linguistic scholarship. Interestingly, these novels are not the highest scoring literary works by an American. That spot is reserved for Ezra Pound's *Cantos*, a cycle of poetry written over the course of thirty-five years. The *Cantos* notched 244 mentions in the MLA index. The top American play of all time is Eugene O'Neill's *Long Day's Journey Into Night*, with an overall score of 47. The highest scoring novel by a woman writer was Kate Chopin's 1899 work *The Awakening*, with 81 points. The book was harshly criticized upon publication for its frank discussion of female sexuality, and it took sixty years for *The Awakening* to be rediscovered. Also scoring highly on the list were *The Sun Also Rises* by Ernest Hemingway, with a score of 83, Melville's *Billy Budd* (75) and two more novels by Henry James, *The Turn of the Screw* (74) and *The Ambassadors* (71).

Novel/Author	Score
1. *Adventures of Huckleberry Finn* Mark Twain	240
2. *Moby Dick* Herman Melville	225
3. *Gravity's Rainbow* Thomas Pynchon	177
4. *The Scarlet Letter* Nathaniel Hawthorne	168
5. *Absalom, Absalom* William Faulkner	139
6. *The Great Gatsby* F. Scott Fitzgerald	122
7. *The Sound and The Fury* William Faulkner	111
8. *Portrait of a Lady* Henry James	95

The Great American Novel.

9. *As I Lay Dying* William Faulkner	89
10. *Light in August* William Faulkner	87

Source: "Best and Worst" original.

NUCLEAR POWER
Till They Glow: America's Largest Nuclear Power Plants

Although paranoia (or plain concern) about the safety of nuclear plants has diminished somewhat since the era of Three Mile Island and *The China Syndrome*, an informed hard core of activists still work fervently to ensure the reliability and viability of our utility nukes. The growing quandary involved in the disposal of nuclear waste, combined with fears enhanced by the disaster at the

THINGS

Soviet power plant at Chernobyl, keep nuclear power from becoming a mainstay of America's energy production. In fact, with the years of red-tape and regulatory battles that must go into building a plant and eventually bringing it on line, experts expect few, if any, new plants to be built in the foreseeable future. We may have to wait until the day that fusion, rather than fission, is perfected. Herewith, ten of the top concerns for the no-nuke crowd.

Plant	Capacity (Kilowattage)
1. South Texas 1	1,250,000
2. Palos Verde 1 (AZ)	1,221,000
3. Palos Verde 2	1,221,000
4. Palos Verde 3	1,221,000
5. Perry 1 (OH)	1,205,000
6. Sequoyah 1 (TN)	1,148,000
7. Sequoyah 2 (TN)	1,145,000
8. Calaway (MO)	1,142,000
9. Grand Gulf 1 (MS)	1,142,000
10. Millstone 3, CT	1,129,000

ODDS
Biggest Poker Longshots

It is always important to know where one stands. The merits of this precaution are especially obvious in connection with quicksand and toxic waste seepage, but even in the wacky world of wagering, it is nice to know on what foundations our feet have been planted. So next time you draw a card, idly wondering, "What are the chances?," please be advised. These are the odds for being dealt various hands on the opening deal in regular five-card poker, with no wild cards. We haven't calculated odds when "Deuces, Jacks and the King with the Ax" are wild. For you poker faces out there, here are your odds:

Hand	Odds against
1. Royal flush	649,739 to one
2. Other Straight Flush	72,192 to one
3. Four of a Kind	4,164 to one
4. Full House	693 to one
5. Flush	508 to one
6. Straight	254 to one
7. Three of a kind	46 to one
8. Two Pairs	20 to one
9. One Pair	4 to 3
10. No matches	1 in 1

POLITICAL ACTION COMMITTEES
Freest Spending P.A.C. Groups

The American social and political systems are based around the free competition of disparate ideas. These days, such ideas don't get far without the support of self-interested groups. Political Action Committees—the PAC's— exist to lobby for the interests of one group or another at the pantheon of U.S. policy, the Capitol. Some are innocuous and impartial, others only sound so.

PAC	1988 Disbursements
1. Democratic/Republican Independent Voter Educ. Comm.	$4,041
2. Campaign America	$3,295
3. National Cong. Club	$3,186
4. Am. Citizens for Pol. Action	$2,888
5. American Medical Association	$2,856
6. Realtors Public Action Comm.	$2,684
7. National Security Political Action Committee	$2,634
8. League of Conservation Voters	$2,570
9. National Conservative Political Action Committee	$2,127
10. AT&T PAC	$2,046

Source: Federal Election Commission.

POLITICAL ACTION COMMITTEES—DEFENSE
Most Generous

Who are the most powerful people in Washington—senators, representatives, cabinet members, White House staffers? In many ways, the true power lies not with our elected officials, but with the people who make our elected officials' campaigns possible—political action committees. Now, we're not implying in any way the existence

THINGS

of a quid pro quo – you supply the campaign bucks and I'll supply the vote in Congress for that expensive new missile or submarine contract. No, no. Not in the illustrious chambers of the United States Congress. What Lockheed, Rockwell, General Dynamics, Northrop and other defense contractors seek when shelling out big bucks to congressional campaigns is spelled out clearly – *good government* – good government, of course, being, one assumes, that which best promotes our vital national defense interests. Each of the PACs listed below has received at least 10 million dollars in Defense Department contracts.

PAC	Campaign Contributions)
1. AT&T PAC	$847,340
2. Philip Morris PAC	$573,780
3. Tenneco Employees Good Govt. PAC	$455,150
4. Lockheed Employees PAC	$434,224
5. Rockwell Intl. Corp. Good Govt. PAC	$422,150
6. Textron Inc. PAC	$376,500
7. General Dynamics Vol. Political Cont. Plan	$372,278
8. Amoco PAC	$351,500
9. Northrop Employees PAC	$315,854
10. FMC Corp. Good Govt. Prg.	$287,045

Source: *Congress and Defense, 1988.*

POLITICAL ACTION COMMITTEES – LABOR

Largest Labor PACs in Washington

PACs work for us and against us. They are, in fact, simultaneously "us" and "them". PACs work for and against abortion, for the Democrats and the Republicans, to sell weapons and to ban them. A number of pacts look out for the concerns of the working class. These, then, are the top ten labor-related political action committees laboring on Capitol Hill, for the interests of unionists nationwide.

PAC	1990 Total dispersals (millions)
1. Democratic Republican Independent Voter Educ. Comm.	$4.04
2. UAW Voluntary Independent Voter Educ. Comm.	$1.56
3. Machinists Non-Partisan Political League	$1.56
4. National Educational Association	$1.53
5. Am. Fed. of State, County and Municipal Employees	$1.38
6. Intl. Brotherhood of Electrical Workers	$1.34
7. Committee on Letter Carriers' Political Education	$1.30
8. Political Contributions Comm.	$1.23
9. Airline Pilots Association	$1.23
10. Transp. Political Educ. League	$1.08

Source: Federal Election Committee.

PLASTIC SURGERY

Most Popular

For whatever reason, a large number of Americans are not content with the physical features God gave them. Whether contending with the rages of age or illness, or simply in pursuit of an ideal of beauty, tens of thousands of us turn to the surgeon's scalpel (or, more and more these days, laser) to improve our appearances. The most popular facial plastic surgery continues to be the venerable nose job. Nearly 100,000 Jimmy Durantes a year elect to improve the schnozz, normally by trimming it down. In this procedure, bone and cartilage are reconstructed and excess is removed from the nose to achieve a new shape. In the 1950s, reconstructive nose surgery consisted mainly of a uniform, stylized nose with a turned-up, ski-jump angle and a highly sculpted tip. These days, through the magic of computer imagery, a plastic surgeon can individualize the nose-job, giving the patient a wider bridge, a stronger, fuller nose, a gently refined tip. Some patients even choose, ironically, to make the nose longer. Other elective procedures that are growing in popularity include mentoplasty, or chin implants (often in conjunction with a facelift and rhinoplasty to improve the profile), blepharoplasty, or eyelid surgery, which eliminates fat and excess skin around the eye to remove bags and pouches, and dermabrasion, or face sanding, in which wire brushes or diamond fraizes gently scrape the face, removing the outer layer of skin, smoothing its texture and removing superficial scars and age lines. Procedures that have declined in popularity over the past several years include eyebrow surgery, hair transplants and surgery on birthmarks.

Procedure	# Performed, 1988
1. Nose Surgery	99,358
2. Head/Neck Tumors	70,247
3. Head/Neck Trauma	43,012
4. Injectable Fillers (Zyderm)	42,529
5. Head/Neck Reconstructive	41,929
6. Eyelid Surgery	38,732
7. Scar Revision	30,187
8. Facial Fractures	26,711
9. Facelift	21,025
10. Face Sanding	15,393

Source: American Academy of Facial Plastic and Reconstructive Surgery.

POEMS
Most Anthologized Poems in English

Poetry has always been one of the more esoteric of linguistic media, which is why anthologies, rather than works by individual poets, are popular. The anthology allows the reader to sample the styles of a number of different poets from different eras and different places. Still, most anthologies of poetry in English feel the need to include a number of "greatest hits," some of which are familiar to the general reader, while others may be more obscure. The following are the ten most anthologized poems in the English language, as registered by *The Concise Columbia Book of Modern Poetry: The Top 100 Poems*. The list is replete with pre-20th

century poems; topping the list is English Romantic poet William Blake's "The Tyger." Only one American, Robert Frost, has a poem in the top ten; his is also the only 20th-century poem to make the list.

Poem/Poet

1. **"The Tyger"**
   William Blake

2. **"Sir Patrick Spens"**
   Anonymous

3. **"To Autumn"**
   John Keats

4. **"That Time of Year Thou Mayst in Me Behold"**
   William Shakespeare

5. **"Pied Beauty"**
   Gerard Manly Hopkins

6. **"Stopping by Woods on a Snowy Evening"**
   Robert Frost

7. **"Kubla Kahn"**
   Samuel Taylor Coleridge

8. **"Dover Beach"**
   Matthew Arnold

9. **"La Belle Dame sans Merci"**
   John Keats

10. **"To the Virgins, to Make Much of Time"**
    Robert Herrick

Source: The Concise Columbia Book of Poetry.

POLICE
Most Dangerous Police Activities

Police work is an inherently under-appreciated, over-anxietal task. Aside from the aggravation and degradation of constant contact with society's surliest, most intractable elements, the peace officer must face the real and constant danger of grave bodily harm. Although interruption of felonies in progress represents the most dangerous side of police duty. Even routine traffic en-... has proven extremely perilous. ... numerous ... face, ... killed in ...

1978-87

131
124
122
ons   100
86
81
59
54
soners 36
27

...eports.

POLICE

Police Response Times for Common Incidents

Americans have evolved a highly schizophrenic posture in their relations with peace officers. On the one hand, they are discomforted by the presence of police on routine occasions. On the other, the are out-raged by delays in response, during criminal or medical emergencies. In the years ahead, a more meaningful middle ground must be cleared. Ironically, the popularity of such "reality" television programs as *Rescue 911*, by making people more aware of the emer-gency services available, may be contribut-ing to even greater lag times for emergency personnel in responding to threatening situations, by the mere fact that more people are calling into 911 services for frivolous reasons. Such calls clog the phone lines and send police on calls that do not require im-mediate attention. Below we have listed the incidents in which police officers respond the quickest, measured by the percentage of incidents in which officers responded within 10 minutes of receiving the radio report.

Incident	Percent
1. Simple Assault	59
2. Aggravated Assault	58
3. Robbery	51
4. Personal larceny with contact	46
5. Burglary	36
6. Personal Larceny without contact	35
7. Motor Vehicle Theft	35
8. Household larceny	32
9. Rape	31

Source: Re-Designed National Crime Sur-vey, Dept. of Justice.

POLLUTION

Main Sources of Water Pollution

The great lakes are representative of the freshwater bodies in the industrial world, and they are taking a beating. This largest group of freshwater lakes in the world are absorbing an incredible amount of con-tamination every year. The main sources of pollution come from two places, industrial plants and sewers. The most flagrant viola-tions are the result of sewage—only 3% of all major pollution spills in the Great Lakes are from sewers, but they account for 33% of the waste. The top five sources of pollu-tion spills account for 3,577,252 tons of waste, or 89 percent of the total.

Spill Sources	#	Tons
1. Industrial Plant	1683	1,604,008
2. Sewers	157	1,299,046
3. Mine, Well	359	268,877
4. Storage Facilty	435	226,599
5. Train	419	68,722
6. Motor Vehicle	540	n/a
7. Tank Truck	462	n/a
8. Aircraft, Ship	187	n/a

Spill Type	#	% all
1. Overflow	670	14%
2. Discharge	518	11%
3. Pipe Leak	515	10%
4. Container Leak	503	10%
5. Fitting	459	9%

THINGS

6. Overturn	396	8%
7. Tank Leak	291	6%
8. Derailment	202	4%
9. Other Accident	182	4%
10. Other Sources	1206	24%

Source: Environmental Protection Agency.

PRICES
Highest Consumer Prices

The consumer price index measures what food, fuel and shelter cost to people who live in various countries. In this survey, the United Nations gave the United States a score of 133, a rating similar to that of much of the industrialized world. In parts of Latin American where inflation reaches the triple digits, U.N. scores for consumer prices are reaching four, five and even six digits. What that means is that even consumers with good jobs must struggle to provide for basic needs. The consumer price index does not measure what it would cost for a foreigner to live in these countries. Just the opposite: High prices for residents often mean a good exchange rate and bargains for foreigners visiting the country.

Country	Consumer Prices (U.S. = 133)
1. Bolivia	616,005
2. Argentina	256,314
3. Israel	33,322
4. Brazil	16,509
5. Perú	5,991
6. Sierra Leone	1,403
7. Mexico	1,195
8. Uruguay	1,123
9. Ghana	1,132
10. Yugoslavia	1,321

Source: U.N. Statistical Yearbook

PRODUCTS
Most Popular Grocery Store Items

In this day and age, supermarkets are so spacious, and the lines they carry so repetitious and plentiful, that there is quite nearly too much too choose from. Faced with such a bounty, many shoppers retreat into the familiar. Indeed, there are a few staples on everyone's shopping lists. Soft drinks, coffee and cigarettes are, in the main, the most popular grocery store items—not quite what the dietitian would order. On the whole, it seems, most of the times that we go to the supermarket, neighborhood grocery or convenience corner, we really are interested in only a very few core items. Such as:

Item	1990 Sales (Millions)
1. Marlboro Cigarettes	$1,509
2. Coke Classic	$1,278
3. Pepsi	$1,222
4. Kraft Cheese	$1,168
5. Diet Coke	$996
6. Tide	$970
7. Campbell's Soup	$964
8. Folger's Coffee	$824
9. Winston Cigarettes	$780
10. Tropicana	$685

Source: Information Resources Inc.

PRODUCTS
Most Popular Foreign-Made Products

Politicos and economists often implore this country's producers and consumers to become more *self-sufficient*. Reliance on foreign suppliers in the marketplace, the adage goes, simply puts us at the mercy of uncontrollable economic and political events overseas. After petroleum products, the supply of which is at the mercy of the Gulf states, the corners of the consumer market most worrisome to pundits and prophets are those which contain big-ticket items like cars, televisions and stereos. But despite all the hand-wringing in this country over tightening grip foreign producers are having on the automobile and electronics markets, these are not the markets most dominated by foreign producers. Less than a quarter of all cars sold in the U.S. are

THINGS

foreign-made (although that percentage is expected to increase steadily in the coming years). No, it is America's addiction to java that is most exploited by foreign producers: more than 70 percent of all coffee sold in the United States is imported. Other highly imported items include small-ticket items like ties, dolls and chocolate. Not, it seems, items the denial of which would tear apart the fabric of American society — though the lack of a cup of coffee may make it harder for the average worker to get kick-started in the morning. These are the top imported consumer products, measured by the percentage of sales to foreign producers.

Product	% from foreign producers
1. Roasted Coffee	72.5%
2. Neckwear	55.5%
3. Dolls	48.3%
4. Motorcycles	47.8%
5. Jewelry materials	45.3%
6. Chocolate	44.4%
7. Nonmetallic minerals	40.9%
8. Watches	39.8%
9. Wool (Broadwoven)	39.7%
10. Recording Media	36.7%

Source: Census of Manufacturers.

PROTESTANT CHURCHES
Largest Congregations

When Martin Luther tacked his 95 theses to the church door in Wittenburg in 1517, he sought to cut out the middle-man — the priest — in the relationship between God and man. Each individual should seek a more personal relationship with God, and not rely on good works or indulgences for salvation, Luther professed. Little did Luther then realize that his call for a more personalized spiritual life would give rise to the phenomenon of the Protestant "Mega-Church." But then again, little did he probably realize the diversity and mobility, or the sheer size, of today's worshipping public. In large but widely spread-out towns such as one finds in Southern California, the church serves as an anchor for the com-

munity — sometimes the only place (besides the mall) in which citizens of these haphazard municipalities feel they are *part* of a community at all. The drawing power of a dynamic pastor, such as the First Baptist Church's Rev. Jack Hyles or the Thomas Road Baptist Church's Jerry Falwell, also plays a part in the vastness of the Sunday flock (although in the latter case, some in the congregation might be motivated by the chance to get on TV). Herewith is a list of the largest Protestant congregations in the United States.

Church/City	Avg. Sunday Attendance
1. First Baptist Church Hammond, Ind.	20,000
2. Willow Creek Church S. Barrington, Ill.	14,605
3. Calvary Chapel Costa Mesa, Calif.	12,000
4. Thomas Road Baptist Church Lynchburg, Va.	11,000
5. First Assembly of God Phoenix, Ariz.	10,000
6. North Phoenix Baptist Church Phoenix, Ariz.	9,500
7. Chapel in University Park Akron, Ohio	8,700
8. Second Baptist Church Houston, Tex.	8,500
9. Grace Community Church Sun Valley, Calif.	8,000
10. Mt. Paran Church of God Atlanta, Ga.	7,850

Source: International Mega-Church Research Center, Bolivar, Mo.

PUBLISHERS
Largest Publishing Groups

The eighties shall go down in the dank annals of publishing as the great decade of consolidation. As mountains moved and

THINGS

moguls merged their less-than-certain assets, the curtain drew abruptly closed on independent facets of the industry. Houses small and mid-sized, in short, were put asunder. Their legacies, if lucky, survived in the expanding corporate halls of the remaining publishing giants, the biggest of which is Simon and Schuster, whose revenues in 1989 topped $1.3 billion.

Company	Revenues (millions)
1. Simon and Schuster	$1,320
2. Time Publishing Group	$1,140
3. Harcourt Brace Jovanovich	$885
4. Random House	$850
5. Reader's Digest	$844
6. McGraw-Hill	$740
7. Encyclopedia Britannica	$650
8. Bantam Doubleday Dell	$630
9. Times Mirror Corporation	$575
10. The Thomson Corporation	$598

Source: Reed Publishing 1990.

RADIO
Most Popular Radio Formats

Although it is often said that radio has become generic, and devoid of meaningful artistry, "commercial radio" today subsumes some truly diverse formats. Despite widespread popularity among the young of such musical styles as rap and heavy metal, radio programming goes where the money is, and, these days, the money is in non-threatening formats like country and the ambiguous "adult contemporary." The most notable effect of this target formatting is the arrival of the nostalgia craze. Seems the aging baby-boomers still want to hear the songs that made them happy in their heyday. Call it classic rock, oldies, psychedelic flashback or what have you — it's still re-run rock 'n' roll to me.

Format	# of Stations
1. Country	2,452
2. Adult Contemporary	2,135
3. Top 40	824
4. Religion	745
5. Oldies	659
6. Rock	429
7. News/Talk	405
8. Adult Standards	383
9. Spanish and Ethnic	342
10. Urban, Black	294

Source: M Street Radio Directory.

RADIO
Most Listened-To Radio Stations

T.V. stations get all the stares, and radio stations get all the ears. This pun aside, radio still very much holds its own amid the media circus. Whether it be drive time, lunch, late-night and early-morning, radio is a hard habit to break. The recent Persian Gulf war boosted the fortunes of numerous news radio stations, but it is yet to be determined if those listeners will stay tuned to news radio in the coming "New World Order." But one thing is for certain: Radio is alive and well in America. From Larry King talk shows to hot mix ho-downs, the wireless is still where it's at. These are the ten most-listened to stations in the U.S., measured by total audience. Eight are in New York, while two span the Los Angeles listening area.

Station	Market
1. WINS-AM	New York
2. WHTZ-FM	New York
3. WCBS-AM	New York
4. KIIS-AM/FM	Los Angeles
5. WPLJ-FM	New York
6. WCBS-FM	New York
7. KOST-FM	Los Angeles
8. WXRK-FM	New York
9. WLTW-FM	New York
10. WPAT-AM/FM	New York

Source: Amusement Business Magazine.

RESTAURANTS
Largest Franchised Restaurant Chains

Fast food is everywhere — there is no escape. On the strength of crispy fries, wispy burgers and unfailing fast pitches, chains like

THINGS

McDonald's and Burger King have established themselves as credible forces in the international economic arena. At those airy heights, competition is fierce, and the chains compete savagely for market share and public awareness, all the while counting up the billions of burgers, drumsticks and pizzas dished out to a hungry world. These are the biggest of the fast-food franchisers, in total annual sales—led, of course, by the ubiquitous Golden Arches. We've also listed the number of franchises for each chain.

Restaurant	Sales	Stores
1. McDonald's	$11,000	8,901
2. Burger King	$3,990	4,225
3. KFC	$3,100	6,396
4. Wendy's	$2,700	3,459
5. Hardee's	$2,200	2,411
6. Pizza Hut	$2,100	4,912
7. Dairy Queen	$1,572	4,822
8. Taco Bell	$1,140	2,173
9. Big Boy	$1,135	870
10. Domino's Pizza	$1,097	2,816

Source: Restaurants and Institutions.

RESTAURANTS
America's Busiest Restaurants

Every town has its dining hot spots. If a restaurant, diner, or other gastronomic haunt can maintain quality, business expands, word spreads, tables are added and a dining institution is born. And so are the giants created: around treasured family recipes, off-key highways and overlooking scenic attractions. Here are the largest restaurants in the land; make sure to reserve your table early.

Restaurants	Meals Served in 1990
1. Hilltop Steak House Saugus, MA	2,427,600
2. Rascal House Miami, FL	1,750,000
3. The Omega Niles, IL	1,543,360

Table for 2 million, please: America's busiest restaurant, Hilltop Steak House.

4. Kelly's Roast Beef Revere, MA	1,152,685
5. Canter's Los Angeles, CA	1,140,546
6. The Kapok Tree Clearwater, FL	1,019,397
7. Phillips Harborplace Baltimore, MD	990,000
8. Zehnder's of Frankenmuth Frankenmuth, MI	990,000
9. Spenger's Fish Grotto Berkeley, CA	910,000
10. The Berghoff Chicago, IL	900,000

Source: Resaurants and Institutions.

THINGS

RETAIL STORES
The Clothiers: Most Popular Apparel Retailers

In the last decade, large department stores, upscale cosmopolitan clothiers and other traditional retail leaders have faced major slumps and cutbacks. At the same time, aggressive, streamlined, discount merchandisers like Marshalls, the Limited and the Gap have made enormous economic inroads, by playing to a younger, more fashion- and price-conscious crowd. The result has been the displacement of those stalwart department stores in the retail apparel business by these upstart stores.

Store	1990 Sales (millions)
1. Marshalls	$7,500
2. The Limited, Lerner	$4,647
3. T.J. Maxx/ Hit or Miss	$2,148
4. The Gap Stores	$1,586
5. Wallach's	$1,297
6. Petrie's, Marianne	$1,257
7. Fashion Bug	$808
8. Ross Dress for Less	$741
9. Burlington	$480
10. Merry-Go-Round	$479

Source: Superbrands 1990.

RETAIL STORES
The Druggiest Chain Stores in America

The corner pharmacy, owned by Mom and Pop America, always well-stocked with Hershey Kisses and cherry fountain Cokes, is a fundamental part of our national mythos, herald of a bygone, more innocent time. These days, drug stores, by and large, are hardly Mom and Pop shops. Chains predominate in today's pharmaceutical retail climate, and size and service mean all. With the loss of innocence, though, comes better service, in the form of wider selection, more diverse product lines, and computerized prescription systems. You may not be able to hop up to the counter and get a Cherry Coke at your local pharmacy any more, but you can get your film developed, buy a six-pack, and pick up a Sony Walkman. Such is the march of progress. The following are the largest pharmacy chains in the country, measured by number of stores nationwide.

Chain	Stores
1. Walgreens	585
2. Osco Drug	235
3. Eckard	150
4. Rite-Aid	125
5. Thrifty	120
6. Revco	120
7. Shopper's Drug Mart	110
8. Long's Drug Stores	110
9. CVS	105
10. Pay Less NW	105

Source: Chain Drug Review.

ROADS
Most Scenic

One of the great pleasures in the American experience is taking the car out on the open road to enjoy the scenic wonders of our land, rolling along through our purple mountains and along our shining seaboards. The following list presents the roadways that offer the richest such experience, according to the Rand McNally Road Atlas. Topping the list is the majestic Pacific Coast Highway, which winds up and down nearly 800 miles of the still-pristine shores of California, pitching and rolling along sheer cliffs and over canyons, with, for the lucky driver, perhaps a glimpse of a migrating whale colony or a school of dolphins frolicking off shore. Just don't get stuck behind a mobile home along these twisting, turning roads with few places to pass; you might end up spending a little more time on these beautiful byways than you bargained for.

Road/Location

1. Pacific Coast Highway, California
   (Cal. Hwy. 1; U.S. Hwy. 101)

2. Columbia Gorge Highway, Oregon

THINGS

(U.S. 30)

3. Coastal Highway, Maine
(U.S. 1)

4. Going-to-the-Sun Road
Glacier National Park, Montana

5. Skyline Drive/Blue Ridge Parkway
Virginia

6. Million-Dollar Highway, Colorado
(U.S. 550 between Ouray and Silverton)

7. Oak Creek Canyon Drive, Arizona
(U.S. 89A between Sedona and Flagstaff)

8. Highway 7, Arkansas
Source: Rand McNally Road Atlas.

SHAKESPEAREAN PLAYS

Greatest

In another rating we saw that Shakespeare rates as the greatest writer of all time. And in this rating, we note the greatest works of that greatest of writers. Topping the list is the tragedy *Hamlet*, the tale of the tragic Prince of Denmark, which contains, among innumerable other great quotations that have become part of the Bard's cultural legacy, the immortal soliloquy "To be or not to be." From the list below, which rates the plays according to the number of citations for each work in the MLA International Bibliography, Shakespeare's most lasting and important plays turn out to be primarily his tragedies—after *Hamlet*, the next greatest Shakespearean plays are *King Lear*, *Macbeth* and *Othello*. Comedies also appear in the top ten list; absent from the list of bests are the historical dramas. If Shakespeare's sonnets were included in this list, they would rank seventh, with an overall score of 173. However, his other poetry does not fare so well. "The Rape of Lucrece" scored a measly 24, while "Venus And Adonis" tallied 21, "The Phoenix and the Turtle," 8, and "The Lover's Complaint" a meager 4. The rating

does not include plays of doubtful or composite authorship, such as *Edward III* or *The Two Noble Kinsmen*.

The Greatest	Score
1. Hamlet	724
2. King Lear	423
3. Macbeth	271
4. Othello	265
5. The Tempest	210
6. The Merchant of Venice	181
7. A Midsummer Night's Dream	166
8. Measure for Measure	153
9. Romeo and Juliet	151
10. The Winter's Tale	132

The Most Ignored	Score
1. Henry VI, Part I	18
2. Henry VI, Part III	20
3. Henry VI, Part II	23
4. The Comedy of Errors	24
5. The Two Gentlemen of Verona	26
6. Henry VIII	28
7. Timon of Athens	35
8. Much Ado About Nothing	38
9. Pericles	39
10. The Merry Wives of Windsor	42

Source: "Best and Worst" original.

SNAKES

Most Venomous Snakes

Most people have an in-built horror of snakes, and that fear is rather more justified than not. Snakes attack in one of two extremely unpleasant ways: Either they coil around the victim, crushing it to death before ingesting, or they bite, injecting a paralyzing or death-dealing poison through the fangs. No wonder the snake is the symbol of evil in the Judeo-Christian heritage. Most venomous snakes are relatively small, but just because a snake is shockingly big does not mean that it isn't also appallingly toxic: the Black Mamba grows to 14 feet, but the venom will get you right off the bat. These, then, are the most venomous members of the serpent world.

THINGS

Species
1. Coral Snake
3. Rattlesnake
4. Cottonmouth Water Moccasin
5. Copperhead
6. Bushmaster
7. Fer-de-Lance
8. Asian Pit Vipers
9. Sharp-Nosed Pit Viper
10. Puff Adder

SOFT DRINKS
Best-Selling Soft Drinks

Coca Cola is not merely a soda, it is an unshakable American icon. In fact, these days, Coke is the most recognizable brand name in the world. Pepsi has nipped at the giant's heels for decades, but somehow, Coke has always managed to stay on top — this despite some enormous strategic and marketing gaffs in the past decade. First and foremost was changing the tried-and-true formula to create the brief, unpopular "New Coke." Then there was the Magic Cans promotion fiasco, in which consumers could win money inside of cans of Coke. The winning cans were filled with a non-potable water so that you couldn't tell which were winners just by feel, but some winners consumed the water anyway, making them sick; the campaign also violated one of the great rules of marketing — people who paid money for a Coke didn't get a Coke. And then there was the pompous 1991 Super Bowl spot that replaced the culmination of a lengthy customer contest with a stark announcement that the Persian Gulf war was too serious an issue for the Coke contest to continue. What better forum for making such a pronouncement than the Super Bowl? Pepsi, on the other hand, used the same forum to introduce a popular new ad campaign. Yes, Coke has stumbled of late, but never yet has the giant fallen. These days, indeed, "Coca Cola" is no one single thing. Classic, New, Cherry, Diet, decaf — all are valid options in today's bubbly market.

Brand	1990 U.S. Sales (Thousands)
1. Coca-Cola	$14,200
2. Pepsi-Cola	$11,300
3. Dr. Pepper	$2,200
4. Sprite	$2,000
5. Mountain Dew	$1,800
6. 7-Up	$1,800
7. RC	$1,100
8. Canada Dry	$932
9. Shasta	$710
10. Slice	$710

Source: Superbrands 1990

SOLID WASTES
Most Abundant

Everyone knows American society is awash in garbage. The landfills are about full, and there is no place left to put the stuff. The following is a list of today's most prevalent types of garbage from residences and commercial enterprises (which comprise the major portion of typical municipal collections), measured by percentage that each type of waste makes up in the dump. As the listing shows, the majority of all garbage, (paper, leaves and grass clippings) is either easily recycled or degradable in yards. The rankings exclude mining, agriculture and industrial processing, demolition and construction wastes, sewage sludge and junked autos and obsolete equipment wastes.

Waste	Percentage
1. Paper and paperboard	35.6
2. Yard Wastes	20.1
3. Metals	8.9
Food Wastes	8.9
5. Glass	8.4
6. Plastics	7.3
7. Wood	4.1
8. Rubber and Leather	2.8
9. Textiles	2.0
10. Other Wastes	1.8

Source: "Characterization of Municipal Solid Waste in the United States 1960-2000, U.S. Environmental Protection Agency.

THINGS

SPORTS — PARTICIPATORY
Most Popular

Baseball may be the great American sport, but for the average Joe, swimming is really where it's at. In our exercise-conscious culture, non-competitive pastimes like swimming, exercise walking and bicycling garner far more participants than classic, highly-organized team activities like baseball, basketball and football. Perhaps because one can do them alone. As we age, it just seems to be more and more difficult to gather up the requisite numbers to engage in such team sports.

Sport	% of Americans participating
1. Swimming	32.8
2. Exercise Walking	28.7
3. Bicycling	24.8
4. Camping	19.5
5. Fishing (Fresh Water)	18.3
6. Bowling	17.5
7. Exercising with Equipment	13.3
8. Aerobic Exercising	11.2
9. Basketball	10.7
10. Running/Jogging	10.6

Source: National Sporting Goods Association.

SPORTS — SPECTATOR
Most Popular

Have you wondered why about a third of every newspaper and a fifth of every newscast is devoted to sports? Why there is a sporting newspaper on every corner and a rack of sporting magazines at every newsstand? Why every pause in a conversation is inevitably filled with the phrase: So what about those Cubs? Giants? Mets? The reason sports are so ubiquitous, if you haven't already guessed it, is because Americans love sports! They love to root for their favorite teams and bet on their favorite horses, dogs and Jai Alai players. More than anything, they love to go to the track, the park or the stadium. Here then are America's ten most popular spectator sports, measured by annual attendance.

Sport	Attendance
1. Horseracing	69,946,000
2. Major League Baseball	53,800,000
3. College Football	35,581,000
4. Men's College Basketball	32,504,000
5. Greyhound Racing	26,477,000
6. National Football League	17,024,000
7. Professional Basketball	14,051,000
8. National Hockey League	13,741,000
9. Jai Alai	6,414,000
10. Women's College Basketball	3,301,000

Source: Statistical Abstract of the United States.

STOCK EXCHANGES

Biggest Stock Exchanges

When the big boys throw their money around they don't call it money, they call it

New York's is the second busiest stock exchange in the world. Photo © N.Y.S. Dept. of Economic Development, 1991.

THINGS

capital. Capital is what you use to start businesses and make them go. Indeed, one of the first things the free-marketeers in the newly capitalized Hungary did after throwing off the cloak of communism was to set up a stock exchange; and in Poland, the government plans to give each and every citizen a share in each of the once state-owned companies, with stock that eventually will be traded openly. The world is becoming one big market. It used to be that Americans invested their capital in New York, Japanese invested in Tokyo, the Swiss in Zurich, and so on in that fashion. But in the age of the electronic money transfer, the fax machine and sophisticated computerized investment programs, money speeds around the world in the blink of an eye. So if you get the urge to make a wager at midnight, you don't have to take the red-eye to Vegas any more. Just call your broker and he'll by some stocks for you on the Tokyo exchange. Indeed, many markets around the world are now flirting with the idea of night-time, or even 24-hour, trading. The technology's there, and so is the money and the demand. It's only a question of will. Here are the world's ten biggest exchanges.

Market	Value (Billion)
1. Tokyo	$3811.6
2. New York	$2596.9
3. London	$766.1
4. Paris	$229.4
5. Frankfurt	$226.8
6. Toronto	$226.6
7. Zurich	$142.0
8. Milan	$130.1
9. Sydney	$123.6
10. Hong Kong	$82.9

Source: Dow Jones-Irwin Business and Investment Almanac.

STOCKS
Top Performing Stocks, 1990
The drops were fairly breathtaking in this year's Dow Jones Bop-Until-You-Drop, Free Market Open, but the rises were comparably meteoric. Effort and achievement, in last year's touchy-feely market, were rewarded in spades. With twenty-twenty hindsight, here's your chance to wave "good buy" to the yesterday's winners, measured increase in the price of the stock from 1989 to 1990.

Company	Percent Increase
1. Cabletron Systems	204.0
2. US Surgical	160.7
3. Signal Apparel	147.1
4. EMC Corporation	146.2
5. Foxboro Corporation	126.8
6. LE Meyers Group	124.1
7. Oregon Steel Mills	97.9
8. Clayton Homes	96.4
9. International Rectifier	91.3
10. Fabri-Centers of America	87.3

Source: The New York Stock Exchange.

STOCKS
Top Stocks of the Decade
Everyone who ventures into the market looks for the singular, sizzling hot tip to place him on the path to financial higher-consciousness. While few of us are cursed with the temptation of genuinely inside information, the astute among us might have perceived the promise of these 1980's super stocks. These bets paid off better than most lotteries.

Company	Price Change, 1979-1989
1. Mylan Laboratories	6,496%
2. The Limited	6,122%
3. Mark IV Industries	4,996%
4. Marion laboratories	3,974%
5. Wainoco Oil	3,768%
6. Gap, Inc.	3,722%
7. Dillard Department Stores	3,707%
8. Servicemaster Ltd.	3,557%
9. Dreyfuss Corp.	3,098%
10. Hannaford Brothers	2,723%

Source: New York Stock Exchange

THINGS

STOCKS
Most Widely-Held
American Stocks

The ability to acquire small equity shares in the juggernauts of commerce is an egalitarian privilege that many take to heart in this country, but which still rests for the most part in relatively few prosperous hands. It's estimated that the bottom 50 percent of the population own only about 3 percent of the country's capital. Like political democracy, the bylaws of corporatism insure that even the smallest of stockholders has a say in the affairs of the institution which he invests with his hard-earned greenbacks, but, of course, those with the most shares have the biggest say. These are the most widely-held stocks traded in America. What stands out are the number of communications companies in the top ten, the "Baby Bells" upon which so many have counted since the break-up of the parent "Ma Bell."

Company	Shareholders
1. AT & T	2,702,000
2. General Motors	1,725,500
3. Bellsouth	1,491,000
4. Bell Atlantic	1,280,000
5. NYNEX Corp	1,249,900
6. Southwestern Bell	1,169,000
7. American Information Tech.	1,164,000
8. Pacific Telesis Group	1,027,000
9. U.S. West	1,007,000
10. IBM	834,000

Source: New York Stock Exchange.

STRESS
Most Stressful Events

In 1967, Doctors Thomas Holmes and Richard Rahe published their findings about how stress can effect your health in an article called "The Social Readjustment Scale," printed in *The Journal of Psychosomatic Research*. Drs. Holmes and Rahe gave stressful events point values and found that any combination of points totaling 300 or more would in all probability lead to a major illness. Holmes' and Rahe's findings have stood the test of time and are now widely regarded and reprinted. If your point total seems to be getting up there, perhaps you out to consider taking a vacation—that is, if you can afford the 13 stress points it will cost you.

Event	Point Value
1. Death of a Spouse	100
2. Divorce	73
3. Marital Separation	65
4. Jail or other Institution	63
5. Death of Close Family Member	63
6. Major Injury or Illness	53
7. Marriage	50
8. Being Fired at Work	47
9. Marital Reconciliation	45
10. Retirement	45

SUBWAYS
Busiest Subway Systems
in the World

Moscow has always prided itself on its subway system. Even when the rest of the country was falling apart, Kremlin cronies could always point to the clean, efficient public transit system built in the 1930s. Perhaps the reason for all the crowding on Moscow's underground is that the country has only one automobile for every 18 comrades. And try fitting them all in a Trabant, Skoda, or other East European clunker. In Tokyo, whose trains carry 2.5 billion passengers per year, the transit system hires people to shove passengers from platforms, sardine-like, into the crowded trains. Makes the New York subway seem kind of cozy by comparison.

Subway/Train System	Passengers/ yr.
1. Moscow	2.6 billion
2. Tokyo	2.5 billion
3. New York City	1.5 billion
4. Mexico City	1.5 billion
5. Paris	1.2 billion

6. Osaka	948 million
7. Leningrad	821 million
8. London	815 million
9. Seoul	810 million
10. Hong Kong	630 million

Source: Urban Transport Systems, 1990.

SUPER BOWLS
Top Ten Televised Super Bowls

Among all professional sporting events, Super Bowls are without question the most watched games in broadcast history. Of the top ten most-watched television programs of all time, according to A.C. Nielsen figures, Super Bowls account for eight of those programs. Each of the top ten Super Bowl games have drawn more than 100 million viewers. Our list ranks the top ten according to shares and ratings, the standard measures for determining audiences for a given program. A share is the percentage of all households watching television generally when the program is on, and ratings reflect the percentage of people who are watching the specific program.

Game/Date/Opponents	Share/Rating
1. XVI 1/24/82 San Francisco/Cincinnati	73/49.1
2. XVII 1/30/83 Washington/Miami	69/48.6
3. XX 1/26/86 Chicago/New England	70/48.3
4. XII 1/15/78 Dallas/Denver	67/47.2
5. XIII 1/21/79 Pittsburgh/Dallas	74/47.1
6. XVIII L.A. Raiders/Washington	71/46.4
7. XIX 1/20/85 San Francisco/Miami	63/46.4
8. XIV 1/20/80 Pittsburgh/L.A. Rams	67/46.3
9. XXI	66/45.8

N.Y. Giants/Denver

10. XI Oakland/Minnesota	73/44.4

TELEVISION
Largest Cable Operators

Once upon a time there were three big guys in TV town, and things were very simple. But in this age of exploding information, the media that carry that information have exploded in kind. Today, we face programming super-saturation. The Big Three—NBC, CBS and ABC—have been watching their shares of the television market dwindle over the past two decades. The Fox Network is on the scene now, stealing a lot of network thunder (and viewers) with ultra-hip risk-taking audience favorites like *The Simpsons* and *Married With Children*. And from humble origins, such cable networks as the all-sports ESPN and the all-news CNN have achieved true network parity. ESPN's gained its biggest coup—and its entrée into the big time—by earning the rights to broadcast NFL—as in National Football League—games in 1988. No longer the network solely of sporting esoterica such as professional ping pong and monster truck and tractor pulls, ESPN could now count itself among the big boys of network sports. Soon thereafter, Major League Baseball entered the ESPN fold. And CNN truly achieved newsroom equality with its non-stop coverage of the Persian Gulf war. As even many network news veterans will admit, CNN's total commitment to news allows it to be at the scene of the news quicker and with more than the overburdened networks often can muster. Perhaps the single most important moment in cable's history—the moment that legitimized CNN, and all of cable TV, for that matter—was when the Iraqi authorities cut the three news networks' lines out of Baghdad, while CNN remained on the air from the stricken city. From that point forward, television will never be the same. The

THINGS

following are the top cable stations in the country, in terms of total number of subscribers.

Network	Subscribers (millions)
1. ESPN	55.9
2. CNN	54.4
3. TBS SuperStation	54.0
4. USA Network	51.5
5. Nickelodeon/Nick at Night	50.8
6. MTV	50.4
7. The Nashville Network	50.0
8. C-Span	49.7
9. The Discovery Channel	49.7
10. The Family Channel	49.1

Source: National Cable T.V. Association.

TELEVISION PROGRAMS
All-time Longest-Running T.V. Series

These days, network shows are lucky if they can live out the premiere season, no less survive for fifteen or more of those golden semesters. Of the ten all-time longest running series, only two are still in production, *60 Minutes* and *Meet the Press*, and these are both news-oriented shows, not as susceptible to the ratings crunch as entertainment programs. *The Wonderful World of Disney* left the air for a time before being reincarnated. The rest, *Gunsmoke* included, have gone to glory, death and dust.

Series	Seasons
1. *Walt Disney*	32
2. *The Ed Sullivan Show*	24
3. *Gunsmoke*	20
4. *The Red Skelton Show*	20
5. *60 Minutes*	20
6. *Meet the Press*	18
7. *What's My Line?*	18
8. *I've Got a Secret*	17
9. *Lassie*	17
10. *The Lawrence Welk Show*	17

Source: Baseline II, Inc.

TELEVISION PROGRAMS
Top-Rated T.V. Series of the 50's

Today's TV generation is, in fact, made up of the children of yesterday's TV generation. So, in the name of mutual understanding — and in attempt to bridge the generation gap with a single span — here are the golden hits of Ma and Pa's couch potato past. The list is notable for its preponderance of the now extinct variety show, as well as the prime-time quiz show.

Program	Average Rating
1. *Arthur Godfrey's Talent Scouts*	32.9
2. *I Love Lucy*	31.6
3. *You Bet Your Life*	30.1
4. *Dragnet*	24.6
5. *The Jack Benny Show*	22.3
6. *Arthur Godfrey and Friends*	19.5
7. *Gunsmoke*	15.6
8. *The Red Skelton Show*	15.2
9. *December Bride*	13.8
10. *I've Got a Secret*	12.9

Source: A.C. Nielsen.

TELEVISION PROGRAMS
Top-Rated T.V. Series of the 70's

The Seventies are back!!! Run away!!! On the music scene there is Dee Lite, as well as other neo-psychedelic, seventies-flashback culture kids. Across the country, bell-bottoms, leisure suits, long side-burns and, worst of all, disco, are re-emerging from well-earned hibernation. All this hubbub has awoken a parallel interest in that era's questionable-classics of the small screen. From *The Brady Bunch* to *Batman*, the reruns are rolling back the years, shifting gears and transporting us the era of Convoy and Convy (Burt). Indeed, a Chicago theater group has been packing its houses for several months with weekly performances of *Brady Bunch* episodes, word for word from the original scripts. Next year, watch out for the Sonny and Cher reunion tour.

THINGS

Program	Average Rating
1. *All In The Family*	23.0
2. *M*A*S*H*	17.6
3. *Hawaii Five-O*	16.6
4. *Happy Days*	15.9
5. *The Waltons*	14.0
6. *Mary Tyler Moore Show*	13.7
7. *Sanford and Son*	13.4
8. *One Day at a Time*	11.4
9. *Three's Company*	10.8
10. *60 Minutes*	10.0

Source: A.C. Nielsen.

TELEVISION PROGRAMS
Top Shows, 1980-1990

The top television shows were rated according to three factors: (1) Emmy Awards; (2) Nielsen Ratings; and (3) television critic's evaluations. In the first category, 15 points were awarded for each Emmy Award. In category two, ten points were awarded for each year the show was in the top ten in Nielsen's annual year-end ratings. In category three, each television critic's vote counted for four points—six critics's judgments were used. Although *The Cosby Show* consistently had the highest Nielsen ratings from 1986 through 1989, it garnered only one Emmy for best series. *Nightline's* ratings, on the other hand, were not as high, but it is considered by critics as one of the best news shows on the air. What began as a response to the 1979 Iranian hostage crisis has turned out to be an intelligent and much-needed alternative to Johnny Carson's monologues.

Show	Total Score
1. *Cheers*	131
2. *Hill Street Blues*	119
3. *The Golden Girls*	108
4. *Cagney & Lacey*	78
5. *The Cosby Show*	73
6. *L.A. Law*	71
7. *thirtysomething*	69
8. *The Wonder Years*	43
9. *Nightline*	24

Lonesome Dove	24

Source: "Best and Worst" original.

TELEVISION PROGRAMS
Highest-Rated T.V. Shows, 1990

Popularity isn't everything, but on tube it's often the only thing. At the TV tippy-top, this year, comedy is king. Although the veteran crews from *Cheers* and *Cosby* held their own at those airy heights, top honors went to bullysome big girl, Roseanne Barr.

Series	1990 Overall Rating
1. *Roseanne (ABC)*	23.4
2. *Cosby Show (NBC)*	23.1
3. *Cheers (NBC)*	22.9
4. *A Different World (NBC)*	21.1
5. *Funniest Home Videos (ABC)*	21.0
6. *Golden Girls (NBC)*	20.1
7. *60 Minutes (CBS)*	19.7
8. *Wonder Years (ABC)*	19.2
9. *Empty Nest (NBC)*	19.1
10. *Chicken Soup (ABC)*	18.2

Source: Nielsen Media Research.

TELEVISION PROGRAMS
Highest Rated Syndicated Programs

These days, as any network honcho will tell you, the real money is in *syndication*. Inexpensive to produce but highly lucrative in the long-run, the games shows *Wheel of Fortune* and *Jeopardy!* are estimated to be worth several hundred million dollars in syndication rights. That has made Merv Griffin, the man who has controlled those rights, a rich man. Syndicated programs often develop their own highly devoted following, those folks who slip through the prime-time net, and get their TV at all hours of the day and night. Rights to reruns of network programs are also hot commodities. The first time around is great, but the second is so much sweeter. On their first run, network programs need to recoup the enormous production dollars spent to bring them to the small screen. On the rebound, however, the price is paid, the path paved and the profits pure. But, despite desperate battles among syndicators for the rights to many a popular prime-time target, only one sitcom resides in the top ten in the syndicated ratings, that being the ever-lovable *Cosby Show*.

Series	Rating
1. *Wheel of Fortune*	14.5
2. *Jeopardy!*	12.7
3. *Star Trek: The Next Generation*	10.0
4. *The Cosby Show*	9.5
5. *Oprah Winfrey Show*	9.4
6. *A Current Affair*	8.8
7. *Wheel of Fortune (Weekend)*	8.8
8. *Universal Pictures Debut Network*	8.7
9. *Entertainment Tonight*	8.4
10. *Columbia Night at the Movies*	7.0

Source: Amusement Business Magazine.

TELEVISION PROGRAMS
All Time Highest-Rated Television Shows

It has often been said that we are settlers in an electronically bordered "global village," but little has been said about what it is like to live among so many virtual "neighbors." For truly, certain televised events quite nearly unite us all. Some moments are emotional, others, revealingly ritualistic. Watching Kennedy, Canaveral and Cosby in 19-inch diagonal slices, we are bound together through the electronic signal. This then is our common heritage—the Super Bowl, Who Shot J.R.?, Kunta Kinte, Rhett Butler, and, of course, Hawkeye Pierce.

Program	Date
1. M*A*S*H (final episode)	2/28/83
2. Dallas ("Who Shot J.R.")	11/21/80
3. Roots (Episode 8)	1/30/77
4. Super Bowl XVI	1982
5. Super Bowl XVII	1983
6. SuperBowl XX	1986
7. Gone With the Wind (Part I)	11/7/76
8. Gone With the Wind (Part II)	11/8/76
9. Super Bowl XII	1978
10. Super Bowl XIII	1979

Source: Nielsen Media Research.

TELEVISION VIEWING
Most Popular Viewing Days

In many households, every night is TV night. Viewing for many mainstream Americans, in point of fact, has come to closely resemble a second full-time occupation, with the number of hours logged in front of the television rivaling, or even surpassing, that spent in the work place. In any case, those who have assumed this laborious entertainment burden seem to be holding up well as they log their dozens of hours of hard core viewing each week. These are the most popular days of the week for video viewing, in descending order.

Day	Viewers (Millions)
1. Sunday	106.4
2. Tuesday	99.2
3. Monday	95.6
4. Thursday	95.5
5. Wednesday	94.1
6. Friday	89.8
7. Saturday	89.1

Source: Nielsen Media Research.

TOYS
Best-Selling Toys

Toys may be just kid stuff, but they are also big business. An honest-to-God marketing hit can mean tens—even hundreds—of millions of dollars in annual revenue. Among the leading toys in the land, Barbie has held tenaciously to her spot as king of the doll hill, finishing second overall. Only the poker-hot Nintendo Video Action system sold better in last year's boom market. Seems toyland is split in a struggle between traditional playthings such as dolls and houses and the new high-tech wizardry of the video system.

Toy	Manufacturer
1. Nintendo Ent. System	Nintendo

THINGS

High-tech Nintendo may be number one, but America is still in love with Barbie, the best-selling doll on the market. Where's Ken these days?

2. **Barbie** — **Mattel**
3. **Super Mario Brothers 3** — **Nintendo**
4. **Teenage Mutant Ninja Turtles Figurines** — **Playmates**
5. **Game Boy** — **Nintendo**
6. **Teenage Mutant Ninja Turtles** — **Ultra**
7. **Tetris (video cartidge)** — **Nintendo**
8. **Magic Nursery** — **Mattel**
9. **My Pretty Ballerina** — **Tyco**
10. **Go-Go My Walking Pup** — **Hasbro**

Source: Toy and Hobby World.

TRAINS
Fastest in the World

The fastest trains in the world are in France and Japan, where governments have spent millions to create fast-moving rail systems for the general citizenry. Overall, Europe and Japan have better rail systems than we do. And they know how to name those fast trains, too. The French high-speed train, for instance, is called TGV for "Train Grand Vitesse," or High-Speed Train. What a way with language the French have. It's true that cities in Europe and Japan are much closer to each other than American cities and are therefore better served by rail transit. In the United States, Amtrak's Northeast Corridor is our fastest moving, best organized train system. Between Washington, D.C. and northern New Jersey, there are about twenty trains traveling faster than 87 miles per hour. Not all were included here since many repeat the same or similar routes.

Name/Service	Avg. Speed (Mph)
1. **TGV Train (France)** Paris/Macon	135.4
2. **/Yamabiko (Japan)** Morica/Sendi	127.6
3. **High Speed Train (UK)** Swindon/Reading	108.3
4. **Metroliners 112-116 (US)** Baltimore/Wilmington	102.4

France's "Train Very Fast." Photo: French Govt. Tourist Office.

THINGS

5. Intercity Trains (Germany) 102.3
Celle/Ueizin

6. 27 Metroliners (US) 100.1
Wilmington/Baltimore

7. Five Trains (US) 95.7
Metro Park/Trenton

8. IC501 (Italy) 94.7
Milan/Bologna

9. High Speed Train (USSR) 88.7
Leningrad/Moscow

10. Seven Trains (Sweden) 88.5
Skvode/Hallsberg

Source: Information Please Almanac.

VEGETABLES

Most Calories per Serving

When your mom made you eat your vegetables, she certainly wasn't trying to fatten you up. Vegetables have one of the highest ratios of nutritional value per calorie — the biggest bang for the buck — and most lack the fat and sodium so harmful to the common American diet. These are the vegetables with the most calories per serving; compared to dessert items and fatty meat products, even the top-rated potato comes out smelling sweet.

Vegetable	Calories
1. Potato	145
2. Sweet Potato	115
3. Corn	85
4. Parsnips	63
5. Brussels Sprouts	60
6. Artichoke	55
7. Winter Squash	40
8. Broccoli	40
9. Onion, cooked	30
10. Carrot	30

Source: Human Nutrition Information Service, U.S. Dept. of Agriculture.

WARS
Longest

One of the frightening elements of our modern era is the speed at which everything happens. In the most recent Persian Gulf War, the land battle took 100 hours. It seems that in the days of yore, people took their time about things, wars included. The longest continuous conflict in history was the Crusades. In a way, the struggle is still going on, because the contestants are still fighting: Christianity against Islam. The Crusades took place over a period of nearly 200 years, from 1096 to 1291, during which four separate excursions from Europe to the Middle East failed to regain the Holy Lands. Imagine the difficulty CNN would have had continuously broadcasting *that* conflict! Like today's battles between East and West, the Crusades were an indecisive war, with each side claiming its own victory. Of the notable wars through history, the following list is organized by duration.

War	Duration (yrs.)
1. Crusades	195
Christianity v. Islam, 1096-1291	
2. Hundred Years War	115
England v. France, 1338-1453	
3. Thirty Years War	30
Catholics v. Protestants, 1618-1648	
4. War of the Roses	30
Lancaster v. York, 1655-1685	
5. Peloponnesian War	27
Sparta v. Athens, 431-404 B.C.	
6. First Punic War	23
Rome v. Carthage, 264-241 B.C.	
7. Greco-Persian Wars	21
Greek States v. Persia, 499-478 B.C.	
8. Second Great Northern War	21
Russia v. Sweden & Baltic Allies, 1700-1721	
9. Napoleonic Wars	19
France v. rest of Europe, 1796-1815	

10. Second Punic War   17
    Rome v. Carthage, 218-201 B.C.

Source: Funk & Wagnall's Standard College Dictionary.

WARS
The Deadliest Conflict: World War II Deaths

Total military deaths in World War II are estimated at around 20 to 25 million. The truly shocking fact is that civilian deaths roughly equaled that figure. The reasons are many. In Yugoslavia, two-thirds of all deaths were civilians, the tragedy being that the German invasion of that country sparked a civil war between Communist and Royalist forces, in addition to unleashing inter-ethnic warfare between Croatians, Serbs and other nationalist groups there. In Russia, Yugoslavia, Poland and elsewhere under the Nazi yoke, populations of entire villages and towns were massacred in response to partisan and resistance attacks on German occupation forces. Other civilians died in bombing campaigns against cities—including atomic bombings of Hiroshima and Nagasaki, and the even more devastating fire-bombing of Tokyo, which caused an estimated 100,000 civilian deaths. Of course, the largest number of civilian victims perished in the Holocaust—6 million Jews from all over Europe.

Country	Total Dead
1. Soviet Union	15.0 million
2. Poland	6.6 million
3. Germany	6.2 million
4. China	2.2 million
5. Japan	2.0 million
6. Yugoslavia	1.4 million
7. Hungary	850,000
8. France	650,000
9. Romania	640,000
10. Britain	450,000
11. United States	408,000
12. Austria	405,000
13. Czechoslovakia	280,000
14. Italy	220,000
15. Netherlands	206,000
16. Belgium	200,000

Country	Military Deaths
1. Soviet Union	7.5 million
2. Germany	4.75 million
3. Japan	1.5 million
4. China	1.35 million
5. Poland	600,000
6. United States	408,000
7. Yugoslavia	400,000
8. Hungary	400,000
9. Britain	350,000
10. Romania	340,000
11. Austria	280,000
12. Czechoslovakia	250,000
13. France	200,000
14. Italy	150,000
15. Belgium	110,000
16. Netherlands	6,000

Country	Civilian Deaths
1. Soviet Union	7.5 million
2. Poland	6.0 million
3. Germany	1.47 million
4. Yugoslavia	1 million
5. China	800,000
6. Japan	500,000
7. Hungary	450,000
8. France	450,000
9. Romania	300,000
10. Netherlands	200,000
11. Austria	125,000
12. Britain	100,000
13. Belgium	90,000
14. Italy	70,000
15. Czechoslovakia	30,000
16. United States	0

Source: World Military and Social Expenditures.

WARS
Deadliest U.S. Wars

War is always a great calamity, but it surprises many to learn that one of America's most calamitous losses of men and material came at the hands of its own

THINGS

generals. Beyond the vast global destruction of World War II, the War Between the States has been this country's most devastating conflict. Such is the power and tragedy of a nation of brothers turned to arms.

Conflict	U.S. Battle Deaths
1. World War II	291,557
2. Civil War*	140,414
3. World War I	53,402
4. Vietnam	47,382
5. Korean War	33,629
6. Revolutionary War	4,435
7. War of 1812	2,260
8. Mexican War	1,733
9. Spanish American War	385

* This includes only Union casualties; Confederate deaths are estimated at abouth the same number, although accurate figures were often not kept by the Confederacy.

Source: Department of Defense

WEAPONS
Deadliest Weapons in the U.S. Arsenal

Military historian Col. Trevor N. Dupuy has devised a formula for evaluating the relative effectiveness of weapons in war. Using values that are either published or known by experience, his formula takes into account a weapon's rate of fire, number of targets hit per single strike, the incapacitating effect of a single strike from the weapon, the weapon's effective range, accuracy and reliability. In addition, for a mobile weapon such as a tank or armored personnel carrier, the formula considers the weapon's speed, distance without refueling, armored protection, rapidity of fire, fire control, amount of ammunition carried. Aircraft also are affected by their operational ceiling. The resulting figure— the "Operational Lethality Index", as Dupuy calls it—can be used to compare the relative lethality—the killing ability—of weapons systems. According to Dupuy's formula, ground attack aircraft are more lethal than tanks—thus

demonstrating the value of air superiority in the theatre of combat. One need only look at the devastation visiting on Iraqi ground forces in the Persian Gulf War to see an example of the lethality index in practice. The A-10 Warthog's high score results from the incredible array of ground-attack weapons it carries—from bombs and cannons to missiles—combined with its high amount of protective armor and its great mobility. Below are the operational lethality scores for weapons in the U.S. arsenal.

Weapon System	Lethality Score
1. 1 Megaton Nuclear Airburst	173,846
2. B-52 Bomber	10,063
3. A-10 Ground Attack Plane	2,697
4. F-111E Bomber	1,922
5. A-6E Navy Bomber	1,484
6. F-16 Fighter-Bomber	1,359
7. M1A1 Abrams Tank	1,049
8. A7 Navy Bomber	707
9. M60A3 Tank	650
10. M3 Bradley Fighting Vehicle	597

Source: T.N. Dupuy, *Numbers, Prediction and War: Using History to Evaluate Combat Factors and Predict the Outcome of Battles,* New York: Bobbs-Merrill Co., 1979; and T.N. Dupuy et al, *How to Defeat Saddam Hussein: Scenarios and Strategies for the Gulf War,* New York: Warner Books, 1991.

WINES
Most Popular Wine Brands

Although we may not be on par with the French or Italians in per capita consumption of wine, the U.S. market is booming. The acceptance of wine as a companion to meals is on the rise, and scads of new and revamped vineyards are competing to quench the national thirst. Leading the bunch are the powerful growers of California's Napa Valley.

Wine	1990 U.S. Sales ($ millions)
1. Carlo Rossi	$240
2. Gallo	220
3. Almaden	190

THINGS

4. Sutter Home	185
5. Inglenook	155
6. Moet Chandon	150
7. Reserve Cellars	150
8. Beringer	140
9. Richard's Wild Irish Rose	140
10. Glen Ellen	135

Source: Superbrands 1990.

WINES
The World's Best Wines

A noted wine connoisseur was once asked, "What is the greatest wine in the world?" He replied, "Who is the most beautiful woman in the world?" Naturally, preferences are largely a matter of opinion, but certain vineyards and wines keep coming up with the experts. The most famous ranking, the Grand Cru or "Great Growths," were officially appeared in 1855 and is still generally valid. But because of wine technology, today's experts have reshuffled the order and added a few of yesteryear's "lesser wines." The following rating is from Frank Schoonmaker, one of the world's most respected wine experts. All are from France, but few independent wine critics will dispute that the French are the undisputed champions at grape growing and winemaking. So Gallic pride should be satisfied.

The Best Reds (From Bordeaux)*

1. Chateau Lafite
2. Chateau Margaux
3. Chateau Latour
4. Chateau Haut-Brion
5. Chateau Mouton-Rothschild
6. Chateau Rausan-Segla
7. Chateau Rauzan-Gassies
8. Chateau Leoville-Poyferre
9. Chateau Leoville-Barton
10. Chateau Dufort-Vivens

* The Burgundy region of France is also considered among the great wine producing regions, but the widespread variance of opinions about its wines precludes their being rated as "best" here.

The Best Whites (From Burgundy)

1. Chambolle Musigny
2. Vougeot
3. Nuit-Saint George
4. Aloxe-Corton
5. Beaune
6. Auxey
7. Meursault
8. Puligny-Montrachet
9. Chassagne-Montrachet
10. Santenay

Source: Frank Schoonmaker's Encyclopedia of Wine, Hastings House, 1982.

THE 100 BEST

The list below represents the top rated entries from the main text in *The Best and Worst of Everything*.

◄══════════ People ══════════►

ACTOR (Highest Paid): Sylvester Stallone
$20,000,000 Per Film
ACTRESS (Highest Paid): Julia Roberts
$7,000,000 Per Film
ARTIST (Top Living): Willem De Kooning
"Best & Worst" Index Measure of Achievements
ATHLETE (Highest Winnings): Evander Holyfield, Boxer
$60,000,000 (Fight Purses)
BASEBALL PLAYER (Most Valuable): Will Clark (S.F. Giants)
Best Batting Average/Most RBI's with Two Outs (.380/89 -1988-90)
BASKETBALL COACH (Winningest College Record): Jerry Tarkanian
"Best & Worst" Index Measure of Achievements
CELEBRITY, FEMALE (Highest Profile): Madonna
Most Press Coverage (1986-90)
CELEBRITY, MALE (Highest Profile): Woody Allen
Most Press Coverage (1986-90)
CEO (Highest Paid 1980-90): Charles Lazarus
Toys 'R' Us, $156,200,000
CONCERT PERFORMERS (Top Gross): New Kids On The Block
$58,600,000 (1990 Season)
FANS (Most Avid Sports Fans): Chicago
Editors' Poll
FOOTBALL COACH, (College, Highest Winning Percent): Tom Osborne
Nebraska, 80.9% Wins
FOOTBALL PLAYER (Highest Paid): Joe Montana (S.F. 49ers)
$3,500,0000
GOLFER, FEMALE (Highest Winnings): Beth Daniel
$863,578 (1990)
GOLFER, MALE (Highest Winnings): Greg Norman
$907,977 (1990)
HOCKEY PLAYER (Highest Salary): Wayne Gretzky (L.A. Kings)
$3,000,000 (1991 Contract)
JOCKEY (Highest Winnings): Gary Stevens
$12,146,703 (1990)
LAWYER, FEMALE (Most Influential): Judith Areen
Dean, Georgetown University Law School
LAWYER, MALE (Most Influential): Robert Cox
Chairman, Baker & McKenzie
PHILOSOPHER (Most Influential): Jacques Derrida
Deconstructionist Founder
PROFESSIONAL (Most Trusted): Druggist
Opinion Poll
RACE CAR DRIVER (Highest Winnings): Ayrton Senna
$12,000,000 (1991 *Forbes'* Projection)
TENNIS PLAYER, FEMALE (Highest Winnings): Monica Seles
$1,600,000 (1991 *Forbes'* Projection)
TENNIS PLAYER, MALE (Highest Paid): Stefan Edberg
$1,400,000 (1991 *Forbes* Projection)
WEALTHIEST (American): John Kluge

THE 100 BEST

Owner, Metromedia; $5.6 Billion Estimated Net Worth
WOMAN (Highest Paid): Margaret H. Hill
$55,000,000 (Oil/Real Estate)
WRITER, AMERICAN FEMALE (Top Living): Eudora Welty
Author, *The Ponder Heart*
WRITER, AMERICAN MALE (Top Living): Thomas Pynchon
Author, *Gravity's Rainbow*

Places

ABORTION RATE (Lowest U.S. State): Wyoming
5.1 Per 1,000 Women of Child Bearing Age
ACTIVITIES (Most Things to Do): Los Angeles
"Best and Worst" Index Measurement
ARCHITECTURE (Best U.S. City): Chicago
"Best and Worst" Index Measurement
ARTS (Best U.S. City): New York City
"Best and Worst" Index Measurement
BANK TELLERS (Fastest): Chattanooga TN
"Pace of Life" Ranking (1989)
BEACHES (Cleanest): Connecticut
95 lb. of Debris per Mile (National Average, Approx. 1,000)
BLUE SKIES (Lowest Rainfall): Phoenix
7.11 Inches Per Year
BUSINESS LOCATION (Best in U.S.): Atlanta
Winner of CEO Poll
CHILDREN (Highest Percent, School Age): Utah
26% Of Population
CITIZENS (Best Smelling): Pittsburghers
Highest Per Capita Soap and Deodorant Sales
CONDOM USAGE (Highest): Japan
44.65% of Married Couples
ELBOW ROOM (Lowest Population Density, U.S. City): Butte-Silver Bow, MT
47 Per Sq. Mile
ENTERTAINMENT (Most Entertainment Opportunities): Los Angeles
"Best and Worst" Index Measurement
ETHNIC DIVERSITY (Most Diverse Population, U.S.): New York City
"Best and Worst" Index Measurement
FISH CAUGHT (Most): Japan
11,798,902 Tons (1984-86)
GRADUATION RATES (High School): Minnesota
91.4 % of Enrollment
HOME COSTS (Lowest New House Cost): Louisville
$63,600
INCOME PER CAPITA (Highest U.S. State): Connecticut
$18,521 (National Average: $12,300)
IRS AUDIT (Lowest Rate): Maine
Odds 1 In 2,493
LIFE EXPECTANCY (Longest): Japan
77.2 Years
POVERTY RATE (Lowest By Percent, U.S.): Sheyboygan WI
4.9% Below Poverty Rate
REAL ESTATE INVESTMENT (Best): Los Angeles
Ernst & Young Survey
SAFEST AMERICAN CITY:(Least Violence): Wilmette IL

THE 100 BEST

6 Violet Crimes Annually
SALARIES (Highest): Washington DC
$30,254 Average Annual
TAXES (Lowest Municipal): Sayreville Borough NY
$28.00
TEEN PREGNANCY (Lowest Teen-age Rate): San Francisco
8.1 Per 1,000 Population
UNEMPLOYMENT BENEFITS (Best): Massachusetts
$255-382 Weekly, Dependent on Average Income When Working
WEALTHIEST (American City): Stamford CT
$91,549 Average Household Income
WINING & DINING (Highest U.S. Expenditures): San Francisco
$3,354 Per House Hold
ZOO (Best U.S.): San Diego Wild Animal Park
"Best & Worst" Index Measurement

Things

AIRLINES (Best U.S. Carrier): American Airlines
Best Food/Best On Time Record/Most Cities Served
ADVERTISER (Highest Expenditures): Philip Morris Corp.
$2,072,000,000 (1990)
AMUSEMENT PARK (Most Popular): Walt Disney World
28.5 Million Visitors
APPAREL (Most Popular): Levi's Dockers
$3,628,000,000 (1990 Sales)
AUTOMOBILE (Best Mileage): Geo Metro XFi
53 Mi City/58 Mi Highway
AUTOMOBILE (Fastest Acceleration): Chevy Corvette
0-60 Mph/4.4 Seconds
AUTOMOBILE (Fewest Fatalities): Tie: Audi 5000/ Cadillac Fleetwood
Chevrolet Cavalier Wagon/Toyota Cressida /VW Jetta
AUTOMOBILE (Top Tire): Goodrich Comp H4
Index Measure
BEER, DOMESTIC (Most Popular): Budweiser
50 Million Barrels (1990)
BEER, IMPORTED (Most Popular): Heineken
4.6 Million Barrels (1990)
BRAND NAME (Most Powerful): Coca Cola
Landor Consumer Poll (1990)
CHICKEN (Best, Fast Food): Chick-Fil-A
Satisfaction Index
COFFEE (Most Popular): Folgers
$1,130,000,000 (1990 Sales)
COLLEGE (Most Selective): West Point, Annapolis
U.S. Army & Naval Academies, Respectively
COLLEGE (Smartest Students): California Institute of Technology
Highest Aptitude Scores
COLLEGE (Most Ph.D.s Produced): Harvey Mudd College
41% of Baccalaureates eventually earn doctorates.
COLLEGE (Top Research Institution): Johns Hopkins University
$557,016,000 (1990 Expenditures)
DRUG CHAIN (Best Overall): Walgreens

THE 100 BEST

585 Stores/Best Service
ENCYCLOPEDIA (Best Overall): Encyclopedia Britannica
  44,000,000 Words, 36 Volumes
FAST FOOD (Healthiest): Wendy's Chef Salad
  Nutripoint Survey
FOOD (Healthiest): Turnip Greens
  Nutripoint Survey
FOOD (Highest In Fiber): Pumpkin/ Squash Seeds
  25.5 Grams per Serving
FOOTBALL, COLLEGE (Most Pro Potential): Notre Dame
  "Best & Worst" Index Measurement
HAMBURGER (Best, Fast Food): Wendy's
  Satisfaction Index
HIGH SCHOOL (Smartest Kids): J.J. Pearce H.S., Richardson TX
  48,946 Score, Academic Decathlon
HOTEL CHAIN (Best Overall): Holiday Inn
  Editor Poll
JOB (Highest Paying, Nonathletic Profession): Law
  $83,383 Average Professional Salary
JOB (Least Stress): Musical Instrument Repairer
  Job Index
LIBRARY (Best in U.S.): Harvard University
  11,781,270 Volumes
MAGAZINE (Best All Round): *Time*
  Editor Poll
MAGAZINE READERS (Classiest): *New York Times Magazine*
  Hightest Demographic Profile: Income, Education, Life Style
MOVIE (Top, 1980-90): Rain Man
  "Best & Worst" Index
SHIPPING SERVICE (Best Overall): UPS
  Most Ubiquitous, Dependable
RADIO STATION (Most Listeners in U.S.): WINS-AM New York
  2,600,000 Listeners (1991)
ROAD (Most Scenic): Pacific Coast Hwy (Calif. Rte. 1)
  Counterpart: U.S. Highway 101
STOCK (Top Investment, 1980-90): Mylan Laboratories
  6,496% Appreciation
TOURISTS, U.S. (Foreigners Visiting U.S.): Japanese
  2,247,000 Visitors (1990)
TOY (Top Selling): Nintendo
  Widest World Wide Sales
TRAIN (Fastest): TGV Train France
  Paris/Macon (135.4 Mph)
TV SERIES (Highest Rated, 1990): Roseanne (ABC)
  23.4 Rating Points
WINE (Highest Rated): Chateau Lafite
  Overall Expert Opinions and Official "Grand Cru" Rating
WORD PROCESSING SOFTWARE (Best Overall): Word Prefect
  Editor Poll

THE 100 WORST

The list below is drawn from the entries in the main text of *The Best and Worst of Everything*.

━━━━━━━ People ━━━━━━━

BASEBALL TEAM (Most Overpaid): Houston Astros
"Bang per Buck Index"
CONGRESSMAN (Worst Attendance): Jim Courter (NJ)
24% Attendance Record; Lowest of Full Term Congresspersons
FANS (Worst): Phoenix
Editor's Poll
FOOTBALL SALARY (Lowest Paid NFL Position): Punter
$233,000 Annual Average
REPRESENTATIVE, U.S. (Top Pac Contributions): Robert Michel (R)
$523,466
REPRESENTATIVE U.S. (Most Outside Speaking Fees) Dan Rostenkowski (D-IL)
$309,850 (1990)
SENATOR U.S. (Most Outside Speaking Fees): Ernest Hollings (D- S.C.)
$82,200 (1990)
SENATOR, U.S. (Top Pac Contributions): Lloyd Bentsen (D-Tex)
$2,144,016
TRUST (Least Trusted): Tie (Ad Man, Car Salesman, State Politician)
1988 Gallop Poll.

━━━━━━━ Places ━━━━━━━

AIDS (Most Victims, U.S. City): New York
25,595
AIDS RISK (Highest World Wide): Uganda
84% of Population at Risk
ABORTION RATE (Highest in U.S.): Washington DC
16.3% of Pregnancies
ABORTION RATE (Highest World-Wide): Romania
56.7 % of Pregnancies
ABORTIONS (Most World-Wide): China
10,394,500 Per Year
ACCIDENTAL DEATHS (Highest U.S. Rate): New Mexico
35.1 Per 100,000 Population
AIRPORT (Worst On-Time Record): Philadelphia Int'l. Airport
24% of Flights Late
ALCOHOL (Highest U.S. Consumption Rate): Washington DC
9.017 Liters Per Adult Per Year
ALCOHOL (Highest U.S. Spending Rate): Miami
$546 Average Annual Consumer Expenditure
AUTOMOBILES (Fewest Per Capita): Bangladesh
1,608 People Per Car
BANK FRAUD (Most Reports): California
2,277 FBI Investigations (1987, Latest Available Data)
BANKTELLERS (Slowest): Los Angeles
"Pace of Life" Study (1989)
BEER CONSUMPTION (Highest Per Capita): New Hampshire
52.4 Gallons
BIRTH RATE (Lowest): Sweden
10.1 Per 1,000 Population

THE 100 WORST

BUSINESS FAILURES (Highest U.S. Rate): Colorado
248 Per 10,000 Businesses
CHRISTIAN POPULATION (Lowest National Percent): China
.2% of Population
CIGARETTE PRICES (Highest World-Wide): Oslo, Norway
$5.35 Per Package
CLOCK WATCHERS (Most Watches): New York
"Pace of Life" Study
CONDEMNED PRISONERS (Most in U.S.): Florida
290 Prisoners
COST OF LIVING (Highest World-wide): Tokyo, Japan
$50,800 Average Per Person
CRIMES OF VIOLENCE (Most in U.S.): New York NY
135,152 (FBI Uniform Crime Report, 1989, Latest Available Data)
CRIMES PER CAPITA (Highest in U.S.): Atlanta
1,919 Crimes Per 100,000 Population
DEATH RATES (Highest U.S. Rate): St. Petersburg FL
18.1 Per 1,000
DIVORCES (Highest U.S. Rate): Nevada
14.1 Per 1,000 Population
EDUCATIONAL ATTAINMENT (Lowest U.S. City): Newark NJ
6.3% with 16 Years or More of Schooling
ELBOW ROOM (Least, World Wide): Hong Kong
43,443 People per Sq. Mile
ELECTRIC BILL (Highest U.S. City): New York
$86.37 Average Monthly Cost
FISH CAUGHT (Least): Luxembourg
Less Than 1 Ton Annually
GARBAGE (Highest Per Capita, U.S.): Los Angeles
300 Kilograms per Capita
GASOLINE COSTS (Highest in U.S.): Hawaii
$1.65 Regular, Unleaded
HAZARDOUS WASTE (Most): Japan
292,312,000 Tons Annually
HIGHWAYS (Worst Condition): Missouri
43% in Need of Repair
HOME COST (Highest New-House Prices): Ventura County CA
$249,498
HOME FORECLOSURES (Highest U.S Rate): Arizona
12.85 % Of Home Loans
INCOME PER CAPITA (Lowest): Mississippi
$8,929
INFANT MORTALITY (Highest Rate World-Wide): Afghanistan
183 Per 1,000 Live Births
IRS AUDIT (Highest U.S. Rate): Utah
Odds: 1 In 21
JUVENILE DELINQUENCY (Highest U.S. Rate): Washington DC
991 Per 100,000 Population
LEGAL SYSTEM (Worst in U.S.): Tie (MS, NE ,WY)
H.A.L.T Index Measurement
LIFE EXPECTANCY (Shortest): Sierra Leone
36.0 Years
MARIJUANA (Most Medical Emergencies): Washington DC
843 (1989)
MARIJUANA (Softest Laws): Alaska

THE 100 WORST

Personal Use Fine, $0-$100
MURDER CAPITAL (Highest Per Capita): Washington DC
59.5 Per 100,000 Population
POLLUTION (Most Toxic Waste): Texas
792,000,000 Lbs.
POLLUTION (Worst Air): Kuwait City
War Result From Burning Oil
POPULATION (Least Populous Nation): Holy See
890 Persons
POPULATION DECREASE (Highest U.S. Rate): Newark NJ
-16.4% (1980-90)
POPULATION GROWTH (Lowest Nation): Tie (Sweden, Germany)
-0.11%(1988-89)
POVERTY (Highest Rate World-wide): Addis Abbaba, Ethiopia
90% Below Poverty Rate
POVERTY (Highest U.S. Rate): McAllen TX
35% Below Poverty Rate
PRISON ESCAPES (Most): Michigan
1,488 (1987, Latest Available Data)
PSYCHIATRIC DISORDERS (Highest per Capita) Washington DC
1,374 Per 100,000 Population
PUBLIC TRANSPORTATION (Busiest): Moscow, USSR
2.42 Billion Passengers Annually
RADIATION (Highest U.S. Rate): Detroit MI
.5 Tritium Level
RAINFALL (Highest U.S. Rate): Mobile AL
64.64 Inches Per Year
SALARIES (Lowest U.S. Rates): South Dakota
$15,424 Average Annual (U.S. Average: Approximately $21,000)
SEGREGATION (Highest U.S. Rate): Chicago
Demographic Population Index, 1989 (latest Available)
SNOWFALL (Highest U.S. Rate): Sault St. Marie MI
114.9 Inches Per Year
SULFUR DIOXIDE (Highest World-Wide Rate): Milan, Italy
Fossil Fuel Emission Measurement
TAXES (Highest Municipal, U.S.): Washington DC
$1,894 Average Per Person
TAXES (Highest National): Sweden
$8,385 Per Person
TEEN "TROUBLE" (Highest Percent Teenage Population): Utah
37% of Populace
TRAFFIC (Most Cars per Km.): Monaco
402 Cars per Km. of Roadway
TRAFFIC FATALITIES (Highest World-Wide Rate): Portugal
1,163 Per Million Vehicles
WEAPON EXPORTERS (Largest World Supplier): Soviet Union
35% of World Total
WINDIEST U.S. CITY: Cheyenne WY
12.9 m.p.h, Average Wind Speed

Things

AUTOMOBILE (Lowest Mileage): Rolls Royce
10 m.p.g City/13 m.p.g Highway
AUTOMOBILE (Slowest Acceleration): Suzuki Sidekick

THE 100 WORST

0-60 Mph in 15.8 Seconds
BIRDS (Rarest): Condor
One known in Wild
CANCER (Most Prevalent Variety): Stomach
669,400 Cases Per Year
COLLEGE COSTS (Highest in U.S.): Bennington College
$16,495 Per Year
COLLEGE LOANS (Most Defaults): Rose State College, OK
69.9% of Loans
DOG ATTACKS BY BREED (Most Fatalities): Pit Bull Terrier
37 Known
FOOD (Unhealthiest): Sweetbread
Nutripoint Measure
FRUIT (Most Fattening): Figs
48 Calories Each
FUR COAT (Most Pelts Per Garment): Mink
60 Pelts Per Coat
GROCERY STORE ITEM (Most Popular): Marlboro Cigarettes
$1,509,000,000 (1990 Sales)
HIGHWAY (Busiest): I-95 at George Washington Bridge (NY-NJ)
249,000 Cars Daily
INFLATION RATE (Highest By Item): School Books/Supplies
69.8 % Since 1982
JOB (Fastest Declining): Electronic Assembler
44% Decline (1990s)
JOB (Lowest Paying): Child Care Worker
$10,486 Average Annual
JOB (Most Injuries): Ship Building/Repairing
40.1% Of Workers
JOB (Most Stressful): Firefighter
Job Index/Death/Injury/General Conditions
JOB (Worst): Migrant Farm Worker
Overall Pay/Work Conditions
MAMMAL (Most Endangered): Florida Panther
30-50 Living
MOVIES (Costliest Production): Die Hard 2
$70 Million
POLICE BUST (Most Dangerous): Burglary In Progress
131 Officers Killed 1978-87
SNAKE (Most Poisonous): Coral Snake
Most Paralysises/Fatalities
SOLID WASTE (Worst Pollutant): Paper
35% of All Pollutants
VEGETABLE (Most Fattening): Potatoes
145 Calories Per Serving
WORLD WAR II (Most Casualties): Soviet Union
15,000,000 Fatalities

The 50 ALL-TIME BEST & WORST

The list below represents both the most outstanding and and most dubious achievements of all-time from the main text of *The Best and Worst of Everything*.

━━━━━ People ━━━━━

ACTOR (Highest Paid): Sylvester Stallone
 $20,000,000 Per Film
ACTRESS (Highest Paid): Julia Roberts
 $6,000,000 Per Film
ADMIRAL (Best): Horatio Nelson
 Most Significant Victory: Battle of The Nile, 1798
AMERICAN (Greatest): Abraham Lincoln
 "Best & Worst" Index of Achievements
ATHLETE (Top Annual Winnings): Evander Holyfield (Boxer)
 $60,000,000 (Fight Purses 1991)
AUTOGRAPH (Most Valuable): Greta Garbo
 $3,000 (Autographed Picture)
BASEBALL PLAYER (Greatest Hitter): Babe Ruth, N.Y. Yankees
 "Best & Worst" Index
BASKETBALL COACH (Best College Record): John Wooden, UCLA
 "Best & Worst" Index
BASKETBALL PLAYER (Best College Record): Pete Maravich, LSU
 3,667 Points Scored
BASKETBALL PLAYER (Best Professional): Wilt Chamberlain
 "Best & Worst" Index
CEO (Highest Paid): Charles Lazarus
 Toys 'R' Us, $156,200,000 (1980-90)
EDUCATOR (Most Influential): John Dewey
 "Best & Worst" Index
FOOTBALL COACH (Best College Record): Knute Rockne, Notre Dame
 88.1% Win Record
FOOTBALL PLAYER (Highest Paid): Joe Montana, S.F. 49ers
 $3,500,000 (1991)
GENERAL (Best): Alexander The Great
 Most Significant Victory: Persia
HOCKEY PLAYER (Greatest All Round): Wayne Gretzky
 Highest Paid Player/Top Scorer in Game
ROCK MUSICIAN (Most Influential): Chuck Berry
 Editors' Poll
WEALTHIEST (American): John Kluge
 Owner, Metromedia; Estimated Net Worth: $5.6 Billion
WRITER (Greatest): William Shakespeare
 English Playwright/Poet
WRITER, AMERICAN FEMALE (Greatest): Emily Dickinson
 Collected Poems
WRITER, AMERICAN MALE (Greatest): William Faulkner
 Author, *The Sound And The Fury*

━━━━━ Places ━━━━━

ABORTIONS (Most World-Wide): China
 10,394,500 Per Year
CONDEMNED PRISONERS (Highest State): Florida
 290 Prisoners
CRIME (Most Violent Crimes): New York City
 135,152 (1989)

339

The 50 ALL-TIME BEST & WORST

FISH CAUGHT (Most): Japan
  11,798,902 Tons (1984-86)
GARBAGE (Most Waste): Los Angeles
  300 Kilograms Per Capita
LIFE EXPECTANCY (Longest): Japan
  77.2 Years
NAVY (Largest): Soviet Union
  2,414 Ships
POLLUTION (Worst Air): Kuwait City
  War Result of 1991
POPULATION (In Year 2,100): India
  1,631,800,000
PRISON ESCAPES (Most): Michigan
  1,488 (1987)
PUBLIC TRANSPORTATION (Busiest): Moscow, USSR
  2,426,000,000 (1989)

━━━━━ Things ━━━━━

BATTLE (Bloodiest): Battle of Ypres (WWI)
  1,800,000 Casualties
BOOK (American Novel, Greatest): *Adventures of Huckleberry Finn*
  Mark Twain, Author
BOOK (Best Seller): *Baby And Child Care* by Dr. Benjamin Spock
  39,200,000 In Print
BOOK (Best Selling Children's): The Tales of Peter Rabbit by Beatrice Potter
  9,000,000 In Print
BOOK (Most Influential): *Structure of Scientific Revolution By Thomas S. Kuhn*
  855 Citations
FOOTBALL, COLLEGE (Top Team): Notre Dame
  75.9% Wins
FOOTBALL, COLLEGE (Worst Team): Kansas State
  37.4% Wins
FOOTBALL, NFL CHAMPIONSHIP (Biggest Blowout): Chicago/ Washington (73-0)
  Chicago 70/Washington 0 (1940)
MOVIE (Longest Ever): Cure For Insomnia
  85 Hours
MOVIE (Top Gross): E.T.
  $367,000,000
NOVEL (Greatest By Dickens): *Bleakhouse*
  "Best & Worst" Index
PLAY, BROADWAY (Longest Running): A Chorus Line
  Over 6,100 Performances
POET (Most Anthologized): The Tyger
  By William Blake
SHAKESPEAREAN PLAY (Greatest): Hamlet
  "Best & Worst" Index
TV PROGRAM (Highest Rated): M*A*S*H (Final Episode)
  February 28, 1983
TV SERIES (Longest Running): Walt Disney
  33 Seasons
WAR (Most U.S. Fatalities): World War II
  291,557
WAR (Longest): Crusades
  195 Years